Indigeneity in African Religions

Also Available from Bloomsbury
The African Christian Diaspora,
Afe Adogame
Innovation and Competition in Zimbabwean Pentecostalism,
edited by Ezra Chitando
Religion and the Inculturation of Human Rights in Ghana,
Abamfo Ofori Atiemo

Indigeneity in African Religions

Ọza Worldviews, Cosmologies and Religious Cultures

Afe Adogame

BLOOMSBURY ACADEMIC
LONDON • NEW YORK • OXFORD • NEW DELHI • SYDNEY

BLOOMSBURY ACADEMIC
Bloomsbury Publishing Plc
50 Bedford Square, London, WC1B 3DP, UK
1385 Broadway, New York, NY 10018, USA
29 Earlsfort Terrace, Dublin 2, Ireland

BLOOMSBURY, BLOOMSBURY ACADEMIC and the Diana logo are
trademarks of Bloomsbury Publishing Plc

First published in Great Britain 2022
This paperback edition published 2023

Copyright © Afe Adogame, 2022, 2023

Afe Adogame has asserted his right under the Copyright, Designs and
Patents Act, 1988, to be identified as Author of this work.

For legal purposes the Preface on pp. ix–x constitutes an
extension of this copyright page.

Cover design: Tjasa Krivec
Cover image © Shegun Joshua

All rights reserved. No part of this publication may be reproduced or transmitted in any form or by any means, electronic or mechanical, including photocopying, recording, or any information storage or retrieval system, without prior permission in writing from the publishers.

Bloomsbury Publishing Plc does not have any control over, or responsibility for, any third-party websites referred to or in this book. All internet addresses given in this book were correct at the time of going to press. The author and publisher regret any inconvenience caused if addresses have changed or sites have ceased to exist, but can accept no responsibility for any such changes.

A catalog record for this book is available from the British Library.

A catalog record for this book is available from the Library of Congress.
Library of Congress Control Number: 2021945664

ISBN: HB: 978-1-3500-0826-7
PB: 978-1-3502-7435-8
ePDF: 978-1-3500-0828-1
eBook: 978-1-3500-0827-4

Typeset by Newgen KnowledgeWorks Pvt. Ltd., Chennai, India

To find out more about our authors and books visit www.bloomsbury.com
and sign up for our newsletters

This book is dedicated to Ọza ancestors
Ọza mayi ki uzekọ
Ọza oke ze ọda yedi
Ọde keke shemi fi inẹnẹ Ọza, ma ke kwe abọ gbe!

Contents

List of Plates		viii
Preface		ix
1	Decolonizing history, memory and method	1
2	Historical origins, migration narratives, relationship with neighbours	41
3	World views, religious cosmologies, spiritual agency	77
4	Genealogies of kinship and sacral kingship	99
5	Kingship myth, leadership succession and legal imbroglios (1991–2011)	137
6	Rituals of passage	169
7	Gendering rituals	191
8	The future of Ọza indigeneity in the face of African modernity	213
Notes		235
Oral Sources		255
Select Bibliography		257
Index		267

Plates

1a   Map of Ọza Okeme (Old Ọza site)
1b, 1c   Map of Ọza Okeme and 2019 satellite image of the old Ọza-Okeme site
2a   Map of Nigeria 1910, London National Archive
2b   Map of Northern Nigeria, London War Office, 1909
3a, 3b   Map, Benin Province, endorsed by Directorate of Military Survey May Library, 26 November 1954
3c   Extracted Map of Kukuruku and Ishan Divisions from Benin Provincial Military, 1954
4a, 4b, 4c   The Edo-speaking peoples of South-Western Nigeria
5   *Ọbu Evba* (diviner) with paraphernalia and client
6a, 6b, 6c, 6d, 6e, 6f, 6g   Variations of *Ẹrẹma* clay products for domestic and aesthetic purposes
7   A male *osokuru* initiate with *egere*, traditional outfit
8a, 8b   *Irimi/Erimi* (masquerade(s) in their ritual paraphernalia)
9a, 9b   The long *Agba* drum used during the *Osọ* rite
10   A female *oruvie/ibishika* initiate with *egere*, traditional outfit during *Ukpe Oruvie/Ukpe Ọza*
11   A female *oruvie/ibishika* initiate during *nya akpa* (public appearance of oruvie) during *Ukpe Iruvie/Ukpe Ọza*
12   *Ẹrẹsha* (Ẹrẹsa) sacred lake in Ọza Okeme

Preface

The enduring journey that brought this book to fruition is one that has taken two decades, from the incubation stage of the research idea in 2001. If there is anything I have learned as an ethnographer in the past decades, it is that having great research ideas does not require a substantial amount of money, but sometimes you just need a little bit of help to see your idea come to maturation. Such an enterprise usually takes 'many hands in the pot'. While space would not permit mention of all or most of them, one must however not remiss to acknowledge the major inputs of a few.

First, my warmest gratitude goes to the twenty-five graduating students of Oza Comprehensive High School in 2004, who assisted in initial data gathering, and the interviewees who chronicled stories and provided invaluable historical, indigenous knowledges and epistemological wealth that this book embodies. Collaboration with Olusegun Lawani to co-author the book at its formative stages were very promising. However, this did not come to fruition in the end owing to logistic and pragmatic reasons. Nonetheless, I am very indebted to him for his passion in documenting Oza cultural history and for the several brainstorming sessions we had in Bayreuth and Paris during the formative years. We had secured a book contract which was later revoked as it became clear that such a prospect dimmed by the day. Nonetheless, his two master's degree dissertations at the University of Paris and other primary documents he availed were highly invaluable. I took the liberty to use and quote from them generously as necessary in this book. Thank you for the enormous wealth of experience and cultural knowledge you shared with me.

My several informants and interlocutors, endowed with cultural and intellectual capital, enriched several aspects of the book, and I am immensely grateful for their impartation. I am indebted to my graduate research assistants in Princeton: Ruth Amwe and Byung Ho Choi, who provided enormous editorial support; Amidu Elabo, who provided GIS and map illustrations; and Olanike Ogunnowo (University of Ibadan), who assisted in sourcing relevant archival resources at the National Archives, Ibadan. My candid appreciation to my colleague and friend, Prof. Olutayo Adesina (University of Ibadan) who recommended Olanike to me as an archival research assistant. Your contributions to different aspects of this book are unforgettable. The British National Library and Archives, London, were very helpful in availing colonial maps of Nigeria, Benin Province and Kukuruku Division. The tremendous support of Shegun Joshua, Ignatius Oshiomogwe and Shadrach Oladungbehin in sharing vital information, arranging focus group discussions and meetings with other interlocutors is much appreciated. Shegun Joshua sourced and made available, *gratis*, several cultural images used in this book. I am deeply grateful.

My family stood by me during the research and writing stages, particularly during the final writing phase which coincided with the Covid-19 crisis. The pandemic took a debilitating toll on our everyday lives, holding one somewhat hostage from research trips during my sabbatical semester in the fall of 2020. Perhaps there are two things one might be thankful for, or maybe what the pandemic era was good for: first, keeping me and my family safe and well under one roof for an entire year. Second, I took this luxury of being home to write and write until I saw the light at the end of the tunnel, the completion of the book. I discussed several aspects of the book with Esther, my dearest wife, and our dear children – Pamẹhasẹ Faith, Ọnọshimijẹ Blessing and Midafẹ Precious – and benefited from their robust insights and inputs. The eagle-eyed editing and sharp and priceless criticisms provided by Pamẹhasẹ indeed lifted me up and convinced me that I have geniuses under my roof. Thanks to you guys for your endurance and encouragement throughout this tortuous and torturous academic safari.

1

Decolonizing history, memory and method

The burden of history and memory: A cursory note on method

The history of Ọza people in Edo State of Nigeria is a dynamic story, an unfolding narrative in motion that entails a critical and reflexive reminiscing into a real and imagined historical past with a view to reconstructing, looking forward to the future of that past as well as the past of the present and the future. We pay crucial attention to the complexities, burdens of history and memory in attempting to reconstruct Ọza historical, cultural and religious imagination. I employ social, cultural and epistemic reflexivity in exploring Ọza indigeneity, and in locating their complex religious, sociocultural and political history within decolonising discourse. My locationality and positionality helps to plug the book within decolonizing knowledges and indigeneity discourses, thus unpacking the complexity of 'indigeneity' and contributing to its conceptual understanding within socioreligious change in contemporary Africa. This often involves a delicate process of retooling, retracing, reinterpreting and retelling. This book privileges the voices of Ọza people in telling their own stories, histories and narratives through their own cosmological imaginaries, mental maps of their cosmos, and how this is shaped by people they encounter and who live around them. Several themes dominate Ọza historiography: world views, cosmologies and religious cultures. As a category of analysis for the study of Ọza culture and society, religion is quintessential to our understanding of its indigenous cultures. I contend that the perception of religion as a phenomenon separate from culture, language and politics is not a suitable reflection of the embedded nature of 'religion' in Ọza indigenous cultural imagination.

Based on scanty extant published material on the historical origins and migration of the Ọza (Ọja/Ọjah)[1] people, this book has depended largely on oral traditions, storytelling and historical myths in reconstructing this mostly undocumented history. Information gleaned from archival sources, and the few existing published and unpublished works, is contrasted and critically appraised with the robust data gathered through extensive field ethnography including interviews, focus-group discussions and participant observation at various rituals, ceremonies and festivals. Perhaps two of the earliest published secondary sources with sparse information on Ọza are the two volumes of Northcote W. Thomas's (1910) *Anthropological Report on the Edo-Speaking Peoples* and Ray E. Bradbury's (1957) comparative ethnographic survey of the *Benin Kingdom and the Edo-Speaking Peoples of South-Western Nigeria Including the Ishan, the Northern Edo, the Urhobo and Isoko of the Niger Delta*.[2] These books, the former by a government anthropologist and the latter being part of a larger publication project – the *Ethnographic Survey of Africa* – are fairly dated and provide a limited and sometimes inaccurate treatment of these diverse peoples and contexts in many places. They nevertheless serve as colonial information banks about the early histories and cultures of the Benin Kingdom and the Edo-speaking peoples. As D. Forde noted about Bradbury's book then,

> despite the fame of the sculptural art of Benin and the considerable travel literature on Benin City, there has hitherto been very little scholarly work and publication on the culture and social institutions of the kingdom or of the other Edo-speaking peoples. The present account benefits from the lengthy and intensive field studies of its author and represents a preliminary outline of the results of his researches so far ... During these three years, while working most intensively in the capital and in the villages of the kingdom, he made an ethnographic reconnaissance of the other Edo-speaking groups. (1957: vi)

Nevertheless, the dearth of published works on the Benin Kingdom or the Bini-Edo has shifted with the growing proliferation of research publications over the last few decades. The history and cultures of Ọza people, one of the Northern Edo towns as described by Bradbury, share commonalities with several towns and villages in Northern Edo but also among Benin and other Edo-speaking peoples. Herein lies the import of this early colonial ethnographical survey in documenting the early history and cultures of Ọza people, particularly during the colonial era and interwar years. The historical myths of origin and migration, and cultural, social organization and political systems have contrasting features. It is therefore logical to attempt to reconstruct Ọza traditions of origin and history within the broader historical tapestry of Benin and Edo-speaking peoples. This book has relied mostly on mixed methods and multiple sources in gathering, synthesizing and analysing primary and secondary data, albeit reflexively. The sources avail robust data, but we have also used the data with some caution and circumspection, paying careful attention to the pitfalls of hagiography, emic-etic dilemma, power dynamics, accuracy and precision in detail, memory and the politics of remembering and forgetting in the process of redacting the multiple source texts and narratives.

Any decolonizing knowledges project, such as in this book, must take due cognizance of how the official archivization of memory has the potential of privileging certain aspects of historical and cultural memories, while at the same time producing archival silences and in that process trapping other forms of historical and cultural memories into oblivion, the dustbin of history. Decolonizing knowledges is an intentional, intricate negotiation process of 'messing things up', that is problematizing imposed, hegemonic epistemologies with a view towards uncolonizing, reinterrogating and relearning indigenous epistemologies within the framework of multiple, contested ways of knowing and knowledge production. It is a delicate process of first decentring colonial European knowledges, often taken for granted as the *be-all* and *end-all* of knowledge production; and then recentring and reimagining indigenous epistemes within embodied knowledges. Such a delicate process has the potentiality of envisioning and unpacking the blind spots and upsides of memory. We shall briefly highlight some challenges in the methods we utilized in collecting, harnessing and analysing oral and written sources, and reflect on their downsides as the burden of history and memory.

Generally, the historiography of African religions and spiritualities provides a significant template for understanding and deconstructing indigenous epistemologies within global academic studies (Adogame 2015:1813–26). The growth, development of old and new forms of religions and spiritualities in Africa, and the academic, public, insiders'/outsiders' discourses they engender are laced with interpretational powers that are often conflictual in nature. This historiography is burdened, on the one hand, by competing claims for the power of interpretation between African and non-African scholars, and, on the other hand, the different academic orientations, scholarly approaches and historical phases aimed at defining, explaining, interpreting and (de)legitimizing African religious beliefs and ritual systems.

Encumbering historiography: Africa as object, Africa as subject

The historical trajectory of the study of religions in Africa has evolved through several phases, each involving different purposes and points of view. Jan Platvoet best categorized these overlapping epochs paradigmatically as 'Africa as Object' and 'Africa as Subject' when its religions were studied virtually exclusively by scholars and other observers from outside Africa, and as 'Africa as Subject' when the religions of Africa had begun to be studied also, and increasingly mainly, by African scholars (Platvoet, Cox, and Olupona 1996: 105). Descriptions and theories of Africa's religious history have been essential elements of the cultural contacts since the very first encounters and remain so up to the present (Ludwig and Adogame 2004: 2). As Platvoet demonstrated, travelogues and missionary and colonial historiographies of the late eighteenth and early nineteenth centuries pioneered the study of and writing about the religions of Africa. These early genres were essentially non-scholarly collections of random observations, superficial opinions and inaccurate information often impregnated with cultural bias and prejudices. Such accounts by Victorian travellers such as Sir Samuel Baker, Richard Burton and James Hunt, and Christian missionaries including Thomas Bowen and David Livingstone had their target audience. They were designed to appeal to the popular Western mind and so were written for this specific public. While some accounts denied Africans any modicum of religion, others made African religions appear as a morass of bizarre beliefs and practices. Most scholars in this phase were 'children of their age', ultimately regarding Africans as culturally 'degraded', thus reinforcing popular prejudice. Nevertheless, their accounts were useful to the extent to which they served as an 'information bank' upon which several scholars later depended. The traits of prejudice that dominated these accounts continue to haunt some learned minds and the academia today. The basic terminologies such as 'primitive', 'nonliterate' and 'premodern', which still find some space in contemporary scholarship, are hardly value-free. They still characterize Africa as the sharp opposite of the West, or the 'heart of darkness' (Conrad 1993), thus reinforcing a negative perspective.

It is therefore expedient that (African) scholars reinterrogate the concepts and terminologies we employ in describing African histories, religions and cultures. The earliest phase, as described by Platvoet, was supplanted by armchair ethnographers and evolutionary anthropologists who propounded theories on the origin and evolution of human culture following evolutionary paradigms.

One feature of this phase was classical approaches championed by nineteenth-century theories such as those by Edward B. Tylor and James G. Frazer. This era produced a barrage of opprobrious labels including animism, fetishism, idolatry, primitivism, totemism, superstition, heathenism and magic to designate the indigenous religions of Africa. These incongruous terms stamped indigenous religions of Africa with an appearance of sameness and primitiveness, and a stigma of inferiority, especially in comparison with Islam and Christianity.

With the decline of evolutionary theory and the advent of social anthropology, systematic fieldwork studies of African societies took root in the late nineteenth century. Anthropological approaches developed in different directions such as the fieldwork approach of Bronislaw Malinowski and the social-functionalist theory of Alfred Radcliffe-Brown. Edward Evans-Pritchard developed a new approach characterized by a shift from function to meaning. A new crop of British scholars including John Middleton and Victor Turner emerged. French anthropologists focused on African cosmological systems and implicit philosophies demonstrating that African religious systems are not simply reflections of socio-economic relations but form coherent and autonomous spheres of thought and action. A notable example is the work of Marcel Griaule among the Dogon of Mali (Griaule 1965). These systematic field studies slanted fieldwork studies according to author's nationality and imposed a 'colonialist' structure upon the interpretation of African social and religious systems. Different colonial policies, backgrounds and experiences significantly affected the study of and research on religion in postcolonial African contexts.

While the government anthropologist Northcote Thomas's report on the Edo-speaking peoples of Nigeria (Thomas 1910) was a product of an earlier phase of colonial historiography, Bradbury's book was a product of the third phase in the study and writing about Africa. They represent the findings of the systematic fieldwork studies of the Benin Kingdom and Edo-speaking peoples of Nigeria. As one of the several volumes of the *Ethnographic Survey of Africa*, Radcliffe-Brown chaired a committee of the International African Institute to determine the scope and general arrangement, and undertook the editing of the *Survey* (Forde 1957: v). The generous collaboration of several research institutions and administrative officers in Europe and in the African territories, as well as the services of senior anthropologists, was secured. The project received collaboration from French and Belgian authorities and ethnologists such as Griaule and others. Forde aptly remarked, 'Since the unequal value and unsystematic nature of existing material was one of the reasons for undertaking the Survey, it is obvious that these studies cannot claim to be complete or definitive; it is hoped, however, that they will present a clear account of our existing knowledge and indicate where information is lacking and further research is needed' (1957: v–vi).

The 1950s and 1960s onwards marked the era of integrated and consolidated research on the history and religions of Africa, the transition from *Africa as Object* to *Africa as Subject*. The word *religion* is a latecomer to the scholarly discourse about Africa. It was only in the late colonial period of the 1950s that scholars began to use the terms *religion* and *philosophy* to characterize African religions in a positive way. Attention shifted to more recent limited forms of cultural and religious change through specially designed fieldwork projects, utilizing oral traditions, political history and contemporary socio-religious analysis. A small number of philosophically and theologically oriented comparative studies by both European and African scholars developed. Their interpretations greatly influenced European understanding of African religions. European scholars did not only dominate this endeavour, viz., the academic study of religions in Africa, but they also impinged their methodologies and brought their world views and epistemologies to bear. In fact, the academic study of religion in Africa has its roots outside the continent, just as the very category of religion itself has a European history.

Within this critical historical milieu, the colonial and missionary machineries invented ways of knowing and meaning-making that anchored and facilitated processes of subjugation, exploitation and expropriation. Alien forms of reasoning were entrenched while also laying claims to a 'civilizing mission'. The 'European' knowledge introduced into Africa came on a collision course with indigenous knowledge systems in a spate of ideological contestation, culminating in a bricolage of knowledges. The knowledge funnelled through the colonial process took centre stage, assuming a dominant epistemology that marginalized and almost silenced alternative world views and conceptualizations of the universe. Such a hegemonic way of knowing and meaning-making was even presumed to be able to turn indigenous epistemologies on their head (Adogame 2015: 1815). In short, the colonization of memory has been clever in assaulting world views and religions (Falola 2007).

Legacies of the European Enlightenment filtered thought patterns that legitimized tropes of Otherness and binaries of difference espoused as tradition versus modernity, primitive versus civilized, superiority versus inferiority complex into the very fabric of the dominant knowledge. It was characteristic of the forms of reasoning that it privileged and superimposed on other cultures. This dominant knowledge was liberating and transforming but also entrapping.

The contestation that ensued in the production of knowledge produced a chasm of epistemological richness and bankruptcy at the same time. Indigenous epistemologies hardly witnessed their obituary in the face of the knowledge encounter that ensued. This scenario produced multiple discourses and theories of knowledge, and through this knowledge production it is continually negotiated in ways that result in the reification of some meaning-making systems, the invention of others, and in a kind of 'hybridized' epistemologies. This (re)production and contestation of ways of knowing and meaning-making has dire implications for unpacking and decolonizing indigenous epistemologies. Thus, the process of deconstructing indigenous epistemologies is largely congruent with, to borrow Cynthia Dillard's phrase, 'learning to (re)member the things we've learned to forget' (2012: 4).

The experience of colonization and sustained interaction with the West has produced and continues to perpetuate an imagined culture in transition from tradition to modernity. The chasm created between tradition and modernity is now being turned on its head as such binaries of opposition are no longer very convincing. It is more useful in some sense to talk of the modernity of African cultures and traditions in an era of social-cultural flux. A proper grasp of indigenous epistemologies is central to the conceptual issues that modernization then and globalization now raises. Processes of transformation and change are not merely driven by sociopolitical agendas but are informed distinctly by the knowledge closest to the people. The sociocultural landscape, including indigenous knowledge and technologies of diverse communities and groups, correlates directly with the dynamics of change and the transformation of individuals' as well as groups' cultural meaning systems and sense of belonging. The spiritual, physical and animal worlds, as well as local geographies are central in this consideration too. Therefore, any analysis or interpretation of existing or changing cultural patterns and societal institutions, terrestrial and extraterrestrial worlds, how they are conditioned and who conditions them, cannot claim validity without full recognition of the important role indigenous knowledge systems play – a fact largely discarded by colonial knowledge hegemony.

In the intellectual enterprise highlighted above, it is important to mention that European scholars did not only dominate this endeavour but also impinged their methodologies and brought their world views and epistemologies to bear. The very concept 'religion', like 'Africa', is a Western invention, an academic construct involving both misconceptions and changing perceptions that hardly does justice to the complexity of African spiritualities. The perception of religion as a phenomenon separate from culture is not a suitable reflection of the embedded nature of 'religion' in African cultures. In most African societies, religion is variously conceptualized as a spiritual, epistemological and philosophical phenomenon. As a category of analysis for the study of societies, religion is, therefore, quintessential to our understanding of African cultures in a global context. While we continue to use the concept 'religion' to embrace African spiritualities, one should be aware of its limitations and tendency to obscure its dynamism. To explain African political, social, cultural and religious life in Western categories can be informing, illuminating and offering useful insights, just as it could be misleading and obscuring. African modes of thought, ritual patterns and symbolism that are integral to their religious worlds are sometimes puzzling to Western ethnography.

Undoubtedly, European scholars have contributed significantly to the understanding of African histories, cultures and religions, but they have also paved the path in its obscurity and public misunderstanding. Certainly, while we stress the need for African scholars to take vantage positions in telling 'their own story' and in (de)constructing indigenous epistemologies, there is an inherent danger in this endeavour if caution is not taken. We do not suggest that all Africans necessarily speak in the same language, have the same voice or reason in the same way. The challenge for Africans to take a vantage position in contesting dominant epistemologies and in knowledge (re)production is a pertinent one indeed. It will certainly allow more Africans to speak for themselves, although this 'speaking for oneself' could run the risk of romanticizing and essentializing African histories, spiritualities and religious cultures.

However, it is expedient that scholars of African history, religions, societies and cultures constantly reinterrogate the dynamic phenomenon that forms the basis of their research. They must be reflexive about the theories they utilize, the very concepts they embrace and the conclusions they come up with. African history, religions, societies and cultures are hardly static and unchanging; rather, they are dynamic and constantly in flux. Religion is not a museum piece or tourist-trod monument but a vibrant force in the lived experiences of many African people around the world; many religious traditions such as indigenous African religions are presently experiencing a renaissance. Old approaches to understanding and explaining history and religions are being increasingly challenged. Theories and interpretations from classical works on histories and religions of Africa may be turning moribund and need urgent revisiting on the basis that these histories, beliefs and rituals have been changing and transforming all the time. Besides the power contestation in telling, researching and writing the story of Africa, the Arab and trans-Atlantic trade in humans had a devastating blow on the continent. When millions of people were enslaved and when their continent was forcefully conquered, it was a strategy both of justification and domination to deny the people a past, a memory. The maintenance of power also meant the creation of a new history to erase the previous. Africans were told they had no history and that they made no significant contributions to world civilization. This leads us to the second critical point, memory.

Remembering and forgetting: The politics of memory

Memory is a dynamic process. When we remember, we select, organize, omit, imagine and sometimes invent aspects of our past experiences according to what we need, feel and believe in the present moment. Thus, the memories of the past are fluid (Hamilton 2002: 209–28). How do memory and imagination play out against the backdrop of traumatic encounters in varied postcolonial African contexts? To what extent do these encounters shape processes of 'dismembering' and 'remembering' of the future's past? Virtually all African societies, histories and religious cultures are concerned with memory, although in different degrees. There are varied ways in which the discourse on memory is embedded and embodied, and it has always been integral to understanding histories, religio-cultural sensibilities and lifeworlds in Africa. One of several forms through which we can approach memory is as mnemonic devices employed in the oral preservation of texts. Myths and legends, stories, folk tales, proverbs, riddles and songs found in large numbers among African peoples and societies are repositories of memory and serve as sources for indigenous histories, cultures and religions. They are handed down or transmitted orally, sometimes through storytelling. While it is important to explore the relationship between myth and memory, there is also a link between myth, history and ritual. The politics of memory also invokes a stark unpacking of historical, cultural and cognitive memories in decolonizing indigenous knowledges and religious imagination. It enables us to raise ethical, race, gender and power enigmas and inherent biases in archival methodologies. Paying attention to hierarchies of knowledge production, especially one that privileges the primacy of archives, leads to the discovery of formal archival public projection and silences, lost and unsung voices, voices of disloyal and subversive elements. It also illuminates how the conscious institutional exclusion of certain sensibilities and forms of expression, as archival repositories, were consequential in narrative lacunae, inherently void in our grasping and comprehending of historical past and present.

Maurice Halbwachs (1877–1945) is one of the pioneering scholars of contemporary memory studies who defined memory as a social phenomenon 'which grows into us from outside'. Memory is always a social and collective endeavour in which '[social] frameworks are ... the instruments used by the collective memory to reconstruct an image of the past which is in accord, in each epoch, with the predominant thoughts of the society' (Halbwachs [1925] 1992: 40). In exploring the social framework of memory and collective memory, he opined that our memory only develops through our intercourse with other people. Most memories depend on a social environment to live through. In the act of remembering, we do not just descend into the depths of our own most intimate inner life, but we introduce into that internal life an order and a structure that are socially conditioned and that link us to the social world ([1925] 1992: 40). The complexity of remembering is partly because memory is not an intrinsic individual act influenced by our personal needs and perspective but one (re)shaped by contextual social exigencies and constructed world views. The enigma is not only about the 'W-questions' – 'what', 'when', 'why' and 'where' we remember – but also the 'H-question' – 'how' we remember. This is also coterminous with the 'W' and 'H' questions on forgetting. These variables ingrain the mental acts and politics of remembering to forget and forgetting to remember. We bear these intricacies of history and memory in our mind as we attempt in this book to reconstruct Ọza history, religious world views and cultures.

Decolonizing from my locationality and positionality

I have engaged in three decades of robust religious ethnography, carrying out longitudinal studies that resulted in this book. My engagement with such a decolonizing enterprise involves constant reflecting on my social, epistemic and cultural locationality, on the one hand, and positionality as a scholar of religion (a historian of religion), an ethnographer and as an Ọza indigene, on the other hand. As Malory Nye aptly remarks, 'decolonization requires scholars to recognize their own structural location within the disciplinary history and the institutions where they teach and research' (2019: 5). I hail from Ọza (both parentage), which qualifies me as an indigene (a 'native') in the first place. I belong also to the Ọza and Nigerian diaspora, having lived in Germany and the UK (Europe) and the United States for almost three decades. At the same time,

I currently hold dual citizenship as Nigerian and British. All these instances of multiplex, intersectional identities shape my structural locationality and positionality in complex, myriad ways. The complicated positionality tension that one faces as an indigenous researcher points one to considering cultural and ethical responsibilities at the same time (Tachine, Bird and Cabrera 2016: 278).

As an Ọza indigene, male, Christian, Okuroshọ, Ọkpameri, Edo, Nigerian, African and now British scholar teaching in European and American universities, researching in Africa and the African diaspora in Europe and the United States in particular, these diverse cultural, social and geographical contexts and intersectional identities have informed and shaped my sociability. At the same time, these social, cultural and epistemic locations are instrumental to rediscovering and reconfiguring the inventiveness of Ọza religious imaginaries and cultural ambience. I have come to relearn, in a rather hard way, that the best way to learn about and appreciate oneself, who you think you are, is by learning and knowing about others. The more you learn about and encounter other peoples, societies and cultures, the more you come to understand, treasure and appreciate your cultural mien, self-identity, who you are in contradistinction with what people think of you and how they have come to know you and learn about you. My first-hand encounters, experiences and instantiations of institutional and non-institutional xenophobia often exacerbate nostalgic feelings and quest for self-identity and preservation of my cultural, ethnic and religious identities. Such embodied exigencies of life evoke rhetorical reverberations – 'Who I am, where I am coming from, and who/what do I wish to become?' – in my very subconscious. One starkly confronts delicate choices under prevailing conditions and social power dynamics. There is a tendency of people wanting to shut you up or shout you down for obvious but also opaque reasons. One option is to capitulate, cave in to cajoling and repudiating the identity of the Self. The alternative is to affirm your dignity and self-worth, reclaim and reaffirm your self-identity, as well as your religio-cultural and ethnic identities. To be able to do the latter entails the resilience of never quitting. You constantly have to receive, resist and remember what people say but also what they fail to and did not say. One way of staying woke and in combating the scourge of systemic and institutional racism is to disburden oneself, resist and not allow the burden of racism define you or weigh you down. This is expedient in building one's epistemic immunity and cognitive vaccine against the noesis of hegemonic intellectualism.

As an African with dual Nigerian and British citizenship (if you like, an African with a British passport) living as a permanent resident in the United States, one is often getting numb to the literal phrase of being 'sick and tired of being sick and tired', the resounding noise of silence in staying woke to a human emergency of removing 'the knees off the necks of black bodies', wanton inhumanity and of the many contradictions and hypocrisy unleashed in perceptibly 'modern' democratic societies such as North America and Europe. For instance, the 'white replacement' conspiratorial theory in the United States is an invented myth of self-preservation, social insecurity and timidity; human despondency and survival instinct that increasingly segue toward an unwarranted epidemic of racial-laden hate crimes, mass gun shootings, indiscriminate killings and waste of human bodies; gun profiteering, racial violence, domestic terrorism and a deeply ingrained misogynistic mindset. The delusional claims to liberty, individual freedom and rights, and second amendment phantasmagoria that validate gun hoarding, primitive accretion of weapons of mass human destruction and senseless gun mass killings appear to be setting America on the tripod of self destruction and debasement of humanity, and in which an imagined 'land of the free and home of the brave' is witnessing the mother of all civilizational and social collapses. In Europe, especially in the case of the UK, the ghost and relics of Empire are resilient and hover nostalgically around the imperial choreography of the Commonwealth of Nations as former territories of the British Empire. Such improvisation and manoeuvring of remnant coloniality of power leave some adopted members of the Commonwealth to query whether and what is indeed common about the Commonwealth. Is Commonwealth common to all member nations, or is it more common to some than the others? Who pays the piper and who dictates the tune of Commonwealth? What concretely is 'the common good' of the Commonwealth beyond political-economic trappings and face-saving gimmicks cushioning colonial hegemony?

The observable, stark paradoxes of contemporary Western societies remind one of *afẹ kafẹ* (home is home), my ancestral abode, and the reality of not taking anything for granted. This is against the backdrop of the incessant waging of war on peace, the erosion of humaneness and truth, racial injustices and social inequities within contemporary political, socio-economic and religious landscapes. This is rather daunting as a cross-section of society endorse and seek to institutionalize 'falsehood' at the expense of truth-telling. This reification of tropes of falsehood, the QAnonization of unreality, the falsification of and conspiracy against truth, myths of 'white' replacement theory, incidences of racial injustice, police brutality and wasting of Black human bodies, misogyny, unbridled hate, bias and prejudice, culture wars, abject denialism, indiscriminate endorsement of 'cancel culture' and the demagoguery of political opportunism is rather grotesque. The global commodification of untruth, in other words, the truth of lies and the lies of truth, is indeed part of devious stratagems that have gone berserk. Wanton reverberations of public silence are resoundingly pronounced, bereft of spontaneous vocal bemoaning of moral bankruptcy. Such public quietude and numb passivity towards an emerging culture of conspiratorial dissembling is complicity, and they thus undergird the antinomies of a fragile democratic experimentation and the re-institutionalization of 'modern' authoritarianisms in so-called developing neoliberal economies. In fact, one is unsure if this unprecedented development is integral to and constitutive of 'modern', 'developed', 'civilized' societies.

I am persuaded about the urgency of deconstructing and discarding the racialized categories of 'Black', 'brown', 'white' and 'coloured' bodies or peoples. The European enlightenment and imperialism projects bequeath to the consternation of the world the indiscriminate stigmatization and diabolization of the Black skin and Black human bodies, *tout court*. This was to perpetually stamp Black bodies with a stigma of inferiority and condemn them to infinite subjugation, slavedom and eternal manipulation. The premise of my argument is simply put: if white, Black, brown and yellow bodies are inherently colour variations, where is the logicality in depicting Black/brown bodies as coloured and white as colourless people? This makes no logical and empirical sense whatsoever. With a coruscating kaleidoscope of colours that we behold, any claim therefore that depicts the opalescence of white people as colourless and the others as coloured is a tacit endorsement of implicit, racial Othering and malignant politics of difference. In other words, such a perception induces an artificial raciality that reinforces and validates a false sense of superiority, securitization of white supremacy and white normativity at the behest of invented inferioritization of an imagined people of colour. From my social location, the appropriation of such race-infested binaries, by its very conscious and unconscious utility, re-intensifies the institutionalization of systemic racism and the colonial matrix of power, with a backlash of seismic dimensions on the identity of the Self and the racialized Other. The unbridled myth of a white replacement stratagem is partly framed and flamed around racial intolerance, implicit bias, domestic terrorism and the politicization, diabolization and criminalization of immigrants. I contend that the convoluted binary of race, in terms of Black/brown/white, is rather simplistic and too narrow to unpack the gravity in meaning of colonial-induced racial differentiations, injustices, implicit bias and ingrained prejudices that has come to delineate, dominate and invade public and private spaces.

A better nuancing is imperative and expedient in further problematizing the somewhat tortuous intra-racial racisms, unwarranted sentiments, vicious bias and prejudices resulting from a backlash of the politics of institutional, non-institutional and systemic racisms, injustices and implicit bias and prejudices, in the face of fragile local-global political economies. The vulnerability of international faculty, students, immigrants and workers to double racisms deserves further attention. There is a subtle politics of differentiation and reification of Otherness that goes on intra-racially. Even when racialized categories continue to be appropriated, there is a contemporaneous power tension and inherent politics of identity and re-Othering in which self-styled gatekeepers engage in and decide 'who is Black and who is not Black enough', 'who is Asian and who is not Asian enough', 'who is white versus who is not white enough' and 'who is coloured and who is colourless'. The messiness and mussiness that go with such a scenario of re-Othering complicate a rather simplified white/Black/brown/coloured binary of racial Otherness.

From my social location, one can observe an inverse proportionality in the racial categorization and differentiation of human bodies as legacies from the colonial lexicon. In my home town, Ọza, Europeans and others involved in the coloniality of Western power were often dubbed as *Obo, Obo ọfọmi lẹkẹ-lẹkẹ* (literally European, white-yellow, coloured). Thus, in Ọza people's mental imagination, the Europeans and white-yellow Westerners are Othered as white-yellow coloured, while in some sense the black colour is perceived as authentic, original and thus colourless of some sort. The racialization of colour and the colourization of race signify iterations and instantiations of colour blindness. This politics of inversion is not peculiar to Ọza people; we can observe a popular utility in the sense that *obo* is even an inflection from Yoruba, *oyinbo/eniyan alawo funfun* (white, yellow people). Europeans and Westerners are generally referred, albeit pejoratively, in Igbo/Ibo language as *onyeochia/ndi ocha*, Hausa as *bature/pature/fararen mutane*, Akan/Twi as *obroni*, Zulu as *abelungu*, Xhosa as *abantu abamhlophe*, Swahili as *muzungu/wazungu* and Shona as *vachena*, respectively.

This racial imagination inverts identification of the human person through skin hyperpigmentation. This engenders binaries of colour ordering and disordering in terms of superior/inferior, original/artificial, authentic/inauthentic and good/bad. The symbolic values oft-ascribed to 'white' came to denote socially desirable, pure; 'Black' denoting the very opposite as socially undesirable, inauthentic, bad; while 'red' could symbolize ambiguous, danger. White colour is depicted as *ọnọfọmi* in Ọza, *Fitaa* in Akan/Twi and *Funfun* in Yoruba, although it is atypically inflected as racial categorizations of the Other, in this case 'white' Europeans and Westerners. In short, Europeans and Westerners are people of colour by virtue of their perceived white and yellow colour differentiation. Such signification depicts the narrative of Self against the hegemonic Other at the intersection of the colonial matrix of power or the coloniality of power. At the same time, while the racial delineation of Africans, all African descendants (diaspora) including African Americans, stamps them with a racial-coloured identity as Blacks, such a collective, public-ascribed identity has gained some currency in the western hemisphere, albeit with some contestations and varied permutations. The interiorization of this colour blindness has resulted in an internalized inferiority/superiority complex, indiscriminate skin permutation, the endemication of mental slavery and the alterity and mentality of a double-colour consciousness that the late Afro-beat musician, social critic and philosopher, Fela Anikulapo Kuti,[3] aptly captures in his song lyrics as 'Yellow Fever', 'double colour' syndrome,

> Fela deplores the fashion among African women for skin-whitening creams, an example of the post-colonial inferiority complex he believed was holding back the country's development. The song addresses the fashion much as 1973's 'Gentleman' berated African men for adopting European suits and ties. Fela explains that if you catch an 'original' fever such as jaundice, you will suffer but, with luck, survive, and your symptoms will fade away. But if you catch an 'artificial' (self-inflicted) fever, such as the craze for skin bleaching: '*Artificial catch you ... na your money go do am for you, you go pass yellow, you go catch moustache for face, you got get your double colour, your yansch go black like coal, you self go think say you dey fine (but) who say you dey fine?*' Whitening creams make you look sick on the outside, says Fela, and are symptomatic of being sick inside, too.[4]

As I have indicated, Ọza people turn this public colour racialization of human bodies on its head. Africans' racial imagination of Europeans and Westerners is generally depicted with white/yellow colour, while Europeans and Westerners generally identify Africans as Black/coloured. In this case, the European, white, Western bodies is *obo ọfọmi lẹkẹ-lẹkẹ* (white, coloured, European, Western), while Ọza, Nigerian, African, African American, Black human bodies are somewhat colourless. Who is not coloured? Are white, Black, yellow and brown not variations of colour? Such racializing tropes of Otherness in terms of colour depictions remain problematic, in my view, in that it essentializes the human body, the natural skin pigmentation, in which one is coloured and the other colourless. Thus, we need to reinterrogate how and to what extent we perpetuate such racially ingrained categories of human bodies, as this binarial delineation falls into tatters as self-induced colour blindness. Make no mistake, I am not unsympathetic to how such colonial colour signification is now emblematic of power, empowerment and identity constructs as 'Black Power', 'Black is Beautiful', 'I am Black and Proud', and even the recent popular slogan and movement 'Black Lives Matter'. These are useful instantiations and contestations of the coloniality of power that continues to perpetuate systemic racial, social, economic and epistemic injustices and implicit prejudices against the racialized Other. White, people of colour, Black and brown are racialized categories of ambivalence that predicate power and powerlessness, empowerment and disempowerment, privilege and disprivilege. However, should we not engage in decolonizing these clichés of Otherness and tropes of racialization as significations of Otherness, an Othering that continues to reify power dynamics and the colonial matrixes of power? Should we not discard from our epistemic lexicon and disenthrall ourselves from such public racial clichés of Otherness, as we engage in anti-racism and decolonizing discourses within academic and public landscapes?

The decolonization enterprise is reminiscent of, and could be likened to, stark life-threatening outbursts best captured in Rev. Al Sharpton's powerful eulogy at the memorial service for George Floyd on 4 June 2020. This was an emotionally charged event characterized by mixed poignant memories and humorous life moments with unapologetic calls for genuine social justice. In a rather sharp tone, he retorts,

> George Floyd's story is the story of black folks ... You all talk about making America great, great for who and when? We gonna make America great for everybody ... You kept your knee on our neck. We had creative skills, but we couldn't get your knee off our neck ... The reason we could never be who we wanted and dreamed of being is you kept your knee on our neck ... Like George, we couldn't breathe ... You wouldn't take your knee off our neck. It's time for us in George's name to stand up and say, get your knee off our necks. We don't want favors, just get off of us, and we can be and do whatever we can be.[5]

This is a poignant remembering and forgetting that indigenous peoples, Africans and people of African descent cannot breathe until the coloniality of power take knees off their necks so that indigenous lifeways can breathe and speak for themselves.

The fetishization of race, ethnicity and identity of indigenous peoples, Africans and people of African descent as 'people of colour' is a racial virus, a conundrum that needs a vaccine urgently. This involves speaking the bitter truth, however irksome it might sound to some, to the coloniality of power and highlighting how this perpetuation of racial stereotyping concatenates systemic racism, implicit bias, prejudice and the institutionalization of white supremacy and white normativity. The time is now, I would argue, to adopt a rear-view mirror gaze at this malignant colour blindness which rather fetishizes, diabolizes and denigrates a people group than edify them. It is against this backdrop that I contend that the sustained appropriation of such racialized categories evokes nostalgia of institutionalized apartheid ('distantiation' in the Afrikaans language) and egregious colour bar polarities of difference as in South Africa, and the horrendous 'separate but equal' racial segregation laws of Jim Crow. There is nothing inherently wrong, bad or defective with being 'Black', with being African, 'BLACK' human bodies or even the colour 'black,' except in the instrumentalization and inferiorization that makes some people think, sense and feel so.

Nonetheless, caution is expedient in telling and retelling the (his)tory of Ọza people, their social and religious imagination, and meaning-making subjectivities. Self-reflexivity is quintessential so as to avoid slipping into romanticizing and essentializing Ọza world views, cosmologies and religious cultures. Thus, this raises the question of how I employ social, epistemic and cultural reflexivity (cf. Spickard 2021: 180–94), in navigating my in-betweenness status as a dispassionate scholar, my avidity in privileging a 'native' narrative, while negotiating emic-etic dynamics and the insider-outsider enigma. In methodological terms, I position myself as an 'insider-outsider' and 'outsider-insider' contemporaneously. This enables social, cultural and epistemic reflexivity, thus confronting cognitive dissonance and/or psychological ambivalence. As Mpoe Keikelame and Leslie Swartz aptly remark, 'the importance of reflexivity and self-reflexivity as a transformative approach in a decolonizing process cannot be over emphasized' (2019: 6). As a 'native' scholar exploring Ọza community, it is not simply an issue of being inside or outside of the process but the knowledge and awareness I bring as a researcher to my study. It is a delicate balance of conducting and analysing research in a culturally appropriate way (cf. Tachine, Bird and Cabrera 2016: 279–80). I explored alternative methods for individual and group discussions that incorporated storytelling and the cultural nuances of Ọza people. Besides, I have a mastery of Ọza language which is central to storytelling, as story and knowing/meaning is intricately connected.

After almost three decades of my academic hiatus, I cannot take it for granted that I know about the Ọza cultural and social universe, *in toto*, as if it is static and undynamic. I am in touch with home and endeavour to visit Nigeria frequently, almost every other year; however, this does not give me a mastery of Ọza culture as I hardly live there anymore. Christmas time was the most opportune time to visit the village as it is a festive time filled with pomp, a time when you catch up with family, friends and close acquaintances you may not have seen for years. It is also a time to eat good, fresh food, 'real food' indeed. Here I am, the last time I spent Christmas at home, Ọza, was probably thirty years ago. As an Ọza indigene who has sojourned in Europe and North America for the past twenty-six years, sociocultural and epistemic reflexivity enables me to unlearn, learn and relearn. I needed to navigate emic-etic positionality and my old/new social locationality. This entails opening up to the cultural, religious and social universe in order that each respective phenomenon opens up to me. This has helped me to uncover multiple layers of hegemony, coloniality of power, as I delved into the foregrounds and backgrounds of Ọza historical, cultural, political, economic and religious imaginaries.

As we shall see in this book, I went a step further to delineate and name colonization and hegemony from outside (European imperialism) but also from within (Nupe, Yoruba and Benin hegemonies) at the intersection of race, power, ethnicity, economic, political, religious, social and gender identities. Kimberle Crenshaw's (1991) 'intersectionality' denotes how race, class, gender and other systems combine to shape people's experiences through vestiges of bias, discrimination and privilege. This is a useful framework for grasping how intersectional identities overlap with one another and with systems of power that (dis)advantage Ọza people in the face of exogenic and endogenic dynamics. One of the ideas of intersectionality is for individuals, groups and communities to self-identity. Intersectionality helps to frame gender power identities in relation to patriarchy, the public objectification of female bodies and the social construction of femininity through initiation rituals of the female gender. However, gendered power contestation and women's sociality play out in the Ọza cultural, religious and social universe. Women's social positioning is intricately tied to their contribution, influence and identity-making. This means how they carry and position themselves, as well as their economic, political and ritual powers. This sociability produces embodied sensibilities around Ọza cultural, ritual and gendered spaces.

Second, my academic sojourn abroad has helped to shape how I read, teach, operationalize and refine thinking about colonization and decolonization. As an African who finds himself in these Western citadels of learning that are in dire need of deconstruction of power structures, I confront the rude challenge of speaking up or keeping quiet about these forms of hegemony and racialized structures that continue to dominate the ivory tower. The politics of knowledge acquisition, production, consumption and dissemination is a dynamic, intricate and contested terrain. It is bold, active, intense and zestful, but at other times it is messy, convoluted and discomfiting. The building of intellectual capital is also often accompanied by intellectual or cognitive smuggling, surplus accumulation, monopoly of production of knowledge of the Other, rights to intellectual property and the politics of research boundary policing and protection. It can be likened sometimes to an enterprise, a man-made artificial tussle of 'survival of the fittest' in which 'the big fish swallows the small fish'. Academic hegemony translates into one who has the right resources, mentoring and enablement. It translates into he who pays the piper dictates the tune, the parade of intellectual know-how and priding under false pretences as the 'expert' and 'authority' in the field. Haythem Guesmi (2018) offers a stark caution about the gentrification of African studies, borrowing from the Marxist sociologist Ruth Glass's (1964) coinage of the term 'gentrification' to interrogate the forced displacement of working-class occupiers by middle-class residents – the gentry – in parts of inner London and the resulting changes in the social structure and housing markets. Guesmi aptly observes that the gentrification of African studies is a threat to the field's social and political contributions and therefore requires an urgent and thoughtful intervention.

According to Guesmi, 'the gentrification of African studies has altered the social character of its community and generated a new set of problems such as visa issues, academic hipsterism, and restricted access to critical research, which risks to permanently exclude continent-based scholars, undermine their critical contributions, and eventually converts African studies into another impotent, banal field' (2018: 2). As he argues further, 'this process of gentrifying African studies calls into attention the shift toward an intellectual hegemony that marginalizes the academic presence and input of African scholars ... African studies is now a thinking machine whose postulates and propositions are largely defined outside the continent'. He hones in on the intersectional identities and dynamics that govern global African scholarship. He is quite apt, direct and convincing. Nevertheless, he offers a stern warning towards the re-ownership and re-institutionalization of an important academic and cultural field of African activism and emancipation: 'Shouting "decolonize this" or "decolonize that" in neoliberal spaces will not advance the African cause but contribute to a new grammar of reified identity politics. The gentrification of African studies has insidiously altered the revolutionary potential and goals of knowledge's decolonization' (2018: 5).

My teaching and research interests tend to focus on interrogating new dynamics of religious experiences and expressions in Africa and the African diaspora, with a particular focus on African Christianities and new indigenous religious movements, and the interconnectedness between religion and migration, globalization, politics, economy, media and the civil society. For over three decades, I have been teaching graduate courses on such themes as 'Vitality of Indigenous Religions of Sub-Saharan Africa', 'African Indigenous Churches and Globalization', 'Understanding Research Methods, Techniques and Data Analysis', 'Rethinking Religion in the Public Sphere: A Cross-Cultural Perspective', 'Concepts, Methods and Themes in World Christianity', 'The New African Christian Diaspora: Trajectories, Themes and Trends', and 'New Religious Movements in Global Perspectives' concurrently. Besides, my epistemic locationality revolves mainly around the interdisciplinary fields of Religious Studies, African Religions and Religions of the African Diaspora, Indigenous Studies, African Studies, World Christianity, New Religious Movements, and Sociology of Religion. Owing to the above, my research and teaching expertise agglutinates and evokes epistemic, but also social and cultural, reflexivities. Who am I teaching? What am I writing? Who I am writing for? In other words, who are my academic and ethnographic interlocutors and target audiences? How do I privilege and make indigenous voices heard and let them speak for themselves? How am I navigating my insider-outsider, etic-emic positionality in teaching and research? What research methods, research methodologies and analytical tools are best suited for my religious ethnography? To what extent do I pay attention to ethics in research especially working among indigenous people groups and vulnerable, marginalized and gendered communities? What ethical challenges and dilemmas do I face? These questions are very pertinent and germane. The topicality of themes such as indigenous, indigeneity, decolonizing knowledges, local agency, gender, power dynamics, spiritualities, religion, cosmologies, world views, research methodologies and so forth make them vital reference points in my teaching and research ethnography. I ruminate on and think with these and other pertinent questions as my 'checklist' or 'boxes to tick' at the intersection of my teaching and research.

Guesmi is perhaps also speaking indirectly to other epistemic communities such as Religious Studies, Indigenous Studies, African Religions, World Christianity and African Diaspora Studies that I identify with and subscribe to. There is a real, imagined gentrification of these disciplinary fields by some Western (European) captains of academic industries who often claim to know Africa better. They shape the trajectory of African religious studies, Indigenous religions and World Christianity in hegemonic ways that challenges 'African', 'indigenous', 'native', 'ethnic' scholars to be on their toes constantly. Natalie Avalos provides a decolonial and Indigenist approach to pedagogy, urging us 'to teach about power from your own position. Complicate your positionality and relation to power' through decolonial autobiography (2018: 6). In this way, Avalos suggests that we can better serve as models of, and for, decolonizing the production of knowledge in religious studies classroom. She contends, 'A decolonial approach makes the mechanisms of colonial power visible. It denaturalizes our assumptions about Indigenous peoples and their religious traditions ... Native-centered narratives often provide a more nuanced and tribally specific framework to understand sacred and interdependent relationships with land and spiritual power. Teaching these ideas is a layered and cumulative process' (2018: 4).

Avalos calls us to take a critical indigenous and ethnic studies approach to decolonizing religious studies (2020). Area or ethnic studies helps us to both illuminate and guide against macrocosms (microcosms) of hegemony. While Yoruba, Benin, Nupe, Hausa/Fulani Studies and so forth, but in particular studies on Yoruba religion and culture, dominate the Nigerian knowledge production economy, this book seeks to populate and contribute to that mix, the visibility of Ọza as one of other minority people groups whose histories, cultures and spiritualities are yet to be inscribed within the global academy. By invincibilizing Ọza histories, cosmologies and religious cultures, we attempt to demonstrate their indigeneity, while also underscoring the inherent homogeneity and heterogeneity of African religions and spiritualities.

As the title suggests, Nye's 'Decolonizing the Study of Religion' (2019) aptly underscores the urgency and pertinacity of a decolonizing knowledges project from the disciplinary standpoint of religious studies. As he aptly observes, 'the study of religion – like much of the humanities – is a disciplinary area with roots in the high period of European colonialism. The disciplinary formation of religious studies is a product of empire (Nye 2017), and so the questions it asks, its key concepts, and its presence within universities reflects this origin' (2019: 10). He notes further that 'although the study of religion serves an important function in exploring and transmitting ancient sources and philosophies from Asia, Africa and elsewhere, at the same time the discipline does so within a framework of colonially structured modernity' (2019: 12) Thus, Nye contends that one starting point for decolonizing the study of religion is to recognize and explore the discipline's historical contingency. One part of exploring and understanding this is to question and contextualize some of the terms and ideas that are 'taken for granted' within the discipline (2019: 14).

Nye raises very pertinent, pragmatic issues on the trajectories of decolonization and decolonizing the study of religion that we cannot fully unpack in this section. Perhaps his unpacking of decolonization could be best summed up in one sentence: 'Decolonization is about changing how people think, talk, and act through a radical engagement with a plurality of voices and perspectives that have been historically marginalized and silenced' (2019: 5) The section 'Reproducing the canon' of the essay is rather compelling methodologically. He hints that 'most programs in the study of religion require some consideration of the tools that are required for research and scholarship, what is often called "theory and methodology". Often these rely on assumptions and ideas that have not moved very far from the colonial beginnings of the discipline' (2019: 17). Nye was probably too harsh and sarcastic in observing that 'the study of religion is a room full of white people sitting around talking about things that people of colour do', and that 'in the study of religion there never has been any previous effort to decolonize' (2019: 22). He submits nonetheless,

> A process of attempting to decolonize the study of religion should require a methodological awareness of the historical and academic legacies within the discipline, in terms of the ways in which it is taught and researched, along with key assumptions about the subject matter (such as the concepts of religion and world religions) … Decolonizing is not an optional add-on: the discipline came into being through empire and colonialism, and the contemporary 'colonial matrix of power' is very often how the study of religion continues to justify itself … .decolonising requires a rethinking of the canons of both theory and methodology, and in particular the processes by which scholars engage with and frame their research. (2019: 27–8)

Akin to other humanities and social science disciplines as Nye points out, the contemporary study of religion is the product of European colonial history and remains firmly embedded in what Anibal Quijano described as the 'colonial matrix of power' (2000: 533–80). Avalos (2020) notes how such critiques remind us that the field was built upon colonial misreadings of the Other:

> As religious studies scholars, it is critical for us to explore the racialized perceptions of non-western religious traditions and peoples as well as to trace how these peoples continue to be structurally dispossessed as a result of those perceptions. Decolonizing religious studies means making the hierarchies that exist materially among peoples and their knowledge systems legible. It also means reclaiming and re-centering Indigenous epistemologies, given their historically violent subjugation.

She warns that 'scholars of religion must take seriously the real material effects of their contributing to constructions of Indigenous peoples as anything less than fully cogent, agentive, and as having rights to their lands. ... A decolonial framework articulates clear critiques of colonial power at the level of epistemology, visibilizing the need for Indigenous knowledge reclamations.'

In the same vein, Abdulkader Tayob (2020) asserts that the colonial imbrication of the discipline is ignored or only briefly acknowledged. Thus, one of the challenges of decolonization is to address this desire for an alternative method and theory against the reality of a distorted field, an enterprise in which scholarship monitors the intrusion of theology into the discipline, while allowing colonialist assumptions to go unchecked and unthought. As he aptly suggests,

> colonialism is often euphemistically represented as modernization or a benign intervention that changed the world. ... Paying close attention to the intellectual labour of critical voices from colonized contexts leads us to new insights on how to think about religion. ... I paid attention to the intellectual labor of Muslim critical voices instead. In a decolonial gesture, I turned my gaze away from Western scholars on religion, and paid attention to how religion was theorized in different political and social contexts. I have since realized that taking these critical voices seriously as intellectual labor goes against a dominant view of the study of religion. (Tayob 2020)

It is against this backdrop that the next section will briefly engage in historicizing the decolonizing discourse and anchor the decolonizing research methodologies that were integral in the research that led to this book. To this we shall now turn.

Engaging the decolonizing discourse

Discourses of decolonization, modernization and modernity are hardly novel. This is against the backdrop of the brutal legacies of colonialism and imperialism; their undercurrents and crosscurrents manifesting global economic, political and social inequities; and uneven power structures, fragile democratic experiments and authoritarian regimes under the so-called neoliberal age. As Walter Mignolo remarks,

> the crooked rhetoric that naturalizes 'modernity' as a universal global process and point of arrival hides its darker side, the constant reproduction of 'coloniality'. In order to uncover the *perverse logic* – that Fanon pointed out – underlying the philosophical conundrum of modernity/coloniality and the political and economic structure of imperialism/colonialism, we must consider how to

decolonize the 'mind' (Thiongo) and the 'imaginary' (Grunzinski) – that is, knowledge and being. (2007: 450)

Mignolo aptly concludes, 'The struggle for epistemic de-colonization ... is to link analysis from the perspective of coloniality and the grammar of de-coloniality (its ethical, political and theoretical consequences), with strategies, strategic plans towards the future. Such strategies will and are already taking place in different locals and histories ... and in diverse geo- and biopolitical genealogies of thought and action' (2007: 500).

From a historical perspective, the term 'decolonization' gained currency in reference to political processes following the apogee of European colonialism around the mid-twentieth century, an era when several countries under colonial rule wrestled political independence from the British, French and Dutch repressive colonial regimes. Political independence hardly supplanted colonization; rather, it has endured as a continuing process in the twenty-first century, eating cancerously deep into the economic, social, religious, cognitive and epistemological fabrics of erstwhile colonized subjects, contexts and countries. Jan Jansen and Jürgen Osterhammel's *Decolonization: A Short History* (2017) note that the pallid term 'decolonization' refers to a particularly unwieldy process in twentieth-century history in which a plethora of meanings, ambiguities, conflicting memories and competing narratives makes it the focus of political and scholarly disagreements. The book seeks to provide a concise comparative interpretation of decolonization that inserts this dramatic process of global change into the wider history of the twentieth century (2017: viii). They both highlight the manifold legacies and memories that decolonization left both in former colonizing and colonized societies (2017: x).

Ostensibly, postcolonial and decolonial arguments have been explicit in their challenge to the insularity of historical narratives and historiographical traditions emanating from Europe. The traditions of thought associated with postcolonialism and decoloniality are long-standing and diverse, with the notable works of Edward W. Said, Homi K. Bhabha and Gayatri C. Spivak (Bhambra 2014). The groundbreaking works – Edward Said's *Orientalism* ([1978] 1995), Homi Bhabha's *The Location of Culture* (1994) and Gayatri Spivak's provocative article 'Can the Subaltern Speak?' (1998) – reset the postcolonial discourse tone that was birthed and echoed by their forebears including Frantz Fanon ([1952] 2008, [1961] 1963), Albert Memmi ([1957] 1965) and Aimé Césaire ([1955] 1972). As Jansen and Osterhammel remark, 'one leitmotif to which postcolonial thinking has adhered is a critical interest in colonial forms of representation and knowledge as well as in "identities" and "subjectivities" that developed both among the carriers and the victims of colonial rule (and their successors)' (2017: 168). 'Decolonization bequeathed shared and divided memories' (2017: 186), and 'there is a strong variation in the concrete relationship between the colonial past and the politics of remembrance' (2017: 188).

The postcolonial discourse took on a theoretical distinction, modernity/coloniality paradigm and later 'decoloniality turn' when 'since the mid-1970s, the idea that knowledge is also colonized and, therefore, it needs to be de-colonized was expressed in several ways and in different disciplinary domains' (Mignolo 2007: 450). The pioneers and disciples of the new paradigm of thought, the coloniality/decoloniality turn, include Anibal Quijano, Enrique Dussel, Talal Assad, Boaventura de Sousa Santos, Maria Lugones and Walter D. Mignolo, and their contemporaries.

In the late 1980s and early 1990s, Quijano birthed the intriguing concept 'coloniality' (the invisible and constitutive side of 'modernity'), explicitly linking coloniality of power with the coloniality of knowledge (2000: 540). As Quijano aptly remarks, 'this coloniality of power, expressed through political and economic spheres was strongly associated with a coloniality of knowledge (or of imagination), articulated as modernity/rationality' (2007:168). The conception of modernity is squarely impregnated within the parameters of colonization of space and time to create a narrative of difference. As Mignolo notes, the spatial/temporal and imperial/colonial differences are organized and interwoven through what Quijano has articulated as the colonial matrix of power. He adds,

> The rhetoric of modernity with its various distinctions, goes hand in hand with the logic of coloniality, which allows me to make the strong claim that coloniality is constitutive of modernity; that there is no modernity without coloniality ... The 'colonial matrix of power' is the specification of what the term 'colonial world' means both in its logical structure and in its historical transformation. (Mignolo 2007: 476)

Mignolo develops and builds upon Quijano's earlier theoretical conception of modernity/coloniality within the framework of epistemic decolonization. He points out how Quijano's project articulated around the notion of 'coloniality of power' moves in two simultaneous directions – *analytic* and *programmatic* (2007: 451–2). At the same time, he underscores rather persuasively how 'the concept of coloniality has opened up, the reconstruction and the restitution of silenced histories, repressed subjectivities, subalternized knowledges and languages' (2007: 451). While Quijano proposes a 'de-colonial epistemic shift',

Mignolo grounds the decolonial shift as a project of 'de-linking', 'epistemic de-linking', 'a delinking that leads to de-colonial epistemic shift and brings to the foreground other epistemologies, other principles of knowledge and understanding and, consequently, other economy, other politics, other ethics' (2007: 453). While Mignolo describes coloniality in this detailed, impressive article as 'the darker side of modernity', he argues further, 'Delinking then shall be understood as a de-colonial epistemic shift leading to other-universality, that is, to pluri-versality as a universal project' (2007: 453). Pluriversality is then envisioned via the decentred nexus between local histories and oriented around 'the decolonial option'.

Mignolo asserts, albeit provocatively, that the hegemonic modern/colonial and Eurocentred paradigm needs to be *decolonized*. Thus, he posits the grammar of decoloniality as a prolegomenon to the decolonial shift, arguing that the first step in the grammar of decolonization could be cast as *learning to unlearn* (2007: 484). In the ambitious task of 'rewriting global history from the perspective and critical consciousness of coloniality and from within geo and body-political knowledge', Mignolo hones in on a bottom-up approach and contends that 'the grammar of de-coloniality (e.g., de-colonizaton of knowledge and of being – and consequently of political theory and political economy) begins at the moment that languages and subjectivities that have denied the possibility of participating in the production, distribution, and organization of knowledge' (2007: 492).

The decolonizing knowledges project has blossomed considerably, thus opening new vistas of theoretical frameworks based on new gold mines of ethnographic research. Mignolo and Catherine Walsh, in *On Decoloniality: Concepts, Analytics, Praxis* (2018), interrogate the hidden forces of the colonial matrix of power, its origination, transformation and current presence, while posing the crucial questions of decoloniality's how, what, why, with whom and what for. Interweaving theory-praxis with local histories and perspectives of struggle, they illustrate the conceptual and analytic dynamism of decolonial ways of living and thinking, as well as the creative force of resistance and re-existence. Marcus Scauso's *Intersectional Decoloniality* (2020) assesses diverse ways to think about 'others' while also emphasizing the advantages of decolonial intersectionality. He emphasizes the potential implications of intersectional decoloniality, highlighting its relationship with discussions that engage postcolonial, decolonial, feminist and interpretivist scholars. He demonstrates ways in which intersectional decoloniality moves beyond limitations found in other discourses, proposing a reflexive, bottom-up, intersectional and decolonial possibility of action and ally-ship.

The very rich and intriguing essays in *Contending Modernities*' new series 'Decoloniality and the Study of Religion'[6] vividly illuminate, first, 'how modern, Western conceptions of religion reinforce a global system of power that decolonial thinkers refer to as modernity/coloniality, revealing the complicity of the academic study of religion in these enduring patterns of violence'. Second, they 'contribute to a burgeoning focus on the possibilities of imagining religion de-linked from the universalizing logics of modernity/coloniality' (*Contending Modernities* 2020) As Garrett Fitzgerald aptly summarizes, 'bringing a decolonial lens to Contending Modernities opens up crucial new sites of analysis and engagement, as we consider how the academic study of religion – and the concept of religion itself – has helped to perpetuate modernity's violences, and might yet contribute to the project of decoloniality' (Fitzgerald 2020: 1).

Quijano's influential conceptualization of 'the coloniality of power', 'the colonial matric of power', resonates and reverberates robustly within contemporary academic discourses. His perspective on decolonization of knowledge has produced interesting iterations such as the 'colonization of the imagination' and knowledge, the idea of coloniality of power through the prisms of 'coloniality of Being' (Maldonado-Torres 2007: 240–70), 'decolonial feminism (Lugones 2010: 742–59), 'Decolonising the Mind' (Beier 2005), 'decolonising history' and other perspectives that space will not permit detailed elaboration here.

At the same time, these perspectives have generated fascinating discourses and histories around decolonizing indigenous methodologies (Smith [1999] 2012; Denzin, Lincoln and Smith 2008; Dunbar-Ortiz 2014; Tachine, Bird and Cabrera 2016; Barnes 2018; Sefa Dei and Jaimungal 2018; Chilisa 2019; Keikelame and Swartz 2019; Windchief and San Pedro 2019; and Scauso 2020, to mention a few). Decolonizing methodologies attempt to bring together a number of critical, indigenous, transformative, liberation, feminist and critical methodologies to strengthen decolonizing research. A number of innovative and creative research methods have gained traction, including photovoice, autoethnography, visual methods, storytelling and participatory approaches, to strengthen decolonization scholarship. Decolonizing methodologies have potential, but it is important to be aware of possible limitations (Barnes 2018). If decolonizing methodologies are to meaningfully contribute to decolonizing knowledge production, the movement has to be aware of potential blind spots (Barnes 2018: 380).

Linda Smith's trailblazing book, *Decolonizing Methodologies: Research and Indigenous Peoples* ([1999] 2012), critically examines the basis of Western research and the positioning of the indigenous as 'Other'. A decolonizing research methodology is an approach that is used to challenge the Eurocentric research methods that undermine the local knowledge and experiences of the marginalized population groups (Smith [1999] 2012: 2–5). Smith challenges traditional Western ways of knowing and researching and calls for the 'decolonization' of methodologies and for a new agenda of indigenous research. To the colonized, the term 'research' is conflated with European colonialism; the ways in which academic research has been implicated in the throes of imperialism remains a painful memory. The book explores intersections of imperialism and research – specifically, the ways in which imperialism is embedded in disciplines of knowledge and tradition as 'regimes of truth'. As Carla Wilson (2001: 215) observes, Western research brings with it a particular set of values and conceptualizations of time, space, subjectivity, gender relations and knowledge. Western research is encoded in imperial and colonial discourses that influence the gaze of the researcher (Wilson 2001). The book illuminates how colonial paradigms continue to evolve and to marginalize indigenous groups, and thus calls on non-indigenous researchers to consider how their 'world view' may (re)inscribe the dominant discourse of the Other.

Norman Denzin, Yvonna Lincoln and Linda Smith's *The Handbook of Critical and Indigenous Methodologies* (2008) draws connections regarding many of the perspectives of the 'new' critical theorists and emerging indigenous methodologies, and its focus transcending qualitative inquiry to exploring the indigenous and non-indigenous voices that inform research, policy, politics and social justice. To be able to promote effective anti-colonial and decolonial education, it is imperative to employ indigenous epistemologies that seek to threaten, replace and reimagine colonial thinking and practice; a more radical decolonial education and practice that allows for the coexistence of, and conversation among, 'multiple-epistemes' (Sefa Dei and Jaimungal 2018). Bagele Chilisa (2019) provides a crucial foundation in indigenous methods, methodologies and epistemologies, and situates research in a larger, historical, cultural and global context to make visible the specific methodologies that are commensurate with the transformative paradigm of social science research.

Sweeney Windchief and Timothy San Pedro's (2019) *Applying Indigenous Research Methods* focuses on the question of 'How' indigenous research methodologies (IRMs) can be used and taught across Indigenous studies and education, exemplifying the ways IRMs can enhance scholarship in fields including education, Indigenous studies, settler colonial studies, social work, qualitative methodologies and beyond. Amanda Tachine, Eliza Bird and Nolan Cabrera (2016) employ sharing circles as an IRM approach to understand the stories of Native American students as they transitioned into college. Sharing circles is an open-structured, conversational-style methodology that respects story sharing within a tribal cultural protocol context (Kovach 2009).

Dunbar-Ortiz's (2014) *An Indigenous People's History of the United States* is the first history of the United States told from the perspective of Indigenous peoples and reveals how Native Americans, for centuries, actively resisted expansion of the US empire. The book is an essential resource providing historical threads that are crucial for understanding the present. Dunbar-Ortiz challenges the founding myth of the United States and shows how policy against the Indigenous peoples was colonialist and designed to seize the territories of the original inhabitants, displacing or eliminating them. Spanning over four hundred years, this bottom-up peoples' history radically reframes US history and explodes the silences that have haunted our national narrative.

Africanists and African diaspora scholars are making indelible imprints towards the decolonizing knowledges and methodologies project. Some instantiations of this deconstructing religions project are through the works of Jacob Olupona, Ogbu Kalu, Oludamini Ogunnaike, David Chidester, John Peel, W. E. B. Du Bois, Charles Long and a host of others. Owing to space, I will focus briefly on three inspiring attempts at decolonizing the field of African religions here. Perhaps one of the foremost scholars in this contemporary decolonizing enterprise is Olupona. For instance, Olupona's *African Religions* (2014) offers a wide-ranging look at the myriad indigenous religious traditions on the African continent. Drawing on archaeological research, historical evidence, ethnographic studies and archival materials such as missionary records, he provides a vivid sense of African religious belief-exploring myths, gods and local deities, ancestor worship, rites of passage, festivals and divination, and underscores the role these religions play in everyday African life. The book also examines the spread of Christianity and Islam throughout Africa, which have had a dire effect on African life.

In a detailed ethnography that challenges Western epistemologies, Olupona's *City of 201 Gods* (2011) adroitly focuses on one of the most important religious centres in Africa and in the world: the Yorùbá city of Ilé-Ifè in south-west Nigeria. The spread of Yorùbá traditions in the African diaspora has come to define the cultural identity of millions of Black and white people in Brazil, Cuba, Puerto Rico, Trinidad and the United States. Seen through the eyes of a 'native' scholar, this book exemplifies how Ilé-Ifè went from great prominence to near obliteration and then rose again as a contemporary city of gods. Olupona corroborates the nexus between religion, cosmology, migration and kinship as espoused in the power of royal lineages, hegemonic state structure, gender and the Yorùbá sense of place, offering the fullest portrait to date of this sacred African city.

Ogunnaike's *Deep Knowledge* (2020) is an in-depth, comparative study of two of the most popular and influential intellectual and spiritual traditions of West Africa: Tijani Sufism and Ifa. Employing a unique methodological approach that thinks with and from – rather than merely about – these traditions, he argues that they contain sophisticated epistemologies that provide practitioners with a comprehensive world view and a way of crafting a meaningful life. Appropriating theories from within these traditions as well as contemporary oral and textual sources, Ogunnaike unpacks how both Sufism and Ifa answer the questions of what knowledge is, how it is acquired and how it is verified. The book illuminates how these traditions represent viable perspectives on knowledge, metaphysics, psychology and ritual practice.

Chidester's *Savage Systems* (1996) unpacks the conceptual genealogy of 'religion' and 'religions' on colonial frontiers, and provides a detailed analysis of the ways in which European travellers, missionaries, settlers and government agents, as well as indigenous Africans, engaged in the comparison of alternative religious ways of life as one dimension of intercultural contact. With primary focus on the nineteenth century, he demonstrates that the terms and conditions for comparison – including a discourse about 'otherness' that were established during this period – still remain. In another impressive book, *Empire of Religion* (2013), interrogates how knowledge about religion and religions is produced, authenticated and circulated through documenting and analysing the emergence of a science of comparative religion in Great Britain during the second half of the nineteenth century and its complex relations to the colonial situation in southern Africa. Chidester provides a counterhistory of the academic study of religion, an alternative to standard accounts that have failed to link the field of comparative religion with either the power relations or the historical contingencies of the imperial project. He underscores how race, rather than theology, was formative in the emerging study of religion in Europe and North America.

Unmasking indigeneity

Indigeneity and indigenous, in conceptual and theoretical terms, are fluid, in constant flux, being continually contested and negotiated glocally. In this book, I explore indigeneity as a relational concept deriving from colonial and postcolonial milieus, through the prism of Ọza spirituality and the ecologies of indigenous knowledge systems. I engage the discourse on Ọza world views, cosmologies and religious cultures as a way of interrogating indigeneity. Indigeneity is lived experiences and embodied memory, often ritualized and performed in their lifeworlds. It is rooted in Ọza self-identity, claims to autochthony, chains of collective memory and narratives of existence, presences, world views and cosmologies, and gendered identities, as well as their historical, cultural, religious, social, economic and political imaginaries. Thus, indigeneity occupies embodied, real and imagined space in ways that valorizes the sociality of Ọza religious cultures in everyday life.

Language is a significant marker of indigeneity and cultural identity. Language, as an expression of culture, is core to this research. As an Ọza indigene, I am very conversant with Ọza spoken and written language, a cognitive capital and a useful asset for data gathering, interpretation and analysis. The bilingual researcher, as a living part of the study, a 'native' speaker, translator and interpreter, assumes the role of a cultural broker during the process and within the context of data production. Issues of interpretation and translation are important in cross-cultural and cross-language qualitative research. As Lincoln and Elza González remark,

> interviewing in one's own language gives the researcher grammatical liberty, access to colloquialisms, and idiomatic freedom, so that deeper meanings … and other languages may be exposed when you read the original data. In virtually every instance, the researcher's native language affords opportunities for linguistic subtleties that may be (or are likely) lost in subsequent translation, no matter how sensitive, fluid, or fluent the translation. (2008: 792)

As a bilingual researcher, I favour the use of bilingual texts for the analyses and presentation of data. When indigenous concepts, phrases, quotations or actual pieces of qualitative data are presented in the original language as well as in the language for presentation, the local or indigenous-speaking reader will have available the complete meaning of the text and its context. Some meanings, interesting but not useful to non-local audiences, may carry enormous significance for local consumers of the research, simply because the words may tie into larger events, circumstances, customs, issues, problems or relationships. Non-local consumers of the research cannot know what kind of actions will be triggered via the original language or what social action may be prompted. Only local users can understand what the words, especially untranslatable, idiomatic terminologies, might mean, or what positive forces might be enabled (González and Lincoln 2006). Even when researcher/translators continue explaining how they approach the context of their participants, looking for personal memories and other strategies can help in a closer interpretation of data (Lincoln and González 2008: 803).

For research to be relevant and thus improve the quality of life of indigenous people, it should be driven by indigenous world views, cultural values and a language that is relevant to the indigenous group with whom research is undertaken (Khupe and Keane 2017). Constance Khupe and Moyra Keane identify issues of power, trust, culture and cultural competence, respectful and legitimate research practice, and recognition of individual and communities' assets as important structures in decolonizing research methodologies.

Indigeneity is also rooted in conceptions and negotiation of land, ecology and spatial configurations. As Nye aptly notes, 'Decolonization is about land issues: it is pragmatic and political, aiming to redress profound inequalities of history. It is about recognizing the many forms of cultural and political indigeneity' (2019: 8). Ọza people link indigenous epistemologies in relation to land, autochthony and language. Ancestral land had both a material and spiritual significance, and within this duality, we can understand their group and sociocultural identity, giving them an aura of invincibility. The personalization of ancestral land as *Ekẹ Ọza* (Ọza land) or *Ekẹ mai* (our ancestral land) endears custodianship, ownership and autochthony. It serves also as an invincibilizing insignia of indigeneity. Ancestral land is not ephemeral or transient but an enduring spatial configuration with significations as *afẹ* (home), *afẹmai* (our home) or a place of abode to nourish and maintain.

As we shall demonstrate, the sovereignty, land issue and identity of Ọza people has remained a point of contention through the colonial and post-independence period partly owing to the commodification, politicization and plantationization[7] of arable land. This is analogous to the saying attributed to Desmond Tutu, 'When the missionaries came to Africa they had the Bible and we had the land. They said "Let us pray." We closed our eyes. When we opened them we had the Bible and they had the land.'[8]

The retention and sustenance of land is critical to the maintenance of Ọza culture, group and gendered identities. Unlike the treatment of land as a commodity by the colonizers and exogenous hegemony, land was an integral part of Ọza group identity and belongingness. An old aphorism suggests, *A desa ame de gbọ Ọza ekẹ zu* (It is a taboo to sell any parcel of land in Ọza). This is qualified by the saying, *Ame de ha ekẹ Ọza nọ ọfa/ọgbọ ovo zu* (It is a taboo to sell any portions of Ọza ancestral land to a non-indigene, foreigner). Such a caution evokes narratives of self and the Other. The commoditization of Ọza ancestral land is indeed an aberration. The restrictions by social custom regarding sale of ancestral land to non-indigenes has a strategic import in that selling ancestral land is tantamount to saleability, mortgaging your ancestors who are custodians of society. Ọza people believe that such illicit transactions could incur the wrath of the ancestors, since the living dead are capable of impacting on the physical world. Ọza people desire to be buried in *Afẹ Ọza*, their ancestral home, as this roots them to the land of the ancestors. This establishes continuity and a kind of socio-religious morphology between the terrestrial ecosystem and extraterrestrial spheres of existence.

Ancestral land, bounded or unbounded, was not the possession of any one person, not even the chief, for the sake of trade. Although certain families and the chief are symbolic custodians, land was the commonality that kept Ọza people together. Land was for the use of all those living on it, even if one did not belong to the original family group within that particular community. As my interlocutors are often quick to indicate, *Afẹ ni nyani ekẹ imede ha ufuru kamisẹ* (Familial custodians of land are not predisposed to pinpoint land boundaries between families). This illuminates the fluidity, boundedness and unboundedness of the land tenure system in Ọza spatial configurations. Land was also a religious symbol – a gift from *Oshukunu Ọpashi* – that connected Ọza people to the Supreme Being. The sacrosanctity of ancestral land is intrinsically tied to its use and abuse: its preservation and maintenance, on the one hand, and commodification, manipulation and exploitation, on the other. The epistemologies of land is therefore connected to the spiritualizing of ecology. In this vein, to 'sell ancestral land' is considered an abuse and an aberration. It is important to underscore how public ascription and Otherization shape how Ọza people make sense of their lifeworlds, and the contestations that ensue partly from the precarious proximity with neighbours. Thus, emic-etic categories and insider-outsider dynamics are instrumental to discourses of autochthony and politics of indigeneity.

The definition and provenance of 'indigeneity' as a concept/term so far has no universal acceptability besides a common understanding of its derivation as an abstract noun version of the adjective, 'indigenous'. Hilary Weaver (2001) cautions that indigeneity is a very complex term which is the subject of controversy and that it can have different interpretations. Future research should explore how the term 'indigeneity' is understood and perceived by the researched and the researchers in our context (Keikelame and Swartz 2019: 2). The relationality of such terms as 'indigeneity', 'indigenousness', 'indigenism', 'indigenous identity' and 'indigenous people' renders them as contested and vaguely defined. The indigenous people's debate transcends the theoretical and ideological sensitivities of anthropologist-scholars of the Western academy (Kuper 2003: 389–402; 2006: 21–2; Guenther 2006: 17–32; Delgado and Childs 2012).

In response to Adam Kuper's critical engagement with the concepts of 'indigenous' and 'primitive', and during a 2006 anthropological debate on the indigenous, Barnard writes, 'It is the idea of definition itself that is the problem' (Barnard 2006a: 7; 2006b: 29–31). He proposes moving beyond debates revolving around essentialism, on the one hand, and a political economy and historical approach, on the other. Alberto Gomes remarks that the concept of indigeneity, with its multiple interpretations and local inflections, not only has attracted much debate and contestation but also has become a significant political strategy in the counter-hegemonic indigenous social movements against oppressive and repressive regimes throughout the world. He adds that in some contexts, indigeneity is complicated by its conflation with racialized identities (Gomes 2013: 5–15). The politics of indigeneity is also partly heightened in its delineation by the United Nations Charter (United Nations 1981, 1986, 2004[9]), the International Labor Organization 169 Convention and the World Bank in 1991. Nair suggests that the UN conception of indigeneity is linked to territoriality, a primeval quality of defence of territories against others of the same species (Nair 2006).

The historicity of African spirituality has always been in flux, negotiating resilience, transformation and change. Any exploration of the concept of indigeneity, at least in African societies, that fails to come to terms with this dynamism and fluidity will be rather fraught. African spirituality simply acknowledges that beliefs and practices touch on and inform every facet of human life, and therefore African religion cannot be separated from the everyday or mundane.[10] Thus, the process of deconstructing indigeneity and indigenous epistemologies is largely congruent with, to borrow Dillard's phrase, 'learning to (re)member the things we've learned to forget' (Dillard 2012: 4). African societies 'possess, practice and protect a total sum of knowledge and skills constitutive of their meaning, belief systems, livelihood, constructions and expression that distinguish them from other groups' (Osman 2009). African indigenous knowledge systems is informed by and relate to all domains of life and the environment. The contemporary politics of indigeneity and identity are as such that people have multiple and overlapping identities shaped by the present political and economic dynamics and their manifestation on the sociocultural context (Nel 2005: 2–14; Ngulube 2016, 2017).[11] Catherine Odora Hoppers aptly defines indigenous knowledge systems as a 'total of knowledge and practices, whether explicit or implicit, used in the management of socioeconomic, ecological and spiritual facets of life' (Hoppers 2005: 2–3). He suggests that the dynamics of African indigenous knowledge systems operate on two entwined levels: the empirical and the cognitive.

Indigeneity is taken to imply first-order connections usually (at small scale) between group and locality, (un)boundedness. It connotes belonging and originariness and deeply felt processes of attachment and identification, and thus it distinguishes 'natives' from others (Merlan 2009: 303–33). We can perhaps advance science and development by tapping reservoirs of knowledge present in indigenous cultures such as that of Ọza, a body of knowledge that had hitherto been repudiated as myth and superstition. Indigenous knowledge refers to the knowledge of ritual performances constitutive of their meaning-making, belief systems, as well as the substantive dimension of their livelihood constructions. Indigenous traditions, often labelled as local or traditional knowledge, have developed over time adapting to their unique environments and conditioned by specific cultural moments and ecological, economic, social, religious and gendered contexts in which they develop and thrive.

The subtle compartmentalization of sacred and mundane domains is one external import into indigenous world views that deserves a deconstruction. Just as the dichotomy between sacred and secular is sometimes blurring, it is problematic to pigeonhole indigenous epistemologies. It embraces beliefs, practices, technologies, values and ways of knowing and sharing, in terms of which communities have survived. It is informed by and relates to all domains of life and the environment, including the creative and artistic aspects of music, dance and oral tradition. It also includes philosophy, ethics and world view – concepts of life, death, cosmos, environment, spiritual world, spirituality, divination, transfer of religious knowledge, rites of passage, etiologies of sickness and disease, and traditional healing systems. This book demonstrates how Ọza world views, cosmologies and ritual praxis, and new ways of knowing make sense as a continuum in the contestation of indigeneity.

The road map

In this book, Chapter 1 begins with decolonizing history, memory and method, by paying crucial attention to the complexities, burdens of history and memory in attempting to reconstruct Ọza historical, cultural and religious imagination. This book relies on mixed methods and multiple source texts, privileging the voices of Ọza people in telling their own stories, histories and narratives, through their own cosmological imaginaries, and how this is shaped by people they encounter and who live around them. We have used these sources reflexively, paying careful attention to the pitfalls of hagiography, emic-etic dilemma, insider-outsider power dynamics, memory and the politics of remembering and forgetting. My locationality and positionality in the decolonizing knowledges project helps to plug this book within the wider historiography of decolonization and indigeneity discourses.

The historical and contemporary encounters, and the relationship between Ọza peoples, her neighbours and multiple colonial hegemonies demonstrate one framework of understanding Ọza indigenous religious and cultural imaginaries. Chapter 2 explores oral narratives, including myths of origin, which explain Ọza historical origins, migration and traditions; relationships with neighbours in historical perspective; encounters with multiple colonialisms, histories and influences; and the transmission and translation of Christianity and Islam in Ọza society.

Ọza understanding of the cosmos and its complexities is expedient in order to appreciate their religious world views, thought patterns and praxis. In describing Ọza religious lifeways, how the people live and act within these frameworks, it is important to show how such worlds consist of spiritual agencies, special powers, beings with which special human actors form prescribed relationships. A dominant element in Ọza religious epistemology is the belief in spiritual entities and underlying life forces including a Supreme Deity, the multiplicity of divinities, spirits and ancestors, and rituals or practices concerning them. Chapter 3 explores how ritual spaces, roles, powers and actions are expressions of a coherent system of thought that informs the religious lifeways of Ọza people who participate in them. The centrality of indigenous healers, diviners and other functionaries are shown as spiritual reservoirs of Ọza indigenous society.

While African societies are often lumped together and their social organizations generally described as patrilineal/patrilocal, it is expedient to underscore that their kinship structures are rather more complex and dynamic. Kinship lineage groupings play an important role in indigenous governance systems while the extended family structure is quintessential. The myth of sacral kingship institution is very central in Ọza cosmological tradition. In Chapter 4, we explore Ọza kinship system as a bilateral lineage structure. We demonstrate how and to what extent *Ireme* as maternal lineage, within Ọza matrilineal/patrilineal pedigree, is centrally important to Ọza social, cultural and political life. The prominence of the female gender within kinship genealogy is analogous to the especial ritual role and place of women within Ọza religious map of the cosmos. Ọza women are renowned for traditional crafts like clay pottery produced for domestic, commercial, aesthetic and ritual purposes. The chapter illuminates feminine ingenuity through the sacrality and aesthetics of *Ẹrẹma* pottery making. The rest of the chapter focuses on how Ọza indigenous polity negotiated the colonial matrix of British powers as a complex exercise that displays hegemony, against the backdrop of inherent vulnerabilities of indigenous political, sociocultural and religious systems. The coloniality of power and labour also makes sense against the backdrop of contestation, negotiation and resilience. The subjugation by the British colonial machinery was hardly devoid of sociopolitical unease and wanton mayhem. Rather, it was a period characterized by dogged resistance and reluctant capitulation.

The British coloniality of power, its duplicity, consciously impinged on the indigenous justice system and eroded its power, authenticity and legitimacy, thereby truncating the juridical process. The encounter between the Empire and local power trajectories espouse the intricate politics of indigeneity, induced multiple hegemonies and loyalties, thus demonstrating the upsides and downsides of that experience. While the Empire was unsuccessful in obliterating and wiping out the indigenous systems of justice, they were nevertheless successful in juxtaposing the British and indigenous structures of justice within a hierarchy of power, influence and authenticity. The hierarchization of power is most consequential in facilitating multiple hegemonies and competing loyalties. Native courts and customary courts are imbrications of a colonial juridical construct, and an invented machinery of subjugation, exploitation and expropriation that continue to bear the imprints and vestiges of imperial power.

The *Ọpashi Ọza*, vested with temporal power and sacral authority in Ọza, had his jurisdiction eroded and debased, through incarceration, and the consequent humiliation in which reinstatement in the Native Court became controversially politicized. This manipulation of the indigenous legal system and paradigms of justice had both intended and unintended consequences. One of such inadvertent after-effect is the protracted legal tussle regarding Ọza chieftaincy leadership succession discussed in Chapter 5. We contend that such intrusions weaponized and represented the spark that ignited further leadership rivalry and competition that has continued until contemporary era. Therefore, a better grasp of the antecedents and precedents of Ọza kingship myth and the royal genealogical tradition – the fissure, friction and change that characterize the process – are expedient if we are to appreciate the complexities of the legal imbroglios that followed from the early 1990s onwards.

The next two chapters, Chapter 6 and 7, turn attention to rituals of passage. Myths and rituals operate within sacred space and time and occupy a conspicuous place in Qza religious life. Rites of passage involving birth, puberty, marriage and death are central and point to the ritual attitude in maintaining cosmic harmony and balance at individual and collective levels. In both chapters, we demonstrate how myths, often enacted in rites of passage, festivals and ceremonial activities, link the creative powers of the deities, divinities and ancestors with the needs of the people; and how notions of time and ritual cycles are embedded in Qza religious cosmos. We also examine how some rituals of passage create rigid and valid renewal in the life cycle – birth, marriage, death and burial processes – in Qza, and highlight the fluidity inherent in their ecological and temporal cycles by examining some rites associated with some major festivals, seasonal changes and individual achievements and sanctity, especially women. Qza indigenous thought and praxis subsume and reconstruct religious sensibilities and attitude towards ritual praxis and performance at various life stages and community's existence. While we describe the *Osokuru, Okutu* and *Osọ* transitional rituals of incorporation which are exclusive for young boys and men, the next chapter has its focus on more elaborate, exclusive rituals for the transition of young girls into women, the *Ukpe Iruvie, Ọmọnugere* and *Ibishika* ritual festivals, respectively.

Also, we argue in Chapter 7, that performative ritual action, bodily objectification of femininity and the aesthetics of indigenous culture and tradition hardly delimit gendered power of women in Qza society. Rather, female ritual power should be situated in its broad, indigenous political economy, social, cultural and religious configurations, and against the backdrop of fluid power dynamics, interpersonal relationship and intersubjectivity. It is within these ambiences that gendered power contestation and women's negotiation of their sociality play out in ritualized space and time. We demonstrate how the political and social role of *Ọdejọ* and her ritual power and function loom large in Qza community. The *Ọdejọ* serves in an advisory capacity to *Ọpashi* and his *Eja*, and through her political and spiritual responsibility foreground women's involvement in social and political debates. Recognition of such gender dynamics is necessary for negotiating social and political equipoise of power. At the same time, the gendered matrilineality of *Ireme* genealogy unpacks the ritual power, social positionality and cultural locationality of women in Qza.

The concluding chapter, Chapter 8, on the future of Qza indigeneity in the face of modernity, critically explores the resilience, change and transformation of Qza indigenous religions and cultures against the backlash of encounters with colonial modernities: British, Nupe, Yoruba and Benin hegemonic incursions and influences, as well as contestations with exogenous religious cultures such as Christianity and Islam that are increasingly engaged in religious competition within contemporary Ọza society. We attempted to reconstruct these contestations between the colonial enterprise, missionary transmission and indigenous agency and (re)appropriations reflexively. Any theorizations of this encounter must take due cognisance of instantiations of indigeneity politics and the dynamics of identity, culture, tradition and power.

2

Historical origins, migration narratives, relationship with neighbours

The historical and contemporary encounters, and the relationship between Ọza indigenous peoples, her neighbours and multiple colonial hegemonies demonstrate one framework of understanding Ọza indigenous religious and cultural imaginaries. This is an integral part of, and within, the context and processes of globalization. The chapter explores oral narratives, including myths of origin, which explain Ọza historical origins, migration and traditions; relationships with neighbours in historical perspective; encounters with multiple colonialisms, histories and influences; and the transmission and translation of Christianity and Islam in Ọza society. Prior to this exploration, the introductory section will locate Ọza within the precincts of colonial, pre- and post-independence Nigeria.

Locating Ọza within colonial, pre- and post-independent Nigeria

In 1914, what later became Nigeria existed as Northern and Southern Protectorates of the British Colony, until their amalgamation on 1 October 1960. In 1939, the Southern Province was divided into Eastern and Western Regions. In 1963, the Benin Province separated from what was then the Western Region, and the Mid-West Region was created on 27 May 1967. On 17 March 1976, the Mid-Western Region was renamed Bendel State, formed from Benin and Delta provinces of the Western Region, with its capital in Benin City. Edo State was created on 27 August 1991 when the former Bendel State was split into Edo and Delta States.

As the Resident of Benin Province best describes its geography in 1939,

the Benin Province was bounded on the East by the River Niger which separates it from the Onitsha and Kabba Provinces. The Northern boundary, also with the Kabba Province, follows a line from the Niger North of Agenebode till it meets the Osse River which with the Siluko River forms the Western boundary with the Ondo Province. The Southern boundary, with the Warri Province, follows for the most part the Benin, Ossiomo and Ethiope Rivers, thence a general Easterly line until the Niger is reached just below the 6th parallel. The Provincial boundaries were changed during the year.

Benin Province with headquarters at Benin City was made up four divisions, namely Asaba Division, Benin Division, Ishan (Esan) Division and Kukuruku (Auchi) Division. In 1939, it had an estimated total population of 489,665: Benin with a population of 118,000, followed by Ishan – 117,111, Asaba – Ogwashi-Uku (80,000) and Agbor (52,054) – 132,054 and Kukuruku – 122,500, respectively. As the Resident, Benin Province further remarked, 'the inter-divisional boundaries were usually not marked by conspicuous natural features, and some of the boundaries, as defined by Gazette Notice, differ widely from the actual boundaries'.

In 1919, the Kukuruku Division was established with headquarters in Fugar. Until this period, much of Edo North, including Ọsọsọ, Okpella, Uzairue North and North Ibie were administered, under the British from Lokoja, as part of Northern Nigeria. Under the British colonial era, Ọza (Ọja/Ọjah) was in Akoko-Edo District under Kukuruku Division of the Benin Province within the Western Region of Nigeria. According to the Resident, 'the Kukuruku Division may be divided broadly into three areas occupied by the Etsako, Iviosakon (Ivbiosakon) and the Akoko groups respectively. The first two are peopled mainly by refugees from Benin, and the last, which has not been reorganised by an assortment from Ife, Benin and Igala.' In 1946, the Kukuruku Division had an estimated population of 155,000, inhabiting an area of 2,105 square miles, and forest reserves approximating 70 square miles. Kukuruku villages are divided into Quarters which may 'regard themselves as being of one family' (extended) or may consist of several such families. Quarter boundaries are presumably natural features (Rowling 1948: 12–13).

In 1954, H. L. M. Butcher, the Resident of Benin Province, suggested the etymology of the name 'Kukuruku', that 'the name evokes memories of trouble times 100 years ago when Nupe warriors swept down from the northern plains on horseback to invade the hilly countryside of this Division'. He continued,

The invaders met and subdued scattered hamlets of peaceful farmers who had already sought security among these hills from tyranny in their own lands. Today the old men will tell you how their father defended themselves and their families against the Nupes in fortified villages amongst the rocky hilltops: how with fear in their hearts they listened at dawn to the cock-crow call Kukuruku echoing round the rocks as the invading bands assembled to attack.

The Nupe warriors settled in the Kukuruku environ for many years and established a crude form of administration under local leaders. This first unifying influence was later adapted by the establishment of seven District Heads during the early years of this century when the area was administered as part of the Protectorate of Northern Nigeria. In 1920, the Kukuruku Division was formally established within the Southern Provinces, romance rather than reason probably fathered the name of the Division and during 1954 there had been suggestions that it should be changed for something less reminiscent of the hostile invader. In 1921, the Kukuruku Council comprising the seven District Heads was recognized as a Native Authority. In no way representative of the people it was 'regarded as an instrument of Government to be sparingly employed' until it was superseded in 1943 by the establishment of Native Authorities on Clan and Village levels. The year 1954 saw the death of the last surviving District Head, Chief Afẹgbua of Ukpilla, not long after he had fulfilled his ambition to make pilgrimage to Mecca.

> During all these years since the Nupe invasions, the villages scattered amongst the hills in the northern part of Kukuruku Division have maintained their tradition of individual independence; in 1943 when the basis of local government was broadened it was found necessary to establish no less than 31 separate Native Authorities in the Akoko area alone. The change in outlook that developed during the next ten years may be reasoned by the universal acceptance in 1953 of the proposal to establish a Divisional Council under the Local Government Law; and the fact that this Council had to win the allegiance of these northern clans at its first meetings in 1954 was not to be wholly unexpected in the light of history.[1]

The present-day Ọjah is now situated in Akoko-Edo Local Government Area (LGA), the northern fringes of Edo State in Nigeria (an area formerly referred by Bradbury (1957) as Northern Edo). The LGA shares interstate boundaries with Ondo and Kogi States in the West and North, respectively. It is bounded by Etsako and Owan LGAs in the East and South, respectively. Akoko-Edo LGA consists of fifteen clans, out of which the Ọkpameri ethnic cluster (one of the Afẹnmai peoples of Edo State) are found in five clans, namely North East Akoko, North Akoko, Okurosho, Eastern Akoko and Central Akoko. One source indicated that the Okpameri were traditionally known as Akoko. The 'Akoko' referred to here is quite different from Akoko in Ikare area of the old western region, now in Ondo State. Folashade Saba suggests that 'Akoko' or its original form 'Ikoko', which means a unit came into being as early as the fourteenth century, derived from the coming together of the various Akoko peoples living together in a defined geographical area (Saba 2003: 7–8). According to Chief Ogunnubi, this name was adopted when the Okpameri people were in their old settlement sites. One tradition suggests that Okpameri came about when the various communities came together to form a formidable defense pack to resist external invasion by the Nupe warriors. Other traditions have it that the Okpameri successfully repelled domineering incursions from the Bini, the Nupe, the Igala and the Yoruba. In the course of time, due to the population strength and prosperity of the people, some other ethnic groups were attracted and had to come into a close relationship with them. They also settled with them. With the advent of some other ethnic groups, 'Edo' was appended to 'Akoko' to give 'Akoko-Edo.' In later years, all these ethnic groups were brought under the umbrella of Akoko-Edo Division. Another source suggests that the idea of coming together originated with the old Western Region of Nigeria in 1948.

Saba (2003: 6) provides a much broader description of 'Akoko' as a frontier region at the intersection of the boundaries of Ondo, Ekiti, Edo and Kogi States, covering all the people who live in the area bounded in the North by Kabba in Kabba/Bunu Local Government of Kogi State, in the West by the Ekitis, in the South by Owo and Ose Local Governments of Ondo State and in the East by the Akoko-Edo LGA of Edo State. Besides any claims to historical, linguistic and cultural affinities, the proximity and inter-trade between them helps to explain a certain kind of Yorubanization process as we shall discuss later. Thus, Akoko is populated by people who, for centuries had migrated to an area which had come to represent a meeting ground for diverse peoples and cultures. Their common traditions of origin often group Akoko towns and villages into three: tracing origins to either Ife from the West, Benin from the East and Kabba in the North (Akintoye 1969: 539–53; Olomola 1976: 40). According to one tradition, the migrants from Benin arrived directly around the thirteenth century, carrying with them relics of Benin culture, including the Edo language. This tradition asserts that this group left Benin because of succession disputes to the stool of Oba of Benin. Some of them settled in Afenmai (Kukuruku) region in the first instance (Saba 2003: 7).

The Ọkpameri, within the Akoko-Edo LGA, are perhaps the largest ethnic grouping in terms of population and geographical spread. Out of a projected population of 158,885 of Akoko-Ẹdo LGA in 1976, the Ọkpameri towns and villages comprise 71,129 people (twenty-two towns and villages), while the remaining ten clans have a population of 87,756. In 1976, the North East Akoko clan comprised Lampese, Imọga, Ekpe and Bekuma towns/villages (with a projected population of 16,885); the North Akoko clan comprised Ibillo, Ikiran, Ekpesa and Ekor (population 19,803). The Eastern Akoko clan comprise Somorika, Onumu, Eshawa and Ogbe (13,669); Central Akoko is made up of Aiyegunlẹ, Ugboshi and Ogugu (8,900); while the Okurosho clan comprise Ojah, Makeke, Dagbala, Ojirami and Oyanvbuza (11,872), respectively.

Oza people have historical, cultural and linguistic affinities with the Okurosho clan and the Ọkpameri ethnic cluster in general. As R. E. Bradbury notes, 'the three communities, Oja, Dagbala and Ojirami are together called Okulusọ [sic. Okuroshọ], a term apparently connected with the Ukpe festival which is common to them all. They are closely related in dialect and culture though they claim different origins' (Bradbury 1957: 114). 'Ọkpameri' is coined from 'Ọkpa' (one) and 'meri' (we are), meaning literally 'We are One'. In a broader sense, however, the name connotes a people of common descent, language, tradition and culture, and among whom all kinds of cultural procedures are similar (Adogame 1987: 8). One who defined himself as an Ọkpameri citizen corroborated this assertion, 'Our inherited culture, traditional ceremonies, art, artists, music, legends, folk-lore and crafts really make us one – Ọkpameri' (Ajibolu 1985).

Owing to the dearth of written records, the origins of Ọkpameri people continue to be enshrined in oral traditions and historical myths. One tradition has it that 'Ozuehan, the founder of Ọkpameri, came from Edo (Bini) in about 1490, during the reign of Oba Ozolua of Benin. He was said to have settled in Ibillo. His children and other grandchildren founded other Ọkpameri towns and villages. His senior son, Ekpese, founded Lampese.' A second oral narrative speaks of early migration from Ilé-Ifè. The collapse of the Old Oyo Empire prompted the petty vassal states to migrate to different areas. Somorika, an Ọkpameri town, is believed to have been settled by one of these early migrants who left Ilé-Ifè because of its fall. The tradition has it that the people first settled in Benin, but owing to certain factors which vary from the unsuitability of Benin because of further military expansion and subjugation by the Benin leading heroes of the new arrivals, they moved on to more conducive areas. J. U. Egbarevba, claiming that the sociopolitical conditions in Benin brought about by

Oba Ewuare prompted migration to different directions by some discontented Benin citizens (1947: 25–6), popularized this narrative. These migrations were hastened consequent upon the harsh laws enacted by Oba Ewuare 'the Great' of Benin (1440–70), who was also regarded as 'the Warrior', 'the Selfish' and 'the Tyrant' (Okogie 1960: 101–10).

A common feature in both traditions of origin is the fact that one traced the origin to Benin while the other was traced from Ilé-Ifè through Benin. This partly explains the ancestral descent of the Ọkpameri people. The narrative of a common origin could have some validity because several words in Ọkpameri dialect have the same pronunciation and meaning as in Edo language (Adjoto 1976: 2). Some examples will suffice here: uchi (moon), ọmọ (child), amẹ (water), ise (may it be) and so forth (Adogame 1987: 10). The myth of a common origin is further buttressed by the similarities, which exist in customs, traditions and many other spheres of life. 'The unifying factors of the Ọkpameri include language, festivals, songs, traditional dances, marriage etc. This agrarian tribe (ethnic grouping) is noted for its traditional hospitality, hard work and honesty. Therefore, the name Ọkpameri denotes oneness, kindness, peacefulness, altruism, magnanimity, egalitarianism, rationality and impregnability' (Agbi 1986: 6). The Ọkpameri people exhibit similar cultural features such as in traditional festivals of Ori, Ukpe, Ọmọshe, Irimi and Imu. Notable among their dances are Uvie, Ododo, Uke, Uhen, Ikpoko, Ukpukpe and Igoro (Adogame 1987: 11–14). Inhabitants of Ọjah village are noted for pottery and terracotta figurines, just as Ọgbe village is famous for material art and Somorika for cultic divination.

Generally, Ọkpameri people revere the Yoruba and the Bini as convenient allies, while they hold the Nupe, the Igala and the Unẹmẹ as adversaries. This is not unconnected with the Nupe and Igala infamous slave trading, and the alleged conspiracy of the Unẹmẹ in furnishing instruments of war to either embattled communities. The fact that the Yoruba had some influence in Ọkpameri area is reflected in place names like Ikiran-Ile and Ikiran-Oke, Igboshi-Ile and so on, with the suffixes 'Oke' and 'Ile' being Yoruba referents for 'uphill' and 'downhill', respectively. The original Ọkpameri name for the two Ikiran villages was Umha (Lewis 2013: 9). Other examples of Yoruba language inflections of town/villages names are Ọjirami Ugbo (now Ọjirami-Afẹ) and Ọjirami Pẹtẹsi, Ugboshi Oke (now Ugboshi-Afẹ) and Ugboshi Salẹ (now Ugboshi-Ele), Aiyegunlẹ (formerly Osi), Ọjah Oke (formerly Ọza Okeme) and Ọjah Salẹ. In addition, the [ʤ] in Ọjah was a Yoruba loan as the village was originally referred to as Ọza – a name still borne by the local secondary school, Ọza Community High School. In a latter section, I shall further explore this sociocultural, religious and political influence as Yorubanization.

Myths of historical origins and migration narratives

Ọza myths of origin and migration traditions derive mainly from oral narratives, local histories partly corroborated by a few archival sources. While the ancestral descent of the Ọkpameri people, of which Ọjah is an integral part, is traced to Benin, on the one hand, and from Ilé-Ifè through Benin, on the other hand, virtually all oral histories interview narratives trace Ọza's historical origin to Benin, though with different emphasis and migratory trajectories. None of the primary sources indicated the specific year, period and ambit of this migration. According to a local historian,

> 'Ọjah migrated from Benin City which is Ogegere, from there to another place called Ọza-nogogo and Ọzanise near Agbor. They lived here for a good number of years and from there some families left to another settlement called Ọza Orogbe. This hilly settlement called Orogbe is close to Okene, along Oruku hills near Ọsọsọ, but as at then Ọsọsọ people were not there.[2]

The migration history that connects Ọza people to Ọza-nogogo is rather speculative and thus might need further investigation. Therefore, the Ọza that is the focus of this book is different from the Ọza-nogogo mentioned above in terms of current geographical location and history in many respects.[3] However, besides the name semblance, there is some affinity in the narrative: both communities tracing their migration from Benin.

Omo-Aghe Isaac's book *Ọza History Nigeria. Ọza History in Delta and Edo State, Nigeria* chronicles the ethnic origins and history of Ọza people in Ọza Nogogo of Ika South LGA in Delta State, Ologbo in Ikpoba-Okha LGA and Ọza-Aibiokunla of Ohionmwon LGA in Edo State, respectively. He traces their origins to Benin Kingdom.[4] He links the founding of Ọza Nogogo with situations in which some army generals deserted Ubini (Benin) with their followers and other persons having desires to gain freedom from oppressive, tyrannical rule of the reigning Oba (King) to start their lives in new found villages and towns. Omo-Aghe notes further that 'Ọza was one of the bulwark places from which the Obas of Benin recruited their army to maintain, expand their Kingdom and ultimately form the Benin Empire. Ọza people also contributed in no small measure to the social, political and economic welfare of the kingdom and the

Empire' (2016: 2). This establishes Ọza Nogogo people as a vassal state of the Benin Kingdom. Nonetheless, in spite of the affinities in the migration history and motives, there is so far no established historical connection or ethnic/cultural relationship between Ọza Nogogo (of present day Ika South LGA in Delta State) and Ọza/Ọjah (of present day Akoko-Edo LGA of Edo State).

There was a variant migration narrative of Ọza people from Benin to Ọza Orogbe. Historically, the inhabitants moved from Benin for safety during the interethnic wars.[5] Oral tradition suggests also that Ọza migration from the Benin Kingdom was prompted by the refusal of the village head to comply with the outrageous demands of the Oba of Benin in terms of royalties and tributes (Alonge 2002: 5). Thus, owing to the high-handedness of the ruling class to the various local communities outside the Benin moats (also traditionally known as *Iya*), many peoples felt insecure and migrated to other places.[6] Benin City, during the peak of the Benin Kingdom, had an external moat[7] and an internal Wall (known as the Great Benin Wall) built around the City as a defensive fortification to keep away invaders. While the inhabitants within the inner City had remarkable security, towns and villages located outside and beyond the moats and inner Wall were vulnerable to adversaries and slave raiders. This vulnerability happened from at least two perspectives. In times of slave raiding, many felt vulnerable since they did not receive the same level of security as compared to those within the inner city. Some inhabitants of villages and towns, including slaves, often fell prey as ritual objects of sacrifice to local deities and during funeral rites of a deceased Ọba.

These reasons partly explain why Ọza people migrated to different locations. Some oral traditions claim that even those who had moved to Ọza Nogogo continued to witness constant harassment under the domineering power of the Ọba of Benin. This resulted in their upward migration to Orogbe, an area very close to Ajaokuta, before they finally settled down at the new place (Alonge 2002: 5). They lived here for several years fighting the surrounding communities during interethnic wars. Later on, they moved southwards in search of water. The scarcity of water in Orogbe made habitation and subsistence farming an arduous task. Three strands of oral narratives explain the subsequent migration from Ọza Orogbe to Ọza Okeme.[8]

The first strand claims that a renowned hunter, Ọgbọmiyan, during a hunting expedition came across a waterlogged area, later named Lake *Ẹresha*, and thought it a better settlement for Ọza people (see Plate 12). He struck his spear to the ground and found water oozing out instantly. To ensure that this would be arable land, suitable for settlement and farming, he took out *Ọlọlọ* (a fruit seed), from his neck-chain and planted it on the spot, invoking the local deity that 'if this place will be good for my people to live, in three days let this seed germinate and bring out leaves'. Just as he rendered this invocation, he saw an enemy, Azanọmhọ, a slave raider approaching, and he had to hide and disguise himself. It was claimed that the enemy overheard his invocation but pretended. When Ọlọlọ germinated, the enemy went there before him and cut off the roots. On Ọbesa, the third day,[9] Ọgbọmiyan returned to the spot and to his amazement, the Ọlọlọ had germinated with sprouting leaves but withered away at the same time. However undeterred by the enemy's act of cowardice, he went home and reported that since the Ọlọlọ germinated, the place would be ideal for human habitation.

The second strand[10] narrates that when the hunter, Ọgbọmiyan, reached the swampy location he was enervated from the long hunting expedition. He climbed up a huge tree to take some rest on one of its boughs. After a while, he woke up abruptly and saw a kidnapper, Azanọmhọ, planting a fruit seed, Ọlọlọ. Ọgbọmiyan carefully watched and listened without revealing his presence there. After planting the seed, Azanọmhọ invoked the spirits, saying, 'If this place will be good for his people to live, let the seed germinate and grow by the time I return here on the ninth day.' After the perceived enemy's departure, he came down from the tree and went home. A few days later, Ọgbọmiyan returned to the spot and found the seed sprouted as the kidnapper had invoked. Instantaneously, Ọgbọmiyan cut the plant from its taproot with his knife and returned home, in a bid to outwit the enemy. When the kidnapper arrived on the ninth day, he met that the seed had actually germinated but the sprout had withered. This outcome led him to conclude that the environment would not be habitable for his people to live and farm. He left in anguish and disappointment. Ọgbọmiyan returned to the site afterwards and found that the seed had sprouted again miraculously. This gave him the audacity to recommend to his people that it was a potentially conducive and fertile settlement place. He returned home and managed to convince some of his people about the newly found settlement. Ọgbọmiyan consulted the diviners and indigenous healers to confirm that the new settlement was indeed the right choice that the ancestors and deities will accept. With their endorsement, they arrived and dug the lake, naming it Ẹrẹsha. Ọgbọmiyan's immediate family and others started to move in groups to inhabit the new settlement, Ọza Okeme (which literally means Ọza uplands, signifying the topography of the new settlement). Some of the earliest families who moved included Ọkọkọ, Unuayinoka, Emoko, Imakẹrẹ, Okidi and some others.[11]

The migration narrative from Benin City towards the Northern fringes of the Benin Kingdom is even more complex. Another oral source noted that some

Ọza peoples settled at Ọjirami, while others went to a hill called Onya ekẹ (now Dagbala). Those that form the present Ọjah settled in five groups, some were at Omune, Ishiki, Afẹke, Udu and Orogbe.¹² As Alonge further elaborated, the groups that later formed Ọjah settled according to their families at different places. Those at Omune were the Osu family; those at Orogbe were the Ọsuruka family, they are also called the Emei; the one at Udu were the Ọbuẹri family; and Afẹke were the Ogbodo family. However, the factors that prompted their reunion vary from family to family that settled as a group. For instance, the Ishiki and Afẹke family migrated from their former place to settle with their brother at Udu, as a result of the effects of the nineteenth-century Jihad. They fled to seek refuge on the hilltop where their brother, the Udu family, resided. The same oral accounts suggested that after some years of unification between the Afẹke, Ishiki and Udu, a hunter named Ọgbọmiyan from Orogbe came to Ọnya-Ọza (Ọza hill) at Udu to hunt. It was there that Ọgbọmiyan found a water spring (lake) which he named 'Ẹrẹsha', according to the same oral account. This was how the Ọsuruka family left Orogbe for Udu. The last group that joined their brothers was the Osu family.

While the migration trajectories remain contentious, there is also no consensus as to the etymology of the name, Ọza. One source suggested that the name was a latter appropriation. The people were first known as Ogegere when they lived in Benin, and then Orogbe when they migrated outside of Benin and then finally to the hilly settlement, Ọza Okeme, where the name was derived.¹³ According to the source, 'the original name of Ọza was Ukarugu. We came from the place known as Ogegere and when we were there, we were called citizens of Ogegere. From Ogegere, we came down to Orogbe and we were known and called by its name. Finally, we came to the hilltop (Ọza) and we are called by its name (Ọza citizens).' Another source suggests that Ọza simply means a village set up on a hill, Oyan Ọza.¹⁴ Yet another source opined that Ọza is an offshoot of the word '*anamajeza*', literally meaning 'since we have been moving from one place to another this is the place we will stop'.¹⁵ Ọgbọmiyan named the site 'Ọza' meaning that the *Ọlọlọ* survived or germinated when the Azanọmhọ planted it.¹⁶ Nonetheless, the name 'Ọza' later became known and called Ọjah by the missionaries who perhaps found difficulty in pronouncing the letter "z." While retaining Ọza in the local language, the anglicized form 'Ọjah' is now adopted for official communication.¹⁷ The British colonial administration, the impact of the missionaries – mostly local Yoruba Christian agents – and traders largely contributed to the entrenchment of the name 'Ọjah/Ọja' instead of its original derivation, Ọza. As we shall discuss later, the proliferation of mission churches and schools, mostly led by Yoruba catechists and teachers, was instrumental to the Yorubanization of Christianity and naming culture in Ọza and other parts of the region.

Generally, several accounts corroborate the view that migration from Benin was a gradual process and attributed the impetus for migration to a number of factors including the high-handedness of the ruling Ọba (King) of the Bini monarch, the imperatives of slave trade and interethnic wars. Osarhieme Osadolor places emphasis on the war potential in early fifteenth century, showing that the development of the military during the era of warrior kings from c. 1440 to 1600 was a period that witnessed the expansion of the state through warfare mounted virtually in all directions (Osadolor 2001). From AD 1440, the Kings of Benin pursued expansionist policy, probably after the consolidation of internal control necessary for assistance in war because territorial expansion required a well-organized army. According to Osadolor, the war value of the royal regiment largely depended upon the value of the Edogun whose leadership role in war as a front commander assured them of possible victory. The strength of the royal regiment varied because it was not based on recruitment but on conscription by birth. The warrior chiefs were generally conferred with the grade of titles referred to as *Egie Ologhoro* within the group of titles known as *Ibiwe n'Ekhua* headed by the Edogun. One of the *Ibiwe n'Ekhua* titles was Ọza (Eweka 1992: 45; Osadolor 2001: 102-3).

J. U. Egharevba (1934: 13-23) and E. B. Eweka (1989: 20-2) made references to 'Ọza of Benin City' among the personages, remembered events and accomplishments attributed to Ọba Ewuare's reign and part of Benin's rich oral tradition about famous kings. 'Ewuare brought out many leaders, warriors, and heroes, some of whom were later deified as spirits in the towns and villages where they performed their deeds. This list included Ọza of Benin City and many others' (Egharevba 1968: 13). Ọba Ewuare the Great (c. 1440-73) was reputed to have been a 'mystic, physician, traveler, and warrior to many parts of present day Nigeria, Dahomey (the modern Republic of Benin), Ghana, Guinea, and the Congo' (Egharevba 1968: 13). As a renowned warrior Ọba he expanded the territorial boundaries of the Benin Kingdom, conquering towns and villages as far as Igboland to the west of the Niger River and far-flung to Yoruba towns and villages including Ọwọ, Akure, Ijebu-Ode and their environs (see also Kaplan 2003: 181-99). It is, however, unclear if there is any connection between the mentioned 'Ọza of Benin City' and what latter became Ọza (Ojah) people that migrated from Benin City. It is also a matter of conjecture if the aggressive rule and expansionist policies of warrior-like Bini Obas such as Ewuare the Great in the fifteenth century led to the migration of Ọza people.

Ọza land tenure system

Family land ownership defines Ọza land tenure system, although the *Ọpashi* (Village Head) and *Eja* (council of chiefs) remain overall custodians and arbitrate in cases of family land disputes. Land in Ọza is ownable property conventionally segregated by *Afẹ* (patrilineal families) including *Afẹ Ọbuẹri*, *Afẹ Ọburẹsẹ (Ọtaru)*, *Afẹ Osu*, *Afẹ Osobo*, *Afẹ Ekẹ* and *Afẹ Ọpashi* (four titleholders).[18] There are no existing, concrete natural or artificial physical boundary demarcators between Ọza and their neighbouring Ọsọsọ, Makeke, Ukpilla (Okpella), Unẹmẹ-Osu and Dagbala peoples. However, Ọza, through oral narratives based on historical and cultural memory, are able to identify what they consider as original, fluid geographical boundaries with their neighbours. Chief Abiodun Joshua delineated Ọza land mass as stretching historically from the northern fringes: Ọgashi River, Opo Ela (literally 'River of Cattles'), which is the present-day location of Filani Hotels in Ọsọsọ, and through Egbetua to Iduru River towards Ukpilla (Okpella) on the western fringes.[19] He claimed that on the eastern fringes, Ọza originally had physical boundaries with Ekpe as Makeke people later migrated from Imọga. *Afẹ Obuẹri* owns the expanse of land between Ajoyo Quarters and *Ọyonba*, although Makeke also now lay claims surreptitiously to parts of the land until *River Obure*. In the southern fringes, *Afẹ Oburẹsẹ (Ọtaru)* owns the land mass between *Ọyonba* and *Ẹrẹvia Origbe* and *Agbọkodọ*; while *Afẹ Osu* and *Afẹ Osobo* own the land between *Ishipo River* in *Agbọkodọ* and Ọnya *Odumu*, physical boundaries with Dagbala. Other land ownership families are *Afẹ Ufeshi* who owns *Ofẹmi* until the *River Iduru* from one end, while *Afẹ Ọpashi* (titleholders) and other families own land around Iduru from the other end.[20]

Chief Abiodun Alleh corroborated similar cultural memory of family land ownership in Ọza. He, however, cautioned that *Ọza Afẹ* family landowners rarely physically demarcate natural boundaries. There is a somewhat 'commonsense' agreement between families not to make artificial boundary demarcation but rely on family land boundaries intuitively.[21] According to Chief Alleh,

> The Osu family hosted some Ineme immigrants for several years in Ọza Okeme (Ọza uplands). The Osu family owns most of the landmass stretching beyond Ishipo river, at the end of Agbọkodọ quarters in Ọza and Dagbala, although a portion of the land also belongs to *Afẹ Osobo*. *Afẹ Ọburẹsẹ* and *Afẹ Ọbuẹri* own current land mass from Ishipo upwards to Ajoyo. Three families: *Afẹ Osu*, *Afẹ Osobo* and *Afẹ Ekẹ* exist in both Ọza and Dagbala and lay claim to proximate geographical land boundaries between Ọza and Dagbala. As benevolent hosts,

our fathers who later inhabited Ọza and Dagbala, gave them a portion of their farmland, *Ochi-Osu* (Osu garden or farm) to inhabit. Thus, the existence and settlement of Unẹmẹ-Osu at the current site is mostly owing to the benevolence, generosity and warm reception accorded the Ineme immigrants by our Osu family ancestors. The relationship between the host family Osu and the new Ineme immigrants was mostly cordial until the Nupe raids when Ineme blacksmiths posed as subversive elements by producing and selling war implements such as swords, knifes for the invading forces. This betrayed the trust of their host family and thus severed relations with the emigrant settlers and the entire Ọza. Such severance of relationships partly resulted in the designation of the Inemes as *ẹbẹ nikara* [literally, dried leaves], a derogatory name depicting them as social outcasts. This means intermarriage and social interactions with the *Ilẹmẹ* became a taboo. Ọza people strictly adhered to such taboos and defaulters face grave ritual consequences. However, this seems to be changing in recent times as there are now instances of intermarriages, and aspects of the taboo have now been relaxed.[22]

Chief Alleh further remarked, 'A few male ancestors of *Afẹ Osu* in Ọza and Dagbala are Thomas Ogbezuode, Ayesufu, Alleh Okigi, Akelemu, Omodara Okigi, Ademola Omodara; while surviving elders of the *Afẹ Osu* in Ọza and Dagbala include Emmanuel Agboju (Inugu), Ojo Omodara, Paul Balogun; and Pa Olori and one nicknamed "Lawyer" respectively.'[23] Women do not own land as family land ownership is a patrilineal prerogative. Nonetheless, by virtue of the fact that women make up patrilineal and matrilineal families, they are also in a position to appropriate farmlands, with permission from *Afẹ*, family landowners, for agriculture and domestic use.

While it is commonly known that these *Afẹ* (families) traditionally own the segregated land mass, any Ọza indigene could make use of any of these lands for housing, farming and other uses with appropriate request and approval from the respective families. For instance, in a letter dated 3 January 1977 from the Ọbuẹri paternal family to the Ọkọgbe of Ọjah, titled 'Donation of Land between the Anglican Church and Ufa Quarters Ọjah to the Entire Ọjah Community for Communal Development', they stated unequivocally,

> This is to certify that we members of the Ọbuẹri Paternal family of Ọjah, the traditional owner of the parcel of land between the Anglican Church and Ufa quarters in Ọjah, do hereby give the said parcel of land to the entire Ọjah Community (of which we are a part) for communal development. (2) That we have agreed to give out the parcel of land free of charge to the entire Ọjah Community on the understanding that it will not be used for a personal economic

venture but a venture that will be benefit the sons and daughters of Ojah and Bendel State at large. (3) That the parcel of land is to be used specifically for the establishment of a post Primary Institution in Ojah. (4) That on no account should the Okogbe of Ojah who traditionally holds land in trust for the various paternal families in Ojah allow trespassers to encroach on the parcel of land.[24]

It is clear from the above correspondence between the Obueri family and the Okogbe of Ojah that even though land is *pro bono*, it necessarily must have the approval of the family landowner. This is the case even for land required for communal use and irrespective of the source of the request, including the *Opashi* who in symbol terms 'traditionally holds land in trust for the various paternal families'. The family, on the understanding that it will not be exploited or used for commercial purposes, approves such land. The approved land in question now hosts Oza Community High School. Upon family request, a parcel of land is approved and obtained free of charge for use, although social change is affecting such formerly free transactional relationships.[25]

Originally, land given to strangers or immigrants by a family landowner, such as the parcel of land, *Ochi-Osu*, granted to Ileme immigrants (now Uneme-Osu settlers) by the Oza *Afe-Osu* (Osu family), was not sold, a lease or any outright purchase of any sort, but was land that was given *gratis*, free of charge and without compensation. Nonetheless, recent, indiscriminate land expansionist strategies of Ileme people and boundary squabbles have rendered what was initially an act of generosity now increasingly contentious, leery and unnerving.

Rowling's (1948) concise notes on land tenure,[26] compiled in August 1947 during a tour of the Benin, Kukuruku and Ishan Divisions, are very instructive in unpacking the land tenure system in Oza. The report indicated that the control of land in Benin City is entirely in the hands of the *Oba*. The *Oba* is the ultimate authority: but detailed application of the *Oba's* policy and administration of town lands is left to the Quarter Elders without whose recommendations the *Oba* would not normally make a grant (Rowling 1948: 19). This slightly contrasts with the land tenure system in Kukuruku, where letters from Divisional Officer to Resident Benin indicated that 'when a village was first settled the land round was shared out between the heads of the original settle families ... Kukuruku villages are divided into Quarters which may "regard themselves as being of one family" (extended) or may consist of several such families' (Rowling 1948: 42–3). Rowling remarked further that

> quarter boundaries are presumably natural features. Any fellow villager from another Quarter has to obtain leave of the Quarter Elders if he proposes

to work their land, but would pay no dues for the privilege ... Farmland is communal in the sense that any member of the community is free to take it up without payment; but community rights are broken down among the Quarters.

In the case of Akoko, Rowling suggested in his notes the existence of exclusive family rights over land. If these in fact exist, individual family heads probably enjoy a degree of independent discretion not recognized elsewhere in the division (1948: 44). He noted, for instance, that the introduction of cocoa on any scale began in about 1935 – though some palms and kola are being grown, cocoa remains the principle plantation crop – and at first created suspicion because of the restriction it imposed on the community's general farming rights. There was accordingly some suggestion, endorsed by the Divisional Officer with a proposal for the Native Authority Order, to this effect that consent of the elders should be obtained before any villager planted such crops.

Rowling also underscored an important feature about ownership of permanent crops in Kukuruku Division.

> Sale, pledge or lease of land are, with two exceptions which do not affect the rule, unknown in the division: the exceptions being a statutory one (Cap. 89) where lease to an alien is concerned, and a single instance of group purchase during the Nupe wars when Enwan, a village of Ukpilla immigrants, settled near Igarra and obtained land from them in exchange for slaves. Otherwise the principle is very clearly insisted upon in discussion. (47)

Bradbury corroborated this observation, noting that 'among the North-West Edo, there appears to be a differentiation of land rights below the ward level. "Family" groups are said to hold exclusive rights over farming tracts and family heads have discretion over the alienation of tree crops by sale or pledge' (Bradbury 1957: 120). Concerning inheritance, rights of inheritance depend upon the form of marriage entered into: *Onabo, Amoya, Isumi*. Patrilineal and matrilineal systems existed side by side. Generally, women do not inherit rights in land but may obtain plantations by purchase, gift or employing paid labour (Rowling 1948: 50).

Strangers follow the already examined pattern of controls: viz., through Quarter Elders to Village Council who share between them the yearly tribute of yams and palm wine payable (Rowling 1948: 51). The commodification of plantation tree crops and the politicization of relationships between landowning groups, strangers and immigrants was most consequential in boundary disputes and inter-village squabbles. Rowling aptly remarked, 'This likelihood is enhanced by the spread of permanent crops since ... the development of palm products industry and, more recently, the planting of cocoa has created an interest in the ownership of land and a desire to define boundaries that never before needed defining' (1948: 55). He was somewhat emphatic and detailed in making certain qualification about inter-communal relations of landowning groups among the Akoko people. Rowling observes,

> Ineme immigration during the Nupe raids has introduced a complicating factor in the form of concurrent land rights held by different villages. 'Village after village', says the Ineme Intelligence Report speaking of the social dislocation caused by these raids, left the lowlands and fled to the protection of the hills; they returned to find others farming where they had farmed. A collection of immigrant groups from Benin, the Inemes, thus found themselves settled on land claimed by the Akoko people. They could not be turned off; and though it seems they were until quite recently regarded as enjoying no more than 'stranger rights', the present position (?since administrative reorganization?) is that they are, within their clan areas, allowed all the rights and powers normally exercised by other Kukuruku villages provided they raise no boundary disputes. Their claims are further subject in certain instances to concurrent Akoko rights in both land and/or forest produce. 'Ineme-Ekpe has little land to which it can claim absolute ownership though it has farming rights over about 10 sq. miles ... Ineme-Ogbe has occupational rights over about 5 sq. miles of land but shares the land and palm products in common with the Akoko people ... Egeni has about 10 sq. miles, most of which is shared in common with the neighbouring village of Oshin ... Ineme-Osu has about 30 sq. miles but Dagbala lays claim to ownership of most of this'. (1948: 54)

In view of the geographical proximity between Dagbala, Unẹmẹ-Osu and Ojah, it is very improbable that Unẹmẹ-Osu can make any ownership claims to about 30 square miles. This is against the backdrop of oral narratives that the Osu kindred, a family inhabiting Oza and Dagbala, lays claim to original ownership of the expanse of land inhabited by Unẹmẹ-Osu and gave a portion of their farmland, *Oki-Osu* (Osu garden/farm), now renamed as Unẹmẹ-Osu. Here is a case in point of Rowling's caution that his notes 'cannot – obviously – claim completeness' (1948: 3).

Rowling was himself skeptical about some of the claims about sharing of rights in forest produce among the Akoko as indicated above. He queries,

> In view of previous statements about family claims over palm and locust bean (paragraph 46) this sharing of rights in forest produce appears difficult to

understand. Presumably it holds only in regard to tracts of what was wholly virgin bush, not previously cleared by any Akoko family before the Ineme's arrival. If so, private and concurrent collective rights in undemarcated areas must constitute an involved pattern very liable to cause disputes. (1948: 54)

However improbable any claims of sharing or collective rights to forest produce might be among the Akoko, Bradbury aptly observes a decade later, that the relation, in respect of land, between North-West Edo and the Ineme communities interspersed with them, was indeed an uneasy, cautiously optimistic one, as the Ineme appear to have few undisputed claims to the ownership of either land or water (Bradbury 1957: 124). I shall return to this below.

Ọza and its neighbours: A precarious proximity

Ọza people's relationship to their neighbours in both historical and contemporary eras is relatively serene and congenial, on the one hand, and turbulent and contentious, on the other. Ọza (Ọjah) is bounded on the north-west by Makeke and on the north-east by Ọsọsọ, while it is bounded originally in the south-east by Ukpilla (Okpella) and in the south by Unẹmẹ Osu, although originally by Dagbala. Bradbury lists Ekpe and Makeke (from Umorga) and one ward of Ọjirami (from Lankpese) among five communities with the most unusual historical traditions, which suggests that they are descended from age-sets, which broke away from their parent communities (1957: 113). This claim makes clear that Makeke and Ọjirami migrated to their present settlements, in this case from Imọga and Lampese, both Ọkpameri-speaking communities. Makeke and Dagbala have some linguistic affinities with Ọza and other Ọkpameri languages. The proximity with Ọza community has resulted in intermarriages and old/new kinship relations, especially visible in some Makeke quarters such as in Ife, Ileteju and in a section of Ajoyo quarters, a predominantly Ọza community. The *Afẹ Osu*, *Afẹ Osobo* and *Afẹ Ekẹ* are three patrilineal families represented historically and present time in Ọza and Dagbala, respectively.

While intermarriages, cultural exchanges and ethnic influences are common denominators of these communities, such historical and cultural affinities and geographical proximities have also fuelled land disputes, encroachment and arbitrations witnessed in the litigations, for instance, between Makeke and Ọjah in Ajoyo, Ife and Ileọrọ (Ufa) Quarters. Such contestations are also rife between Ọjah, on the one hand, and other neighbouring communities of Ọsọsọ, Unẹmẹ

Osu and Okpella,[27] on the other hand. Nonetheless, the close proximity of these communities has also enhanced the local trade economy with its rotational market-day calendar between Ọsọsọ, Makeke, Ọjah, Unẹmẹ Osu, Dagbala and Ojirami Afẹ (Ekunu-Ofami).

Ọsọsọ is strategically located on the elevation in the north-eastern fringes of North-West Edo. The Ọsọsọ people are said to have migrated from Idah (current Benue State), but it is doubtful whether this was their ultimate origin. Bradbury notes that 'indeed the present Olososo (King of Ọsọsọ) says that his ancestors came from Benin, but that they had once claimed an Idah origin from a fear of being placed under Benin: in the course of their wandering they had crossed and re-crossed the Niger' (1957: 113). Lore has it that the people of Ọsọsọ earned their name from an ancestor, Oshiọsọr, who discovered their present location during a hunting expedition about 150 years ago (Lewis 2013: 10).[28] The same source indicated that the people have enjoyed intermittent epochs of prolonged peace, interrupted by a Yoruba invasion (1875), Nupe occupation at the turn of the nineteenth century and British colonization in the 1920s.

Bradbury remarks that the whole of the North-West Edo area came under the Nupe during the latter half of the nineteenth century. The Nupe invasions preceded the incursions from Ibadan. The Ibadan raids seemed mainly to have been confined to the north-west corner of the region, but the Ọsọsọ people claimed their ancestors were driven away and their houses burnt by the Yoruba forces before the Nupe arrived. While many villages were sacked, Ojah was not mentioned among the several communities who were scattered or had their settlements sacked by the Yoruba (Bradbury 1957: 112). Some of these scattered groups returned to their old sites after the Yoruba raids passed, only to submit to or be driven out again by the Nupe (see a later section on Nupe invasion). When the Nupe *ghazi* (raids) arrived, some villages submitted; some inhabitants abandoned them and fled to the tops of the neighbouring rocky hills. The Nupe intruders sacked other villages and dispersed their populations. However, Nupe hegemonic power ended only with the appearance of the Royal Niger Company's agents in the 1890s.

While Bradbury (1957: 113) documents that most of these communities accepted Nupe rule and paid tributes mainly in slaves, Ojah was unnamed among the villages and communities that fell to the Yoruba and Nupe raids. Several oral sources corroborated this view that Ọza escaped these external attacks, incursions and direct exposure to slave raiding. The relocation to Ọza Okeme settlement probably coincided with the era of interethnic wars and slave raiding that involved Nupe, Yoruba and Benin Kingdoms. Oral sources claimed that Ọza Okeme was largely unscathed owing to its strategic location, with the hills serving as a natural bulwark for its inhabitants and some of its neighbours.

Sources indicate that several families from neigbhouring villages such as Ogori (Oshiedu 1980: 28) and Ọsọsọ sought refuge in Ọza Okeme. Baba Oshiedu refers to the protracted interethnic wars unleashed in succession by the Nupes on Yagba and Kabba country, and Akoko region, which stretched to the borders of Ọwọ in Yoruba domain and Auchi in Kukuruku (Afẹnmai or Akoko-Ẹdo) territory. He notes, 'An Ogori hero, Agiri humiliated Ojibo (Ejibo) the Nupe warrior, he proved a march for the Nupes whom he held at bay for a long time. With his prowess, he and his army successfully brought to nought several campaigns of the invaders which at certain times drove Ogori to Ọja and other places for refuge' (Oshiedu 1980: 28). Ọza people inhabited Ọza Okeme during the era of British conquest of Benin Kingdom in 1897. Following the internecine wars, Yoruba and Nupe slave raiding, and the British conquest of Nupe and Benin kingdoms, Ọza people gradually migrated to settle at Ọza lowlands, which forms the present-day settlement. The rest of this section will focus on Ọza's relationship with Ilẹmẹ (Unẹmẹ-Osu), an ambivalent relationship that has proved elusive, unwieldy and prolonged owing to obvious reasons as will be discussed below.

Ọza people and Ilẹmẹ (Unẹmẹ-Osu)

We can better grasp the history of Ilẹmẹ, now Unẹmẹ-Osu as a relatively recent immigrant neighbour of Ọza, by charting the general history, location, nomenclature and language of the Ineme (Unẹmẹ) briefly here. Charles Temple (1919: 7)[29] indicates that the Unẹmẹ are scattered all over Akoko-Ẹdo, Etsako, Kabba, Ọwọ, Ishan and Asaba. Bradbury also notes historically that

> The Ineme (Unɛmɛ or Ulɛmɛ) inhabit a number of villages in the northern and south-eastern parts of the Kukuruku Division, widely scattered, and separated from each other by the territory of various Etsako and North-West Edo communities. They are undoubtedly an intrusive element in the population of this area and probably represent a more recent migration from the vicinity of Benin. The Ineme are united by common traditions of origin, by their traditional craft as smiths, in their dialect, and in certain other social and cultural features. In a sense they represent an endogamous caste, for their non-Ineme neighbours refuse to intermarry with them. (1957: 123)[30]

While the extent of the Ineme's geographical spread to Northern Nigeria may not be the case in present-day Nigeria, Bradbury indicates that 'other Ineme settlements are to be found in Ishan, parts of North-Eastern Yoruba country and in the neighbouring parts of Northern Nigeria'.[31] Demographically, he classifies Southern Ineme as comprising the following villages: Alagbeta, Imiava, Udochi North, Udochi South and Uzanu; while Northern Ineme is made up of Ineme-Ogbe, Ineme-Ekpe, Egeni, Ineme Osu, Eturu and Ineme Ogbe, respectively. Lewis suggests that there are at least ten Uneme settlements in the Afenmai area (Northern Uneme) and another five in the Etsako region (Southern Uneme).[32] Despite their diaspora spread and trade links with many Akoko-Edo villages, the Uneme are not much liked by their neighbours, who are too quick to be dissociated from them (Lewis 2013: 13). Temple accounts earlier that

> the Uneme too would not trade their independence for anything. ... but Ineme-Ekpe, Ineme-Ogbe and Egeni are separated from each other and are for the most part surrounded by the land of the Akoko clan. There are objections, therefore, to the three of the Northern Ineme villages being included in the re-organisation of the Ineme clan, but not only do they strongly desire it, but also the Akokos have no wish for the Ineme to join with them. (1919: 7)

In terms of their traditions of origin and history, Bradbury aptly remarks that Ineme probably migrated to this area at a later date than neighbouring peoples. The Inemes descended from a group of blacksmiths from Obadan in Benin Division who fled from the wrath of an *Oba*. They settled first at Inyele, in what is now Asaba Division and later at Ugboha in Ishan, where there are still some Ineme.[33] Their own traditions and anomalous position in respect of land tenure attest to this. Bradbury contrasts names of certain *egware* (wards) within the northern and southern villages, suggesting either that the northern villages are composite settlements containing elements from different southern villages or that the latter are derived from particular *egware* in the northern villages. According to him,

> traditions collected by government officers in 1911-15 suggest the latter since they indicate that all the Ineme formerly lived in the north. Mr. D.P. Stanfield, who lives in Kukuruku Division, supports this view and suggests that Ineme who had crossed and recrossed the Niger probably founded the southern villages after 1865. But much fragmentation and regrouping appears to have taken place during the latter half of the 19th century as a result of Nupe raids. (1957: 124)

The fact that these accounts alluded to the Inemes as recent immigrants who arrived at this area in the post-1860s is most plausible, in view of Ọza-Osu family narratives of encounter above. It is against this backdrop that Hakeem Harunah's description of Unẹmẹ Aki-Osu's founding in about the early 1400s, as well as the migration, founding and early growth of new Unẹmẹ communities outside Benin since the 1370s (Harunah 2003: 183–346), is fundamentally flawed, historically speculative, strategically dubious and disingenuous.

Bradbury aptly observes about land tenure of the Inẹmẹ,

> The Inẹmẹ appear to have few undisputed claims to the ownership of either land or water. The fishing-ponds which the Southern Ineme use are disputed with the Uzia, Ekperi, and Ifeku people, and most of the Northern Ineme share their farming and palm produce rights with neighbouring North-West Edo communities ... This situation does not appear to have caused much friction, but in recent years the increasing importance of palm-produce has resulted in a desire to establish boundaries which were formerly vague. (1957: 125–6)[34]

This land contestation and boundary disputes seem to be a characteristic of all Inemes and the neighbours they met in their current settlements until date. Such land and boundary disputes are concomitant with the crisis of Nigeria's political economy and the ensuing politics of land grabbing particularly in the last decades. Below, we shall demonstrate this tendency in the relationship between Ọza host community and the new immigrant settlers, the Unẹmẹ-Osu (Ilẹmẹ) people.

A recent work that attempts to capture the complex history of the Unẹmẹ was Harunah's *A Cultural History of the Unẹmẹ: From the Earliest Times to 1962* (2003),[35] which is mostly hagiographical and inherently skewed with robustly distorted and sensationalized history. The book's foreword was apropos in noting, 'The author does not and cannot claim, that he has written all that can be said or written about the Unẹmẹ.'[36] Nonetheless, even what he wrote, based on some conspiracy theories, is hardly devoid of historical inaccuracies and spurious claims. A brief critical appraisal of the book will suffice below.

The author attempts to provide a comprehensive insight into the historical and cultural past of Unẹmẹ communities from the precolonial period to 1962, highlighting, among other topics, origins, patterns of migration and settlement patterns of the Unẹmẹ; evolution and development of the Unẹmẹ indigenous culture; and the role of iron technology in shaping the growth of ancient Unẹmẹ. Harunah explores the migration and early growth of new Unẹmẹ villages, towns and clans outside Benin since the 1370s. He identifies six new villages and towns founded by Unẹmẹ migrants in Akoko-Ẹdo LGA as Unẹmẹ Akpama, Unẹmẹ Aki-Osu, Unẹmẹ Erhurun, Unẹmẹ Nekhua, Unẹmẹ Ekpẹdo and Unẹmẹ Aiyetoro, respectively (Harunah 2003: 212).[37]

First, with the book's detailed exploration of the history of the Unẹmẹs, their migratory narratives and their relationship with neighbours, it is both unconscionable and inconceivable that the author escaped any mention of Ọza (Ọjah) as having common geographical borders with Unẹmẹ Aki-Osu (Unẹmẹ Osu) in Akoko-Ẹdo South. Robust oral narratives[38] and a lot of evidence (see colonial maps) lend credence to Ọza people as a hosting community to the Ineme immigrants. An extract from Map of Nigeria London War Office (Map E) 1910,[39] a British colonial map published under the direction of the Inspector General of Surveys[40] Nigeria showing Benin Province with the geographical boundaries of Kukuruku Division and a third map of Edo-speaking peoples, South-Western Nigeria,[41] originally produced in Bradbury (1957: 165) are noteworthy. It is hardly by accident or error by design that all three maps listed Ọja (Ọza/Ọjah), but none listed Unẹmẹ-Osu or Unẹmẹ Aki-Osu. Two maps clearly indicated Ọja as bounded in the north by Ọsọsọ, in the south by Dagbala, in the east and west by Makeke and Egbetua (an Ọsọsọ Quarter), respectively. Either we can infer from the non-inclusion of Unẹmẹ-Osu (Unẹmẹ Aki-Osu) in colonial historical maps that they were probably new immigrants whose emerging community was relatively small, in transition, or that the Ineme community was non-existent in their current location at that time. As Bradbury aptly underscores, the Inemes 'are undoubtedly an intrusive element in the population of this area and probably represent a more recent migration from the vicinity of Benin' (1957: 123). The far-fetched narrative that the Unẹmẹ people did not meet any groups of autochthonous settlers in their new abode was common in the history of Unẹmẹ Ekpe (Ekpẹdo) in relation to their Ekpe neighbours, Enegi (Unẹmẹ Nekhua) in relation to their Osi (Ayegunle) neighbours, and Unẹmẹ Akpama.[42] Such a similar narrative smacks of hagiography and a distorted historical account that further undercuts the book's scholarly integrity and rigour.

Harunah recounts Unẹmẹ Aki-Osu community's oral traditions and their migration trajectory from Unẹmẹ Akpama to Unẹmẹ Osu.[43] The author indicates variously that 'the Unẹmẹ Aki-Osu people, like their kith and kins in neighbouring Unẹmẹ Akpama', 'Unẹmẹ Aki-Osu is situated in the north of Unẹmẹ Akpama'. It is rather cynical and suspect to paint such a picture that vividly obliterates the geographical existence of the proximate neighbours – Dagbala and Ọjirami to the south and Ọza (Ọjah) to the north. Even more contentious and unseemly is the specious claim 'that (like the founders of Unẹmẹ Akpama), they did not seem to have met any autochthones or earlier settlers at the site on which they founded Unẹmẹ Aki-Osu'.[44] This is indeed a grevious misplacement of historical facts as the present Unẹmẹ Osu were originally *Oki-Osu* (Osu gardens or farmland) originally owned by *Afẹ Osu* and *Afẹ Osobo* kindred families in Ọza and Dagbala and given *pro bono* to the new Ineme immigrant families. The fact that the original name, *Oki-Osu* (Osu garden/farmland), belonging to Ọza's *Afẹ Osu* has been recasted as *Aki-Osu* (to mean Osu market) and linked to their migration narrative from Akpama deserves further critical scrutiny and historical emendation.

Second, oral narratives and written sources point to existing trading and social relations between the Inemes and their surrounding neighbours, except for intermarriages. Oral narratives, largely corroborated by Tempel, Bradbury, Lewis and other scholars' works, share a similar view that the non-Ineme neighbours refuse to intermarry with the Inemes on grounds of caste prejudice and other obvious explanations. Such narratives have, however, been upturned and distorted with an Inẹmẹ counternarrative that 'the refusal by the Unẹmẹ people to allow their girls and women to be married by non-Unẹmẹ men is to prevent the leakage of the Unẹmẹ iron technology, through the processes of inter-marriages'.[45]

Several oral narratives allude to the claim that earlier Inẹmẹ immigrants were given some pieces of land to farm and inhabit by respective *Afẹ Osu* and *Afẹ Osobo* family landowners in Ọza and Dagbala. Some Ineme migrants served as casual workers in farmlands owned by Ọza and Dagbala people, while others served as babysitters for Ọza and Dagbala farmers. No sooner, they expanded and started to encroach on land spaces to their host's chagrin and disapproval. This earned them strict restrictions to land expansion and acquisition.

Another oral narrative on the caste prejudice and intermarriage is the myth built around Inemes as blacksmiths and builders/traders in iron implements. Owing to their perceived complicities during interethnic wars and slave trade, it became a taboo to intermarry with them. In earlier times, it was recounted that Ọza farmers left their children in the custody of house helps in Unẹmẹ Osu, but it was a taboo to leave the children there to sleep or stay overnight in Unẹmẹ Osu. Some commentators even mentioned that where that happens by mistake, the child is abandoned and changes identity as Unẹmẹ-Osu. Oral tradition also claimed that if you had an Osu person as a guest, you must wash clean the seat to avoid any contamination. Such myths have so much fear and trepidation built around them. People believe that any breach of these taboos will result in mysterious death. Such prejudices and taboos continue to dominate narratives today although such beliefs are less strictly adhered to in recent times. Oral tradition has it that the Ọkpameri withstood domineering incursions from the Bini, the Nupe, the Igala and the Yoruba. Curiously, though, the Ọkpameri still rever the Yoruba and the Bini as friends, while they hold the Nupe, the Igala and the Unẹmẹ as archenemies (Lewis 2013: 8–9). This perception resonated with the Nupe and Igala infamous slave trading, and the readiness of the Unẹmẹ to equip two sides of any battle with instruments of war and invasion.

Ọza during the Nupe invasion and hegemony in the nineteenth century

There are no existing written records of the Nupe incursion into and invasion of Ọza or direct encounter with Ọza people. However, oral traditions abound that date the Nupe invasion and hegemony of far-flung lands and non-Nupe communities in the nineteenth century. Prior to the termination of the Nupe raids in the late 1890s and the conquest by the British forces (Royal Niger Company) in 1897, the Nupe warlords had harassed, tormented and made extortionate demands for slaves, commodities on neighbouring communities for almost half a century. S. F. Nadel wrote that

> 'the people of Nupe obtained their slaves by two methods: first, there were the slaves captured in the war, who became the property of the man to whose share in the booty they had fallen; and second, there were slaves bought in the markets of Bida … Slaves were also sold abroad, mostly to the South. Many Nupe men of rank were engaged in professional slave-trading; they acted as middlemen between the slave markets of the north, Kano, Katsina, and others, and the buyers in the south, on the river and coast. (1942: 103–4)

Consequent upon these random slave raids, many communities were sacked, while several inhabitants were forced to flee their homes to seek refuge on hills, mountain tops and in caves.[46] The impact of the Nupe wars and the Islamic jihad expansionist policies on North-Eastern Yorubaland, the Akoko and Afẹnmai has been fairly captured.[47] Michael Mason provides a chronology of nineteenth-century Nupe military and political activities in North-Eastern Yorubaland and Afẹnmai, relating them to the history of the central Nupe Kingdom. The essay also outlines the forms of administration employed by the Nupes in these areas and suggests some of the most enduring effects of the years of Nupe hegemony (Mason 1970: 193–209). Ade Obayemi remarks, 'Undoubtedly, the slave raiding activities of the Fulani-led Nupe armies created a lot of problems for the northeast Yoruba. Depopulation, relocation of settlements to barren and hilly terrains and disruption of indigenous industries are but a few examples of the effects of the Fulani-led Nupe activities in the area' (1978: 61–87). Inevitably, southward expansion threatened established political alliances and economic partnerships (Kolapo 1999: 69). The North-East Yoruba and other communities gave their moral and material support to the British with the hope of bringing Bida domination to an end. It never mattered to them whether the British were imperialists or not. Their target was to get rid of the Fulani ruling dynasty (Idrees 1989: 69–82).

Generally, the Nupe wars, which occurred in several phases between 1810 and 1857, began as a civil war between members of the *Etsu* Nupe (Nupe kings) royal family. However, foreign Muslim clerical immigrants and revolutionary jihadists from Sokoto to the north-west soon intruded into the fray, immediately giving the wars an altogether new and complex character. 'Nupe occupied an important position in the overall prosecution of the jihad – both through its own military campaigns and the support it provided to the central government and especially to Gwandu' (Kolapo 1999: 71). In 1842, Caliph Muhammad Bello outlined official policy and declared intent to extend the jihad southward to the coast. He was quoted as saying, 'God has given me all the land of the infidels' (Kolapo 1999: 72). The general progress and outcome of the Nupe wars were henceforth closely impacted by the factor of Islamic jihad. This was demonstrated in the successful establishment of the five Nupe emirates as members in the Sokoto caliphate.

Nonetheless, other ideological motivations were also important. Thus, nationalist, cultural, militarist and economic sentiments all asserted their influence on the Nupe wars and produced the unrelenting, vicious and complex character that the Nupe wars of the first half of the nineteenth century assumed (Kolapo 2012: 16). The jihadist's intervention in the Nupe wars was premised on Islamic ideology and their entire political agenda was based on the ideological justification and political legitimization of Usman Dan Fodio's jihad. The administrative arrangement of the Sokoto caliphate placed the Nupe emirates under the charge of the emir of Gwandu (Kolapo 2012: 28). The factionalization of Nupe into multiple poles of political, economic and demographic power contributed in a large measure to the intense and prolonged nature of early-nineteenth-century Nupe wars. Thus, several elements constituted the internal dynamics of the early-nineteenth-century Nupe wars (Kolapo 2012: 34). The internal Nupe wars were concurrent with raids launched by the Rabah and

Lade jihadist factions against non-Nupe communities on their borders. These Nupe against non-Nupe wars have been variously described in the literature as raids, razzias, expansionist wars, jihad and slave raids; they were perpetrated against weak and defenseless communities at the southern frontiers of the Nupe (Kolapo 2012: 24).

To a large extent, the Nupe emirate of Bida partly emerged because of the nineteenth-century Sokoto jihad and was in the making for almost half a century, from 1810 until 1857. By the 1840s most of the towns in North-Eastern Yoruba as well as in Afẹnmai had become aware of the military threat of the Nupe armies emanating from the north-west (Mason 1970: 204). These years were filled with chaotic military and political activities among several contenders for the Nupe throne and the position of *Etsu* (Kolapo 1999: 69). Of the five Nupe emirates, Bida was by far the largest and most populous. Its territory covered areas far beyond Nupeland across the Niger to the North-East Yorubaland, Afẹnmai in the (former) Bendel State and Akoko in Ondo State. Each of these groups were politically independent before they were conquered or absorbed into Bida emirate system (Idrees 1989: 70–1). In a series of raids into non-Nupe territories, Masaba, one of the *Etsu* Nupe (kings), expanded his sphere of influence by bringing the North-East Yoruba and South-Eastern Kakanda, and some Igbira and Bassa groups under his political sway. Mason (1970: 197) noted that the two most notable of Masaba's military undertakings were his unsuccessful expedition against the Igbirra of Okene (*c.* 1861–2) and his more successful confrontation with the Ibadan military leader known as 'Aggẹ' (1863–4). The most concerted assault against the Igbirra heartland failed as a result of the unsuitability of the terrain to Nupe cavalry tactics and the effectiveness of the Igbirra bowmen, fighting undivided by geography or local loyalties, against an acknowledged common enemy (Mason 1970: 197). One of the least known features of Masaba's emergence as the dominant figure in Nupe involved his campaign to extend the jihad to the Niger Delta between 1843 and 1844. Masaba's southern campaigns were not simple slave raids, but these forays were consistent with the policies of Sokoto and Gwandu (after 1817) that attempted to extend the jihad south, and specifically with various diplomatic initiatives involving the abolition of the slave trade (Kolapo 1999: 69).

By the third decade of the nineteenth century, the continuous search by the Nupe contenders for personnel, equipment and allies during their wars was already directing attention of Nupe military to the potentialities of having access to guns. The relocation of the captives and slaves from place to place within the advancing or retreating military forces was inextricably part and parcel of the military-political programmes of the various Nupe political contenders. Raiding, capture and transfer of captives and slaves constituted an important avenue by which mercenaries (and regular soldiers) were remunerated. The forced migration of both freed and slave/captive population was thus both a war policy and an effect of war, and Nupe urban centres benefited from these movements during the wars. The demographic factor was an important factor for Masaba and other contestants in the Nupe struggles for wooing foreign conscripts, seasoned mercenaries and volunteers from across the Nupe borders.

Thus, the half century before 1957 was very volatile in Nupeland. The jihad was waged by military means, accompanied by slave raiding, slave tribute, enslavement of the vanquished and the transfer into internal or foreign servitude of masses of enslaved individuals (Kolapo 1999: 74). Masaba needed a constant flow of resources to realize his ambition of attaining the sole control in central Nupe. Thus, he extended his sphere of influence outside of Nupe, raiding and enslaving people, conscripting some into his army, selling others and forcing the remainder to pay tribute (Kolapo 1999: 77). In short, Masaba's military activities towards the south were determined by political factors within Nupe as well as the grand aims of jihad proposed in Gwandu and Sokoto. There were also economic factors relating to the abolition of slave trade and the expansion of legitimate commerce. So, he excised the Kakanda from Igala, harboured imperialistic designs on the Igala kingdom and mounted expeditions against Akoko and Afẹnmai (Kolapo 1999: 80).

E. G. M. Dupigny reinforces the accounts of how the Nupes under their ruler, Abu Bekri, raided the Afẹnmai in about 1885-6, compelling the Northern Edo peoples to pay tribute to Bida (1920: 15-16). The last expedition sent southwards in the reign of *Etsu* Masaba was into Kukuruku. The reign of Etsu Umaru Majigi (1873-82) saw not only further extension of Nupe hegemony in the south but also the more effective exploitation of the peoples who had already surrendered to the Nupe. His first undertaking (1874) was an expedition, led by himself, against the indomitable Igbirra of Okene (Mason 1970: 198). Armed with guns recently purchased from European traders and reinforced by contingents from both Ibadan and Ilorin, the Nupe seemed to have every chance of success. Indeed, they may have even enjoyed some initial gains (Dupigny 1920: 18). However, the allied expedition ended in an almost total failure. In the years succeeding their frustrations among the hills of Okene, Nupe influence seeped gradually over more and more of Northern Yorubaland from time to time, encountering, as it did, competition from territorially ambitious military leaders from the south (Mason 1970: 199).

Mason suggests that the stages of Nupe influence in Afẹnmai may not have been well documented as the area was of little interest to either missionary, southern trader or colonial agent (1970: 199). This area was initially attacked in the 1830s, but regular tribute may not have come out of it, however, until after Masaba's reign at Bida (1859–73). One account of the area indicates that Agbede, at least, may have sent slaves to Bida from as early as the 1860s (Mason 1970: 199). The 'Ajẹ' of Ibadan, who were so active in Akoko, invaded Kukuruku between 1856 and 1863 (Bradbury 1957: 112–3). From the 1870s onward Agbede and the areas to the north of it had fully accepted their tributary status vis-à-vis Bida. It was not until *c.* 1878 that *Etsu* Umaru's forces undertook another major campaign southwards (Mason 1970: 199). Subjugated villages and communities, in each case, had to pay *amana* (peace), tribute to the Nupe military administration as a sign of submission. Agents, variously known as *ajeles* or *ogbas* (in Yorubaland) or *azeni* (in Afẹnmai), were installed or elected to manage the collection and dispatch of annual tributes (Mason 1970: 204–5). It was in the period extending from the 1840s when Masaba had his headquarters at Lade until the reign of Umaru Majiki (1873–82) that the larger part of North-Eastern Yorubaland and Afẹnmai were brought under Nupe dominance. In many Kukuruku villages, slaves were remitted right from the beginning of the period of Nupe overrule (Mason 1970: 205).

Narratives of encounter of the Nupe military forces and immigrant Fulani Jihadists by neighbouring communities/people lend credence to the argument of a possible encounter with Ọza people. One tradition suggests that the Nupe forces attempted to capture Ọjah around 1840, though unsuccessfully. The Nupe admired Ọza pottery as an article of trade but could not have much incursion owing to the hilly, rocky topography of the old Ọza settlement. Oral narratives state that the old Ọza settlement served as a place of refuge for people fleeing from neighbouring towns such as Ogori.[48] The Magongos south of Okene sided with the Nupes against their neighbours, the Ogoris (Mason 1970: 204). Another tradition suggests that the fears of a repeat attack made Ọza people to enter into a defence pact or alliance with her immediate neighbours of Dagbala, Ojirami and Makeke, an alliance called the Okuroshọ sacred pact. Again, the desire to strengthen this alliance made these Okuroshọ clan group to reach out to other villages with similar or identical dialect.

Oral tradition, according to Lewis, has it that the Ọkpamheri (*spelt elsewhere in this book as Ọkpameri*) withstood domineering incursions from the Bini, the Nupe, the Igala and the Yoruba (Lewis 2013). Thus, the entire

Ọkpameri communities then formed a very formidable defense pact to resist any invasion from the restless Nupe warriors. Prior to this time, there had been inter-village skirmishes among Ọkpameri villages, which include Ekor and Ibillo war, and Ogugu and Somorika war, among others. Some traditions believed that the word 'Ọkpameri' was first coined and used in 1840 to end hostilities among the Ọkpameri villages. It was also used as a defense bond to resist the Nupe invasion of Ọkpameri villages. The word was used as a sacred oath that forbids one Ọkpameri village from attacking another. Other traditions situate Nupe invasion of the area and, indeed, of the entire Afẹnmailand in 1860.

From 1897, the Royal Niger Company, and from 1900, the British colonial administration, effectively ended Nupe colonialism south of the Niger (Mason 1970: 204). Bradbury records that

> the Nupe domination came to an end only with the appearance of the Royal Niger Company's agents in the 1890s. After the departure of the Nupe the area was controlled by the Royal Niger Company, which had officers at Ikaram, now in Ọwọ Division. When the Company's charter was withdrawn (c. 1900) the greater part was attached to Kabba Province and administered at various times from Kabba, Okene and Iddo. There was considerable opposition to British rule until 1909 when a military patrol captured Somorika which had been the chief centre of resistance. Taxation was introduced about 1910, each community being assessed for a lump sum. (Bradbury 1957: 113)

He reports further that until 1918 all people in the area (North-West Edo) were regarded as subjects of the Attah of Idah and were required to attend court at Okene (the Igbira capital). In that year they were included in the newly formed Kukuruku Division, whose headquarters were first at Fuga and later at Auchi. In 1920, the Division was divided into a number of districts each under a District Head, and North-West Edo communities were included in five of these districts, some of which contained Etsako and Ivbiosakon tribes (ethnic groups). The District Heads acquired considerable personal authority and appointed their representatives in the villages, often giving them Nupe titles. This system was abolished in 1936 and later each community became a separate Native Authority (Bradbury 1957: 113–4).

Mason cautions regarding the legacy of Nupe imperialism, 'Any generalization about the legacy of several decades of Nupe colonialism must be guarded; yet a failure to make suggestions concerning the impact of the Nupe on their southern subjects would reduce the value of any historical study of Nupe expansionism' (Mason 1970: 206). He notes further,

> While looking at a number of separate spheres in which Nupe influence was strong, it is necessary to remember that their mutual isolation is simply a crude means for examining them and that such isolation does not exist in reality … Besides the uneven effect of Nupe domination, it is necessary to point out that the phenomena of nineteenth century Nupe expansionism, rather than a straightforward invasion by Nupe from Nupeland, grafting aspects of Nupe culture onto the cultures of the conquered peoples, was an invasion of Muslim northerners, whose own religion, political systems, and social organization was an amalgam of borrowings from as far north as the Mediterranean littoral. (1970: 206)

In this way, Mason aptly suggests that this important aspect of the Nupe invasion of the south was the result of the heterogenous nature of Bida army, which was composed of widely diverse ethnic backgrounds. While perhaps mainly a Nupe army, it contained substantial Hausa as well as Kanuri, Yoruba, Kamuku and other elements. It is apparent, as Mason argues, that the main cultural and religious impact of the northern forces was the fostering of Islam (1970: 206). 'The religion of Islam followed the jihadists' flag. After conquest or submission its continued influence was assured by northern, often Hausa, *colon*, traders and missionaries, and repatriated slaves who, while away from home, had adopted the religion of their masters' (1970: 207). Mason suggests that of all the areas colonized, none was more profoundly affected than Afẹnmai, the furthest south and latest to be conquered. Here, in places, the Nupe colonial government seems to have replaced indigenous government to much the same extent that Islam replaced traditional religion (1970: 207).

A final aspect of nineteenth-century Nupe imperialism, Mason concludes, is the influence it had on boundary making in the twentieth century (1970: 208). He asserts,

> While the Nupe rulers were, as early as 1857, deprived of their southern colonies, much of the Yoruba and all of the Igbirra-speaking areas which had been included in them were attached to the British colonial administration of Northern rather than Southern Nigeria. This manifestation of the attempts of the early British colonial policy-makers not to upset the *status quo*, has persisted up to 1967, when the formulation of new states severed at least some ties with the colonial past. (1970: 208)

Thus far, I have provided glimpses into how the Nupe invasion and imperialism of the nineteenth century was consequential in processes of Nupenization. Next, I shall examine briefly how Benin and Yoruba colonialisms, particularly the latter hegemony, also resulted in Yorubanization.

Oza under Benin and Yoruba hegemonies

Obayemi explores the emergence of the cultures of the Yoruba and Edo peoples, and outlines their history, with emphasis on the processes of state formation and in less detail the history of neighbouring Nupe, Ebira (Igbira), Igala and Idoma peoples (1971: 255–322).[49] This extensive comparative essay corroborates some of the earliest, classical ethnographic surveys, such as by Nadel (1942), Forde (1951) and Bradbury (1957). The territories of the Yoruba and Edo peoples display great internal variety (Obayemi 1978: 255). The important rivers that flow within their vicinity play an important part in the consciousness of the people as is evident in their popular and religious oral culture.

'Modern linguistic and archaeological research suggest that Yoruba, Edo, Igala, Idoma, Igbo, Nupe, Ebira and Gbari form a cluster of languages within the larger Kwa group, centred roughly on the area of the Niger-Benue Confluence. Each of these units is itself a cluster of dialects which in some instances are usually unintelligible' (Obayemi 1978: 259–60; see also Ballard 1971: 294–305). In his extensive ethnographic research, Lewis underscores North Edoid (NE) as the linguistic classification of languages with native speakers in North-Western Edo Nigeria (Lewis 2013). This work determines the number of extant NE languages, quantifies effects of geography and contact on vocabulary diffusion and language density, establishes levels of genetic and areal relations, delineates migrant patterns, identifies Edoid homeland and decides on which of Edoid or Yoruboid antedates the other. The Edoid speak languages classified by the same name and reside in all of Edo and parts of Delta, Rivers, Ondo, Kogi and Kwara States of Nigeria. NE is a branch of the Edoid family tree (Elugbe 1989).

As Lewis indicates, its native speakers live in North-Western Edo, Nigeria, and there is accumulating evidence that their homeland is Akoko-Ẹdo. North-Western Edo includes the regions administered by the local governments of East and West Owan, and Akoko-Ẹdo. It is constituted by settlements that straddle the Afẹmai Hills. This area inhabits high-density language varieties in contiguous settlements. Older members of North-Western Edo tend to be bilingual speakers of an Edoid language and Yoruba (Lewis 2013: 2). Their dwelling, the hilly terrain of North-Western Edo with its high density of languages, fits perfectly with prototypical homelands (Elugbe 1979: 82–101). For that matter, the collective name for the hills in this region is *Afenmai*, which means 'our home'. Likely, North-Western Edo served as prehistoric refugium, and its geographical layout is germane to linguistic diversity. As Lewis concludes, 'lexicostatistical, geographical and areal diffusion variables have illuminated North Edoid prehistory to the extent that eleven languages are freshly mapped on the Edoid genealogical tree; ... and Edoid is more ancient than Yoruboid. Therefore, Akoko-Ẹdo was prehistoric refugium for Edoid and Yoruboid migrants' (Lewis 2013: ii).

There has been a continuous debate, largely based on differing interpretations of oral traditions, as to which predates the other between Ifé (Yoruboid) and Bini (Edoid) of South-Western Nigeria.[50] Lewis remarks that based on genetic classification, Edoid is conceived as an offshoot of Benue-Congo earlier than Yoruboid. However, the reverse is the case when viewed from the sociolinguistic platforms of population, prestige and power (Lewis 2018: 2–23).[51] He contends that the minority and largely un-codified Edoid languages of the Bini are often taken to be recent offshoots of the Yoruboid stock, to the extent that, Yoruboid, a huge language family with a cluster of nineteen varieties (considered as dialects because of their homogeneity), is perceived as a parent of Edoid, which is composed of thirty heterogenous languages (Lewis 2018: 3). At the same time, the force of political appropriateness between Bini and Ife has been strong enough to occlude phylogenetic facts, which plot Edoid above Yoruboid in West Benue-Congo (Williamson and Blench 2000: 31).

Lewis contrasts Yoruboid and Edoid, as constitutive of the Benue-Congo language subfamily, by identifying relevant lexicon and phenomena. On the one hand, he concludes that 'the comparison of Edoid-Yoruboid cognate lexicon showed that etyma lexicon is predominantly found in Edoid forms. This strongly indicates that Edoid languages chronologically predate Yoruboid by being closer in form to Proto-Benue-Congo' (Lewis 2018: 22). Pottery is practised today by Edoid (Ọjah and Otuo), as well as Yoruboid (Ijaye in Abeokuta) natives, more by the latter. All three towns as noted by Lewis are situated at the base of hills, and in them, pottery is more associated with the female than with the male gender (Lewis 2018: 12). As he further argues,

> it would then be plausible that occupational pottery is prehistoric to the Edoid. The Yoruba either share this homeland with the Edoid, or they acquired pottery by recent contact. Natives of Ọjah speak of times back in the day when the main

export of Ojah was pottery. Meanwhile, at this time, pottery is scarcely practiced in North-Western Edo, and ornamental pottery is the mainstay of many present Yoruba settlements ... Thus, pottery assessment again points to Edoid ancient and Yoruba nascent practices. (2018: 15)

In the category of occupational vocabulary, Lewis found that Edoid traditions have preserved pottery for functionality while Yoruboid traditions have traded off functionality for aesthetics and ornamentation.[52] He concludes that 'lexical and segmental archaisms underscore the fact that contemporary Edoid populations speak more ancient versions of the common West Benue-Congo linguistic heritage. Therefore, the persuasion is that Edoid languages predate Yoruboid, at least in their present states of complexity or lack thereof' (2018: 22).

Early ethnographic mappings of the societies of the region (Yoruba and Edo) give a picture of the region's political diversity and help to construct a narrative which starts out from that era and provide details of its characteristic patterns of social and political organization. Obayemi makes a significant distinction between what he calls the 'mega-states', that is, the great states with their royal dynasties, highly centralized political systems and large urban capitals. This pattern is to be contrasted with polities of a very different kind, 'mini states', existing as settlements or groups of settlements without powerful royal dynasties or highly centralized governments, lacking urban capitals and much smaller both in territory and in population (Obayemi 1978: 261). As he notes, the mini-state pattern of political organization is typical of the area of Idoma speech (with the exception of the Alago Kingdoms of Doma and Keana); it is prominent in the Edo-language group with Etsakor, Ivbiosakon and Akoko-Ẹdo in the north; Urhobo, Isoko, Egenni and Dekema in the south; and Ishan (Esan) in the centre. The mini state is also to be found at various points on the periphery of the Yoruba-language unit, with Oworo, Ijumu, Abinu, Ikiri, Igbede, Yagba and Akoko in the north-east; and groups like the Egbado, Ikale and Iwori in the south, and is readily discernible within the Nupe and Igala areas. In spite of variations even within the same area, the numerous individual mini-states appear to conform to a general pattern (Obayemi 1978: 261).

Obayemi's analogy of 'mini-state' and 'mega-state' is perhaps illustrative in reconstructing the historical relationship that existed between Ọza, on the one hand, and the Benin and Yoruba kingdoms, on the other. This does not in any way suggest that all societies that existed can be lumped under these two categories. We can also think outside the box in terms of several people groups that existed independently, and who may or may not have been under the influence of 'mega' or 'mini' states. The oral traditions of origin and migration narratives point to some possible inferences that can be drawn on the relationship, coexistence, continuities and discontinuities of links between mini-states and megastates and the surrounding communities, but also in contrasting the affinities and autonomous nature of their cultural and religious world views, linguistic characteristics and sociopolitical organizations.

Obayemi notes that the basic building block of every mini-state is the patrilineage, which is described in its biological-territorial setting by important terms in the different languages, but also sometimes buttressed by maternal links. This is of immense importance to the individual for landholding, land allocation and food production. It is the basis for his identity and membership of the society, and for his political and social rights (1978: 264). This, he argues, is the focus of strongest allegiance: authority is symbolized and to some extent exercised by a lineage head chosen on considerations of age and genealogical proximity to the ancestors. Several such lineages are united to form the community. The morphology of the mini-states is characterised by several settlements at varying distances from one another (1978: 264). Whether we characterise Ọza as a mini-state, a vassal state or an independent settlement is beside the point. More importantly, exploring its historical and contemporary relationship with its immediate and remote neighbours, towns and villages helps us to see how and to what extent this proximity may have resulted in mutual influence and exchanges.

As Obayemi aptly describes, the emergence of homelands politics of speakers of the Edo group of languages is broadly similar to that of the Yoruba-speaking peoples to their west and north (1978: 300). That of Benin is by far the most spectacular. While the oral traditions indicate that Benin, like Ilé-Ifè, was only one among many, it remains the best known because it is the most extensively studied (Egbarevba 1968). The rise of Benin to political eminence was a progressive event dating effectively from about the thirteenth century AD (Bradbury 1959: 263–87). However, the differences displayed within the territorial-linguistic blocs of the Edo group of languages certainly antedate the rise of Benin to political dominance (Obayemi 1978: 300). The overwhelming commitment to theory of origins from Benin, which has now become standard in a region in which Benin City has enjoyed political and cultural supremacy, has effectively obscured the identification of what, properly speaking, should have given us an insight into the steps towards the formation of the states or mini-states of the region. So spontaneous have been the narrations of the stories, which say that founding ancestors came from Benin, that they have been accepted with little questioning (1978: 300). With the exception of the Ineme (Bradbury

1957: 123–6), there were Benin cultural influences, like kingship emblems, on the other polities, but emphatically these do not establish folk movements from Benin as the only cause of the first men settling in the area of the Urhobo, Isoko, Ivbiosakon, Etsakor, Ishan, Akoko-Ẹdo or even the metropolitan area of the Benin Kingdom (Obayemi 1978: 300). Of the mini-states in the area of Edo-speaking peoples (the clans, village groups or chiefdoms), Bradbury and others enumerate thirty-four for the Ishan, nineteen for the Ivbiosakon, twelve for the Etsakor, twenty-eight for the Akoko-Ẹdo, eighteen for the Urhobo and seventeen for the Isoko.

3
World views, religious cosmologies, spiritual agency

Ọza understanding of the cosmos and its complexities is expedient in order to appreciate their religious world views, thought patterns and praxis. In this book, the concept 'cosmology' synonymously denotes world view, thought pattern or system. Thus, cosmologies refers to world views and myths in general, or, more specifically, the assemblage of images concerning the universe held in a religious or cultural tradition. Cosmologies or oral narratives transmit the world view values of Ọza people and describe the web of human activities within a potent spiritual cosmic imaginary. Therefore, to delineate the anatomy of African cosmologies is an attempt to classify and understand the significance of mythical images and religious imaginaries concerning the cosmos, the origin and structure of the universe, how humans relate in and to the cosmos, and how and to what extent their thoughts and actions are shaped by it. Clifford Geertz (1973) designates the cognitive, existential aspects of a given culture, their picture of the way things in sheer reality are, their concept of nature, of self and of society using the term 'world view'. It contains their most comprehensive ideas of order and disorder. Thus, while Ọza indigenous religions and spiritualities encompass phenomena that are defined primarily in terms of their orality, world views and ritual orientation within their specific geo-cultural landscape, we shall explore how the beliefs and rituals associated with spiritual forces constitute a distinctively indigenous pattern of religious thought and action.

Ọza people's discernment of *Ogbẹ* (the world) is the kernel to their religio-cultural imagination, moral compass and constructions of social reality. World views underpin Ọza cultures in that they serve as reservoirs of indigenous epistemologies. Essentially, their cognition of *Ogbẹ* unfolds in their epistemologies, encoded in cosmogonic and cosmological myths, and routinized through ritual action, performance and symbolism. The structure of Ọza religious cosmos is broadly evident in the various folk myths, music, proverbs, veneration and praise songs of spiritual entities, through semantic references and symbolic utterances. The polarization of the cosmos in their world view is a germane feature for a proper understanding of their way of thinking. While indigenous Ọza language has no equivalent word for 'religion', the complexity and dynamism of Ọza indigenous cosmologies and spiritualities render any clear-cut distinction between religion and the 'superstructure' problematic. Religion forms an integral facet of culture. In Ọza indigenous context, religion is a stream or river that flows and coalesces with and into other dimensions of culture. Therefore, to analyse religion as a separate system of beliefs and ritual practices apart from subsistence, kinship, language, politics and the landscape is to misunderstand the indigeneity of Ọza spiritualities and religious cosmologies. Ọza social structures and cultural traditions imbue a spirituality that may not be separated easily from the rest of the community's life and *Weltanschauung* (world views) at any point. Thus, we could describe their indigenous cultures as a complex web of religion, attitudes and behaviour, morality, politics and economy in which their thought systems influence their cognitive processes and life styles.

Generally, cosmologies are mostly local and rooted in space-time imagination, although one cannot generalize on everything about Ọza world views as a whole. This is against the backdrop that local cosmologies are themselves dynamic, complex and variegated at the instance of external cultural contact, influence, synthesis, interethnic trade, marriage and migratory trends. Nonetheless, as local cultures, languages and dialects vary, each reflects its own cosmology, its own way of understanding the local environment to which it belongs. A common denominator of respective local traditions embodies orality, historical specificities and semantic and symbolic representations of elements of their cosmological systems and ritual orientations. These traditions do not have the characteristics of any historical foundation as oral traditions, myths, legends, art, paintings, sculpture, songs and dances transmit beliefs and practices from one generation to another.

In spite of the complexities highlighted above, Ọza indigenous society share common affinities in their religious world views, belief in spiritual entities and the use of concepts to represent them, in rituals and similar attitudes towards their manipulation and control. To understand the complex spatial and temporal constructions of Ọza cosmologies, and the values associated with them, one must comprehend a multiplicity of affinities and peculiarities contemporaneously. Ọza cosmologies also consist of constructed special spaces that provide the setting for ritual action and an enabling environment for ritual enactments, special roles that evince the pertinacity of ritual actors in the religious activity and special powers or beings with which the actors form prescribed relationships within a ritualized context. Inherent in ritual praxis are religious symbols that inform the actions that characterize life stages and patterns. Myths represent one source for understanding Ọza cosmologies, creation of the universe, human origin, death and societal norms and ethos. Ọza creation narratives are located in religious mythology. Myths connect the human and supersensible cosmos. Although there are mythical variations, they, however, provide images of the cosmos and pantheons of supernatural entities. Ọza people perceive myths as the key towards unlocking life and its provenance.

In describing Ọza religious worlds, how the people live and act within these frameworks, it is important to show how such worlds consist of special powers, beings with which special human actors form prescribed relationships. A dominant element in the epistemology of Ọza religious world view is the belief in spiritual entities and underlying life forces including a Supreme Deity, the multiplicity of divinities, spirits and ancestors, and rituals or practices concerning them. Below, we will focus on what constitutes the pantheon of spiritual powers and their interaction with human entities, how this-worldly and other-worldly orientations exemplify the polarization of a religious cosmos and how Ọza people makes sense of their religious lifeways.

Ọza spirit cosmos

Ọza indigenous religions and spiritualities are concerned with underlying life forces, vital forces, energies or other supramundane powers. Such themes as belief in a transcendental reality, a Supreme Being, divinities, spirits, ancestors, magic, sorcery and witchcraft are central, although the names, functions, rankings in hierarchy and emphasis vary from one context to another. Some animals, forces of nature, natural objects and unseen forces qualify as spirits, but Ọza people assign the same objects different hicrarchical ranks and symbolism. Relationships between humans and spiritual entities are expressed and achieved through ritual action. Mediation plays an important role in Ọza indigenous religious systems since people cannot receive the source of power from *Oshukunu Agbalagbala* (Supreme Deity) directly. While *Ehọ* (divinities or deities) and *Erio adẹ* (ancestors) are proxy to the affairs of the living, they mediate between the earth and the sky. People approach these spiritual forces through elaborate ritual action. Ancestors play an intermediary role between the mundane and supersensible realms, and they are the guardians and custodians of moral and religious values of society. The beliefs and rituals associated with spiritual forces constitute a distinctively indigenous pattern of religious thought and action. Ọza indigenous culture is thus a complex web of religion, attitudes and behaviour, morality, politics and the economy.

The creation myth relates the deities to the birth of the first humans. According to Lawani,

> Beings and spiritual representations have an important role in Ọza. The key role is the role of the creator Deity associated with the phrase *Ka Otutukẹ Noi Akẹrẹ* or *Ka Ekẹ Akẹrẹ Ọgbe Duo*. In the beginning there was the *Ema*, the creator. It is him who created the the *Irimi* (spirits); the *Ehọ* (deities), beings who are in charge of the permanent control of the universe. *Ema* is the creator of all natural things. The *Ishẹ* are stemming from him; *Ukunu*, who is living in the sky and sharing it with *Oshi Ukunu*, a deity who functions as a 'supervisor'. Its equivalent on earth is *Oshi Ekẹ*. (1992: 33)

Ọza people trace their mythical ancestry to creation by *Ema* (creator deity), *Oshukunu Ọpashi* (the Supreme King and deity above), *Eya no ma mai so gbe* (the Supreme Father who created humans in this earth) or *Esha mai no di okeme* (our Father who lives up above in the skies). The conceptual imagination of a Supreme Deity is also through chiefly attributes such as *Oshukunu Agbalagbala* (the Supreme Deity who is limitless with creative power) and *Eya Nọporo*, a great, benevolent father. Ọza world view divides the cosmos into *Ọgbe* (earth) and *ukunu* (sky). The cosmos is believed to be the creation of *Oshukunu Ọpashi*, *Oshukunu Agbalagbala* or *Eya Nọporo* (the Supreme Being) and the names and attributes reveal its inherent nature.

Ọza religious world is characterized by a multiplicity of *Ehọ* (divinities or deities), and beliefs and rituals concerning *Ehọ* are a dominant element. While *Ehọ* are numerous, seven popular deities in Ọza are distinguished as *Ehọ Itishove* (seven principal divinities) with special portfolios and functions. The symbolism of *Ehọ Itishove* correlates with the seven family genealogies in Ọza. What characterizes this plurality of divinities as *Ehọ Ọza* (Ọza deities) is their gender, multifarious portfolios, capabilities and functionality. In examining gender in the Ọza pantheon of deities, there is a somewhat gender neutrality and gender sensitivity in the nature and composition of spiritual beings. The *Ehọ* (divinities) and *Eriọ adẹ* (ancestors) could be male, female or a combination of genders depending on the spiritual agency in question. In Chapters 4, 6 and 7, we will focus on the especial ritual role and place of women within the religious maps of Ọza people.

Ehọ Akẹshi, a female deity, is perhaps the most prominent among all Ọza divinities, responsible for protecting Ọza people from oppression, injustice and in fighting against intruders. *Ehọ Akẹshi* therefore wields the insignia of justice and fair play; hence her shrine is not only recognized for oath taking but also attracts so much reverence that no one will venture to disobey her. Ọza people revere *Ehọ Akẹshi*, the divinity within whose sacred shrine oath taking, swearing, vows and covenant making are prevalent. The people seek justice in most vices involving crimes, corruption, immorality, incest, premature deaths, theft, quarrels, family conflicts and acts of misdemeanour before *Ehọ Akẹshi* for adjudication and conflict resolution. Anyone who dares to consult *Ehọ Akẹshi* in their quest for equity, justice, redress and refuge must approach the deity cautiously, with clean hands and without blemish. The *Ehọ* serve as adjudicators when they receive petitions for revenge and justice for havoc caused by a third person (Lawani 1992: 35). The petitioner is seeking revenge and justice, and the special request is made according to precise rules. The petitioner, woman or man, approaches the shrine of *Ehọ Akẹshi* carrying a ritual pot or emblem and chanting '*Ẹkẹshi gbere o*, which literally means 'Bring to justice and punish the person who is responsible for our despair and make him accountable.'"

Ọza people venerate *Ehọ Ọza* but at the same time find the deities awe-inspiring and dreadful for their perceived potency and effectivity in conveying instantaneous justice to appellants against offenders and miscreants. This is often consequential in unprecedented deaths, mental disorders and calamitous conditions. As culprits of her intervention, *Ehọ Akẹshi* mysteriously strikes to death *Ẹfia* (witches), *Egbọ* (wizards) and *Agbọ Enẹbẹ* (sorcerers or evil persons) who kill or prey on others, and their bodies are disposed unabashedly in shallow graves in *Ilẹkpẹ* or *Onumọ*, sacred forests.[1] *Ehọ Akẹshi* also doubles as a war deity who protects Ọza people during interethnic wars.

Ehọ Atakara, also known as *Ukpokpo*, is a male deity that protects people against *Ẹfia*, *Egbọ* and *Agbọ Enẹbẹ*; they are responsible for checking for the morbidity and mortality of Ọza people. This deity is nocturnal and diurnal, hovering day and night, preventing people from potential havoc or harm from witches, wizards, sorcerers and evil people. People believe that *Ehọ Atakara* utilizes the *Ukpokpo* (wooden sceptre or baton), a symbol of power and authority, to strike down the aggressor or its accomplice. Thus, it is a taboo to carry a corpse past or close to the vicinity of the *Ukpokpo* shrine. *Ehọ Atta* takes charge of procreation, as a deity of fertility who grants children to barren women. *Ehọ*

Irugbabọ is a female divinity that protects children and *Erẹnia* (community) as a whole from evil people. Other deities include *Ehọ Eshiọde*, a male and female divinity for agriculture and good harvest, who prevents famine and ensures rain and good harvest. One interesting characteristic of these divinities is that while some are gendered, revealing their peculiar male and female features, others maintain dual gender characteristics in their functionality, capability and portfolio and attend to the supplications of males and female accordingly.

Ehọ Atta doubles as a male and female deity in charge of healing and solving problems associated with sicknesses, illnesses and ailments especially attributed to spiritual causation, while *Ehọ Oke* or *Ọgbename*, another male-female deity, takes charge of the *orere* (public square or arena) and *ise* (dance performance). Some of these deities seem to have overlapping functions. *Ugbo Ovie*, a male divinity symbolized by a python, literally 'vomits' rainbow. He forbids witches and wizards, and he is against theft, burglary and falsehood. Other male deities are *Upiopio*, represented by a massive rock from which cement is processed. This rock deity is located between the physical boundary of Ọza and the neighbouring Okpella community. *Upiopio* is also associated with agricultural products. Two deities have a symbolic connection with natural water. *Amẹ Egẹdẹ*, a female deity, is symbolized by water and a rock, as a source of living spring water, while *Ehọ Ọyonba* literally 'fetches water into stomach', symbolizing protection.[2] *Erimi/Irimi* (spirit/spirits) signified by masquerades are between the human and supersensible worlds (see Plates 8a and 8b). The divinities and spirits are proxy to the affairs of the living; they mediate between the human and spirit worlds.

Generally, *Ehọ Ọza* act on behalf of *Oshukunu Ọpashi* and are approached through elaborate ritual action. According to Lawani, 'Ọza community believe that there is an energy representing *Ehọ* in everything, who mediate between the creator *Ema* and human beings, the end users of this creation. Nature and life seem to be the substance that nourishes this communication' (1992: 33). As he further underscores, 'Being the mediators between *Ema* and the whole of creation, these spiritual forces function as a mirror reflecting the state of spirit of human beings towards the "author" of creation. Intuition seems to be the privileged form of contact between humans and the *Ehọ*. The *Ehọ* are rather numerous and transmit human intuitions to *Ema* and vice versa' (1992: 35).

Ẹrio adẹ or *Eshamai ni inumai ni di irimi* (ancestors) also play an intermediary role between the mundane and supersensible realms. They are the guardians and custodians of moral and religious values of society. Ọza people believe that death does not terminate the relationship between the living and dead. Death is only a stage in life. Only those who lived a good life, lived to a ripe age, died a good death and are accorded a befitting burial can qualify for the status of an Ọriọ adẹ (ancestor). The Ẹrio adẹ are of fundamental significance. Ọza religious life revolves essentially around veneration of ancestors and this attracts extensive ritual obligations. The relationship between the living and the dead is one of mutuality, which excludes non-kin and reflects the major emphases of Ọza kinship and matrilineal/patrilineal organization. As religious powers, ancestors are capable of acting for the good or ill of their kin. For this reason, ancestors are venerated and accorded deference. Special family shrines located in homesteads and rituals exist as sacred spaces and contexts for maintaining proper relationships with them.

Although different and not characterized as *Ehọ*, oral traditions suggest that wild animals such as *Urorogo* (chimpanzee), *Ẹgbesa* (gorillas) and *Odumu*[3] (lion), owned by a certain Ọwọ family, were totemic spiritual forces that served to protect Ọza from external aggression in the past.[4] Lawani also highlights how oral traditions regarding *Ogbesa* (gorilla) as a totem is ritualized in one of the *Ibishika* dance songs as in *Oyibo no ra Uhuoka, Okpe resa kpe rilo Oyibo. Oyibo Oyibo Oyibo* (literally translated as '*Oyibo* (name meaning the white one, but now attributed to Ọgbesa, gorilla) *who lives in Uhuoka, Who claps his hands, Who rings the bells, Oyibo Oyibo Oyibo*'). Tradition indicates that, in former times, Ọza people constructed houses of Ọgbesa in Uhuoka, a quarter in Ọza, as one of the totems that defend the community against external aggressors. In return, the *Ẹgbesa* (gorillas) were propitiated with ritual offerings of live *irobua* (dogs) (Lawani, 39). However, owing to inadequate expiation, the Ọgbesa totems were claimed to have mysteriously retreated from the community into oblivion.[5]

While *Oshukunu Ọpashi, Ehọ, Ẹriọ adẹ* or *Eshamai ni inumai ni di irimi* constitute benevolent spiritual entities, Ọza people also recognize malevolent spiritual forces in terms of *Ẹfia, Egbọ* and *Agbọ Enẹbẹ*. Evil, sorcery and witchcraft are real phenomena. Belief in the reality of evil and witchcraft as nocturnal agencies bridging the human and spiritual domains is rife among Ọza indigenous peoples. Generally, people perceive witches, wizards, sorcerers and evil people as anti-individual and antisocial (society). Notions, perceptions and imaginations of evil and witchcraft as spiritual agencies, and sorcery as human agency are counterbalanced with elaborate rituals and measures towards containing evil manifestations and combating witchcraft within Ọza society. As Lawani aptly noted, in Ọza the *Ehọ* are not the only spiritual powers the community encounter in their everyday life (36). People also contend with *Ẹfia, Egbọ, Agbọ Enẹbẹ, Ori* and *Olidodo*.

Ọfia/Ẹfia (witch/witches) and Ọgbo/Egbọ (wizard/wizards) are inherently malevolent spiritual forces, although with ambivalent demeanour depending on intentionality and functionality. While witches and wizards are claimed to have the capability of protecting their offspring or children from the evil ones, they are seen to be predacious and capable of inflicting harm, horror or causing death. Such evil misfortunes are also linked to the practice of sorcery. Owing to greed, envy or revenge, people may solicit the services of a sorcerer to wreak havoc, misfortune and death on unsuspecting individuals. It is against this backdrop that many have recourse to elaborate rituals to the benevolent spiritual forces – *Oshukunu Ọpashi, Ehọ* and *Ẹrio adẹ* – in their quest for protection and safety from the malevolent spiritual forces – *Ẹfia, Egbọ* and *Agbọ Enẹbẹ*.

Lawani describes how each new baby is accompanied by his/her *Ori* (personality soul) into this world (1992: 37). *Ori* materializes as *Ibienẹmi* (a guardian spirit) through life and is determined through *Evba* (divination). Through a divination ritual, the *Ọbu Evba* (diviner) reveals the appropriate *Ori* of the new baby. This personal guardian spirit, embodied by natural objects such as a rock, a river or a tree is believed to protect the child against evil machinations throughout its life. *Ori* helps to consolidate the relationship between the individual and the family. The individual and family must appease and propitiate the *Ori*, guardian spirit, through *Iyẹsẹmi/uriẹsẹmi* (ritual sacrifices) to keep it active and potent. The child who is protected by *Ori* since birth also benefits from additional guardianship from *Olidodo* (literally, the one who jumps from flower to flower). Spiritual entities and numerous ritual specialists and agents serve as intermediaries between the human and supersensible cosmos, charged with the protection and sustenance of human beings and of plants. As Lawani noted, the presence of the *Olidodo* near children inspires their mothers to create new songs for their babies when they cry: *Owu Ọgbe me ọmọ e, Olidodo noo. ọmọ ode vie o, O sho sho e, Osho sho* (meaning: 'Who hurt my child? It was the Olidodo. My crying child, listen to the Olidodo'). The state of visibility or invisibility that appears throughout the encounter between *Olidodo* and the child in the song becomes even more importantly evident in relation to the ancestors (1992: 37).

As Lawani further demonstrates, Ọza people integrate the notions of the invisible or *Bebe* and the visible or *Fienea* in their belief that makes intelligible the consequences of good and evil acts. In fact, in the afterlife the dead *Ofuegbe* will live in *Egada Oshukunu* (under the sacred canopy of the Supreme Deity), which is the intimacy of the creator or the spirit world. Alternatively, the dead *Ẹfia* take the route to what has been associated with *Irimi Ishomuvi* (1992: 38). It is expected that the *Ofuegbe* who lived a good life, died a good death, received a befitting burial and transitioned to the spirit world will become translated as an Ọriọ adẹ. Contrarily, the Ẹfia who lived a bad life, died a bad death, with the corpse discarded and improperly buried in a shallow grave within Ilẹkpẹ or Onumọ, the sacred forests, remain perpetually in limbo in Irimi ishomuvi, the spiritual abode of malignant, evil forces. As spiritual entities, the Ẹrio adẹ oversee their loved ones, sustain intimate contact; as invisible beings, they protect and guide their earthly families and community in their new capacity as living-dead and guardians of society. Ẹrio adẹ have the capability of being reborn as newborn babies into the human, earthly cosmos. *Ise* and *Agba* dance is one of Ọza community's ritual enactment for honouring and venerating ancestors, living-dead who they believe passed on to the invisible world but at the same time continue to inhabit the visible world, albeit in an incorporeal state.

Erimi/Orimi/Irimi (masquerade/masquerades) occupy a central, although ambivalent, liminal place within the religious cosmos, in that they straddle between the Ọgbẹ agbọ (human realm) and Ọgbẹ irimi (spirit realm) especially within the terrain of ritual action and performance. Ọza people have a rich tradition of masquerades, with an ensemble of masquerade masks, of mostly colourful costumes, designs and patterns that only male guilds wear during ritual festivities, ceremonies and performance, such as the death of a King or Chief, initiation and marriage ceremonies (see Plates 8a and 8b). Specific ritual time and duration is assigned to *irimi* display, performance and other rituals. As Dania notes,

> Orimi is believed to be very supernatural, for the villagers believe that the heavenly bodies act in those who perform it ... There are four types of *orimis* in a year lasting for five to thirteen days each, except for one lasting thirteen days. When observing the *orimis*, the performers do not sleep in the house but in the public place called *Orere* or *Oqua* in order to keep away from women during the period.[6]

Lawani remarks, for instance, that *Orimi Odure* lasts for nine days; *Ukpe Iruvie* for five days; *Orimi Irimizọ, Orimi Afiarọ* and *Orimi Eshiọde* for four days; *Ibishika* for two days; and *Ọbilẹ Ọnọfa* (new yam rites) and *Eruhe* for one day (1992: 47). Other ritual times includes *Orimi Ukpe*, which takes place on a respective market day, and Ọza people await six market days before *Orimi Eshiọde*. Following *Orimi Eshiọde* is the proclamation of *Ọbilẹ Iremi*, the new yam festival. Five days after *Akanumu* is the *Orimi Irruhie* enacted throughout the day, from morning till evening.[7]

With facial or full-body masks, the costume disguises the wearer's facial appearance, identity and social status while invoking and inducing a non-material, other-worldly imagery. The masquerade performance by masked characters takes place during major communal rituals and festivals as outdoor events, performed by men, and mostly limited to the attendance of and public viewing by men/boys (see Plates 8a and 8b). In exceptional cases, female religious leaders, chieftaincy title holders and women who have attained the state of menopause may be allowed to see the masquerade. There are usually dire consequences and fines for women who violate this ritual taboo.

Masquerades provide public entertainment, define sociocultural roles, display aesthetic talents and convey religious meanings and symbolism. *Irimi* can symbolize complex personality traits including elegance, authority, awe, dignity, sophistication and mystery, just as people believe that masquerades exude magical or spiritual power. Masquerade masks represent spirits or ethereal beings that are central to the rituals in which the masks are used. As masquerade masks symbolize a spirit or spirits, people commonly believe that the spirit of the ancestors possesses the wearer and the wearer is able to communicate with the incorporeal entity symbolized by it, or possessed by who or what the masquerade mask typifies. Masquerades both personify the ancestors and embody spiritual entities, while they honour a family or a community's ancestral spirits at the same time. Ritual festivals and ceremonies generally depict *Ehọ* and *Ẹrio adẹ* as other benevolent beings and *Ẹfia, Egbọ* and *Agbọ Enẹbẹ* as malevolent beings believed to have power over humanity.

The *Irimi* speak and sing in a somewhat esoteric language, mostly unintelligible to the non-initiate, what some observers believe have some affinity with the language of the neighbouring Okpella people. The appropriation of a foreign language further camouflages the real identity of the mask carrier, thus inducing the imaginary of a coded, mysterious, unintelligible language of *Ọgbẹ irimi*. This places the *erimi* at the intersection of *Ọgbẹ agbọ* and *Ọgbẹ irimi*, between and betwixt a polarized religious cosmos. Masquerade dance accompanies singing and drumming, and the type of mask shapes the style and nature of the masquerade dance. Dance steps are often spontaneous, improvised in alignment with rhythmic song and music.

Prior to public appearance and performance, the mask bearers converge in *Oqua* (the house of the living-dead), a secluded sacred space for ritual purification and fortification. It is only upon the completion of the appropriate rituals that the masquerades make their public debut. A number of taboos are associated with the identity of the person behind the masks and the public display of masquerades. Although it is formally prohibited to reveal the identity of the persons wearing the masks, the identity of the *Erimiove* (the chief owner of the masks) is obvious as a red cloth is hanging vertically down his face (Lawani 1992: 40).[8] Any physical contact between women and the masquerades is prohibited. Women are forbidden from viewing the masquerade public performance. It is claimed that the spiritual potency of the masquerade could impair a woman's productive capabilities, resulting in infertility or miscarriages. The *Irimi* must avoid visiting specified places within the community, and people are advised not to provoke them, disturb their silence, lay ambush or engage in any sorts of physical confrontation with them. During the *Orimi Odure* festival, characterized by a period of nine days of silence, those who break silence during the special ritual time pay fines to appease the *Irimi*. Lawani maintained that as far as Ọza people are concerned, the deities, spirits, ancestors and masquerades remind us that the visible and the invisible worlds are two sides of a single reality (40). Through the enactment of elaborate rites, festivals and ceremonies, Ọza people strive to live and maintain a good relationship with the invisible, benevolent forces consequential in their protection, peace, social cohesion and human flourishing. Appropriate ritual attention to and veneration of the ethereal powers invoke their guidance and protection from various misfortunes including illness, sickness, accident, poverty, famine, theft, infertility and premature death.

Agbọ (human beings) also occupy a significant position in Ọza cosmological thought. Humans have their own agency and they negotiate their own existence and living by being in constant mediation with spiritual entities. Each human being has a dual make-up: the physical and spiritual mien. The spiritual aspect of humans serves as a nexus between them and the ethereal world. Ọza people distinguish between three aspects of being, which are important for their religious thinking. They distinguish between *ukuru egbe* (the physical body), which perishes or decomposes after death; *udu/uhonemi* (vital force or breath), which keep humans alive; and *ori* (personality/guardian spirit, force or character). Once the *udu/uhonemi* leaves the body, then the person is dead. His/her *ori*, spiritual mien, lives on as an ancestral spirit; it goes to the ancestors who live in the nether world.

In describing the religious worlds of Ọza people, and how they live and act within these frameworks, it is important to think about sacred spaces or places that provide a ritual environment for ritual enactment and performance and how such worlds consists of special roles that define the purpose of ritual actors in the religious drama. Below, we shall explore briefly how ritual spaces, roles, powers and actions are expressions of a coherent system of thought that informs the conduct of the lives of Ọza people who participate in them. We shall demonstrate the centrality of indigenous healers, diviners and other functionaries as spiritual reservoirs of Ọza indigenous society.

Ritual roles and special functionaries

We have demonstrated above how benevolent and malevolent spiritual forces populate Ọza cosmological religious imaginaries. Elaborate rituals and sacrifices involving processes of explanation, prediction and control; and petitions, adoration, praise and thanksgiving to these spiritual agencies are facilitated by people with special ritual roles. Apart from these incorporeal entities, people believe that chiefs, kings, priests, diviners, healers, spirit mediums and sorcerers possess tangible power of one kind or another, and they play special ritual roles within the Ọza indigenous religious praxis. Spirit mediums, spirit possession guilds, diviners and healers form a large section of the indigenous healthcare system and they are integral phenomena in Ọza religious world.

All these special ritual functionaries are means of communicating between two interconnected worlds: *Ọgbẹ irimi* and *Ọgbẹ agbọ*. There is a strong link between gender and spirit possession and mediumship in Ọza indigenous religious traditions, with an overwhelming majority of women. Women's role and status are defined by what is deemed wholesome to the welfare and flourishing of the entire community of men, women and children. As we shall describe in Chapters 4, 6 and 7, women carry out crucial ritual roles and functions in Ọza indigenous society. In many cases, political, economic, cultural, social and ritual functions of religious adepts overlap and intersect in terms of gender. In most of the sacred spaces such as communal shrines or sacred groves, there are usually ritual specialists or priests who undertake special roles in ritual enactment processes. These ritual functionaries serve as caretakers of the communal sacred spaces, as consultants and facilitators of the ritual sacrifices and offerings, and protect the space from desecration and misappropriation.

Ritual and sacrifice operate within sacred space-time and occupy a conspicuous place in Ọza religious life. Through ritual and sacrifice, people aim to counteract the evil machinations of the malevolent spiritual beings on humans and to invoke the benevolence of the deities, ancestors and spirits to ensure and maintain cosmic balance and cohesion in the society. Ritual occurs in sacred spaces which are set apart by symbols making those spaces different from others, and hence an appropriate place for the ritual to occur. Ritual symbols play a very conspicuous role in Ọza cosmology and praxis. The hermeneutics and application of these symbols reflect a whole spectrum of their belief system. Both sacred space and time are non-homogeneous, that is, not of the same kind as other space and time. Most of the rites and sacrifices are enacted at specific ritual times in secluded sacred spaces which vary from family altars, ancestral shrines, village or community shrines, in groves, hills, mountains, rivers, beneath certain trees, sacred forests, road intersections, graveyards and market squares. Ọza people treat these constructed sacred spaces with utmost awe and reverence.

Divination and healing

The pursuit of health, fertility and a balance between humans and nature constitute some of the basic concerns of Ọza indigenous religions and spiritualities. Ritual and sacrifice structures draw upon a philosophy of relationships. Divination is an important ritual activity and the role of the diviner-healer is widespread. Ọza people make recourse to divination, a process that involves, in many cases, the enactment of sacrifice. People divine in their quest to know the behest of the supernatural beings and to inquire about their destiny. Divination is performed in all existential circumstances such as illness and death; in situations of loss, calamity or unresolved conflict; in the corroboration of a marriage choice; seeking employment, promotion in the workplace, admission into schools; embarking on a journey; and in all other life crises and circumstances.

In their quest for prevention against physical and spiritual illness, diseases, death and misfortune, Ọza people rely on two ritual practitioners, the *Ọbu Evba* (diviner) and the *Ọbu Ikumu* (healer), although their roles and functions are not mutually exclusive (see Plate 5). The *Ọbu Evba* has the capability to prognosticate into the future and diagnose aetiologies of illness and disease. *Ẹbu Evba* are able to make a distinction between illnesses or diseases with a natural or spiritual causation. The distinction made on the anatomy of natural and spiritual illnesses/diseases is significant against the backdrop that natural illness could be remedied by both natural (medical) and spiritual antidotes, while spiritual illness can be cured only by spiritual means, rituals of healing.

The *Ọbu Evba* or *Ọbu Ikumu* is also vested with the powers of spiritual prognosis in detecting theft, burglary or deceit. The ritual of *omuno-muno* is a case in point where the diviner, through ritual empowering of certain herbs, gives some to the petitioner and thus induces and brings the petitioner face to face with the offender or culprit. The ritualizing of the herbs gives the necessary potency that discerns the offender. The petitioner becomes spiritually charged and controlled, moving towards the direction of the defaulter until s/he is publicly identified. This often results in public confession of guilt or denial, followed by ritual sacrifice or penalty as the case may be. Failure to accept guilt, delay in returning stolen items or refusal in enacting appropriate sacrifice rites could result in misfortune, dislocation of cosmic harmony or death.

Through divination, an individual finds out what type of sacrifice will ensure that a predicted good fortune will actually come to pass or, alternatively, what type will mitigate the worst effects of a predicted bad fortune. Ray (1976: 110) argues that divination does not pretend to offer a total prognosis about futurity but furnishes advice as to what can be done to secure the most favourable outcome within the limits of a person's given destiny. If the situations are unpleasant, men will be required to offer a sacrifice to change things for the better; and if they are pleasant, a sacrifice will still be offered to retain and improve upon the good fortune.

Following appropriate prognosis, the Ọbu Evba is able to determine and recommend the nature of the ritual sacrifice necessary to heal, cure or rectify the disturbed spiritual state of a person. As Lawani indicates, this kind of healing is legitimated by a common Ọza adage: *Ehue Ono fu Ọfa ikumu* (It is better to have a sane spirit than to use medicine) (42). *Ikumu* refers to the medicinal substance, and the Ọbu Evba or Ọbu Ikumu is renowned for divinatory as well as pharmacological capital, as a person set apart by virtue of formal training in some esoteric wisdom. In spite of their overlapping nature and functions, people recognize a distinction between an Ọbu Evba and Ọbu Ikumu. Although the Ọbu Evba could maintain a dual role/function, the Ọbu Ikeme functions distinctly as the indigenous healer or divine-healer, who is well versed in indigenous pharmacology and prescribes herbal remedies for curing and healing physical illnesses, sicknesses and diseases, and misfortune, with a natural or spiritual causation. While there are several Ọbu Ikumu who are not necessarily Ọbu Evba, it would appear that most Ọbu Evba double as diviners and healers. Therefore, the Ọbu Evba/Ọbu Ikumu (diviner-healer) is a pivotal force for order and rapprochement between man and the spirit world. Both men and women hold the role of diviner/healer, and Ọza people consult or approach them with much awe and respect.

Ọza people recognize *Afẹ Ẹbu* (a guild of diviners), although there is now a proliferation of divinatory practices outside this guild of diviners. The most widespread means of divination in Ọza is the cowrie system in four chains.

Other divining systems include casting of sand and water gazing. Lawani notes that some diviners prognosticate through *Oviese*, an encased being in a bottle (40). Diviners are also consulted when people become victims of misfortune, on the level of familial or social relationships and with regards to loss of property and material possessions. Thus, in order to regain personal harmony, and the affection and protection of one's *Ori, Ẹrio adẹ, Ehọ* and *Ema*, the most useful means is *Iyẹsẹmi*. People enact ritual sacrifice to venerate *Ehọ* and *Ẹrio adẹ*, and honour personal *Ori* who in turn counteract *Ẹfia, Egbọ* and *Agbọ Enẹbẹ. Izobo* is one example of ritual sacrifice against illness or drought. It consists of the offering of concrete ritual objects, including a live or immolated animal or bird, or other agricultural products at a road intersection or sacred spaces such as shrines, hilltop, rivers or the sacred lake *Ẹrẹsha* (Lawani 1992: 43). Ọza people believe that the different systems of divination engender confidence, certainty and effectivity in a world of anxiety and doubt, a world populated by evil and mischievous spiritual forces. Thus, the links between *Evba* and *Iyẹsẹmi* are mostly inseparable. Sacrifice, in its ritual or ceremonial use, means a making sacred, an offering that becomes divinized. In that case, while humans offer their intent and thought in sacrifice, whatever is the object of ritual sacrifice crosses over from the human to the superhuman.

Healing is a sustained ritual process of righting the disequilibrium generated by spiritual, natural, psychological and social factors, which are often expressed in the form of physical or mental problems. Healing practices are part of the complex conceptual framework that constitutes a people's world view, such as in their religious beliefs. In indigenous Ọza society, religion intertwines with disease and illness causation. Beliefs about illness have contributed to health concerns, and the healing methods have addressed the need for healing. Religious world views are quintessential to understanding indigenous healing systems and medicine, how the people make sense of illness and misfortune, and what therapeutic and prophylactic mechanisms they adopt. Traditional healing is holistic, encompassing the physical, mental, psychological, material and emotional aspects that result in total well-being and wholeness. Traditional healing has it focus on symptoms or diseases but also deals with the total individual. In a sense, healing focuses on the person, not the illness.

In most African cosmologies, people link sickness, diseases and other misfortunes to supersensible origins such as the wrath of divinities and neglected ancestral spirits, malevolent spiritual entities, witches, wizards and sorcerers. However, people also recognize non-religious aetiologies of disease. Most Africans view diseases as a direct intervention by the deities or the malevolent spiritual beings, a signal that some adjustment to the person's life is expedient. Diseases or misfortune of any other kind is a signifier that an overhaul of a person's 'psychic motor' is necessary. In the mental and social attitudes of many Africans, there is no belief more ingrained than that of the reality and existence of witches, wizards and sorcerers. All strange diseases, abnormal occurrences, physical disorders, ailments, accidents, untimely deaths, inability to gain promotions in office, failure in examinations and business enterprise, disappointment in love, fertility in women, impotence in men and failure of crops are often attributed to witches and other spiritual agents of malevolence. This explains why they are very much dreaded and feared in the society.

When confronted with illness, impending danger and misfortune, there is usually recourse to divination in a process of 'explanation, prediction and control'. The people divine in their quest to know the behest of the Supreme Being, the divinities and the ancestors, on the one hand, and to inquire about the particular kind of fortune or misfortune involved in their destinies, on the other. The diagnostic process, cure or prevention that follows is often undertaken and supervised by diviners and healers who play an interlocutory role between the physical and spirit world. Most diviners and healers rely on some type of divination in diagnosing client's illness, and a divinatory technique used in determining the appropriate treatment. Those who play these special ritual roles in the society undergo special medical training, which involves the novice being apprenticed to a practicing healer for several years. While epistemologies of healing transmit from one generation to another, diviners and healers sometimes are linked to specific deities responsible for divination and healing.

The prescription by the healer or diviner and the use of the medicinal concoctions by patients for therapeutic or prophylactic means are central to Ọza indigenous healing systems.[9] The methodology of treating patients consists of an enormous variety of medical preparations made of mixtures of roots, leaves, barks, fruits and parts of animals and birds. Such concrete objects accompanied by incantations imbue the medicinal preparation with sacred power and potency. The ritual specialist enacts a divinatory ritual and in the process invokes the appropriate deity to give potency to the concoction before dispensing it to clients. In some cases, the client is made to enact rituals and sacrifices to the appropriate spirit or divinity to sustain the immutability of such power. The treatment may include herbal potion with pharmaceutical properties to deal with the symptoms. People ingest such medical preparations orally, in ointments, by bathing or through bodily scarification. While the diviner-healer is versed in the collection of recipes and their preparation, such pharmacological skills and knowledge remain the prerogative of the ritual specialist. The gradual loss of orally transmitted epistemologies of healing; the influence of Christianity, Islam and other religious traditions; and the introduction of Western medical systems inhibit Ọza indigenous healing practices in some respect. However, indigenous healing systems, the role of healers and diviners, continue to occupy a significant place in present-day Ọza society, especially in a context where governments are incapable of providing adequate medical facilities for its people.

Empowering words, ritual prohibitions and taboos

Ritual is a complexity of words and actions, and not simply a stereotyped behaviour consisting of a sequence of non-verbal acts and manipulations of objects. Ritual communication involves action, practice and performance, but also the verbalization of words and sounds. The utterance of words is itself a ritual (Leach 1966: 407). Ritual words are as important as other kinds of ritual acts. Sometimes, rituals are performed with words alone, though more generally actions and words are not mutually exclusive. Most rituals embody action, performance and words (speech, song, prayer, incantation, invocation), and may show distinct differences in the proportion of words to acts. Thus, a healing ritual or an initiation rite may emphasize words, while a collective rite in which there is mass participation may rely less on auditory communication and more on the display of conspicuous visible material symbols (Tambiah 1968: 176).

The verbal component in a ritual is important. Words really matter; words do things or make things happen. Words are not simply spoken; they are ritualized through rhythmic prose and poetry, songs, invocation, incantations, prayer and meditation. Ritual prescriptions and behaviour encoded in words are narrativized. The relationship between words, as text, and performance implies several different agents and different kinds of agency. Thus, it is important to contrast the author of the spoken word (oral text), the agency of the performer(s) and the agency of the audience, receiver or consumer. Such words, as oral texts, embody and convey translational and interpretational utility. It presents the words (oral texts) themselves, not just as fragments, but as coherent performances of ritual speech acts.

The performative power or force of words are therefore integral to ritual action and processes. Doing things with words is consequential upon the effectivity of words and thus the potency of ritual speech or text. Empowered words through ritual processes can be appropriated to make or mar things.

The intelligibility of sacred words to both the users, officiants and the audience, resonates with how the people think them to possess a special kind of power not normally associated with ordinary language. Thus, for religious adepts, devotees and clients, words rendered as prayer, invocation, incantation, oath or song are not simply verbalized sound or text, but it is quintessentially a coterie of powerful words, what S. J. Tambiah refers to as 'the magical power of words' (1968: 175–208). Perhaps what makes a ritual effective has to do with the belief that the power is in the 'words' even though the words only become effective if uttered in a very special context of other action.

Tambiah (1968, 1985) articulates his interest in myth and ritual as practice, with a focus on the power of words and how they lead to performative power in social contexts, words, not as frozen texts but as behaviour, with power for social action. He aptly underscores that we should not treat ritual words as an undifferentiated category (Tambiah 1968: 176). Rituals exploit a number of verbal forms, which we loosely refer to as prayers, songs, spells, addresses, blessings and so forth. As a battery of verbal devices may appear in a single rite, it is therefore important to explore what recognized categories a ritual is composed of and to analyse their distinctive features in terms of their internal form, meaning, sequence and symbolism. In *A Performative Approach to Ritual* (1979: 113–69; see also Tambiah 1985: 87–116), Tambiah adopts the term 'performative' from the ordinary language philosophy of Austin (1961, 1962), where he teaches that it is by words and (for especially important acts) by the ritual of which the words form a part that people bind themselves to fulfil commitments to one another and thereby create a social order. In Austin's *Performative Utterances* (1961) and *How to Do Things with Words* (1962), he considers statements in which the uttering of words is itself the execution of an act.

For Tambiah, ritual is performative in the sense that 'saying something is also doing something' (1979: 128). He also draws on the multiple meanings of performative to point to parallels between ritual performances and dramatic ones. Tambiah's idea of ritual as a performative distinguishes two aspects of ritual as performative: the 'constitutive' and the 'regulative'. He also develops a theory of human rationality based on the performative approach to ritual (Tambiah 1990). Non-verbal and verbal performances are two aspects of ritual that are both modes of symbolic expression analysable as communicative activity. Tambiah argues that the important feature of this conjunction of word and deed is the manipulation of metaphor and metonym. Specifically, he says that ritual 'actively exploits the expressive properties of language, the sensory qualities of objects, and the instrumental properties of action simultaneously in a number of ways' based on the principles of similarity and contiguity, which underlie the construction of metaphors and metonyms (1968: 189–90).

Within Ọza cosmological imagination, *Akẹrẹ unu* (the spoken word) in ritual and non-ritual contexts is sacrosanct, legitimated by the charm of command, vital force or supersensible entities. Lawani argued that the perception of *Akẹrẹ* (the word) is not simply in light of its sacrosanctity; people also view it in terms of its intrinsic positive and negative aspects (1992: 81). The fact that the potency of Ọza ritual beliefs and praxis also lie in *Akẹrẹ* means that certain precautions are necessary when using *Akẹrẹ*, as unreflected usage of the word could have a dangerous and disastrous impact: *Akẹrẹ unu ọmu f'egbele* (the word is sharper that a knife, cutting tool) is a recurring warning in everyday life conversations. This literally means that just as a bruise sustained by *egbele* (a knife) leaves a scar, the scar caused by *Akẹrẹ* can be devastatingly consequential. In a sense, *Akẹrẹ* has an ambivalence effect: once spoken or uttered, it has the potentiality to bring comfort, healing and redress, while it could also destabilize, demoralize, injure and symbolically harm or kill a human being. The human essence of *Akẹrẹ* lies in the way that Ọza people distinguish themselves from other non-human entities such as *Oromi, Urorogo* and *Ọgbesa* (Lawani 1992: 81). A distinguishing category is *Ọgbo nae Akẹrẹ Unu* and *Ọgbo nae Ehu Ikeme* (human beings with intelligible words or speech and beings with human hair). Lawani aptly described one distinguishing feature in Ọza between the beings with intelligible words and animals or other non-human living entities: the established words in terms of *Unufiemi, Ubiamimi, Ikumumi* and their positive or negative aspects (1992: 81–3).

Unufiemi is verbal utterances aimed at inflicting harm, misfortune, discomfort, pain or even death for others. A parent or an elder who is dismayed may utter the following words or phrase to their son or daughter: *Ako ode shemi awe* (It will not be well with you). People view such pronouncement with much awe and trepidation. *Akẹrẹ* in this sense has a negative connotation. *Unufiemi* is also related to *Unwanomi* (curses or swearing). It is generally believed that *Unufiemi* and *Unwanomi* emanating from religious specialists including the *Ọpashi, Eja, Ebu, Agbọ Enẹbẹ, Ẹrio* and other religious adepts has immense potency and efficacy. Once they are rendered, people anticipate the direct or indirect effect on the addressee. Thus, *Unufiemi* or *Unwanomi* makes bad, awful things to happen, in a cause-and-effect relationality.

Ubiamimi, according to Lawani, is one's intuitive perception to evoke evil acts. It is practised by sorcerers or *Efia* who operate within the seven Ọza family lineages. *Ọza Ishẹ* (customs) prohibit *Ubiamimi* outside the lineage families (1992: 82). Those who resort to sorcery sooner or later become victims of *Ehọ Akẹshi* and *Ehọ Irugbabọ*. Through the will of *Ema*, these *Ehọ* embody natural law and justice, particularly highlighting a cause-and-effect relationship. Ọza community is linked with these beings by *Ehuehue* (intuition). Justice is exemplified by the words or sayings attributed to *Ehọ Akẹshi* and *Ehọ Irugbabọ*: *Ojeme ereshi nae ereshi Ojeme erebe nae erebe* (translated literally as 'Whoever addresses me verbally or intuitively concerning a noble act will be heard. And whoever addresses me concerning suspicious acts will never be disappointed again') (1992: 82).

Ikumumi is the symbolic act of manipulating or invoking elements of nature – *amẹ* (water), *esha* (fire), *oshisho* (air) and *ovo* (sun) – in order to inflict misfortune or harm. This is a ritual practice common among *Ebu* and *Agbọ Enẹbẹ*. But one can also request support against evil intentions of others through *Ikumumi*. Such an act cannot be sanctioned by the *Ehọ* until the person in question is in the position of self-defence. Ọza women are conscious of the potency of *Akẹrẹ* in formulating *Ibishika* polyphony. The messages conveyed by the songs are well intentioned, and the question of *Unufiemi*, *Ubiamimi* or *Ikumumi* hardly arises (Lawani 1992: 83).

A positive and negative aspect characterizes Ọza conception of *Iyẹsẹmi/uyesemi*. Mostly all paraphernalia associated with *Iyẹsẹmi/uyesemi* have symbolic connotations. The positive precepts with regard to *Iyẹsẹmi/uyesemi* also portray their negative facets, evident in the numerous *Asa* (taboos or ritual prohibitions). *Asa* include killing, stealing, lying, sorcery, incest, adultery, jumping over a married woman's legs, obscenities towards married women, distortion of the heritage, revealing secrets to strangers or enemies, having sex in the bush or having two brothers involved in an armed conflict (this also goes for two children of the same maternal line and for age groups) (Lawani 1992: 46). These *Asa*, prohibitions, deserve strict observance and adherence. They may be general or particular, moral or ceremonial, secret or public, or merely imposed by custom. *Asa* are associated with several rites, performances and sacred spaces. Integral to the rites within these sacred spaces are sacrifices and offerings in the form of raw and cooked foods; immolation of animals and birds such as fowls, goats, sheep and cows; and household utensils, farm implements, money and clothes. Some ritual sacrifices take place during the day and others at night-time. People believe that middays and midnights are special ritual times in which spiritual forces are very mobile and active, thus making humans more vulnerable to their actions.

Some *Asa*, of a general sense, apply to the entire community irrespective of family, gender and social status. In some cases, it may apply only to males or females as the case may be. Great festival occasions such as *Ukpe Ọza/ Ukpugbe* (the annual festival) and *Ukpe Iruvie* (marriage festival), linked to certain deities, require a great deal of ritual preparations and prohibitions by the officiating priests and initiates. They have to prepare themselves in order to be worthy and acceptable before the *Ehọ*. They have to observe certain *Asa* or codes of conduct, avoiding, *inter alia*, coition, cursing and fighting, and they abstain from taking certain types of food, fruits and drinks depending on the *Ehọ* in question. For instance, the *Ọbilẹ Iremi* (new yam harvest ritual) features the presentation of the *Ọbilẹ ọnọfa* (new yam) as first crops to the divinity and ancestors before human beings partake of them. Harvest and the consumption of the new yam prior to the appropriate ritual is believed to result in famine, bad harvest, sickness or even death subsequently. Failure to perform the obsequies of a relative is an *Asa*, except if found to be *Ogbo* or *Ofia*. It is an *Asa* or abomination for parents to commit incest, have sexual relationships with any of their children or vice versa.

The particular *Asa* are those prescribed specially for the devotees of the different *Ehọ* and other ritual functionaries. Irrespective of their nature and scope, Ọza people regard *Asa* as prerequisites for the prosperity and human flourishing of the individual or community, and as necessary conditions for maintaining right relationships with the different *Ehọ*. Neglect of *Asa* is fraught with dire consequences. Such neglect and infringement of the *Asa* usually attracts punishment, fines and sacrifice leading to purification, reintegration or even banishment and ostracization. People bring a suspect alleged to have committed fraud, burglary or stealing before *Ọpashi, Eja* or *Ọriọ odo* (the eldest person in the town quarter) for adjudication. In case of any doubts, an *Ọbu Evba* will be consulted. The guilty person will have to return the stolen goods to the owners or face severe consequences.

It is clear that much about *Asa* has to do with keeping moral economy, maintaining ethical values and good, exemplary behaviour. A lie or deceit can also bring disaster or calamity upon a person. A common story that hones in the essence of a good moral compass is rendered as follows. This is the story of a woman whose son was ill and who consulted the *Ọbu Evba* (Lawani 1992: 45). The deity revealed through the diviner to her that she had farted in public, denied it and accused her son of having farted. The woman lied in order to save her face in public. Owing to her misdemeanour, the deity mandated that the woman walk round the entire village to make *Ife* (public confession) of her misdeed or offence recounting, *Owu one efu adaro e? Meme no o a akomo* (Who has farted in the public square? It was me and not my son). *Ife*, the public confession of crimes or offences, is a practice of public shaming of an individual or group. This serves as a preventive mechanism and could also assist in resolving familial or communal problems. To ensure public safety, a complexity of *Asa*, prohibitions, after consultation with deities and ancestors are enunciated.

4

Genealogies of kinship and sacral kingship

While African societies are often lumped together and their social organizations generally described as patrilineal/patrilocal, it is expedient to underscore that their kinship structures are rather more complex and dynamic than frequently contemplated. A number of African societies, including Ọza, are also characterized by matrilineal/matrilocal descents. Kinship lineage groupings play an important role in indigenous governance systems while the extended family structure is quintessential. In this chapter, I explore the Ọza kinship system as another instance of African kinship in which the lineage structure is bilateral, with *Ireme* (maternal kin/matrilineality) as paramount and patrilineality less consequential in the context of their sociopolitical and religious imagination. I shall demonstrate how and to what extent *Ireme* as maternal lineage, within the Ọza matrilineal/patrilineal pedigree, is centrally important to the social, cultural and political lives of the people. The prominence of the female gender within kinship genealogy is analogous to the especial ritual role and place of women within Ọza religious map of the cosmos. In examining gender in African pantheon of deities, there is a somewhat gender neutrality and gender sensitivity in the nature and composition of spiritual beings. A gendered consideration of Ọza pantheon of deities would reveal that divinities, ancestors, could be male, female or a combination of both genders.

In addition, integral to Ọza indigenous sociopolitical organization is the kingship institution. Chieftaincy roles and functions are rife and continue to be relevant in Ọza and among several African societies, even in the face of modernizing tendencies and globalizing trends. The resilience of such institutions in Africa stem not so much from the fact that they are integral to political institutions and governance structures within emerging democratic polity; rather, the sacrality of the myths of origin and the rituals of the sacred associated with kingship imbues the institution with inviolability to contemporary African societies such as Ọza indigenous peoples. Thus, the kingship or chieftaincy institution is far more complex than as a mere political phenomenon. Kingship is a dynamic institution that embodies religious, sociocultural, political and economic fabrics into an integral whole. The King, Chief, Queen or Village Head represents a religious, political, cultural, social and economic head contemporaneously. This chapter will demonstrate how the intricate link between sacralizing Ọza historical myth and rituals of the sacred institution of kingship leverages indigeneity, sacrosanctity, resilience and societal relevance prior, during and beyond the encounter with a coloniality of power.

Rethinking Ọza kinship system

Ọza social and political organization helps to provide a robust context and understanding of kinship and religion. As one significant aspect of Ọza social organization is the kinship system, a brief exploration of the nature of the kinship system is expedient here. Although the idea of kinship has attracted robust debate for decades in anthropology, the biological basis, the ethnocentric biases and the reality of abstract models contested (Schneider 1968), the continuing importance of relatedness to human societies remains clear (Carsten 2003). Kinship has been conventionally seen through the distinction between unilineal descent groups, which emphasize either the male (patrilineal) or the female (matrilineal) line in tracing group membership, and bilateral kinship, which emphasizes both lines. The concepts of matrilineal and patrilineal kinship have been used rather dualistically and simplistically thus far, whilst in the lived experiences of kinship these modes of reckoning relatedness shadow each other and coexist to varying degrees. There is often semantic confusion that has surrounded the terms: kindred, kinship, lineage, extended family and consanguinity. Contrastingly, in broad terms they exemplify the connexion or blood relations of persons descended from the same stock or common ancestor.

As R. E. Bradbury generally observes about kinship in his consideration of the social organization and political system of Edo-speaking peoples,

> the North-Western Edo inhabit compact towns and villages, usually divided into wards which may in turn contain a number of extended families having, as their nuclei, corporate, localized descent groups. The three communities, Ọja, Dagbala, and Ọjirami are together called *Okulusọ* (*Okurosho*), a term apparently connected with the *ukpe* festival, which is common to them all. They are closely related in dialect and culture though they claim different origins. (1957: 114)

Thus, descent systems are germane to an understanding of the overall social structure of Ọza people. One of the most central social units among Ọza people is the lineage group, *Ireme* and *Afẹ*, descent groups consisting of members who trace their origin to a mother and grandmother (*Ireme*) or father and grandfather (*Afẹ*). The lineage group is broken down into family units or kindred in which Ọza is structured under seven *Ireme* or *Ibinonu*, maternal family kindred, and seven *Afẹ* or *Ibinesha*, paternal family kindred. The *Ireme*, maternal kindred, comprise Ibiowe (Ibiozọ), Ibieki (Ibioma), Ibikira (Ibiozọ), Ibiligbe, Ibiadesami, Ibiokeji and Esamizeri, while the *Afẹ*, paternal lineage, is made up of Ọsuruka, Uveshi (Ufeshi), Ukpi, Ọburẹsẹ, Ọbuẹri, Ibiovie and Apara (Akpara), respectively. *Ireme* has two forms that further depict closeness and proximity within the maternal lineage. They distinguish between *Ibinosami*, meaning family under one central mother with their grandchildren, and *Ibinonu*, symbolizing a small unit of persons under a mother.

In fact, every bona fide Ọza indigene can trace her/his *Ireme* and *Afẹ* at the same time. This self-identity is intrinsically important as a member of a lineage is entitled to certain rights and privileges. This kinship identity marker also invokes loyalties, allegiances and responsibilities. For instance, Ọza has an exogenous marriage pattern where a man may not marry within his lineage but can marry within the community. There also distinctive guidelines about inheritance. Bradbury noted that the Edo-speaking peoples universally show not only a marked patrilineal bias in their kinship and lineage organization but also an emphasis on primogeniture. As he indicated,

> almost everywhere the senior surviving son of a dead man is regarded as the chief heir to his property and the successor to whatever offices, privileges and duties he may have had. Hereditary titled offices, where present, pass from the last incumbent to his senior son. Where rights of the other children to a share in their father's property are recognized, the children of each mother generally form a distinct group for this purpose. (1957: 15)

In spite of this generalization, Bradbury remarked, however, 'among some North-West Edo groups there is evidence of a double descent system whereby every individual belongs both to a localized patrilineage and to a dispersed matrilineal group' (1957: 15). It is against this backdrop that we can interrogate Ọza kinship as a bilateral or double-descent system within Ọza social-political and religious milieu.

Kinship lineage in Ọza is bilateral with *Ireme* as paramount, although there is some emphasis on *Afẹ* in another respect. Matrilineality, the tracing of kinship through the female line, correlates with a social system in which each person is identified with their matriline – their mother's lineage. The matrilineal descent pattern is in contrast to the more common pattern of patrilineal descent from which a family name is usually derived. Patrilineality or agnatic kinship,[1] on the other hand, is a common kinship system and social unit in which an individual family membership derives from and is identified through their father's lineage. Although bilateral kinship is common, matriliny rather than patriliny is most significant in Ọza. The maternal kin occupies a very important position in the life of an Ọza indigene, much more than a paternal kin. Birth and blood relatedness determines maternal kin's identity and belonging. One is born into the matrilineal family line, although he maintains virilocality or virilocal residence within a social system in which a married couple resides in the household of the groom's parents, or within the vicinity of the family house, compound or homestead. Thus, the man retains his father's name while the wife takes on husband's surname.

Owing to an exogenous pattern, marriage and cohabitation from within the same *Ireme* is strictly forbidden and considered a taboo. Thus, marriage within the same *Ireme* is mostly discouraged, albeit a taboo, to retain the distinctiveness of their blood relations. Any violation of this taboo is accompanied by a ritual process, *Afẹ Osha*, through which the acceptance of certain rules of behaviour makes it possible to marry a cousin or aunt. The couple is more or less regarded as stemming from the same flesh, but not from the same *Ireme*. They must not engage in divorce, the husband may not expel his wife under any conditions. The couple is thus staying within their own familial bounds, in compliance with social norms.

There has been a common tendency within families or male-headed households, in the past and now, when the man who is expected to play the husband-father role is derelict in duty, leery or simply fails to assume due responsibility in providing the needed financial resources for training or educating the boy-child or girl-child. The excuse is often hinged on a rather evasive dictum, *Esha oke to ọmọ fi oshe a, a ki ode nise oyi, ireme onuo oda nise*, literally translated as 'If a father trains or educates his child and the child grows up, the child will not "know" his father but his/her maternal kin'. In other words, it is needless to invest your resources on or train up your child on behalf of his *Ireme* (matrilineal family). The phrase 'to know' in this sense means that the father may not literally reap the fruits or enjoy the dividends of his investments on his child. Such a thought is rather retrogressive against the backdrop that the boy-child mostly remains in the father's household beyond puberty and marriage. For the girl-child, it is counterintuitive that since the girl-child leaves her father's house to live with the husband upon marriage, she drops her maiden name in place of her husband's family name, hence a variant axiom that *Esha oke to ọmọ ubishi fo oshe a, Ọhọshi wo nai ireme Ọgbe na* (literal meaning, 'If a father invests and trains his girl-child till puberty and beyond, the man has only made investments on behalf of his maternal kin and her would-be husband'). Such maxims are, however, disingenuous but appear to shape a trend which has an adverse impact on human capital building and a drawback in terms of both personal and community development, social mobility, literacy, entrepreneurship and skills acquisition. This complicates familial responsibility, since the negligence by the husband-father figure in a small conjugal family household puts enormous responsibility on the woman to serve as the breadwinner. This abdication of the husband-father role, authority and filial duty undergirds people's perception of the primacy of *Ireme* in contradistinction with *Afẹ*.

There is a sense in which Ọza people exhibit a strong tendency towards matrifocality, similar to what Jacob Olupona describes in the case of Ondo people (Olupona 1991: 36). Matrifocality refers to kinds of relatedness in societies where mothers are structurally, culturally and affectively central (Tanner 1974), and coexists with any formal descent system. Matrifocality designates a type of family or household grouping in which the woman is dominant and plays the leading role psychologically. She is probably the figure who most influences the children in their development. Thus, matrifocality can exist within kinship systems formally designated as patrilineal. It is not simply a quality of intra-household relations, but it exists in contexts where women have extra-household economic, political and cultural roles and opportunities. Raymond Smith was the first to attach the concept (matrifocal) to this type of family structure, partly as a point of departure from Meyer Fortes (Smith 1956, 1996).[2] In his efforts to isolate what he considered the irreducible 'elementary components' of family and kinship, Fortes (1969: 261) argues that an individual is tied 'bilaterally' to both the mother's kinship line (matri-kinship) and the father's kinship line (patri-kinship).

Jimi Adesina (2010) focuses on the idea of matrifocality or matricentricity while examining the contributions of Ifi Amadiume (1987) and Oyeronke Oyewumi (1997) to gender scholarship. He notes that while not a new concept, the idea of matrifocal or matricentric societies acquires distinct valency in their epistemic framework and as the basis for theorizing matriarchy. He contends that matricentricity in Amadiume's works accounts for the structural and ideological conditions of many African societies. Thus, we could also talk about gendered matrilineality, or what Cecile Jackson characterizes as the feminization of kinship (Jackson 2014). The relegation of filial duty by Ọza men, coupled with urban drift of men in search of white- and blue-collar employment and better job opportunities, partly explain why kinship relatedness has largely become feminized.

Historically, Ọza's royal genealogical tradition is located within the *Afẹ*, paternal lineage, first from the Ọbueri to the Ọsuruka kindred. These paternal lineages are situated within different *Odo* (quarters) that constitute the old Ọza village, namely Ọdun, Imejere, Ekpe, Odoshami and Ovopki quarters. Zoning of Ọza village under *Unukpa* (household unit) and *Odo* is for organizational or administrative expediency. For instance, for communal work such as environmental sanitation of the town and road paths to farms and streams/rivers, the community relies on representatives drawn from each *Odo*, *Unukpa* or *Eku* (age grade) to accomplish this.

Ọza political structure and organization is understood in light of the religious dimensions to political authority. Ọza kingship ideology is expressed in various forms through myths, oral traditions, proverbs and songs. Praise names and special attributes articulate the divinity of *Opashi Ọza*. Ọza community evince a complex political structure, the central focus of which is *Opashi Ọza* (King or Village Head of Ọza), a position that is rotational between patrilineal family lineages. The *Opashi* and his *Eja* adumbrate enormous political authority in Ọza. *Opashi*'s authority is partly symbolized by his sacred beaded or woven crown, a sacred staff of authority and other royal paraphernalia. The *Opashi* oversees the day-to-day affairs of the community with the support and advice of *Eja* and the Village Council, which is selected from the seven *Afẹ*, paternal families, and the seven *Ireme*, maternal families. To make vital decisions concerning the community, *Opashi o de yo eba* (summons consultation) with the *Eja* to deliberate on the issues at stake. The political authority of the *Opashi* is also characterized by checks and balances. In most cases, the *Opashi* refrains from making autocratic or unilateral decisions on issues that affect the entire community; he consults with the *Eja* systematically. Every time a decision is being made, they come together and then approach the king and inform him about their decision based on the legal concept of *Ogbele* and censuring injustice, *Orere* (Lawani 1992: 14).

Thus, an incumbent *Opashi Ọza*, in his daily governance, receives support and advice from the *Eja*, a Village Council with title-holding representatives from each respective *Afẹ*, kindred and Village Quarter. The titles they receive indicate the order in hierarchy but also the distinctive portfolio of the title holder. The

Eja serves in an advisory capacity to the *Ọpashi*; they discharge their leadership roles and are responsible to the *Ọpashi*, and serve as liaison between the *Ọpashi* and their *Afẹ/Ibinesha* (kindred or paternal lineage) and Quarters. Each *Eja* has ritual (religious), political and social functions to perform on behalf of *Ọpashi* and their respective *Afẹ*. The structure of *Ireme* and *Afẹ* is identical in the sense that each group is headed by *Ọriọ-Afẹ*, the eldest female in the case of *Ireme* and the eldest male in the case of *Afẹ*. The *Ọriọ-Afẹ* is officially responsible for all matters concerning the kinship group, the sustenance of its structure; wields authority and represents the kin in all communal and inter-family matters; supervises and protects family ancestral land, properties and marriage; settles family and interpersonal disputes; and serves as a guardian and adviser in social, economic, political and religious issues. Lawani demonstrates that representatives of each *Afẹ* are vested with specific political functions on behalf of their families and the entire community (1992: 14). The communal functions and responsibilities of *Afẹ* and *Ireme* intersect on the level of society and of the individual, since every individual maintains a dual identity, belonging and relatedness – paternal and maternal. The patrilineal kin wields political power in the sense that the royal chieftaincy institution is situated within *Afẹ*. They take charge of the security of the community, the traditional army that produces warriors in times of interethnic wars and conflicts. The *Afẹ* are responsible for overseeing the economy and political matters of their village while the *Ireme* take charge of the spiritual and emotional well-being of the community. The *Ireme* also handle issues concerning inheritance, family land and properties.

Another significant aspect of the social structure is the *Eku*, age-set or age-grade system. Bradbury observes that as among other sections of the Edo-speaking peoples, 'men's age-grades and age-sets and title associations are important features of the social organization. In Ọja, Dagbala, Ojirami, Makeke, and Ọsọsọ age-sets are formed at seven-year intervals. The Okulusọ villages – Ọja, Dagbala, and Ojirami – form their age-sets at the same time and with one exception they have the same names' (1957: 114, 118). All Ọza adults, men and women, are divided into *Eku*, age groups that are totally independent of the *Afẹ* or *Ireme* lineage configuration, although members emanate from *Afẹ* or *Ireme*. The age group structure covers all life stages. Upon the attainment of puberty and performance of the necessary rites of puberty, an individual enters the first age grade and moves to the next grade in subsequent years as defined. The main purpose of the age-set is to form a corporate group as a source of solidarity, support and labour for community-oriented projects and to provide a hands-on, formidable security force in the event of emergencies such as external aggression, interethnic wars, epidemics, famines and droughts, and other communal projects and rituals including house-building construction, market and road maintenance, marriage ceremonies, festivals, leisure activities and so forth. Young male and female adults are integrated into community life through elaborate initiation rituals and extensive indigenous education mechanisms where social norms, ethics, moral and cultural values, taboos and notions of respectability are inculcated. Each *Eku* appoints an *Oga*, a leader, followed by an *Ubere*, a deputy, to galvanize the group into action and ensure its social functionality and relationality.

Bradbury notes further that in all villages except Ososo, there are six title-associations or title-grades, those of the Okuluso ([sic] Okurosho) villages having the same names. The first, Isukuru ([sic] Isokuru), is open to boys who have not entered their first age-set and who gain admittance by paying a small fee to the village headman. At Oja, the second association, *Oso*, is joined by a whole or part of an age-set whose members perform masquerades, entertain the town and present two hundred yams to the village headman. On the death of his father, any member of this rank can take the *Eja* title by paying 4 shillings to the village headman. At Dagbala and Ojirami, both these ranks are said to be joined by age-sets rather than individuals (Bradbury 1957: 118). Bradbury remarks,

> All villages have individual titles which 'belong' to descent-groups; they are available to members of the senior title-grade. In Oja, for example, five descent-group have two titles each and the other two one each, the holders being selected by the group from its members who hold the *eja* title. Each of the seven descent-groups of Ojirami 'owns' three titles, *Okogbe* or *Otaru, Obolo,* and *Oka*; the first being that of the headman and the second of his designated successor. At Dagbala the four wards have four titles, *Okogbe, Otaru, Obolo,* and *Ogisua* … One of the title-holders is usually recognized as the headman in each ward and one of these ward headmen is the village head. (1957: 118)

The latter part of Bradbury's remarks above is in connection with the exercise of political authority. While there are obviously affinities and variations on age groupings, title-associations and political organization among the Okurosho clan as described, these structures are dynamic and have been susceptible to change, adaptation and transformation. The political organization, as Bradbury observes, was everywhere complicated by the disturbed history of the last century. Indigenous political offices seem to have been associated with the guardianship of ward and village shrines, priests being selected according to a variety of principles – age, differential ranking between territorial segments, divination and so forth. The members of title-associations, too, played a leading part in the authority structure. As Bradbury remarks, 'throughout this area the age-grades and title associations have declined with the refusal of Christians to undergo the necessary ceremonies of initiation and promotion' (1957: 115). I shall come back to this point in the last chapter where I explore further the cultural, social, religious and political impact of British, Nupe and Yoruba colonialisms, and of Christianity and Islam on Ọza. As I have described, the external exposure to Nupe, Yoruba and British hegemonies and political cultures was consequential in the Nupenization, Yorubanization and Anglicization of Ọza personal family appellations, chieftaincy titles and religious, social and political organizations. Bradbury observes,

> In some cases village headmanship may have been an innovation of Nupe times. At Dagbala the Nupe called the senior *Ọkọgbe Zeike* and the second *Dawudu*. At Makeke they recognised the *Osheku* of one ward as *Zeike* though the *Osheku* of another ward is priest of two of the village deities. At Ọja and Dagbala all *eja* are members of the village council. (1957: 119)

Besides *Zeike* (Saiki) and *Dawudu* (Daodu) titles commonly used in Ọza, other Nupe/Filani chieftaincy titles such as *Otaru*, and Yoruba titles such as *Ọba* and *Olọjah* of Ọjah, came into popular usage.

Myth and sacral kingship

The myth of sacral kingship institution is very central in Ọza cosmological tradition. The *Ọpashi* is *primus inter pares*, doubling as a human-spirit figure that intercedes for *Oshukunu* within the human realm. The idea and imagery of a Supreme Deity is also intelligible through attributes such as *Oshukunu Ọpashi*, the Deity King, *Oshukunu Agbalagbala*, the Deity who is limitless, and *Eya Noporo*, a great, benevolent father. The ritual power imbues *Ọpashi* with the paraphernalia of royal office, including *Agua* (crown) as the most significant of the royal insignia and robes, *Uje* (flywhisk or horsetail) and leather cowhide as fan or umbrella. The *Agua* symbolizes the sacred royal power of the *Ọpashi*. The *Agua* embodies the essence of divinatory prowess, the emblem of the royal ancestral lineage, the moral and political power vested in the person of the King.

Elsewhere, sacral kingship represents one of the most distinctive and widespread feature of Yoruba political organization. The *Ọba* is regarded as *Ekeji Orisa* (the companion of the divinities), set apart from his people by the spiritual powers with which he was endowed at his installation. As the 'deputy of the *orisa*', the Ọba is the supreme head of the social and political hierarchy and is nominally responsible for the welfare of his people. The ascension of a new Ọba was marked by elaborate rites. Throughout his reign, he made few public appearances, and even during these his face was hidden by the *ade* (the crown with its beaded fringe). Olupona's *Kingship, Religion, and Rituals in a Nigerian Community* (1991: 195) deals with the forms, contents and symbols of Ondo ritual life as it is articulated and shaped by their most significant festivals. He is concerned primarily with Ondo religious beliefs and rituals connected to the traditions of sacred kingship, and exemplifies how Ondo civil religion, emanating from the institution and rituals of sacred kingship, becomes the focus of the Ondo-Yoruba multireligious community. As D. Westerlund notes, 'A key aspect of these festivals, Olupona accentuates is the articulation of the sacred power of Kingship, through which the social and religious groups "transcend" their differences and conflicts, thus confirming their solidarity and common Ondo identity' (Westerlund 1991: 9).

In exploring the ideology, iconography and rituals of kingship, Olupona explains how they create an invisible sacred canopy that unites Ondo's multireligious community and contributes to the understanding of Yoruba religious world view and the sociocultural changes taking place in contemporary Yoruba society (Olupona 1991: 14). Olupona vividly demonstrates how the system of government in Ondo is centralized on the election of a divine kingship with a king status, which is a hereditary one, rotating among five ruling houses (genealogies), with an authority partly derived through the legendary foreparent, and in the other part, from Oduduwa, the descent of the Yoruba race who derived (his) from 'Olodumare', the Supreme Being. He contends, 'The most important aspect of Ondo religion today is the system of royal rituals and ideology under which all other aspects of cultural life are subsumed. In the Ondo political system, the King's role is critical in terms of its executive, judicial and ritual functions' (Olupona 1991: 58). The book provides a useful analysis of the kingship ideology, which is relevant to understanding of the rituals of kingship, but also focuses on the myths and rituals of kingship as portrayed in two major ceremonies: *Ifobaje*, the King's installation ceremony, and *Ọdun Ọba*, the annual festival of the King.[3] In the institutional structure and governance process of Ondo Kingdom, women are also highly formidable and influential with their own structure appearing like their male counterparts', playing prominent roles like the installation of a new Osemawe by the 'Lobun', the head of the market and kingmaker.

Women, ritual power and sacral kingship

The role, status and impact of women in Ọza is partly understood in terms of their political, socio-economic and ritual power; through the levels of social and political organizations they belong and sustain; and how they contribute to the shaping, negotiation and resilience of the sacral kingship institution. Lawani remarks,

> Regarding Ọzah social organisation one can say that it is characterized by spaces occupied by *Esami* (women) and *Ehọshi* (men), both of which are recognized as co-creators and partners concerning the construction of society. This engagement of women and men in collective activity is subject to the following rules: (a) sharing of tasks, and (b) respect for the attributes and rights of men and women. These are the two principles that guarantee the continuity of the system. (70-1)

The title/function of the *Okọgbe* as *Ọpashi Ọza* is ascertained by the royal lineage, while at the same time *Ọdejọ* is the royal title assigned to the woman who stands as the head of the women guild, but also the female leader of the community at large. The *Ọdejọ* performs significant ritual, political and social roles and serves in an advisory role to *Ọpashi*. Such a somewhat bicephalous system could lead to a false conclusion that there are two Village Heads (male/female) with equal, identical political power. Each leader exudes charismatic power in their own right; the gender power each garners is mutually reinforcing and can be politically, socially and ritually differentiated. Although direct public authority is absent in many cases, most strategic political decisions are made by *Ọpashi* and *Ejas* with the consent and approval of *Ọdejọ* and the women leadership guild.

Within the indigenous polity, women are highly influential within and beyond their own social circles, playing outstanding roles, prominent functions that have political, social, economic and ritual import. When *Ọpashi Ọza* and his *Eja* meet to deliberate on problems concerning the people, they will withhold decisions until the women express their point of view. Similar issues are brought before *Ọdejọ* and the women leaders for deliberation. It is only when the women's opinion and feedback is received that a final decision or verdict is reached on behalf of the community. In this process the sensibility and sensitivity of women is paramount and is not usually stymied. Ọza women negotiate gender power by utilizing their spiritual authority and responsibility to underline issues that they consider controversial in their interpersonal relationship with the men, regarding the crucial issues at stake. Ọza women have the capability to engage in sociopolitical debates and to revisit and rescind any decisions taken by *Opashi* and *Eja* that they perceive are not in their favour and in the best interest of the community.

Thus, women's negotiation of political power underscores how a local community expresses the need for sustaining a somewhat social equilibrity. To obtain this equilibrity, there has to be mutual consent or even acquiescence between those who hold the instruments of power: the men and the women who are culturally in charge within *Ireme* and *Afẹ* settings. In this regard, mothers of past, present and future generations are respected by the men for taking over this responsibility. For instance, Lawani documents one instance in which the political power of women was expressed in a conflict between a representative of the colonial native authority and Ọza people (1992: 71-2). The local government council had demanded the payment of taxes for community development. Upon receipt of the formal letter notice, the Village Head summoned a meeting of the Village Council to discuss the matter. The *Odejo* also gathered representative women leaders to discuss the same. In the end, the women were totally opposed to the payment of tax, thereby inferring from a similar scenario in previous years, during the reign of Chief Ogundare Lawani, when a tax waiver was consequential upon the vigorous protest by women.

The women then put forward a logical argument which made their vehement rejection of the imposed tax plausible. They contended that the absence of electricity and portable water in Ọza is hardly a good sign of local government efforts and failed to justify tax levies. The government representative failed in his task to retire with the tax and left Ọza disappointingly. This was, however, a temporary success for the village, although taking such a stand did not hinder the procedures set up by the local government for tax collection. In the end, *Opashi* and his *Eja* were unsuccessful in presenting the case forward before the local government. The women stood in defiance and refused to pay tax on grounds that it was unwarranted. The *Okọgbe* convened another meeting with his council in order to examine the women's arguments and to review the whole situation. The *Okọgbe* and his *Eja* were finally convinced of the validity of the women's arguments. Thus, the men and the women now had a unanimous answer for the representative during his subsequent visit to Ọza. It was reported that the women demonstrated remarkable bravery in presenting the same argument before the government representative. He was exasperated by the women's recalcitrance and invited them to visit the local government office at Igarra, (a distance of 18 km from Ọza) to substantiate their case or argument before the local administration. But the women were not receptive to that invitation; feeling unperturbed they told the representative to take the following message to his superiors: 'Those who want us to pay taxes should provide the means (money or transportation) that will make the visit to Igarra possible.' Although this was an affront and an act of gross civil disobedience to the representative and the local administration, the local government did not press their demand for taxes from this community at least for a while. This harsh stance and political consciousness of the women helped to prevent external exploitation through taxation and to ease the suffering and manipulation of the men, some who were already victims of government action and abuse.

The social, political, economic and ritual importance of women is seen in the formation of age groups and in the recognition that the annual *Upe Iruvie*, *Ibishika* and *Ọmọnugere* marriage-related festivals help to build cohesion and a corporate social grouping, consisting of girls/women of similar age, who have a common identity, forge and maintain close ties over a prolonged period, and together encounter a series of age-related statuses.[4] During these rituals and festivities, Ọza women's political consciousness and cultural capital is enhanced. The sociopolitical, religious and economic significance of the annual *Upe Iruvie*, *Ibishika* and *Ọmọnugere* festivals in Ọza is perhaps analogous to the Ondo girl's puberty ceremony, *Obitun*, which is normally integrated into kingship rituals and with which adolescent Ondo are integrated into the cultural life of the community.[5]

The social and cultural learning that forms a core part of these ritual events serves to prepare girls for their immediate and future tasks, responsibilities, rights and privileges as potential women, mothers and leaders. The social and political role of women in Ọza needs to be understood against the backdrop of their significant role in the market economy of the community, quest for relative autonomy and economic independence, but also the need to demonstrate integrity, rectitude and moral uprightness and exude an aura of reassuring solidity. Thus, the role and status of women in Ọza religion and society is defined by what is deemed wholesome to the welfare of the entire community of men, women and children. In Ọza community, women are in charge of some shrines with cultic focus and functions. As religious specialists, women can achieve status and authority that allows them to mobilize important resources within the community. The *Ọdejọ* advises *Ọpashi Ọza* and his *Eja* on matters concerning women. She has economic oversights on the market economy and affairs, but also more importantly social and ritual jurisdiction over the ritual enactment of *Ukpe Iruvie*, *Ibishika* and *Ọmọnugere* ceremonies or festivals.

In the traditional setting, Ọza men generally engage in subsistence farming and hunting. Although women also engage in farming, they are responsible for selling the agricultural products on market days and in neighbouring villages/towns. Ọza operates a four-day market calendar: *Akọ Ebiene, Akọ Anumu, Akọ Afọ* and *Akọ Akpẹ*. There is an economic culture based on the complementarity of men and women in which the sharing of tasks is commonplace. Although most men, but also women, engage in subsistence farming, planting and harvesting cash crops such as Cassava (Latin name, *Manihot esculenta*), the women transform the harvested crops into finished products such as Garri, fermented and fried manioc flour, which is both consumed within the household or sold in the local market.

Feminine ingenuity: The sacrality and aesthetics of *Ẹrẹma* pottery making

Ọza women are renowned for traditional crafts like clay pottery produced for domestic, commercial, aesthetic and ritual purposes. 'Pottery making is largely done by the womenfolk who specialize in the production of earthenware, kike cooking pots, bowls, mugs, water pots, pipes etc. Ojah in Akoko-Edo Local Government of Edo state is known nationally for its fine pottery.'[6] Traditional pottery production is the invention and exclusive preserve of women; the *Ẹrẹma* (clay), a fine-grained natural soil material that contains hydrous aluminium phyllosilicates (clay minerals), is obtained from clay deposits found in designated clay sites in Ọza. The *Ẹrẹma* not only depicts one of the several marks of wealth and splendour of the female earth deity that is believed to be the custodian of the land/earth, but also bequeaths and enriches it with fertility, mineral resources and for agriculture.

As early as 1910, Northcote W. Thomas notes the prevalence of pottery making among Edo-speaking peoples, describing two methods of making pots in Southern Nigeria – the commonest method at Utekon in Benin and larger pots at Sabongida Ora (1910c: 1–15; 1910d: 97–8).[7] He unpacks how pottery in Benin was produced to serve both ceremonial and utilitarian purposes (Bradbury 1957: 20). Thomas generally observed,

> Pot-making is somewhat local in the Central Province. Finely-decorated pots are made at Yaju on the borders of Northern Nigeria, and at Ulola, near Benin City, I saw some highly decorative pots; but as a rule they are more useful than ornamental. In Benin City are made pots with human figures on them (Ulo-Oloku), large round pots (utkodo), yam pots (axe), soup pots (umaua), small

pots to represent an ebo (juju), which are called oviaxe or uluebo, toy, pots of the same shape offered (with a hole in the bottom) to Osan or Obiame, and native basins. Uhumilau, or heads of ancestors, which are frequently made in bronze, are also made in pottery. The uhumilau often have a projection on the left-hand side to represent the white feather worn by chiefs, and one in the centre of the head to support the ivory tusks formerly, found in the shrines of ancestors. The chiefs who talked to me about these matters were unanimous in declaring that the ivory actually rested on the heads. (1910d: 98)

J. O. Ohimai and E. Okunna (2016: 77–87) aptly explored Ojah pottery tradition as an instance of innovation and adaptation in modern usage, examining the practice in relation to the survival strategy of the art form. They remarked, 'Pottery tradition of Ojah people is as old as the community itself. Pottery developed with the oral history of the village. It is an occupation, which distinguishes the people who practice it as well as bring into the limelight the place where it is practiced' (77). Ohimai and Okunna asserted, though with some exaggeration, that Ojah (Oza) is a village where almost every woman is a potter besides farming. The Oza women interlocutors allude to the fact that the origin of pottery is as old as the town itself and the discovery of clay was a big relief to Ojah women who had long abandoned the moulding artistry from the time they migrated from Benin and Ozanogogo to settle in their present location. The soil is quite suitable for agriculture hence farming is also thriving for men along with pottery by women. They stated,

> Clay in Ojah is held sacrosanct. It is most sacred and inviolable. Clay is believed to be connected to gods and deity in the land, hence it is taboo for raw clay to be taken out of Ojah community or given a price for unfired clay or ware … Another important law guarding the handling of clay is that a woman under menstruation is forbidden to touch clay or work on pottery. This is based on the belief that a woman under menstruation is not spiritually clean and so forbidden to touch any sacred item of the land: an attempt contrary to these demands will attract a sacrifice to appease the gods of the land. (Ohimai and Okunna 2016: 78)

The Obueri kindred in Ojah are the custodians of *Erema*, the clay; they control also the usage and all rituals associated with the practice. Pottery production follows a laborious trajectory through which the women potters manually prospect and excavate *Erema* from the clay deposits clay of two colour extractions: *Erema Obibi* (black clay) and *Erema Omeme* (red clay). These are often combined to achieve a better result. The excavated *Erema* is stored in *Iperema*, a clay pit, for a few days to help the clay to slake. Ohimai and Okunna best described the manual hand building; apparatus or working tools; the pottery decoration using the roulette, incised, mould or embossed pattern and burnishing; and the firing and finishing of the pots. They also described the typology and functions of Ojah pots in terms of the forms, shapes and sizes. Some of the common pottery forms and products at Ojah include *Abẹ Osomi, Abẹ Idodo* or *Abẹ Udodo, Enyeamẹ, Iresumu, Abẹ Oka, Agogo, Eruesumu, Abẹ Opẹ, Agere, Onwaja, Oshiaololo, Emashimi, Akomi, Enamako, Ekpakunu, Abẹ-Iwe* and *Amaokomi* (83). There is evidently the women's ingenuity, creativity and innovation involved in Ọza pottery art (see Plates 6a–6g). Ohimai and Okunna noted,

> The Ọja potters are striving to remain relevant in terms of production and adaptation to new demands while maintaining their creative cultural identity. The Ọjah potters are faced with the challenge of survival, pottery being their means of livelihood and social recognition … They are also aware that they are admired for their creative prowess and so with a dogged zeal they have continued and are open to innovations. (2016: 86)

Ohimai and Okunna concludes how Ojah pottery tradition have moved on to achieve relevance in the contemporary world of technology, even though some traditional potters still cling to the old products. They underscore how their methods of production, decoration techniques, materials and ethos of practice remain ancestral and primordial. Ọza pots are essentially for utilitarian and spiritual purposes (2016: 86). At the same time, they explore the disastrous impact of external influences on pottery traditions, demonstrating how the art of traditional pottery in Ojah had been interrupted, abandoned and left to grope in the shadows of uncertainties.

Beyond domestic appropriation, African pottery found relevance in religion, industry and social applications up to the point of traditional architectures as the use of broken pottery shards as pavement in excavations at Ife demonstrated (Willett 2002: 122). Ohimai, I. B. Kashim and T. Akinbogun (2013: 475–83) collected waste pots and potsherds in Ojah, a pot-producing community in their research to determine the suitability of the sample pots and potsherds collected for the construction of the kilns. This study explores the possibilities of designing efficient ceramic kilns with the use of earthenware pots/potsherds and concluded that there were plenty of waste pots and potsherds in local pottery-making centres such as Ojah and Imiegba, which can be harnessed for the production of pots and potsherds kiln. The pots and potsherds sourced were of different sizes and shapes depending on their initial primary function. Their findings also included an illustration of Ojah potsherds dump estimated to be over a hundred years old. The evidence of plenty of waste pots and potsherds in local pottery-making centres such as Ojah is indicative of a once thriving industry that has declined particularly in the last few decades.

Negotiating Oza indigenous polity under a coloniality of power

The encounter between indigenous African polities and European colonial regimes was a complex exercise that displayed hegemonic power, on the one hand, and the vulnerability of indigenous political, sociocultural and religious systems, on the other. The coloniality of power,[8] as Anibal Quijano best describes it, is a model of power with one of its fundamental axes in

> 'the social classification of the world's population around the idea of race, a mental construction that expresses the basic experience of colonial domination and pervades the more important dimensions of global power, including its specific rationality: Eurocentrism. The racial axis has a colonial origin and character, but it has proven to be more durable and stable than the colonialism in whose matrix it was established. Therefore, the model of power that is globally hegemonic today presupposes an element of coloniality. (Quijano 2000: 533)

The coloniality of power and labour also makes sense against the backdrop of contestation, negotiation and resilience.

As discussed in Chapter 2, the entire geographical region of what later became Nigeria collapsed in the face of British incursion by 1900. The British had made significant inroads into the Nigerian hinterland. In 1897, Benin Kingdom witnessed a major military set back in her encounter with the British colonial forces and this was consequential in a discomfiting economic, sociopolitical future for vassal states and neighbouring communities that bore close affinity with the Kingdom, including Oza peoples. This subjugation by the British colonial machinery was hardly devoid of sociopolitical unease and wanton mayhem. Rather, it was a period characterized by dogged resistance and reluctant capitulation.

Local historians claim that Oza Okeme settlement was largely unscathed during the Nupe invasion in the late 1890s and the conquest by the British colonial forces (Royal Niger Company) in 1897 owing to its strategic topography, with the rocky hills serving as a natural bulwark. However, Benin Kingdom and virtually all its environs had succumbed to British rule by the first decade of the twentieth century. Out of colonial administrative convenience, Ọza community became part of the Kurukuru Division of Benin Province of Southern Nigeria. It is so far unclear from historical records when Ọza people first had any direct encounter with the British provincial administration. While not corroborated by any available colonial archival sources, a local historian suggested, perhaps anecdotally, 'In 1839 some representatives of the British Council visited the village. Before and after that year, successive British and government officials visited and still visit the village ... Chief Ọnọbumẹ' was captured in 1897.'[9] According to this source, Chief Ọnọbumẹ of Ọja reigned between 1850 and 1950, and died on 7 August 1951.[10] It is most improbable that *Ọpashi Ọza* (Ọza Village Head/King), the 'Ọnọbumẹ of Ọja', was captured and incarcerated for more than four decades, especially when official colonial government records show enquiries at Ọja on the circumstances subsequent to his release from prison in the early 1930s.[11]

In his official letter to the Resident of Benin Province in 1934,[12] R.B. Kerr, the acting district officer of Kukuruku Division, partly reveals the reasons for the imprisonment of the Ọnọbumẹ of Ọja but also the negotiation of a compromise between colonial and village authorities. According to Kerr,

> All the offences charged against Ọnọbumẹ are traceable to his desire for independence both for himself and for the village. He has offered passive opposition, at least, to his District Head, to the Kukuruku Native Administration, and to Administrative Officers. At the same time, he appears to be a capable and authoritative village head and it does not appear possible to recommend anyone else for Government recognition. To leave the village without recognition will be to encourage its indifference to authority. This situation is largely the result of traditions engendered by an isolated independence maintained for generations on a hill top rendered in-accessible to foes.[13]

Kerr notes that similar traditions are not uncommon 'in villages in the North West of the Division such as Makeke, Dagbala, Omorga ([*sic*.] Imọga), Kakuma ([*sic*.] Kakumo) and others'.[14] The Resident remarks, in his *Annual Report of 1939*, that the Nupe conquest of the Kukuruku Division in the last century still leaves traces of alien imposition of the village head and title system, and in many of the clans there is still a good deal of rivalry and intrigue in attempts to secure individual preference.[15] J. G. Cary, the District Officer Kukuruku in 1939, wrote, 'The present writer as a newcomer to the Division was showered with a rain of petitions, reminiscent of leaflets in an intense election campaign, requesting his support of the petitioner in his endeavour to establish himself in a position on the council or court, or as a clan or village head.'[16] But despite these disputes, which are not very serious and give a spice to life, the people are happy and contented, have ample good land and pay their tax more readily than, say, in the Province. Their previous history has taught them to appreciate the benefits of undisturbed enjoyment of their land.[17] More than a decade later, a new Resident of Benin Province notes, 'During all these years since the Nupe invasions the villages scattered amongst the hills in the northern part of the Division have maintained their tradition of individual independence.'[18] The Resident observes further, 'My own first acquaintance with the Benin Province was in 1925, and I can well remember that it was then universally the case that age and seniority was the only qualification for leadership, whether in Courts or Councils, and that no one ever thought of anything beyond the confines of his own village.'[19]

First, from Kerr's letter we can deduce that offences framed as Ọnọbumẹ's 'desire for independence both for himself and for the village' partly links Ọpashi Ọza's recalcitrance to colonial intrusion and invasion of his political sphere of influence and territorial integrity through taxation and economic expropriation. There could well be other factors or explanations to this 'desire for independence' that are undisclosed in this letter. Ostensibly, Ọnọbumẹ came on a collision course with coloniality of power by refusing to pay Oso obo (white man's tax) for and on behalf of his village. For its colonial economic base, the provincial administration[20] and native administration depended on poll tax, court fees, court fines and revenue generated from taxes imposed on timber trade, tree felling, cocoa, oil palm, palm kernel, rubber, vehicle (bicycle) and other sources of economic exploitation. What seemed to matter most for the colonial interlopers was the unrepentant appropriation of economic surplus at all costs and by all means possible.

Even during the latter decades of the British colonial regime, the Resident of Benin Province continues to report with resounding enthusiasm:

> The past year has been a satisfactory one economically ... Though at the time of collection of increased taxes at the beginning of the year, there was a general complaint the people could not find the extra money, once pressure to pay was applied the tax was forthcoming and it is significant that this year there have not been the same complaints.[21]

During the 1950s, the strategies and prospects for crude oil exploration, to supplant the expropriation of raw materials, were already in process. As the District Officer, Benin Division, wrote, 'one aspect of development which may have profound economic effect in the future is the activities of Shell

D'Arcy Exploration Company. The Company is at present test-drilling for oil at Iguoriakhi, 16 miles from Benin City. They have not reported any results to date, though drilling is still in progress.'[22] G. K. Monro, the District Officer of Kukuruku Division, also wrote in his annual report about relative economic success attained against the backdrop of economic strangulation, deplorable infrastructure and sociocultural, political dislocations of the local people:

> Generally speaking the Division today is enjoying a prosperity such as it has never seen before ... A word must be said about the condition of roads in this Division. There is no single road that can be called an 'all season road' and at the height of the rains in 1954 every Trunk and Provincial road became impassable at many points. In the dry season, their condition is correspondingly bad, and the effect not only on the economic but on all aspects of life is seriously detrimental to progress[23]

The District Officer, Kukuruku Division, remarks, 'Tax has always been collected promptly in the past in spite of the widely varying methods of collection between the Districts, all of which are antiquated and in need of overhaul.'[24] In the same report, the Resident raised an urgency, highlighting the appalling state of the roads as well as the financial difficulties in maintaining the roads. He remarks, 'Kukuruku has been described as a country of hills and swamps: this is true and it makes the maintenance of road communications throughout the 2,105 square miles excessively costly and difficult.'[25] In spite of this lapse, he reports that the total collection for 1953–4 amounted to £48,160.00 compared to £25,655.00 in 1952–3. The assessment for 1954–5 was £50,350. 'Faced with the genuinely difficult problem of balancing their budgets for 1955–56 and reluctant to increase tax or introduce rates at the present time each council has had to resort to large increases in fees and the cost of licences,'[26] the District Officer retorts.

Elsewhere within the Province, the total tax revenue generated in the Benin Division alone increased monumentally from £38,201.00 (1951–2) to £52,646.00 (1952–3) and £67,817.00 (1953–4), respectively. The total number of taxpayers also increased from 49,978 to 58,736.[27] The District Officer, Benin Division, remarks that the increase in amount of tax collected from 1951 to 1952 is gratifying and reflects the growing prosperity of the Division and more efficient collection. The years 1953 and 1954 saw the introduction of an entirely new system of Tax Assessment and Collection in that Flat Rate Tax was abolished and all people paid Income Tax. M. M. R. Haig, District Officer, Ishan Division, reports,

The finances of the Division remain satisfactory largely owing to the continued high yield from timber fees and royalties which produced a total of over £35,000 in the year 1953–54 against an estimate of £7,000, and have in the current financial year produced £20,000 in the first eight months (April to November) against an estimate for the whole year of £15,000. The yield for the first eight months of 1953–54 was over £21,000 so it appears that the peak of the timber boom may have been passed.[28]

Significant revenue figures for the first eight months of 1953–4 were based on Tax (£335), Native Court Fines (£480), Native Court Fees (£4,442), Timber Revenue (£21,292), Vehicle Licences (£411) and Total ordinary revenue (£29,927). In the next fiscal year period, 1954–5, the figures were Tax (£Nil), Native Court Fines (£479), Native Court Fees (£6,683), Timber Revenue (£20,045), Vehicle Licences (£332) and Total ordinary revenue (£33,520). The actual surplus revenue accrued by 1 April 1954 amounted to £59,135.[29]

Second, Ọnọbumẹ's perceived intransigence, resistance and diplomacy displayed through 'passive opposition' is a stark indicator that he was indeed a hard nut for the colonial government to crack. This posture portrays him as a charismatic leader who chose to put the interest and well-being of his community over and above the economic interest and political might of the colonial interlopers. The 'Ọnọbumẹ of Ọja' put his life and royal splendour on the line to defend and protect his people. Of course, he paid dearly for it through incarceration in the end. Third, the District Officer offers a more subtle recognition of and a somewhat deferential approach to 'tradition', which in his reckoning was 'engendered by an isolated independence maintained for generations'. Kerr underscores Ọnọbumẹ's leadership qualities in noting that 'he appears to be a capable and authoritative village head'. At the same time, he cautions, 'It does not appear possible to recommend anyone else for government recognition. To leave the village without recognition will be to encourage its indifference to authority'. The resilience of Ọza tradition in that you cannot replace an incumbent *Ọpashi* except at death or owing to debilitating circumstances is a pertinent one indeed to adhere to. The District Officer was perhaps apt in sounding this warning to his superiors, the Resident at Benin Province, that to do otherwise on grounds of incapacitation such as imprisonment would probably be disingenuous and an action that might land the colonial authorities in unwarranted political risks and turmoil such as 'to encourage the village's indifference to authority'. Thus, the letter partly unpacks the colonial government's recognition and disguised empathy for 'tradition', and the indigeneity of Ọza kingship institution, thereby demonstrating colonial vulnerability to any major disruptions of Ọza cultural and sociopolitical *modus vivendi*. Such circumspection reveals the economic insensibilities and coloniality of power inherent in the imperial experiment. As the letter asserts,

> Ọnọbumẹ is the Village Head by virtue of holding the title of Ọkọgbe which cannot pass to another during his life-time. This title is hereditary to the Ọsuruka family who choose one of their number to present to a meeting of the village for ratification upon the death of the former Village Head. The Ọkọgbe elect then feasts the villagers, after which he is confined to his house for three months, after which further feasting is made to celebrate his assumption of the office. No other person can be appointed to this position during his life time.[30]

The Ọkọgbe chieftaincy title was rotational between two family lineages of the Ọsuruka kindred: Ọkọkọ and Ugbọnọkua. Thus, 'hereditary' in the letter should be seen in terms of this rotational system rather than misconstrued as hereditary directly between father and son. This means that an incumbent Ọpashi Ọza cannot pass on the *Agua Ọpashi* (king's crown) directly to his son during his lifetime or after his demise. The *Agua* must rotate to the next family lineage within Ọsuruka and then return to the former upon the demise of the Ọpashi. No new Ọpashi Ọza can be enthroned while an incumbent is still alive. Liminal, transitional rituals of the sacred, pomp and pageantry and extensive festivities mark the enthronement of a new Ọpashi Ọza, but also the demise of an incumbent King.

When an incumbent Ọpashi Ọza dies, due to either old age or illness, Ọza people describe his death as a passage, journey, transition, 'gone to rest with the forefathers,' thus indicating the resilience of the ancestral lineage, but also the symbolism of death not as an end in itself. Death does not write a finis to life; rather, it is a transitional process to another life, the spirit cosmos. The news of an incumbent Ọpashi Ọza who has 'gone to rest with the forefathers' is concealed among the Ọsuruka kindred, the paternal lineage, and undisclosed to the public until a felicitous time. Any death during the *Ukpe* and *Orimi/Irimi* festivals are abominable. First, the Ọsuruka kindred meets to deliberate on the royal burial (royal funeral process) and the transitional process in which to transfer the Ọpashi's *Ema* and *Ọdumu*,[31] royal paraphernalia necessary for the appointment of a new Ọpashi Ọza by the other ruling family of the Ọsuruka kindred. Through oracular divination, the selection process of a new Ọkọgbe from the incoming ruling house is facilitated.

Once all family plans are in place, the tragic news is then broken to the entire village via the town crier, thus announcing a phase of mourning. On the appointed day of the royal burial ceremony, the entire village assemble at the palace and village square for the funeral, though only the Ọsuruka kindred have knowledge of the grave or specific burial place of the deceased *Ọpashi*. The Ọsuruka keeps this confidentiality from the public for strategic reasons. On the third day of the funeral, the *Aburofemi* ritual takes place amid celebration, dancing and sporadic shots of local guns into the air as a mark of respect and honour of the deceased.[32] On the fifth day of the funeral, there is recourse to oracular divination. It is the belief that by going to rest with the forefathers, *Ọpashi Ọza*, who deputises for *Oshukunu Ọpashi* (the Supreme King/Being) and *Ehọ Ọza* (the divinity), has translated from a corporeal body into the ethereal spirit world.

Following elaborate royal funeral obsequies, the Ọsuruka kindred will remove all the *Ema*, royal antiquities, to a secluded place unanimously assigned to keep them. These antiquities are carried to a secluded place only after *Erimi Ovie* (masquerade) removes *Odumu* (royal insignia) away. It is a taboo for women to see these royal paraphernalia and the *Erimi Ovie*. As the name *Erimi/Irimi* signifies, masquerades are between and betwixt the human and supersensible worlds thus rendering them potently perilous. Twenty-eight days of symbolic daily mourning by *Erimi Ovie* follows the interment of the deceased *Ọpashi*. The apogee of the royal funeral is marked with *Ezọ Isuemi* on the twenty-eighth day. This date also signifies the installation of the incoming *Ọpashi*.

Ọza sacral kingship system is such in which a nominee or successor to a deceased King will first have his political status and social position authenticated and legitimized through recourse to oracular divination in order to gain the consent and approval of *Oshukunu Ọpashi* and *Ehọ Ọza*. The *Ọbu Evba* receives the sacred mandate through the divining process, announces the verdict often received with jubilation. Consequently, the *Ọkọgbe-elect* hosts the village to a royal feast. Afterwards, the *Ọkọgbe* remains confined to his house for a period (sometimes three months). During this interregnum, the new *Ọkọgbe* communes with the supernatural forces, through rituals of incorporation into the spirit world. Thus, the festivities and confinement celebrate his assumption of the office and further legitimize the institution of sacral kingship.

While the District Officer's ingenuity is somewhat plausible in this letter, it nevertheless reveals a stark ambiguity in his disguised subversion of 'tradition' and traditional authority through its reinvention, modification and integration into the colonial legal logic. Reiterating the legal-political import of the Village Head, the 'Ọnọbumẹ of Ọja', Kerr demonstrates how 'in minor disputes in Ọja and other neighbouring villages both parties must on many occasions accept settlement by the Village Head in preference to a toilsome journey to a polyglot Native Court imperfectly acquainted with the affairs of the village.'[33] At the same time, he recognizes the limitations of the imposed colonial Native Court in adjudicating certain local disputes and in providing conflict resolution sustainably. It was against this backdrop that one could better understand the subtle subversion of tradition and traditional authority. The Resident of Benin Province also recognizes the imperfection and limitations of the Native Court in dealing with all village affairs, hence his metaphorical illustration:

> The machinery of Native Administration has been assembled in most of the Province and it is in course of being tested and run in. A few parts require modification or renovation for the machine was not constructed entirely with new parts. As with all new machinery it is unwise to give it the full throttle until the machine has been thoroughly run in. Youth is all for speed and finds irksome the brake of conservatism applied by his elders. The administration has attempted, with some degree of success to find the happy mean.[34]

To augment the limitations and amplify the colonial legal authority (Native Court system) on the one hand, and at the same time undermine and minify village (traditional) authority, the district officer proposes a ragged fusion of traditional and colonial legal systems in a way that further revealed legal, sociopolitical and economic undercurrents. As Kerr opines,

> If the village authorities could be constituted modified 'D' grade courts for the trial of civil cases up to perhaps £5 upon re-organisation it would remove a sense of degradation from them, and would have the effect of increasing the court fees, of which the decrease is a disquieting symptom at the present time. Further, it might appear that this would be of educative value, and promote association into larger courts, when the limitations of the small ones were apparent, better than if this intimate touch had not been made. Such recognition would, in my opinion, provide the best solution at Ọja, by going far to remove the prime cause of Ọnọbumẹ's insubordination in the past, and by giving him an opportunity of acquitting himself well in a smaller capacity within his own village before recommending him for higher authority by removing his suspension from Ọsọsọ Native Court. I have no doubt that in these circumstances he would do well.[35]

To validate his point, Kerr argues, 'Failing any immediate prospect of this, the only ground for recommending the removal of his suspension would appear to be the subjection resulting from his imprisonment.' He notes further,

> 'Fifteen cases of which both parties come from Ọja, have been tried in Ọsọsọ Native Court since Ọnọbumẹ's return in December 1933 as compared with sixteen for the whole of last year when he was absent, and tax has been paid by the village twice since his return without trouble. Ọnọbumẹ appears to be doing his best in the circumstances, and is not likely to give further trouble if re-instated.[36]

One can deduce some important points from this statement. While Ọnọbumẹ's actual date and duration of incarceration is uncertain, it is clear that his release was in December 1933. It is possible to glean from this that the duration of Ọnọbumẹ's incarceration was probably one year. Contrastingly, the number of cases from Ọja arraigned before the Ọsọsọ Native Court were more robust since Ọnọbumẹ's return, than during his absence. It makes about ten months from Ọnọbumẹ's return in December 1933 until the dating of Kerr's letter in October 1934. The statement 'as compared with sixteen for the whole of last year when he was absent' in a sense points to the duration of Ọnọbumẹ's absence. His physical presence and the shorter period since his return makes much economic sense to the colonial administration with less trouble or resistance to the payment of village *Oso obọ* (white man's tax), 'tax has been paid by the village twice since his return without trouble'.

It is probable that prior to his imprisonment, Ọnọbumẹ already served as a member of Ọsọsọ Native Court and was suspended as a result of his alleged insubordination, 'desire for independence both for himself and for the village', and 'passive opposition' to the coloniality of power. Thus, his reinstatement and recognition as 'Ọnọbumẹ of Ọja', coupled with 'removing his suspension from Ọsọsọ Native Court' was considered probably a recipe for boosting colonial revenue, earnings and economic windfall. A brief backdrop of the complexity of colonial politico-economy and revenue generating mechanisms below will help to underscore the severity with which the colonial regime viewed Ọnọbumẹ's perceived offences.

By 1939, there were 204 Native Courts including 96 Village Courts, and 11 Native Treasuries in Benin Province.[37]

> The assumption of financial responsibility by Native Authorities is of utmost importance to the progress of Native Administration. But with a large number of small units in the Province it is impracticable even were it desirable, to give

them all separate Treasuries which are clearly uneconomical and increase the burden of local administration. Interest in Treasuries varies from clan to clan.[38]

Apart from Benin, none of the Native Administrations have large surplus funds and many of them have difficulty in making both ends meet. The flat rates of tax remained unchanged and are 7/- in Benin Division, 6/- in Ishan and Asaba Divisions, and from 4/3d to 7/- in Kukuruku Division.[39] The comparative figures for civil and criminal cases heard in the Native Courts were 21,516 in 1948, 22,381 in 1949 and 23,972 in 1950. These cases generated corresponding revenue figures based on fines and fees averaging at £24,426 in 1948, £26,883 in 1949 and £29,455 in 1950, respectively.[40] The Senior District Officer, Kukuruku Division, wrote, 'A further increase in the flat rate tax and a considerable increase in the amount of Schedule II Tax collected in each of the three Native Authorities have made the financial position more secure. The three Native Authorities of the Kukuruku Division raised their flat rate tax from 10/- to 11/-.'[41]

The slump in the timber trade adversely affected the Benin Native Administration forestry revenue. There was a small deficit in the last financial year, but since the outbreak of war there had been increased demand for timber for export to Europe. Between 2,300 and 2,800 labourers are employed by European firms on timber exploitation, mostly in the Benin Division.[42] These are housed in temporary quarters during the period of exploitation of a particular area. The Forestry Department Working Plan was introduced and 'one of its objects was adequate control of exploitation'.[43] The creation of forest reserves and the popularity of plantation cultivation necessitate a more economical use of land for food crops, for in some villages there is already justifiable complaint of land shortage.[44] Substantial progress made in forestry reservation by the Provincial and Native Authorities often met with vigorous opposition and resulted in a large number of land disputes, especially where forests were given out abruptly without due consent of the owners. Some of the land dispute cases had to be determined under the Inter-Tribal Boundaries Settlement Ordinance.[45]

The Forest Officer, Benin, Mr. R. J. Dewar reports,

> During the first seven months of the year (1950) the demand for timber increased particularly for medium hardwoods like Obeche, Agba, Abura. This demand is a result of the soft wood shortage in the United Kingdom … Nevertheless, the number of trees felled in Benin Division was well over the 20,000 mark, and revenue for the calendar year was £89,888, as compared with £72,952 in 1949.[46]

The District Officer, Benin Division, reports, 'The financial position continues to be very strong, Forestry Revenue again exceeding all expectations. Total Forest revenue for the year amounted to £89,676 as against approximately £70,000 for 1949.'[47] Comparative figures of forest revenue, inclusive of fees and royalties, for the rest of the Province were £15,986 in 1948, £23,653 in 1949 and £25,511 in 1950, respectively. Outside Benin Division nearly £49,000 had been collected by the end of the year out of a total assessment of £63,000, Kukuruku Division being within £1,300 of its £22,303.[48] Such colossal revenue generated annually from tree felling and forest revenue enriched the provincial administration and colonial metropole, while at the same time impoverishing the local communities socio-economically and resulting in environmental degradation.

In 1954, Kukuruku Division continued to witness an upsurge in the amount of tree felling as a steady source of revenue, for export and for local consumption. Forest revenue for the period January–November in the areas of the three District Councils amounted to Akoko-Edo (£1415), Ivbiosakon (£2666) and Etsako (£3065),[49] respectively. Native authorities continued to collect their own revenue outside forest reserves. In October 1954 when the administration of Native Courts passed into the hands of the Divisional Council, the Native Courts remained a stable source and conduit for revenue generation to the colonial authorities. According to the District Officer, Kururuku Division,

> It cannot be said that the courts are efficient and dissatisfaction is probably more widespread than is realised. The total number of cases heard in 1954 was 4,247, both civil and criminal, a decrease of 706 compared with the figure for 1953. The large increases in the rates of court fees introduced in May 1954 have undoubtedly resulted in many disputes being adjudicated by Village Heads out of court and the Chairman of the Divisional Council reports that his council is taking active steps to eradicate this practice. Court revenue has increased from £8,562 in 1953 to £10,252 in 1954.[50]

Colonial revenue drive was also on palm produce and cocoa in addition to rubber. The rate of production and sales increased exponentially. For instance, comparative figures of provincial total tonnages for oil and kernels were from 17,294 in 1948 to 20,005 in the case of palm kernels and from 2,940 to 4,371 for palm oil.[51] Increase in the price of cocoa, combined with spectacular rubber profits, shows an increase in production and the fact that the quality has been both high throughout the Province. Statistics of main crop totals in Benin Province for 1948-9 and 1949–50 were 1,510 and 1,590, while in Kukuruku and Ishan Divisions the numbers 1,241 in 1948-9 and 1,582 in 1949–50, respectively.

In contrast to this remarkable boom in production, sales and export to the UK, the Resident notes on imports,

> For the first time for many years there was no break-down in petrol distribution. Kerosene and flour supplies were not always adequate; cement and corrugated iron became almost unobtainable towards the end of the year save at fantastic prices ... There has been signs of a general fall in prices in 1949, but almost everything was dearer by the end of 1950.[52]

Overall, the provincial administration found it both necessary and expedient to exert rather closer administrative control of the Native Authorities, particularly in financial affairs.[53] All three Federal Councils have been active over legislation – Timber Revenue Collection Rules, Birth and Marriage Registration Rules and Building Rules – and over matters connected with staff conditions of service.

Having provided this brief background above, I shall now return to how the District Officer, through his ingenuity, won the hearts of his superiors with his intelligence report on the Ọnọbumẹ of Ọja. The administrative position of a District Officer, such as Kerr, has some weight and *gravitas* within the colonial system to the extent that the incredulity of his superiors to his logic is out of the question. In order to circumvent any trepidation, Kerr ended his letter with a *proviso* that might intimidate Ọnọbumẹ for any further intransigence towards his District Head, to the Kukuruku Native Administration and to Administrative Officers. He concludes, "If the solution suggested in paragraph 13 [*sic* the in-text quote above] cannot be adopted I suggest that Ọnọbumẹ might be informed that the removal of his suspension will be considered in a year's time if he continues to keep the village in a state of law and order."[54] Undoubtedly, such a contingency as deferring his suspension would give Ọnọbumẹ little wiggle room to consider the best option as a face-saving strategy before his people, but also as a useful revamp of his status and credibility within the colonial Native Court authority. The premise was probably that Ọnọbumẹ would feel deeply humbled, devoid of any choice but acquiesce to their stringent demands. The District Officer's ingenuity paid off when the Acting Resident of Benin Province gave his express consent to the proposal that a 'D' Grade Court would in all probability be the best solution, although giving a caveat that an intelligence report will first be required.[55] The Acting Resident may have found Kerr's admonition and probationary tone compelling and congenial to the subversive colonial strategy. Resident Dickins concurs,

In regard to the last paragraph of your letter under reference I am inclined to think that Ọnọbumẹ might be made a provisional Court member now and be recognised provisionally as Village Head, after being warned that he will only retain this position if he behaves himself and that the least cause for complaint will again result in his suspension.[56]

In this instance, to 'behave himself' is pertaining to Ọnọbumẹ's perceived civil obedience and a promise of uninterrupted facilitation of *Oso obọ* (white man's tax) into colonial government's treasury. In his quest to fulfil the provincial headquarters' mandate to providing an intelligence report, the District Officer visited Ọza on a fact-finding mission and held a meeting with the Ọnọbumẹ and his Village Council. In the intelligence report,[57] Kerr refers to the Resident's letter of 19 January: 'I have the honour to inform you that I visited Ọja on the 13th of May and held a meeting. There were present Ọnọbumẹ and the following elders: Egboje, Usiojeka, Ogbebu, Epekeme, Uyonla, Ajegbe and representatives of the others, who were either sick or dead. Also a great number of old and young men and women.' By listing the participants in attendance with Ọnọbumẹ and the Village Council, Kerr gave it credibility and authenticity as a consultative, representative village meeting that attained a quorum. As Kerr reports,

> It is clear that Ọnọbumẹ is village head and cannot be replaced during his lifetime. He has given a great deal of trouble in the past. His power in the village is absolute and depends apparently on the Ọja *ju-ju* [Ọja divinity], which is not only recognised as a great swearing place throughout the Division (*sic.* Kukuruku) but is feared so much that nobody would venture to disobey it. The elders are a spineless lot and evidently the whole village lives in fear of the *ju-ju*.[58]

Here, District Officer Kerr highlights the centrality of traditional kingship institution while also underscoring the intersectionality of the Village Head, the *Ọpashi Ọza* and *ju-ju*, divinity. *Ju-ju*[59] was an invented, pejorative colonial term to characterize the indigenous African belief systems, thus demonizing them. The '*Ọja Ju-ju*' on which the *Ọpashi Ọza* apparently depends is *Ehọ Ọza*. The *Ọbu Evba*, diviner, consults the deity prior, during and at the death of an incumbent *Ọpashi*. *Ehọ Ọza* also has the insignia of justice and fair play hence it is both recognised as a great swearing place but is feared so much that nobody will venture to disobey it. Ọza people revere *Ehọ Ọza*, the divinity within whose sacred shrine oath swearing, vows and covenant making are prevalent. Most issues that involved crimes, corruption, immorality, incest, premature deaths, theft, quarrels, family conflicts and acts of misdemeanour are brought before *Ehọ Ọza* for adjudication and conflict resolution. Anyone who dares to consult

EhọỌza to seek equity, justice, redress and refuge must approach the deity cautiously, with clean hands and no blemish. Ọza people venerate Ehọ Ọza but at the same time find the deity awe-inspiring and dreadful for its perceived potency in conveying instantaneous justice to appellants against the offender and the miscreant. This is often consequential in unprecedented death, mental disorder and calamitous conditions.

In spite of the District Officer's awkward language, a somewhat misplaced sarcasm employed in characterizing 'the elders as "a spineless lot" and evidently the whole village lives in fear of the ju-ju', Kerr exemplifies the reverential awe, deep *angst* and veneration that Ehọ Ọza inspires among Ọza people and their neighbours. Thus, the mere mention of the deity's name often results in anxious circumspection and trepidation among the people. In the same vein, Ọza people hold the position of Ọpashi Ọza in high esteem, revered, and in some cases formidable and overbearing. As Kerr observes during the meeting at Ọnọbumẹ's palace,

> Everybody said they would like Ọnọbumẹ to be re-appointed to the Court. If a second man is appointed, they are unanimous for Lawani, the prospective village head when Ọnọbumẹ dies. If Ọnọbumẹ is not appointed, he suggested Osogori. All the elders agreed but I think largely because they did not dare to disagree. (This is only based on the look on their faces and the fact that some of them told me at Unguyami last month, that they did not want him).[60]

This stark observation is very revealing of the people's perception of Ọnọbumẹ's power, influence and respect accorded him, to the effect that any public opposition will be tantamount to abomination. As Kerr observes, some of the elders disagreed on his reappointment to the court and had privately disclosed this to him in confidence. Nonetheless, such elders dared to demur in the presence of Ọpashi Ọza as this will be likened to treason, insubordination to traditional authority and by extension sacrilegious to Ehọ Ọza. Ọza people will also interpret such a dissenting voice as conspiratorial with the colonial regime and as a traitor of Ọza village. Moreover, Ọnọbumẹ was possibly thinking ahead of intended and unintended consequences of his membership reinstatement to Ọsọsọ Native Court. While there was consensus about Ọnọbumẹ's re-appointment to the Court, 'if a second man is appointed, they are unanimous for Lawani, the prospective village head when Ọnọbumẹ dies. If Ọnọbumẹ is not appointed, he suggested Osogori.' To this suggestion for an additional member or alternative membership as successor in the Native Court upon his demise, Ọnọbumẹ differed for undisclosed reasons. His preference for Osogori instead of Lawani smacks of hubris, umbrage and rivalry in that it deflects from a routinized rotational system of leadership within the Osuruka kindred.

Although the reasons and circumstances surrounding the incarceration of the 'Onobume of Oja' were inexhaustible in Kerr's letter, his imprisonment nevertheless generated mutual suspicion and considerable distrust that engendered further conflictual relationship within the Osuruka kindred. Some oral sources attribute Onobume's incarceration to a perceived betrayal by the Lawani Ogundare to the colonial government. It was been alleged that the imprisonment was a fine ploy to oust Onobume's leadership, against the backdrop that Lawani Ogundare had become literate in the meantime while working for the colonial administration, serving as interpreter for the colonial establishment. In a private family communication, D. S. Lawani remarks, 'The recent revelation from Pa Adebayo Onobume was that our grandfather Chief Ogundare Lawani imprisoned their father Chief Onobume twice and efforts to get at least one person from the Lawani's family imprisoned failed'[61] So far, there is no corroborating evidence to support such allegation of a betrayal of trust. As these oral sources further allege, Onobume had vowed to revenge what he considers a treachery and familial betrayal. Thus, a conspiracy of silence ensuing from this partly resulted in the withholding of the rotational chieftaincy much later when Unuanoyoka Onobume (Ugbonokua) appointed Oshioma, in this instance as a regent, a decision that temporarily truncated the rotational system that would have ushered in Lawani Ogundare (Okoko). As we shall demonstrate below, it was this poignant controversy that later triggered and exacerbated the legal imbroglio that characterized Oza chieftaincy succession for over three decades.

Nonetheless, the District Officer appeared persuasive in presenting a coherent and logical intelligence report to the Resident and Provincial Administration in Benin City. He weighed carefully the pros and cons of Onobume's re-appointment to the Court, deposition from the village headship or banishment from the village, against the backdrop of implications for sustainable colonial governance. Kerr's cautious optimism led to his rhetorical stance:

> The question is whether Onobume's conviction should operate as an absolute bar to re-appointment to the Court. It is useless trying to depose him from the village headship: it could only be effected by his banishment or by destroying the ju-ju [a deep rock pool] by blasting and by force of arms. This would plunge the village into years of strife but would eventually be for its good as being the only way to purge it. But with no concrete evidence of the ju-ju being harmful

such drastic action could not be justified. Nor is there any ground for banishing Ọnọbumẹ. Since Ọnọbumẹ is unanimously recognised as village head and will continue to be so recognised, I think the best thing is to give him an opportunity starting again with a clean sheet. I recommend his appointment and Lawani's to be members of Ọsọsọ Native Court. I broached the subject of re-organisation the very question which precipitated the incidents reported in my memorandum M.P.No.44/1922 of the 17th of December 1931. I invited the elders to think about it at their leisure and to let me know when they felt a desire the Okulosor Clan to be taken in hand.[62]

The District Officer infers that Ọnọbumẹ's conviction should serve as a punitive measure rather than as a forbiddance to his reappointment into Ọsọsọ Native Court. He reckoned that his ousting would be ineffectual against the backdrop that Ọza tradition recognizes replacement of an incumbent Village Head only at death. Dethronement of the Village Head will flout tradition and the people may not recognize any unconventional reinstatement. Even expulsion from the village or a resort to iconoclasm and brutal force would be implausible. As he reckoned, either choice of action would likely result in further crisis, 'this would plunge the village into years of strife'. While he pondered that this might be the only way 'to purge it', it nevertheless sounded ludicrous to suggest that this 'would eventually be for its good'. The fear of the unknown, the awe and potency of the 'ju-ju', and the capabilities served as a possible deterrent. As the District Officer remarks, 'but with no concrete evidence of the ju-ju being harmful such drastic action could not be justified'. On the one hand, he strongly endorsed the reinstallation of Ọnọbumẹ, while with a dint of a diplomacy Kerr proposed the appointment of Ọnọbumẹ and Lawani to the Native Court, as if to circumvent Ọnọbumẹ's perceived cynical attitude and partisanship.

The District Officer's mention of 'the subject of re-organisation the very question which precipitated the incidents' is a matter of conjecture. It is unclear what incidents he is referring to here, nor what would need a reorganization, although it is suggestive of a conflictual leadership situation. Nonetheless, the District Officer displayed some diplomacy by inviting 'the elders to think about it at their leisure and to let him know when they felt a desire the Okulosor Clan to be taken in hand'. First, the District Officer broached a sensitive subject, in order to leverage and generate a conversation by Ọza elders and the Okulosor ([sic] Okurosho) Clan. Such an invitation 'to think about it at their leisure' demonstrated a somewhat lack of exigency of the matter, a sense of insecurity, but more importantly specious relevancy to the coloniality of power. After all, what seemed to matter most to the colonial authorities is a steady, unimpeded flow of taxes to the colonial treasury rather than who becomes the leader of the village. That meant that any perceived fragility of traditional authority would raise alarm, if and only when it potentially subverts the political economy of the colonial enterprise.

Nonetheless, the District Officer hints at an emerging or already existing crisis in leadership, familial rivalry and power contestation. Whether we speculate on the issue of chieftaincy, membership or representation at Ọsọsọ Native Court, what is important is that by asking for the intervention of the elders and 'Okulosor' clan, the District Officer feigned the pertinence, congruity and capabilities of traditional authority within the hierarchies of colonial power strategy. In other words, he teased out how traditional authority and indigenous power structures could be a boon or bane to the coloniality of power. It is more probable that Kerr insinuated that the elders and 'Okulosor' clan are in the best position to deal with any undercurrents of discontent concerning Ọza chieftainship by reorganizing it. It is no wonder then that the District Officer took ample time to interrogate and report on the intricacies of Ọza traditional authority and power dynamics.

The Benin Province Resident, in his general commentary on the native administration affairs, observed some apprehension felt by local people towards traditional authority as reported in Benin Division and elsewhere in the Province. According to the Resident,

> Under the indigenous system of government the common people were members of one or other of a series of guilds each of which was a territorial and administrative unit which managed its affairs with a minimum of outside interferences. Modern progress has brought in its train the virtual disappearances of the guild, and there has been nothing to replace it.[63]

In the specific case of the Oba of Benin as the Native Authority of the Benin Division, he was assisted by an advisory Council of some fifty title holders. He notes that although it has a traditional basis and contained a number of educated members, it failed to inspire popular confidence. According to the Resident, the main reason for its failure is that it represented only the titled and wealthy classes. 'In the result the progressive elements found that they had no voice in the administration and clamoured for reform.'[64]

In his intelligence report,[65] District Officer Kerr detailed names, titles and families of the members and the respective quarters of the Village Council with which he held a meeting during his fact-finding visit. The table below indicates the order as it appeared during the official visit to Ọza probably in 1931.[66]

	Name	Title	Family*a	Quarter
1.	Ọnọbumẹ	Ọkọgbe	Ọsuruka	Ọdun
2.	Asogbe	Otaru	Obuese*	Imejere
3.	Egboje	Oshimatu	Iviovie*	Odosame*
4.	Usiojeka	Ogbodo	Akpara	Odosame*
5.	Ogbebu	Ijagun	Obuese*	Ọdun
6.	Epekeme	Uga	Ufeshi	Ọdun
7.	Uyonla	Okora*	Obuele*	Ọdun
8.	Ijeru	Ude	Ufeshi	Ọdun
9.	Ajegbe	Oboro	Ọsuruka	Ọdun
10.	Ahareyo	Ogisua	Ukpi	Odora
11.	Obeyuama	Uka	Iviovie*	Odora

a'Family' as mentioned here is correctly used in this chapter as 'kindred' or paternal lineage.

The acting District Officer's letter noted that the order of seniority except for the Ọkọgbe, appears to vary, to some extent at least, with the seniority in the Council of the individual holder, and there appears to be some uncertainty about it among the members themselves. He also observed that there were additional family titles of less significance that were unlisted in his official letter. Although the title belongs to a particular family, the holder performs its functions for the whole village. The letter notes, 'The Ọsuruka appears to be the leading family in the village in fact as well as in theory,' and then highlighted in the letter, the functions of Oshimata, Otaru, Ọga (Uga) and Uka as examples to underscore their importance, 'Oshimata – sacrifices a she-goat every year to the ju-ju [deity] of the River Ilashia [Lake Ẹrẹsha] from which the village gets its drinking water. Otaru – Priest of Oshiegia ju-ju for sticks of titled men after death. Ọga [Uga] – performs burial of titled men. Uka – introduces the new yams.'67 This partly underscores Ọza indigenous governance based on a hierarchical system in which Ọpashi Ọza, the Ọkọgbe who sits at the apex of government, rules with the support of Eja, in which each member performs specific functions. Each respective Eja is responsible to Ọpashi Ọza, the Village Council, Ọsuruka royal kindred and the village as a whole.

The fact that a family dispute or an unhealthy rivalry may have ensued and lingered within the Ọsuruka royal kindred, a development with a tendency to undercut the colonial political economy, necessitates the District Officers' soliciting 'the elders to think about it at their leisure' and inform him 'when they felt a desire the Okulosor Clan to be taken in hand'. This perceptible occurrence may have lingered as a serious cause of disagreement to the following decades. G. K. Monro, District Officer, Kukuruku Division, aptly observes, 'The predilection among some clans for village head disputes at times assumes an unreasonable importance in the minds of their people and has provided a test of the ability of the District Councils to mediate.'[68] He notes further,

> The origins of these disputes may be traced to three causes: (a) family rivalry (b) friction between progressive and traditional elements (c) uncertainty as to the definition of 'senior village head' for the purpose of filling the seat of traditional member on the District Council. Each of the District Councils has proved its competence to settle most of these disputes ... the other Councils have achieved the same result through ad hoc Commissions of Enquiry. This procedure has in many cases rendered unnecessary the interference of an administrative officer.[69]

In the case of Ọza chieftaincy feud, family rivalry seems to have been the primary cause, much more than other secondary motivations. The interventions through the District Council, ad hoc commissions of enquiry did not appear to be successful in weathering the storm of Ọza leadership crisis. On 21 August 1961, an inquiry on 'Ojah Chieftaincy' was conducted by Chief Idogu II the Olokpe of Okpe, Yaya of Somorika, Oba of Unẹmẹ Nekhua at the behest of District Officer Kerr. The letter, 'How Ojah Is Ruled' sent by the Ojah Royal Family to the Chieftaincy Committee of Akoko Oke District Council, Igarra,[70] foregrounded the royal genealogical tradition and honed in on the root of the leadership crisis. The letter states, *inter alia*:

> In the past, Ojah is ruled by Ọsuruka family. In this family, there are three titles plus one that is rotational. 1. Okaku 2. Ogone 3. Obuoro, the fourth is Ọkọgbe ... Furthermore, the following houses in the family use to hold either Ọkọgbe or Saiki or both together if the whole family agreed to do so. 1. Unuayuoka – late Ọnọbumẹ 2. Ifiabeka – Late Chief Lawani 3. Ọkọkọr whose turn it is now. 4. Oshiọma ruled when there was no appropriate person to rule in the other houses and he being a popular member of the family, was allowed to rule. He now claims a separate house in the ruling family. Though not very bad, but the house can be merged with any of the three because he also not own any other preceding title. However, I am not very particular about the house yet. All I am after is that when one is ruling one chooses one's assistant from the next house who eventually takes up the throne after one's death. In case of death and thereby left the village head without assistant, then any popular person can be chosen to rule or hold the title of Ọkọgbe and Saiki together.[71]

However imprecise and controversial the above details may be, they nevertheless accentuated Ọsuruka kindred as the royal lineage, with chieftaincy titles that are rotational. He identified the titles of Ọkọgbe and Saiki[72] and the simultaneity of positions held by two houses within the Ọsuruka kindred. His emphasis was on the fact that once one family lineage house held the title such as Ọkọgbe, the second title 'Saiki' naturally falls on the second family lineage house and vice versa. This reinforced the rotational system between family lineages within the Ọsuruka. An incumbent Ọkọgbe cannot pass on the *Agua Ọpashi* (king's crown) directly to his son or within the same family house during his lifetime or after his demise. The *Agua* must rotate to the second family lineage and then return to the former. In fact, the letter from Ọjah royal family mirrors Oshiọma's reign here as an aberration, a trajectory that is however emendable. The letter concludes:

> If there is struggle as it is now, then one will be Ọkọgbe while the other will be Saiki, (in reference to Unuayuoka and Oshiọma) who will be recognised as the village head. Precedent: Oshiọma was responsible for Egia and home or domestic welfare while the then Saiki was recognized locally, tribally and as nationally. Therefore, Chief Sam Ọkọkọr was Daodu to the late Chief Lawani of Ọjah. He should be recognized as the village head of Ọjah till the prescribed Authority approves of it for payment and other necessaries.[73]

The rationale of the argument presented here seems logical against the backdrop of the premises presented previously in the letter. It seemed to suggest a convergence or complementarity of Unuayuoka and Oshiọma's hiatus as rulers within Ọza sociopolitical history, albeit a terse life span.

The royal contestation and controversy that embroiled Ọsuruka kindred continued even after Nigeria's attainment of political independence from the British regime. Benin was administered as part of the Niger Coast Protectorate, which later became the Protectorate of Southern Nigeria in 1900. From 1906, Southern Nigeria was administered as three main provinces, Western, Central and Eastern, along with the Lagos colony with which it had been merged that year. The old Central province of Southern Nigeria was split into the Benin and Warri provinces. Thus, the Edo-speaking peoples were mainly located in the Central Province of Southern Nigeria. The protectorates and colonies of Northern and Southern Nigeria were later amalgamated on 1 January 1914 to create the political entity, Nigeria (Thomas 1910a; Lugard 1920). Benin Province now came under the Midwest region (with Benin as the regional or state capital) within the new political configuration until the creation of Bendel

State of Nigeria. On 29 March 1963 the Federal Ministry of Internal Affairs of Nigeria was given the responsibility for the organization of a referendum to decide whether a new region should be created out of the Western region in a subregion called the Mid-West. In June 1963, the Mid-Western Region was formed as a new regional administrative Division of Nigeria, as an agglomeration of Benin and Delta provinces of the Western Region. The status of the region was changed to a state on 27 May 1967. On 17 March 1976, the Mid-Western state was renamed Bendel State, retaining its capital in Benin City. Bendel State was again subdivided into the Delta and Edo states on 27 August 1991.

During the post-independence era, the Bendel State Ministry of Local Government and Chieftaincy Affairs commissioned an additional inquiry into Ojah chieftaincy, leading to a hearing at the Customary Court, Dagbala, on 3 June 1970. The Osuruka family vehemently opposed the results of this inquiry on grounds that they perceived the outcome as partisan, prejudiced and disingenuous. As they protest,

> We regret to point out that the general public of Ojah was unaware of the research conducted on 3rd June 1970, hence not well represented. Democracy becomes a sham when minority representation or rule is the order of the day ... We regret that Ojah general community was not informed. We shall, on the day of the 'Research' welcome another inquiry if the authenticity of this letter is doubted. Your reply is eagerly awaited.[74]

They objected to the assertion that one, Aseka,[75] had ruled Oza within the royal genealogical tradition. As they exclaimed, 'Aseka is tipped as to have ruled! No, no, no!' They note further,

> After consultation with the elders of the above family, it is understood that the Osuruka family live in each of the three quarters at Ojah viz. Odosami, Odun and Imiejere, as against the declaration by the present Okogbe of Ojah on June 3rd 1970 at Dagbala Customary Court that 'The Okogbe of Ojah is confined to Odun quarters alone'.[76]

To substantiate their claim, they provided in the letter a list of past and present Okogbes from different quarters of Ojah as follows: Okoko (Odosami), Anemo (Odosami), Imodibie (Odun), Ifiabeka (Odosami), Ugbonokua (Odun), Osioma (Odun), Onobume (Odun), Ogundare Lawani (Odosami) and Adeshina Onobume (Odun), respectively. This historical backdrop suggests instances of the *longue durée* of the dissension around chieftaincy succession within the

Ọsuruka kindred. Therefore, a better grasp of the antecedents and precedents of Ọza kingship myth, the royal genealogical tradition – the fissure, friction and change that characterize the process – are expedient if we are to appreciate the complexities of the legal imbroglios that followed from the early 1990s onwards. To this we shall now turn.

5

Kingship myth, leadership succession and legal imbroglios (1991-2011)

Oral traditions suggest that the earliest known royal lineage that held the *Opashi* (King) Okogbe chieftaincy title in Oza was the Obueri kindred. However, the status quo changed when the reigning *Opashi Oza*, Imodafe of the Obueri kindred, as an act of benevolence, handed over the chieftaincy office to his son-in-law, Okoko from the Osuruka kindred. For indeterminate reasons, Imodafe's immediate family neglected and failed to accord him good care while he was indisposed. Some local sources indicate that Imodafe was sick of an infectious disease, leprosy.[1] Instead, his son-in-law, Okoko, took proper care of him during his illness providing food and attending to his health, necessary to sustain his life. His abandonment by his extended family left *Opashi* Imodafe aggrieved and humiliated. Consequently, Imodafe made breathtaking decisions, on his deathbed, that were to change Oza kingship institution in profound ways thereafter.

First, Imodafe bequeathed the throne to Okoko, his son-in-law, an unprecedented succession scheme that altered the genealogy, thus tilting the royal family lineage from Obueri to Osuruka kindred. Imodafe's umbrage and reprisal had both intended and unintended consequences on the Obueri family as they lost the sole prerogative as the royal family lineage. Second, Imodafe employed an expletive in a somewhat vindictive manner, invoking an 'ancestral curse' that any member of the Obueri family who contests Okoko's enthronement or plots to regain the royal chieftaincy title will have sudden, premature death befall him. Several oral accounts corroborated the claim that all subsequent attempts by Obueri family to usurp the kingly throne or arrogate the chieftaincy title resulted in mysterious deaths. Such unprecedented mortality served as a deterrent to further claims from Obueri as no one dared such a calamitous end. Thus, the Osuruka kindred assumed and sustained a bequeathed genealogical royal tradition and new chieftaincy lineage and titles subsequently. Oral sources point to the inception of Ọkọkọ chieftaincy title into Ọsuruka kindred, from which two main family ruling houses emerged as Ọkọkọ ruling house and the Ugbọnọkua ruling house located in different quarters in Ọza. While such a narrative established the origin myth of Ọsuruka royal kindred, even this royal genealogical tree of Ọbueri kindred and its transition to the Ọsuruka kindred was not devoid of contestation, as we shall see below in the legal controversy that ensued from the early 1990s onwards.

Oral sources and local history generally affirm that there are seven paternal kindred in Ọza. Although the Ọsuruka kindred produces *Ọpashi Ọza* through two lineages of Ọkọkọ and Ugbọnọkua, the representative of each kindred within the village council has a chiefly title attached to it, depicting the specific function and the authority with which he was vested (cf. table in Chapter 4). In the case of Ọsuruka kindred, the titles are Ọkọgbe and Obuoro. Thus, the Ọkọgbe title became the most important chieftaincy title in Ọza as it is the title of the village head.[2] Chieftaincy is rotational between the Ọkọkọ and Ugbọnọkua family lineages within the Ọsuruka kindred. Also rotationally based is the residential quarters from which the ruling *Ọpashi Ọza* emanates. Originally, the Ọkọkọ ruling house inhabited Odoshami quarters while Ugbọnọkua ruling house inhabited Ọdun quarters. Thus, the Ọkọgbe's as *Ọpashi Ọza* emerged from the alternate quarters[3] in a chronological order as follows: Ọkọkọ Aiyejina (Odosami), Ugbọnọkua (Ọdun), Ifiabeka (Odosami), Imodibie (Ọdun), Anemọ (Odosami), Oshiọma/Ọnọbumẹ (Ọdun), Lawani Ogundare (Odosami) and Adesina Ọnọbumẹ (Ọdun), respectively.

There is no accurate and detailed written records of the timing or duration of Ọkọgbe and their reigns in Ọza. Information gleaned from the writings of a local historian dates the reign by Ọsuruka kindred from the fourteenth century onwards.[4] This work, coupled with oral sources and court documents, provide a chronological list of Ọkọgbes though with scanty, incomplete data on the reigning years. After Imọdafẹ's (Ọbueri kindred) bequeath of the royal throne to Ọkọkọ Aiyejina's of the Ọsuruka kindred, the family elders had recourse to divination to ascertain the first beneficiary of the Ọsuruka to be crowned. The divination process resulted in the installation of Ọkọkọ Aiyejina himself as the first to be bestowed with the title of Ọkọgbe of Ọza.[5] Following Ọkọkọ's death and the completion of the burial ceremonies, the elders of Ọsuruka again consulted the oracle as to who was to succeed Ọkọkọ and the oracle approved one Ugbọnọkua, one of the elders of Ọsuruka kindred.[6] Thus, the institutionalization, rotational but not hereditary, of Ọkọkọ and Ugbọnọkua ruling houses in Ọsuruka kindred took place. 'No chieftaincy is hereditary in Ojah as it must go to another house before coming back to the previous house.'⁷ Oracular divinatory processes are central to each phase of separation, liminality and incorporation. Thus, the *Obu Evba* represents the powerhouse within which the kingship institution routinizes and mutates. However, crisis ensued in the rotational system between the reign of Anemo (Osuruka) and Unuanyoka (Ugbonokua), the next rotational ascendancy to the throne. Unuanyoka appointed Oshioma as a regent for his young son, Onobume, since he himself was going to the war front. Court documents further outlined the succession in a chronological order:

> The Okogbe title then descended in that order of rotation from Ugbonokua to Ifiabeka of Okoko then to Imodibie of Ugbonokua and back to Anemo of Okoko. After the death of Anemo the title was to go to Unuanyoka of Ugbonokua ruling house but Unuanyoka being the captain or the teacher of the Ojah army appointed one Oshoma as a regent for his young son, Onobume, before leaving for the war front. The entire people of Osuruka and Ojah protested the appointment of Oshoma as regent and Oshoma was therefore not crowned and not given the chieftaincy regalia and the Odumu earthen pot was hidden away from him by Osuruka in the bush in old Ojah-Oke. When Unuanyoka returned from the war Oshoma was on the throne but when he (Unuanyoka) died, his son, Onobume, had matured and the people of Osuruka consulted the oracle and Onobume was so chosen and crowned in place of his father and the people were happy.⁸

The defendant, Michael Onobume, confirmed through cross-examination that his grandfather Onobume was so chosen and crowned as the Okogbe during Oshioma's lifetime.⁹

This was noticeably the second interregnum within the chieftaincy institution, with the first being the royal genealogical transition from Obueri to Osuruka kindred. The second interregnum marks a period of temporal rupture and discontinuity in the routinization of two family lineages within the Osuruka. Local history attested,

> 'After Okoko and Anemo as the Okogbe's of Ojah, there was a family struggle to shift it to another quarter or household. As a result of this, the grandfather of Ekemieme Agbebu hid the *Odumu*, the traditional jar at Oyina Irobe or Ame Dania. The grandfather of Ekemieme Agbebu since then refused to stay and cultivate the family land in Odoshami because of hiding the *Odumu* jar. They fear, being worried by the ghosts (spirits) of the late Okogbes and elders of the family.'¹⁰

By virtue of the fact of concealment of the *Odumu* throughout Oshiọma's regime, it meant that he was not in custody of the chieftaincy regalia, the paraphernalia of the Ọkọgbe that legitimizes his reign. It was against this backdrop that the claim that Oshiọma ruled Ọza as a regent rather than as an Ọkọgbe becomes plausible.

Although Oshiọma's reign was short-lived, this brief hiatus represented an epochal development that would serve to internalize any future claims for a third ruling house. The rulership of Oshiọma and Ọnọbumẹ, in quick succession, provisionally altered the rotational system of the quarters as both rulers emerge from Ọdun quarters, respectively. While the exact duration of Oshiọma and Ọnọbumẹ's reign is uncertain, a local historian suggested that Ọnọbumẹ lived from 1850 to 1951 and died on 7 August 1951. Chief Lawani Ogundare Ifiabeka II (Odosami quarters) was installed on 4 September 1951, and a public outing ceremony was on 12 September 1951. Lawani Ifiabeka II died on 10 October 1960 and *asuezọ* took place on 1 November 1960.[11] Locate history also accounted for another critical episode that would have derailed the royal genealogical order. While it was the turn of Ugbọnọkua ruling house to present the next *Ọpashi*, Edu Adeshina Ọnọbumẹ Amanirimi (Baba Egbe of Catholic Church, Ojah-Oke), installed himself as Ọkọgbe on 16 October 1960 against Ọsuruka's approval. He was out for public show already on 24 October 1960. Adeshina Ọnọbumẹ ruled for thrity-one years and died on 10 April 1991 during *Ukpe* (festival). Since it was an abomination to bury a deceased *Ọpashi* during *Ukpe*, his family deferred his burial until 2–3 June 1991. *Asuezọ* for Adeshina took place on 7 June 1991.[12]

The demise of Ọkọgbe Adesina marked a major watershed in Ọza kingship institution. The post-Ọkọgbe Adesina era heralded a new historical phase of contestation that sought to obfuscate the authenticity and credibility of the sacred institution. In the following decades, disputes over the rightful successor led to court cases that literally engulfed the Ọsuruka kindred in a protracted legal quandary. On the demise of an Ọkọgbe, the oldest man in Ọsuruka is informed and he in turn conveys the news to the other elders of Ọsuruka kindred. The elders then meet and proceed with other young men to the house of the deceased Ọkọgbe to retrieve the *Ema* on an appointed day.[13] Also invited is the Apara family to identify and remove their property among the antiquities, which is a calabash. Once removed, they will store the *Ema* in a safe and neutral place for safety, pending the burial ceremonies of the late Ọkọgbe. Thereafter the elders of Ọsuruka will meet and deliberate on the modalities for selecting a new Ọkọgbe from the in-coming ruling house through *evba*. After the death of Adesina Ọnọbumẹ, there was claim that they did not adhere to this procedure and did not send or relay any message to the oldest man in Osuruka.¹⁴ Contrary to custom, as the plaintiff claimed, Lawrence Obayemi and other descendants of Oshoma in Ugbọnọkua 'secretly removed the *Ema* and kept same in the house of Paul Agbalajobi also a descendant of Oshoma'.¹⁵ All attempts by the plaintiffs to retrieve the *Ema* from him failed. 'The original *Apesu* or crown is merely placed on the head of the new *Ọkọgbe* and thereafter kept by the Ọkọkọ ruling house who has permanent custody of same.'¹⁶

On 12 June 1991, Ọkọkọ ruling house confined and crowned Jonathan Lawani as the *Ọkọgbe*. 'Although Lawani was duly selected and confined he did not have the paraphernalia of *Ọkọgbe* as same had been secretly removed by the descendants of Oshiọma and kept with one Paul Agbalajobi contrary to their traditions'.¹⁷ The Ọkọkọ ruling house sought the assistance of the police in retrieving the paraphernalia of the Ọkọgbe from Paul Agbalajobi but the police declined.¹⁸ Four days later, the Oshiọma family, with some backing from the Ugbọnọkua ruling house, also crowned Lawrence Obayemi as Ọkọgbe on 16 June 1991, thus laying claims to the throne. They were of the view that 'after the death of Adesina Ọnọbumẹ, the Ọkọgbe crown should come back to the Oshiọma line, as great grandsons of Aseka of the Osuruka kindred'.¹⁹ Thus, Lawrence Obayemi was 'selected, crowned and confined', and 'he performed the Oso festival and also caused himself to be confined contrary to their traditions'.²⁰ The Oshiọma family averred,

> Ọkọkọ was a member of the Osuruka kindred and held the title of Obuoro at the time Imodafẹ gave him the crown of Ọkọgbe. When Ọkọkọ presented the crown to his Osuruka kindred, the kindred deliberated and decided that one Aseka be crowned the Ọkọgbe because he was already old and for fear of the curse placed on the crown ... Aseka was the next oldest man in age to Ọkọkọ. After the death of Aseka the next oldest man in Osuruka was Ugbọnọkua and he took the title. After his death Ifiabekhai took the title and these first three holders of the title in Osuruka constitute the three ruling houses which exist in Osuruka today.²¹

This narrative charted a royal genealogical trajectory, in some respects anomalous to the historical narrative presented by the larger Osuruka kindred. While both traditions concur on the transmutation of the royal chieftaincy lineage from Ọbuẹri kindred to Osuruka kindred through Ọkọkọ, they nevertheless differ on the genealogy within the Osuruka kindred. The earlier traced historically from Ọbuẹri kindred to a dyadic – two ruling houses – Ọkọkọ-Ugbọnọkua family lineages, while the other posit a different slant, a triumvirate, three ruling houses, from Ọbueri kindred, that is Aseka-Ugbọnọkua-Ifiabekhai, respectively. The royal Ọkọkọ family house argued to the contrary that 'Oshiọma is not a member of the Ọsuruka Royal kindred but rather hailed from Ibiovie kindred of Ojah'. The Ọkọkọ family lineage refuted Oshiọma family claims' to Ọsuruka royal genealogical history, arguing,

> The grand-father of Oshiọma who was variously called Oshiozobo or Oshiojobo is from Ibiovie kindred. He wanted to perform a festival called Agbe in Ibiovie kindred but because there were more important members of the kindred who did not have the means to perform the festival Oshiozobo was not allowed to perform it because they were jealous of him. He then approached Ifiabekha his friend who was Ọkọgbe in Ọsuruka at that time. Ifiabekhai accommodated him and allowed him to perform the Agbe festival in Ọsuruka as a tenant in Ọsuruka just like the Osu, Afẹkhe, and Osobo in Ọsuruka. They are not entitled to the Ọkọgbe chieftaincy title in Ọsuruka.[22]

The defendants held on to their assertion that Oshiọma was the grandson of Aseka of Ọsuruka kindred. They disclaimed any blood relationship with Ibiovie or any other kindred in Ojah, and that Oshiojobo, Oshiọma's father at no point performed the Agbe festival since this was unknown to Ọsuruka. They also contended that 'Oshiọma was not a regent and he ruled as the sixth Ọkọgbe and when he died Ugbọnọkua ruling house took over'.[23] They maintained further that Oshiọma was crowned according to tradition and the *Ema* was not hidden from him. The defendants claimed, in an astonishing manner, that there has never been dispute over the succession to Ọkọgbe since inception.[24]

Nonetheless, the successive coronation of two Ọkọgbes in Ọza within the same week was an unprecedented development that generated a very tensile atmosphere, tantamount to creating communal discord and civil strife. The tension that the situation brought about was prevalent to the extent that it threatened peace and tranquillity, generated an astonishing number of duels, but also increasingly polarized Ọza along at least two major opposing sides, depending on which family you pledge allegiance and loyalty. This scenario resulted in a quandary thus necessitating an urgency in which individuals, community and family groups made interventions and mediations towards averting an imminent hostility, belligerence and internal strife. There were a number of interventions within Ọza suing for peace and reconciliation. Most visible among these arbitrations was the role of Ọza Youth Association (OYA), Ọza Community Development Movement (OCDM), Ọza Solidarity Movement,

Ojah (OSMO)[25] and the peace and reconciliation meeting at the instance of Jolly Ashore, then proprietor of Joli Farms Limited Company.

Following Obayemi's installation, Joli Ashore summoned a peace and reconciliation meeting in his house to attempt to resolve the chieftaincy dispute. Although his intentionality, personal motivations and partisanship were unclear at this time, his proclivity soon became translucent, thus exacerbating and further stoking the conflictual situation. By disguising as a much-needed arbiter between the 'duelling camps', Ashore attempted to broker a fragile peace between the warring family factions. He demonstrated amazing ingenuity at the meeting by not betraying his complacency, close acquaintance and long-term friendship with Lawrence Obayemi. At the same time, he posed as a credible adjudicator masked with a somewhat neutral tone, devoid of much sentiment. He seemed to have managed to sway representatives of the Okoko Ruling House to commit to inaugurating a third ruling house (Oshioma) and communicating the decision to the Divisional Police Officer (DPO) as a reconciliatory gesture and guarantee for peace.

His actions, good or egregious as they may have seemed, left many people intensely irritated and frustrated. This somewhat duplicitous mediation was consequential as the spark that ignited a conundrum, an inflection point in the longue durée of the chieftaincy melee. On 18 June 1991, the Okoko ruling house were strategically discreet in a letter titled 'Ruling in Osuruka Family' to the DPO, Divisional Police Office at Igarra. They seized on the opportunity to enlighten the security officials about Oza royal genealogical tradition and rehashed their claim as successors to the village headship. Inadvertently, the Okoko royal family betrayed their naiveté and unbridled restraint. Nevertheless, how preposterous was it that only one of the warring royal family houses but not the other attended such a crucial meeting meant to broker peace? Why were the signatories to the letter only from Okoko ruling house, but not Ugbonokua and even members of the Oshoma family? Presumably, the Okoko ruling house may not have seen the awkwardness and subterfuge in such an arrangement. In the end, they felt very exasperated realizing that Ashore had hoodwinked them.

In their quest for a convoluted truce, the Okoko ruling house had hastened to capitulate or, as they claimed, 'were lured' to concede inventing a third ruling house. Their rationale was that by simply agreeing to the scheme of a third ruling house, it makes their claim to produce the next Okogbe plausible and legitimate. Therefore, they conveyed to the authorities their unanimous resolution to create the third ruling house through a letter. They asserted,

Ọsuruka is the ruling family in Ojah, from time immemorial, there has been two ruling houses in Ojah viz. 1. Ọkọkọ Ruling House and 2. Ugbọnọkua Ruling House. The first Ọkọgbe of Ojah was Ọkọkọ. The second Ọkọgbe was Ugbọnọkua. The third Ọkọgbe was Ifiabekha. The fourth Ọkọgbe was Imodibie. The fifth Ọkọgbe was Anemọ. The sixth Ọkọgbe was Oshiọma. The seventh Ọkọgbe was Ọnọbumẹ. The eight Ọkọgbe was Lawani Ogundare while Oba Adesina was the 9th Ọkọgbe of Ojah.[26]

This chronological history of rotation of royal chieftaincy helped to institutionalize the tradition, but also routinize the practice. The Ọkọkọ ruling house took a rather conciliatory, placid tone in this letter by recognizing Oshiọma as the sixth Ọkọgbe. In other cases, they mostly portray Oshiọma as a regent and not a substantive Ọkọgbe of Ojah. In a rather naïve, unsuspecting manner, the Ọkọgbe Ruling house averred and determined as follows:

> From the onset, the Ọsuruka has never resolved to have the third (3rd) Ruling House. However, it should be noted that the entire Ọsuruka Family after due consultation at Joli Farm's Office on the 18/6/91 unanimously resolved to create the third (3rd) ruling house in Ọsuruka to be known and called Oshiọma Ruling House. It should be noted from time immemorial that Ọkọkọ Ruling House has produced only four (4) Ọkọgbes while the Ugbọnọkua Ruling House has produced five (5) Ọkọgbes. Since the approval to create the 3rd Ruling House was reached on the 18th June 1991; we would wish therefore that Ọkọkọ Ruling House has her 5th turn before the 3rd Ruling House (Oshiọma) takes off.[27]

Ostensibly, Lawrence Obayemi and the Oshiọma family did not take part in this meeting nor endorse such a letter. This further raises major questions about Ashore's original motives for convening such a one-sided meeting at his farm office. It is unclear whether he invited the Oshiọma and Ugbọnọkua families to the meeting or whether they declined to attend. Nonetheless, the Ọkọkọ ruling house would not have envisaged the horrid turn of events that followed.

However, during the next days following Obayemi's announcement as Ọkọgbe, officers of the Nigerian Police, who reprimanded the Ọkọkọ ruling house for their claim to the chieftaincy throne, arrested ten family members.[28] With the downturn of events, the Ọkọkọ family were fully convinced that Obayemi orchestrated the police arrests, exhibiting his influence as a retired police officer himself. The Ọkọkọ family testified in court later that the police cajoled them to sign documents evidencing their consent to creating a third ruling house, through duress and duplicity. According to the report, 'the Divisional Police Officer at Igarra caused them to sign a document the contents of which were not read to them. They were also forced by police to create a third ruling house – the Oshioma ruling house for the defendant.'[29] The fact that the Ọkọkọ family signed a document earlier recognizing the formation of a third ruling house, albeit out of coercion and deception, was in fact consequential. On 2 July 1991, a writ of summons[30] was filed in the High Court of Justice by 'Philip Aiyejina Dania Ọkọkọ and D.S Lawani, in a representative capacity for themselves and on behalf of Ọkọkọ Ruling House, Ọsuruka Royal Kindred of Ọjah and the whole Ọjah community' against Michael Ọnọbumẹ and Lawrence Obayemi.

Prior to a detailed description of the protracted legal affray that transpired for another decade, I will briefly describe two instances of interventionist strategies by the Ọza Solidarity Movement, Ọjah (OSMO), a progressive movement of Ọza elites; and Ọza Community Development Movement (OCDM) (now renamed as Ọza Community Development Association – OCDA), a pan-Ọza sociocultural association comprising sons and daughters in Ọza and beyond. The OCDA as a national, voluntary, not-for-profit, pro-development association charges itself with promoting community development through community-based initiatives; act as liaison with local, state and national government on behalf of Ọza community; and work to sustain peace, progress and development of Ọza community.

External and internal pressures from the state government,[31] the Nigerian Police Force, OCDM, OSMO and individual mediators in Ọza no doubt prompted and pressured the Ọsuruka family to seek and explore internal mechanisms towards resolving the lingering chieftaincy dispute and routinization of leadership. With the re-emergence of the chieftaincy leadership disputes that ensued between the royal lineages following the demise of Ọkọgbe Adesina Ọnọbumẹ, OCDM rose instantaneously to play a mediating role between the feuding royal families and seek an amicable resolution. While OCDM's motivation, as an arbiter in the royal family succession dispute may have been genuine at its inception, some unsuspecting members seemed to have hijacked such a noble intention, thus leading to bouts of partisanship, bigotry, recriminations and rebuttals. Some members did not perceive the OCDM National and State leaderships to be immune from the antimonies that came to characterize the association. Some even alleged that OCDM leadership backed one of the feuding royal families with funds against the other. This perceived bias and preferential treatment eroded member's trust and confidence in OCDM's leadership. It is against this backdrop that the ambivalent role of OCDM in peaceful conflict resolution of the chieftaincy tussle needs a better grasp. While OCDM's intervention yielded positive outcomes in a multiplicity of ways, at the same time OCDM appeared to transmute into an arena of incendiary rage, to the extent that it derailed the reconciliation process to a reasonable extent. In fact, the unprecedented polemical trend convulsed the raison d'être, modus operandi, and the social and cultural capital that OCDM had hitherto built within the community.

The OCDM National body moved briskly to initiate a mechanism to avert a chieftaincy leadership vacuum during the interregnum. First, the National Executive Council of OCDM took a drastic action in dissolving Ojah Town Council. In a letter dated 28 September 1991 to the Chairman of Ojah Town Council, it stated straightforwardly,

> As a result of the National Executive Council (NEC) meeting held on the 28th September 1991 at Auchi the house decided that Ojah Town Council be dissolved with immediate effect. The reasons mitigating against these decisions are: The house observed that there are conflicts in the operations between OCDM home branch and the Town Council. To this end all assets and liabilities are to be taken over by the OCDM Home Branch.[32]

Second, on 2 October 1992, the OCDM National Executive under the leadership of F. A. Edward (President) appointed Chief B. A. Arishe as Interim Honorary Community Leader to oversee affairs of the village pending the final resolution of the chieftaincy dispute. His main duties were enshrined in a letter, to Chief Bokeshimi, the then Chairman of Akoko Edo Local Government Area, seeking official recognition and credence of the Community Leader. The letter titled *Appointment of Community Leader in Ojah* stated, *inter alia*,

> We refer to the court injunction on the Chieftaincy dispute between the Oshioma Family (involving Chief Lawrence Obayemi) and the Okoko family (involving Chief J.O. Lawani) in Ojah, that no one should parade himself as the Chief of Ojah until the determination of the suit before the court. We the entire citizens of Ojah hereby make the following resolutions for the smooth-running of the administration of Ojah ... Sir, this decision have become necessary as a way of alleviating the sufferings, deprivations, and alienation of Ojah as a result of the vacuum created. They are also a way of diffusing the tension created by this vacuum. We thank you, sir, for your usual cooperation. Yours faithfully.[33]

The resolutions stated in the letter were as follows:

1. That we hereby appoint for ourselves a Leader.
2. That such a Leader be in the person of whoever occupies the office of the President of Ozah Community Development Movement (OCDM) Home Branch, which is the supreme legislative body in Ojah.

3. That the incumbent, Chief B. A. Arishe, is hereby appointed as such Leader.
4. That his functions include representing Ojah in any matter where a village Head/Leader is required.
5. That he acts as the referee for all sons and daughters of Ojah.
6. That he receives all visitors, guests, etc. that may visit Ojah from time to time which require a Community Representative/Head.
7. That he functions generally as the overseer of Ojah until such a time as the court resolves the issue of the Chieftaincy dispute in the Community.
8. That he, the Leader, ceases to carry out all these functions immediately the court decides the suit.
9. That these decisions are taken because Ojah lacks a Chief/Head.
10. That Ojah is presently suffering inadequacies/deprivations due to this vacuum.[34]

Chief Arishe served as Community Leader, in honorary capacity, for a couple of months until he was relieved of his position in May 1993. Although he discharged his duties accordingly, some members soon alleged that he demonstrated bias and unfairness in handling matters relating to the chieftaincy dispute. Some members had identified his propinquity and familial intimacy with Obayemi of the Oshioma family as a necessary barrier to fair play and equity. Following robust deliberation on the integrity and perceived partisanship of Chief Arishe in handling affairs of the community, members in attendance voted him out of office at an OCDM National delegates meeting held in Auchi on 5 May 1993. In his stead, Rufus Adogame received unanimous appointment and became Community Leader from May 1993 until 29 September 2002. His letter of appointment as Community Leader was duly signed by the OCDM National President, F. A. Edward, and representatives of the seven quarters in Oza, namely Adeyemi Akintola (Ajoyo), Julius Ishame (Ileoro), Adekunle Balogun (Bamishaiye), John Balogun (Araromi), Lawrence Akpaja (Igodi), Benjamin Omunagbe (Oke Iye) and Patrick A. Obanile (Agbokodo), respectively. Once more, Chief Bokeshimi, in his capacity as Chairman of Akoko Edo Local Government Area, was informed vide a letter of the appointment of a new Community leader.[35] The letter read, *inter alia*,

> We would like to refer to our letter dated 2nd October 1992 (copy attached) concerning appointment of Community Leader in OJAH. The incumbent Chairman of Ojah Community Development Movement is MR. R.S. ADOGAME. He is therefore the Community Leader of Ojah. We like to reiterate that his functions include representing OJAH in any matter where a

> village Head/Leader is required. This letter and clarification is as a result of the verbal message you sent to the Community. We thank you, sir, for your usual cooperation. Yours faithfully.

Thus, Rufus Adogame inherited the hitherto functions by Arishe and continued to carry out the functions of a community leader that included convening meetings with the warring Ọsuruka royal families to explore a road map for peaceful resolution. He represented Ọza in organized meetings on matters affecting the community and discharged laid down functions as enumerated above. Indeed, the honorary role of a community leader was a herculean task in the midst of a seething chieftaincy dispute that continued to polarize both the respective families but also the wider community.

With some determination and charisma, Adogame served as Community Leader for a decade until that time when dissension and friction started to hold sway especially during pan-village meetings. For instance, Agbọkodọ quarters under the leadership of Chief Ojisua publicly displayed loyalty to Obayemi, canvassed for relative autonomy and shunned pan-village meetings. Ojisua and his representatives also started to display overbearing, fractious and recalcitrant tones. Usually, it behoves the Community Leader to convene pan-village meetings often attended by representatives from all seven Quarters. At one time, Chief Ojisua wrote an imperious letter, dated 1 August 2002, to the Community Leader summoning him to appear before him and some *Ejas* at a meeting in Agbọkodọ Quarters. The Community Leader considered this approach as a high level of intransigence and dereliction, and so refused to attend the meeting. This coupled with some rumour about a prearranged altercation and feud made his attendance at that meeting problematic. The Community Leader abhorred such aversion and unprecedented antagonism displayed by Ojisua and his supporters.

Thus, with such instances of disrespect, unresponsiveness and dwindling enthusiasm at meetings, lack of trust and cooperation, neglect and flagrant disregard of his authority as Community Leader coalesced to his resignation.[36] On 27 September 2002, through a letter to the President National OCDM Lagos, Pa Adogame resigned as Community Leader after serving for nine years in honorary capacity. His letter, 'Resignation Letter as a Community Leader', reads,

> You will recall that by an unanimous decision, I was appointed as a community leader with a letter dated 5th May 1993 (about 9 years today). This appointment was necessary in view of the prevailing stalemate experienced in our community Chieftaincy tussle. I wish to emphasize that to the best of my ability, I have discharged my duties creditably, efficiently but unfortunately thanklessly from

the prevailing situations. I hereby honourably tender my resignation as the community leader in follow up to my earlier notification at the NEC meeting on 29 September 2002. I thank you all for the privilege you have given me to serve you in such an enviable capacity. I believe that it is only God that is infallible, and hence who ever I must have offended in the course of rendering my selfless service, should forgive and forget. I wish you all success in life and long life Ojah and continuous progress. God bless. Yours faithfully.[37]

Pa Adogame felt a sense of indignity, as there was no official response to his letter of resignation nor any appreciation for his candour and magnanimity in handling affairs as Community Leader. This is perhaps indicative of the extent to which the ongoing chieftaincy crisis had left a deep abyss and cracks in the corporate existence and functioning of the OCDM, but also heightened tension and communal apprehension at large. Nonetheless, Mr Braimoh served consequently in this capacity, as the incumbent OCDM National President.

Earlier, on 3 December 1996, OSMO Lagos branch sent a letter of appeal 'Request for Peace within Osuruka Kindred Ojah'[38] to the Osuruka family requesting their intervention to withdraw the case from the High Court and explore internal, peaceful negotiation and settlement of the family melee. OSMO also enjoined the family to explore a triangular system of succession between the Okoko, Oshiomah and Onobume ruling houses in Osuruka royal kindred. This plea from OSMO was not ignored but seemed to have swayed the Okoko ruling house of Osuruka kindred into some desired action. They provided a detailed response to the letter but also appeared to have set the machinery in motion towards an internal resolution. In two different communications, they seized the opportunity to provide robust family genealogies regarding succession of the Okogbe Chieftaincy in Ojah.[39] In the earlier, Chief J. O. Lawani attempts to recapture what he considered the crux of the matter:

I refer to your letter dated 3rd December 1996 which was received today, 20th December, 1996. On 12th June, 1991, Chief J.O. Lawani was confined as Okogbe by the King makers (usually from Okoko ruling house) in Osuruka Royal kindred. On 15th June, 1991, when the Okoko ruling went to remove the EMA (the chieftaincy regalia or antiquities) from where the eldest man, Mr. Michael Onobume ordered the Oshioma great great grand children to keep them. They refused to release them. To maintain peace, on 16th June, 1991: the Okoko ruling house went to Ososo police, for escort to remove the EMA. But they met Mr. Lawrence Obayemi: a retired Senior Police Officer and Mr. Paul Agbalajobi at the police station. Immediately Obayemi and Agbalajobi saw the two men sent by Ọkọkọ ruling house, they told the Police that they (Oshiọma) would confine their choice that evening (16th June 1991). The Police warned both parties to suspend any further action until 17th June, 1991. But while Ọkọkọ ruling house observed the order, the Oshiọma great great grand children purportedly confined Lawrence Obayemi as another Ọkọgbe. They and their supporters went round the town booming guns and singing abusive songs.[40]

The letter continues a chronological narration to make their own side of the case. Much of this account corroborated the testimony provided in the High Court earlier. Chief Lawani continues,

> On 17th June, 1991, a report was made at Igarra Police Station. Both parties were invited to Igarra Police Station. The Police referred the parties matter to Ọjah Elders at home to settle, with the instruction that a 3rd ruling house 'Oshiọma ruling house' be created in Ọsuruka royal kindred so as to remove the strife and ordered that a letter should be written to the Police Divisional Officer Igarra, effecting the creation of a 3rd ruling house in Ọsuruka royal kindred. The elders of Ọjah met on 17th June, 1991 with Ọsuruka kindred and could not convince Oshiọma great great grand children to accept the decision, and Mr. Michael Aiyede Ọnọbumẹ delivered; that since Chief J.O. Lawani was the First to be crowned, he should be upheld. The Police on 18th June, 1991 forced the Ọsuruka members who attended Divisional Police Office at Igarra to sign a blind document with which the 'Oshiọma ruling house' was created by and at the instance of the Police Divisional Officer who was clearly a biased interested party. The D.P.O. further threatened that anybody who refused to sign the chieftaincy document would be locked up in the Police Cell. That was how the 3rd ruling house purportedly came into being and which forced the Ọkọkọ ruling house to seek redress in the Igarra High Court. The facts above are made before God and man and without fear, favour or prejudice. I wish you all a Merry Christmas and a Prosperous New Year. Yours faithfully.[41]

I have taken the liberty to reproduce this letter extensively because it helps to make sense of the documented court testimonies somewhat. Besides the mediation of OCDM and OSMO, this account is suggestive of the ambiguous role of the police officers at Ọsọsọ and Igarra in mitigating the crisis. While they advised the family to explore indigenous conflict resolution strategies through Ọjah Elders, we can infer police intimidation. It was obvious that the police exerted coercion diplomatically, both ordering the families to invent a third ruling house and threatening detention for anyone who fails to sign the document. It is against this backdrop that we can unpack the tendentious complicity and manipulation of law enforcement agents in the escalation of the family feud. The second letter from Ọkọkọ ruling house concludes in a cautiously optimistic tone:

> The Ọsuruka royal kindred does not wish to create problems for future generation by increasing the two to three or more ruling houses. Chief J.O. Lawani an indigene of ỌKỌKỌ ruling house of ỌSURUKA royal kindred whose turn it is, to have his turn after the late OBA ADESHINA, while the choice of Ugbọnọkua ruling house will follow. This is the peaceful way forward and once more we are ever grateful to Ọjah peace lovers and more especially the members of O.S.M.O and O.C.D.M. who came, saw and conquered. My God continue to guide us, may his peace reign supreme in Ọjah, Amen.[42]

Although OSMO and OCDM's intentionality and mediatory roles were palpable, their impact, however, was equivocal and convoluted. The intensification of the chieftaincy crisis meant that some members became embroiled and enthralled in the crisis. Such partisan inclinations soon generated suspicion, eroded trust and confidence, developments that rocked the very foundation of both associations for several years that followed.

Nonetheless, the Ọsuruka family seemed to have succumbed to OSMO's missive suing for peace in late 1996 and OCDM's earlier memoranda of action, albeit temporarily, in their attempts at an in-house reconciliation in January 1997. Three successive meetings of the Ọsuruka royal kindred held in a bid towards reconciliation proved abortive in the end. The first of such meetings took place on 20 January 1997 in the home of Chief Pa Michael Aiyede Ọnọbumẹ from the Ugbọnọkua ruling house, who was at the time the oldest surviving male in Ọsuruka royal kindred.[43] Members from Ọkọkọ and Ugbọnọkua Ruling houses and the great-grandchildren of Oshiọma, who was once a regent, attended the meeting. The attendees included P. A. Dania Ọkọkọ, J. A. Ogundare, D. S. Lawani, Felix Killani and Chief J. O. Lawani (Ọkọkọ ruling house); Pa Michael Aiyede Ọnọbumẹ, Adebayo Ọnọbumẹ, James Oka, Matthew Osogori, John Samiyu and Eminefo Samiyu (Ugbọnọkua ruling house); and Paul Agbalajobi, Abudu Daudu, William Lawani, Josiah Agbalajobi and Chief Lawrence Obayemi (great-grandchildren of Oshiọma), respectively. The host, Pa Michael Aiyede Ọnọbumẹ, introduced the purpose of the meeting and 'solicited for maturity of minds and co-operation from each party concerned. He then asked for what the entire House can do in a bid to resolve the problem.'[44]

The initial deliberations were auspicious in that the meeting identified the problem, addressed the impact and seemed resolved for a final resolution. To this end, they contemplated on and discussed the procedures that would be required for withdrawing the lawsuit and coming to terms with in-house family dispute settlement. The meeting was unanimous in the pursuit of a family resolution, with decisions communicated to the public for acceptance. In pursuit of this goal, the meeting constituted and adopted a six-man committee of family elders to facilitate and deliberate on the settlement process and procedure. The meeting adjourned until 22 January 1998, when the terms of agreement will be reached.[45]

Recriminations and oppositions dominated the meeting of 22 January and thus stymied any hopes of in-house settlement and reconciliation. No substantive progress was realized owing to such disruptions. Not even the verbal apology tendered by Adebayo Onọbumẹ, for admitting his failure to send a direct message to Ọkọkọ ruling house at the death of Ọkọgbe Adeshina Onọbumẹ, could assuage nerves that were already sore. One main contention was the existing tradition regarding the appropriate custodian of the *Ema* (royal antiquities) at the demise of both late Ọkọgbe Onọbumẹ and Ọkọgbe Lawani Ogundare. Failure to reach any consensus ended the meeting. The third meeting of 24 January 1998 did not improve matters as the contention remained about the *Ema*. Adebayo Onọbumẹ's assertion that 'the antiquities (Emas) are not carried twice. He and the "Ejahs" crowned Chief Lawrence Obayemi and celebrated his outing ceremony'[46] was met with much indignation and repudiation by the Ọkọkọ ruling house. To avert a rowdy situation that was resulting in an atmosphere of confusion, Pa Michael Aiyede Onọbumẹ, the eldest surviving elder in Ọsuruka kindred, rose to his feet and with a tone of finality opined that the case should rather continue in court.[47] Frustrations about the ineffectuality of these successive meetings in reaching a verdict or resolution was conveyed in the closing paragraph of the minutes. From its first seating on 20 January 1997, Pa Dania raised great hopes when he told the House that the issue is directly between Ọkọkọ ruling house and the great-grandchildren of Oshiọma and we are looking highly unto the Elders of the Ugbọnọkua Ruling House for reasonable intervention.[48] Rather than realized, such hopes 'of reasonable intervention' by Ugbọnọkua were dashed, but also seen as a betrayal of trust. The minutes concluded with wary disenchantment and direct indictment:

> It is a pity that despite the directives from the State Government and Ọza Solidarity Movement, Ọjah (OSMO), to settle the case out of court, for peace to reign in Ọjah, the Ugbọnọkua Ruling House, who was supposed to play the part of a mediator, chose to sit on the fence each time. It should be noted that there are two Ruling Housses in Ọsuruka Royal Kindred, thus, Ọkọkọ Ruling House and Ugbọnọkua Ruling House. The last Ọkọgbe Adeshina Onọbumẹ was from

Ugbọnọkua Ruling House and it is now the turn of Ọkọkọ Ruling House. The coming in of the third House was a complete work of Ugbọnọkua Ruling House to set in confusion in the system.[49]

Nonetheless, the stark failures of mediation and peace initiatives from the OCDM and OSMO, interventions by the State Government and the Nigerian Police, individual arbitrations and in-house resolution by the Ọsuruka kindred further plunged Ọza and the Ọsuruka chieftaincy tussle into an abyss of unprecedented legal fray, social ferment, political disquiet and uncertainty.

While Ọkọkọ and Lawani filed a writ of summons in the High Court on 2 July 1991, the Court hearing proper commenced more than a decade later, on 21 February 2002. The suit hearing based on the issues finally joined in Ọkọkọ and Lawani's (Plaintiffs) Fourth Further Amended Statement of Claim of 10 December 2003, and Ọnọbumẹ and Obayemi's (Defendants) Third Further Amended joint statement of defence and counter claim of 22 April 2004.[50] In the Fourth Further Amended Statement of Claim [paragraph 59], Ọkọkọ and Lawani as plaintiffs, sought several reliefs in their claims as follows:

i. 'A declaration that the Ọkọgbe Chieftaincy title of Ojah is the joint inheritance and property of the descendants of the two ruling houses of Ọkọkọ and Ugbọnọkua both of which form the Ọsuruka royal kindred.
ii. A declaration that by the custom and tradition of Ojah in Akoko-Ẹdo Local Government Area of Edo State, the Ọkọgbe Chieftaincy title rotates between the said two ruling houses of Ọkọkọ and Ugbọnọkua in Ọsuruka royal kindred.
iii. An order directing the 1st, 2nd, 3rd and 4th Defendants to respect and uphold the tradition, customary and constitutional rights of Ọkọkọ ruling house of Ọsuruka royal kindred of Ojah.
iv. A perpetual injunction restraining the 1st, 2nd, 3rd, 4th, 5th and 6th defendants from doing any act in violation of the custom and tradition of Ojah with regard to the succession to the Ọkọgbe Chieftaincy title as found and ascertained by the history of Ọsuruka royal kindred of Ojah.
v. An order restraining the 5th Defendant and other elders and kingmakers from appointing and/or recognising the 6th Defendant as a rightful Ọkọgbe of Ojah.
vi. A declaration that the said letter dated 18/6/92 and addressed to the Divisional Police Officer, Igarra, purporting to create Oshoma Ruling house in Ọsuruka royal kindred was clearly induced by the 6th Defendant as a retired senior police officer who used his undue influence to make Oshoma

descendants a third ruling house in Osuruka royal kindred and that the said letter is therefore incompetent, ineffectual, null and void ab initio.

vii. A declaration that after the late Okogbe Adesina from Ugbonokua ruling house it is the turn of Okoko ruling house to take the Okogbe Chieftaincy title.

viii. An order compelling all those whom the late Paul Agbalajobi aided especially 6th defendant to deliver the 'EMA' (Chieftaincy regalia and properties) in his possession, to the plaintiffs who are of Okoko ruling house to produce the next rightful Okogbe of Ojah.

ix. An order of perpetual injunction on restraining the 5th Defendant or his successor as the eldest man in Osuruka royal kindred from approving, consenting and/or recognising any other appointment of any other person as the Okogbe in violation of the custom and tradition of Osuruka royal kindred in Ojah.

x. An order perpetually restraining the 6th defendant either by himself or his agents, servants or whosoever from any other ruling house than Okoko ruling house from parading himself or themselves as member or members of the ruling house whose turn it is now, after the reign of the last Okogbe Adesina who was from Ugbonokua ruling house, to take the Okogbe Chieftaincy title as a rightful successor.

xi. A declaration that after the death of the late Okogbe Adesina from Ugbonokua ruling house it is the turn of Okoko ruling house and none other to take the Okogbe rulership (Chieftaincy) title and to vest or confer some on any of its qualified member.[51]

Michael Onobume and Lawrence Obayemi, as defendants, also sought reliefs [paragraph 9] of their counter claims as follows:

a. A declaration that there are three Ruling Houses in Osuruka kindred of Ojah for the purpose of selecting an Okogbe of Ojah.

b. A declaration that the three Ruling Houses in the Osuruka kindred of Ojah are:
   i. Aseka Ruling House, frequently called Oshiomah Ruling House
   ii. Ugbonokua Ruling House
   iii. Ifiabeka Ruling House

c. A declaration that by the order of rotation of the office of Okogbe between the three Ruling Houses, it is the turn of the Aseka (or Oshioma) Ruling House to hold the office of Okogbe after the death of Adeshina Onobume from Ugbonokua Ruling House

d. A declaration that the 6th defendant, Lawrence Obayemi is a person qualified and suitable to be appointed as Okogbe of Ojah

e. A declaration that the 6th defendant has been validly selected, appointed and crowned and recognised as the 10th Ọkọgbe from the Ọsuruka kindred of Ojah

f. A declaration that the 'Apesu' is the only crown by which an Ọkọgbe of Ojah may be validly crowned and that the "Apesu" crown confers legitimacy on an Ọkọgbe

g. A declaration that the purported selection and crowning of the late Jonathan Lawani as the Ọkọgbe of Ojah is contrary to and a violation of Ojah custom and tradition and is therefore null and void.[52]

As Hon. Justice Imoedemhe noted further in his submission, the plaintiffs (Ọkọkọ and Lawani) also filed a reply to the Third Further Amended Statement of defence and counter claim. From the pleadings filed, it is clear that the parties agreed on a number of matters. These include the following:

1. That the Ọkọgbe Chieftaincy title originally belonged to the Ọbueri Kindred of Ojah before one Imodafe (then the Ọkọgbe) on his deathbed gave it to Ọkọkọ, his son-in-law, who had taken good care of him during his illness when all his Ọbueri kinsmen abandoned him.

2. That Imodafe at the time he gave the crown to Ọkọkọ placed a curse on the crown to the effect that 'any person' (according to the plaintiffs) and 'any Ọbueri person' (according to the defendants) who attempted to retrieve the crown from Ọkọkọ would meet with death.

3. That by the traditions of Ojah an individual cannot hold two titles and that a ruling house cannot succeed itself or rule twice in succession.

4. That unless an Ọkọgbe is crowned with the Apesu and takes custody of the Ema and Odumu, which constitute his paraphernalia of office, he is not an Ọkọgbe, hence J. O. Lawani was not an Ọkọgbe.

5. That confinement of an Ọkọgbe for nine days is an important aspect of the traditions of Ojah, which confers validity on the appointment of an Ọkọgbe.[53]

The judge aptly observed that arising from their rival claims to the stool of Ọkọgbe of Ojah, however, the parties have joined issues on the following matters which are matters, which in his view, arise for determination in this case: First, the number and the names of the ruling houses within Ọsuruka royal kindred of Ojah. Second, the order of rotation of the Ọkọgbe title or the order of succession thereto. Third, whether or not Ọkọkọ was the first Ọkọgbe of Ojah or an Obuoro. Fourth, whether or not Oshiọma was a regent.[54] Finally, who, as between the plaintiffs 'Ọkọkọ Ruling House' and the 6th Defendants 'Aseka/Oshiọma Ruling

House', is entitled to produce the Ọkọgbe of Ọjah after the death of Adesina Ọnọbumẹ who is acknowledged by both sides as the last Ọkọgbe of Ọjah, and whether the 6th defendant has been validly appointed as the Ọkọgbe of Ọjah.[55]

Hon. Justice Imoedemhe gave careful consideration to the pleadings, evidence led including the exhibits and the submissions of the learned counsel and the learned defence counsel, respectively. The Judge observed,

> In my view the questions raised as to the number of ruling houses in Ọsuruka royal kindred, the order of rotation of the Ọkọgbe title or succession thereto, whether Ọkọkọ was the first Ọkọgbe or an Obuoro and whether or not Oshoma was a regent and what family is now entitled to Ọkọgbe are so closely interwoven that they can safely be considered together.[56]

As a succinct summary of the cases, Hon. Justice Imoedemhe was very ingenious in providing two tables[57] showing the different orders of succession that both parties relied upon.

The judge examined and contrasted the two tables showing the order of succession relied upon by the parties, and this was both illustrative of the rotational nature of the royal genealogical tradition and instrumental to the inferences he made regarding the case. As he observed in the case of the plaintiffs (Table 1), except during the period between the reign of Anemọ of Ọkọkọ and Ọnọbumẹ of Ugbọnọkua when they allege that Oshoma ruled as regent, the table showed a clear order of rotation between Ọkọkọ and Ugbọnọkua ruling houses. However, the same cannot be said of Table 2 for the defence which showed that after the reign of Ifiabekha ruling house as 3rd Ọkọgbe the title skipped Aseka ruling house and went to Imodibie of Ugbọnọkua ruling house; and again, after the reign of Lawani Ogundare of Ifiabekha as 8th Ọkọgbe it again skipped Aseka and went to Adesina Ọnọbumẹ of Ugbọnọkua ruling house as the 9th Ọkọgbe. Nor does the title now going backwards from Adesina Ọnọbumẹ to the 6th defendant of Aseka ruling house display a consistent order of rotation.[58]

Table 1. Plaintiffs' Case

Ọkọkọ	Ugbọnọkua
1. Ọkọkọ	2. Ugbọnọkua
3. Ifiabekhai	4. Imodibie
5. Inemo	6. (Oshoma) Ọnọbumẹ
7. Lawani Ogundare	8. Adesina Ọnọbumẹ

Table 2. 5th & 6th Defendants' Case

Aseka	Ugbọnọkua	Ifiabekhai
1. Aseka	2. Ugbọnọkua	3. Ifiabekhai
-----------	4. Imodibie	5. Anemọ
6. Oshoma	7. Ọnọbumẹ	8. Lawani Ogundare
-----------	9. Adesina Ọnọbumẹ	------------
10. 6th Defendant	------------	------------

Following a robust, profound evaluation of the evidence provided by the parties, Hon. Justice Imoedemhe made conclusions[59] he considered inevitable. First, he surmised that there are two ruling houses in Ọsuruka royal kindred, which are the Ọkọkọ ruling house and the Ugbọnọkua ruling house. Second, the order of rotation of the Ọkọgbe title between the two ruling houses is as stated by the plaintiffs and set out in Table 1 above. Third, Ọkọkọ was the first Ọkọgbe of Ọjah. Fourth, Oshoma who ruled as the 6th Ọkọgbe of Ọjah ruled as regent for Ọnọbumẹ the young son of Unuanyoka. Fifth, following from the above, it is now the turn of Ọkọkọ ruling house to succeed the stool of Ọkọgbe of Ọjah. In his summary findings, the judge asserted, 'It is needless to state that the 6th defendant who has stated that he is neither from the Ọkọkọ nor Ugbọnọkua ruling houses is not qualified to be appointed the Ọkọgbe of Ọjah.'[60] He underscored the fact that the appraisal, findings and indeed the outcome of the case depended essentially on the evaluation of the evidence adduced by the parties and 'the ascription of probative value thereto. It has been held on high authority that the weight to be attached to evidence depends largely on rules of common sense.'[61] The judge cited the case of *Lord Advocate v. Lord Blantyre (1879) 4 App. Case 770 House of Lords* as legal precedence. In Hon. Justice Imoedemhe's view, 'the entire case of the defence smacks of a smart attempt to disrupt the settled order of rotation of Ọkọgbe Chieftaincy stool in Ọjah with the connivance of Ugbọnọkua ruling house; it is totally lacking in merit'. Thus, their claims that Aseka/Oshoma and Ifiabekha are ruling houses within Ọsuruka and that Oshoma was 6th Ọkọgbe as of right are not supported by credible evidence, he concluded.

From the totality of the foregoing and in view of his findings in this case, Hon. Justice Imoedemhe held that the plaintiffs' claim succeeds, and he made the following declarations and orders[62] in their favour:

1. A declaration that the Ọkọgbe Chieftaincy title of Ọjah is the joint inheritance and property of the descendants of the two ruling

houses of Ọkọkọ and Ugbọnọkua, both of which form the Ọsuruka royal kindred.
2. A declaration that by the custom and tradition of Ọjah in Akoko-Ẹdo Local Government Area of Edo State, the Ọkọgbe Chieftaincy title rotates between the said two ruling houses of Ọkọkọ and Ugbọnọkua in Ọsuruka royal kindred.
3. An order directing the 1st, 2nd, 3rd and 4th defendants to respect and uphold the tradition, customary and constitutional rights of Ọkọkọ ruling house of Ọsuruka royal kindred of Ọjah.
4. An order restraining the 5th Defendant and other elders and kingmakers from appointing and/or recognising the 6th Defendant as a rightful Ọkọgbe of Ọjah.
5. A declaration that after the late Ọkọgbe Adesina from Ugbọnọkua ruling house it is the turn of Ọkọkọ ruling house to take the Ọkọgbe Chieftaincy title.
6. An order compelling all those whom the late Paul Agbalajobi aided especially 6th defendant to deliver the 'Ema' (Chieftaincy regalia and properties) in his possession, to the plaintiffs who are of Ọkọkọ ruling house to produce the next rightful Ọkọgbe of Ọjah.
7. An order of perpetual injunction restraining the 5th defendant or his successor as the eldest man in Ọsuruka royal kindred from approving, consenting and/or recognising the appointment of any other person outside Ọkọkọ ruling house as the Ọkọgbe in violation of the custom and tradition of Ọsuruka royal kindred in Ọjah.
8. An order perpetually restraining the 6th defendant either by himself or his agents, servants or whosoever from any other ruling house other than Ọkọkọ ruling house from parading himself or themselves as member or members of the ruling house whose turn it is now, after the reign of the last Ọkọgbe Adesina who was from Ugbọnọkua ruling house, to take the Ọkọgbe Chieftaincy title as a rightful successor.
9. A declaration that after the death of the late Ọkọgbe Adesina from Ugbọnọkua ruling house it is the turn of Ọkọkọ ruling house to take the Ọkọgbe rulership (Chieftaincy) title and to vest or confer some on any one of its qualified member.

In contrast to the eleven claims filed originally by the plaintiffs, Ọkọkọ and Lawani, in the Fourth Amended Statement of Claim (paragraph 59) of 10 December 2003, Hon. Justice Imoedemhe effected some minor editorial changes on claims

7–9 above, although without changing the substantive claims. Moreover, the judge totally expunged two original claims (iv) and (vi), respectively, below as:

(iv.) A perpetual injection restraining the 1st, 2nd, 3rd, 4th, 5th and 6th defendants from doing any act in violation of the custom and tradition of Ojah with regard to the succession to the Okogbe Chieftaincy title as found and ascertained by the history of Osuruka royal kindred of Ojah; and

(vi.) A declaration that the said letter dated 18 June 1992 and addressed to the Divisional Police Officer, Igarra, purporting to create Oshoma Ruling house in Osuruka royal kindred was clearly induced by the 6th Defendant as a retired senior police officer who used his undue influence to make Oshoma descendants a third ruling house in Osuruka royal kindred and that the said letter is therefore incompetent, ineffectual, null and void ab initio.

In his declaration and orders, the judge did not make clear the rationale or reasons for disregarding the omitted claims. He may have deemed those additional claims as ambiguous, unsubstantiated, lacked merit or not proven beyond reasonable doubts. Overall, the denouement was that the defendant's counter claim is dismissed in its entirety. Costs in favour of the plaintiffs against the 5th and 6th defendants is assessed and fixed at N10,000,00.[63] This court judgement hardly laid the protracted legal tussle on Oza rotational chieftaincy to a final rest. Although the verdict ostensibly was a sigh of relief to the Okoko royal kindred (the plaintiffs), it was not well received by the Oshioma family and Ugbonokua kindred (defendants). However, the court ruling seemed to have brought a relative lull to an already charged communal *zeitgeist*. This temporal hiatus was, however, short-lived as familial anxieties and public disquiet brewed in reaction to the court decision. Lawrence Obayemi and the Oshioma family requested the High Court of Justice at Igarra to grant a stay of execution of the court judgement and an injunction to restrain the government from doing her work, formal recognition of the Okogbe of Ojah. The first hearing of the case took place on 2 June 2005 at the same High Court of Justice, Igarra. Consequently, the court denied the stay of execution and injunction.

However, while the verdict was given on 15 October 2004, it took eighteen months (a year and a half), until 14 March 2006, before the formal government recognition of Daniel Suru Lawani as the *bona fide* Village Head, Ifiabeka II – the Okogbe of Ojah. The letter from the Honorable Commissioner, Edo State Ministry of Local Government and Chieftaincy Affairs,[64] stated, *inter alia*, 'I am directed to inform you that the Edo State Executive Council has approved your appointment as the Village Head (Ọkọgbe) of Ọjah with effect from 22nd November, 2004. Appropriate action is being taken to publish your appointment as the Village Head (Ọkọgbe) of Ọjah in the State Gazette. Kindly accept my hearty congratulations.' The appointment of Chief Lawani as Ọkọgbe or Village Head of Ọjah was duly gazetted in 2006. It stated as follows,

> It is hereby notified for general information that in exercise of the powers conferred upon it by Section 22(1) of the Traditional Rulers and Chiefs Law, 1979 and by virtue of all other laws enabling it in that behalf, the Executive Council of Edo State of Nigeria has approved the appointment of Chief Daniel Suru Lawani as the Village Head (Ọkọgbe) of Ọja in Akoko Edo Local Government Area with effect from 22nd November, 2004. [65]

The mere fact that the letter, dated 14 March 2006, actually arrived and was endorsed by Akoko-Ẹdo Local Government Office at Igarra two weeks later, on 29 March 2006, gives some pause for concern on how such a retroactive decision could have an *ex post facto* effect. It is so far unclear whether the time lag in government recognition is simply a question of administrative exigency. What happened in Ọza during this interregnum, between the court judgment on 15 October 2004 and the letter of recognition on 14 March 2006? Did Chief Lawani assume the role of Ọkọgbe of Ọjah at the instance of the verdict but before receiving the official letter, or did Chief Lawrence Obayemi also arrogate himself with the same role prior? Whatever the situation was during this interim period has significant implications for what happened beyond March 2006.

The learned counsel, on behalf of the applicant, Lawrence Obayemi, filed three motions of appeal against Philip Ọkọkọ Anor (respondent).[66] The first motion was filed on 18 September 2006, followed by second and third motions on 20 July 2007 and 20 November 2007, respectively. At its last sitting on 9 July 2007, the first two motions were adjourned for hearing. Subsequent to the last sitting, the applicant filed a third motion on 20 July 2007. The counsel for the applicant was on notice to be in court on 27 November 2007. The respondent, Philip Ọkọkọ Anor, and his learned counsel, Dr S. E. Mosugu, were present in court, but the applicant, Lawrence Obayemi, and his learned counsel were conspicuously absent. Dr Mosugu, the learned counsel, urged the Court to strike out the three applications with costs: 'We are satisfied the learned counsel for the applicant is on sufficient notice to be in court today. He is apparently absent.' This formed a sufficient ground to strike off the case. Thus, on 27 November 2007, 'the three motions filed on behalf of the appellant/applicant are struck out seriation for want of diligent prosecution cumulative cost of N10,000.00 awarded to the 5th and 6th Respondents against the appellant/Applicants.'[67]

On 18 May 2009, Lawrence Obayemi, as an appellant/respondent to the Respondents/Judgment Creditors (Philip Ọkọkọ and D. S. Lawani) in the Court of Appeal Holden at Benin City, both responded to 'Further Affidavit filed on 3rd November 2008' and 'Counter Affidavit in Opposition to the Application for the committal of Appellant for Contempt'.[68] In one of his response letters, he introduced himself as 'I, Lawrence Obayemi, adult, male Christian, Traditional Chief of Ojah Village', while he was mute about 'Traditional Chief' on the other. While the first eight items (1–8) of the two letters were somewhat different, the last six items (9–14) were identical. He acknowledged receipt of the 'Further Affidavit' served by the Respondents/Judgment Creditors on 18 November 2008, alluding that the averments are false. He disclaims,

> 4. That since the judgment was delivered on 15/10/2004; I have never referred to myself as Ọkọgbe of Ojah and have never caused anybody to address me as such or to answer such salutation or perform any function or role reserved for the Ọkọgbe. 5. That I handed over the chieftaincy antiquities (*Ema*) in my possession to the Judgment creditors in total compliance with the terms of the Judgment of the trial court. I have no other antiquity or paraphernalia in my possession ... 8. That it is not true that on the 8/10/06 I bedecked myself and danced as the Ọkọgbe of Ojah. I was not even at the arena where the masquerade danced.

At the same time, he indicated,

> '...11. That I have filed an application for stay of execution of the Judgment and Orders of the trial court made on 15/10/2004. The application for stay of execution was filed on the 18/9/2006 long before the contempt proceeding was commenced on 4/7/07. 12. That my counsel Fola Ajayi informed me and I verily believe him that the application for contempt against me is frivolous and a ploy to delay the prompt hearing of my appeal.

He also alleged that the Judgment Creditors have boasted severally that having assumed the stool they will delay and frustrate the hearing of the appeal by instructing their lawyer to continue to file all types of processes.

The follow-up hearing in the Court of Appeal,[69] which was held on 7 March 2011 at Benin City before their Lordships – Hon. Justice A. Sanusi (presiding), Hon. Justice O. F. Omoleye and Hon. Chioma E. Nwose-Iheme (Justice, Court of

Appeal) – appeared to be the last straw that broke the camel's back, in terms of the legal tussle. In the case between Lawrence Obayemi & Anor vs. the Executive Governor of Edo State & ORS, Lawrence Obayemi, as the appellant/applicant, was represented by D. A. Alegbe (Learned Counsel), while Dr S. E. Mosugu SAN with Mrs B. O. Okoduwa (Learned Counsels) represented the respondents. In the first instance, D. A. Alegbe applied to withdraw the motion dated 11 October 2010 filed on 11 November 2010 and the motion dated 12 March 2007 and filed 12 April 2010. Dr Mosugu SAN had no objection to the request nor ask for cost. In reaction to this plea, the Court struck out the motions upon being withdrawn and awarded N10,000.00 as cost of the 5th and 6th respondents only. With respect to a second plea, Dr Alegbe applied to withdraw his motion 31 March 2011 filed on 11 April 2011. Dr Mosugu also did not have any objection nor ask for cost. Consequently, the court struck out on withdrawal the motion dated 3 March 2011 filed on 11 April 2011, without an order on cost. Thus, the appeal case was dismissed on 7 March 2011 with Hon. Justice A. Sanusi presiding.[70]

On 12 March 2011, barely a week following the dismissal of the appeal case, Philip Ọkọkọ vs. Lawrence Obayemi, the latter through his solicitor B. A. Alegbe Esq., petitioned the Deputy Governor of Edo State.[71] Some claims and allegations were brought against Chief D. S. Lawani, in the petition titled 'Acting in Dual Capacity as a Village Head of Ojah and as a Civil Servant and Receiving Remuneration for both Positions.'" These claims and allegations seem to sidestep and contradict the dismissal of the appeal court case on 7 March 2011, while also alleging duplicity and sharp practice. On the one hand, the petition read,

> We are Solicitors to CHIEF LAWRENCE OBAYEMI of OJAH Village in Akoko-Edo Local Government Area of Edo State, hereinafter called 'Our Client' on whose instruction we petition your office as follows: Our Client is a strong contender to the throne of the village head of OJAH which said position is currently a subject of litigation at the Court of Appeal, Benin City in Suit No: CA/B/229/04. Our Client states that the other contender to the throne is CHIEF D.S. LAWANI who was gazettered as the village head of OJAH during the pendency of the case on appeal.[72]

These two phrases appear to be in flagrant contradiction of each other. First, the reference to 'contenders to the throne' suggests that the court of appeal case was so far inconclusive, being a subject of litigation. This assertion is incongruent with the affirmation that Chief Lawani was already gazettered as the village head of Ojah. However, the substantive aspects of the petition were presented concurrently:

Our Client also states that even though the said Chief D.S. LAWANI is a teacher at the Girls Secondary School Igarra and on the pay roll of the State Government, he is also receiving remuneration as the village head of OJAH without resigning his appointment as a teacher in the employ of Edo State Government. Our Client also state that on the 10th and 11th day of March 2011, the said D.S. LAWANI without any reason gathered a few of his political friends under the influence of DR. TUNDE LAKOJU and started shooting guns sporadically in celebration of a case that is yet to be decided by the Court of Appeal. Our Client says that his action is not only provocative but can cause a total breakdown of peace and order in OJAH community. Our Client is writing this petition because it is with great effort that he was able to calm the frayed nerves of his teeming supports not to react to the provocative actions of D.S. Lawani.[73]

Thus, the petition was urging the Deputy Governor to restrain D. S. Lawani from politicizing the office of the village head and stop his allegedly 'provocative actions'. The letter also appealed for 'an investigation into the activities of D.S. Lawani who is defrauding the Government by receiving salaries from two positions with the State Government'. These allegations centred on perceived fraudulent acts, and provocative actions that could result in a breach of the peace. The Office of the Deputy Governor, through the Permanent Secretary, treated this petition with despatch, requesting the Honourable Commissioner, Ministry of Local Government and Chieftaincy Affairs, Benin City, to investigate and report back to the Deputy Governor, 'the action you have taken and thereafter the outcome of your action on the matter please'.[74]

Although it was unclear if and what immediate action was actually taken in the interim, on 23 May 2011 Chief D. S. Lawani, through his solicitor, Dr Mosugu (SAN), submitted a robust response to the petition. The letter urged his Excellency, the Deputy Governor of Edo State, that 'Mr. Obayemi's petition dated the 12th day of March, 2011 be seen as diversionary, baseless, ill-conceived, unwarranted and lacking of any substance and accordingly same should very respectfully, be discountenanced and ignored'.[75] The response letter provided some background information as a preamble to disclaiming the substantive allegation. First, the letter refuted the claims in paragraphs 2 and 3: 'Obayemi is a strong contender to the throne of the village head of Ojah', and 'the other contender to the throne is Chief D.S. Lawani', indicating that the counsel for Mr Obayemi 'is clearly being economical with the truth and is trying to walk judicial judgment on its head'.[76] The letter recalled that Mr. Obayemi had, on 15 October 2004, lost his case in a judgment delivered by Hon. Justice Imoedemhe, then of Igarra Court, in Suit No. HIG/11/91: Okoko & Lawani v. Lawrence Obayemi.

The letter asserted, 'A person recognized and gazette as a Chief by the Edo State Government (as has been done for Chief D.S. Lawani) cannot, any longer, be described as "contender".'[77] The response letter also drew attention to an appeal filed by Obayemi that is pending at the Court of Appeal Benin. It mentioned that the motions filed by Obayemi 'were serially struck out four or five times' at the Benin Court of Appeal, the last occasion being on 7 March 2011. Second, the letter noted that the striking out orders were accompanied with an award of N20,000 costs against Obayemi, thus revealing that the series of cumulative costs awarded against him were yet unpaid. Third, it was perhaps an ingenious move that Chief Lawani, prior to disavowing that he was acting in dual capacity as a Village Head of Ojah and as a Civil Servant and receiving remuneration for both positions, resolved to incriminate Obayemi in retaliation. The letter appeals to the Deputy Governor,

> We urge that your Excellency do cause the petitioner (Mr. Obayemi) to avail your Excellency with his antecedents or records in the Nigerian Police Force where he once served, such as by production of his Retirement or discharge papers – and on what grounds. Mr. Obayemi is playing the Ostrich. But he who comes to equity must do so with clean hands. Can Ojah Community ever entrust its fate in the hands of such a one?[78]

The letter also dismissed the allegation that he 'gathered a few of his political friends under the influence of Dr. Tunde Lakoju' as 'tendentious claim' and 'cheap black mail'.[79] In respect of his submission on the legal regime on the matter, Dr Mosugu relied upon the Traditional Rulers and Chiefs Law, 1979, highlighting Schedule 2 that makes a distinction between 'Traditional Ruler' and 'Traditional Chief'.[80] Schedule 3 requires a traditional council under the prompting of the State Executive Council to make a declaration in writing stating the customary law, which regulates the selection of a person to be the holder of a traditional ruler or traditional chief title associated with any community. It is against this backdrop that Mosugu identified the Okogbe of Ojah as a 'Traditional Chief' being contained in a list of 'Traditional Chiefs in Akoko-Edo L.G.A. including a total of eleven (11) traditional Chiefs of Ojah'. Moreover, he affirmed that the Edo State Government duly appointed Chief D. S. Lawani as the Okogbe or Village Head of Ojah, and same was duly gazetted by virtue of the *Edo State of Nigeria Gazette (Extraordinary)* 2006 as 'Appointment of Chief Daniel Suru Lawani as the Village Head (Okogbe) of Oja in Okuloso Federated Clan, Akoko Edo Local Government Area'.[81] He raised the technicality that by virtue of his position as traditional chief or village head, Chief Lawani as the Okogbe of Ojah does not earn a salary but receives allowances or stipend.[82] He corroborated this by citing the provisions of the enabling Law on the Stipends and Allowances payable to Traditional Chiefs, which states, *inter alia*,

1. The Executive Council may from time to time prescribe the stipends and allowances to be paid to Traditional Rulers and the manner in which such payments shall be made.
2. The Stipends and Allowances of traditional rulers specified by the Executive Council under sub section (1) shall be a direct charge on the revenue of the Local Government Council.
3. The Local Government may pay to Traditional Chiefs in its area, such stipends and allowances as may be approved by the Executive Council.
4. The stipends and allowances payable to traditional Rulers and traditional Chiefs under sub-sections (1) and (3) of this Section shall be income tax free, and for the avoidance of doubt, the incomes of any traditional Ruler or traditional Chief derived from other sources shall be liable to tax.[83]

Dr Mosugu argued on the behalf of his client, Chief Lawani, that although the Akoko-Ẹdo Traditional Council had made provisions for the Village Head of Ojah's monthly stipends or allowances in its budgetary allocations, he only received accumulated allowances following official response to Chief Lawani's letter to the Permanent Secretary, Edo State Ministry of Local Government and Chieftaincy Affairs, Benin City, in April 2007 requesting for directives or clarification on the allowances issue.[84] In Chief Lawani's letter to the Permanent Secretary, he indicates,

> Prior to my appointment as the Ọkọgbe, I served (and I am still serving, pending effectuation of my disengagement from the service) as a classroom teacher: teaching at the Ọza Comprehensive High School, Ojah. I have been dutifully discharging my royal responsibilities as Village Head of Ojah … All these activities and more necessarily involved expenses on my part some expenses have become impossible to meet from my scarce pay as classroom teacher. Such expenses incurred in the discharge of my duties as Village Head are of a continuing nature. Meanwhile, the Akoko-Ẹdo Traditional Rulers Council has repeatedly contacted me to come and collect my stipends as Village Head. I hope I can proceed to collect the same-pending my receipt from your good offices of any contrary instructions.[85]

Thus, Mosugu put forward the argument demonstrating that Chief Lawani duly satisfies the provision of the Traditional Rulers and Chiefs Edict, 1979, that qualifies him to receive a stipend or allowance, but not salary. In this way, he sought to show that the accusation was erroneous and an attempt to hoodwink the government. Second, drawing from subsection (4) of the Edict, he asserted that

> a traditional Chief does have incomes 'derived from other sources', which is liable to tax, such as the salary earned by Chief D. S. Lawani as employee of Edo State Government Teaching Service Commission. So, the Edo State Law itself acknowledged and recognized that traditional Chiefs can and do derive income from both the official stipends and allowances as well as 'from other sources'. Meaning that such income does not amount to 'defrauding the Government' as the shallow and puerile reasoning of the petitioner has assumed in his solicitors said letter of 12th March, 2011.[86]

Therefore, his submission was that Obayemi's petitions regarding 'politicising the office' and 'defrauding the government' were 'frivolous, totally baseless and malicious'. Thus, his plea was that the Deputy Governor should discountenance the complaints on grounds that they were unsubstantiated and lacked facts.

In a bid to reinforce the antithesis of Obayemi's petition, Chief Lawani opted for a somewhat political turn beyond the redress through his legal counsel. On behalf of the Ọkọkọ ruling house of Ọsuruka royal kindred, Chief Lawani wrote a week later directly to the Deputy Governor of Edo State on 1 June 2011, further reiterating the main issues addressed in the 23 May letter through his solicitor, refuting the allegations and urging the government to dismiss the petitions brought against him. Ostensibly, with some discernment and tact, the letter assumed a political tone by eulogizing the state government on her efforts and success in subsequent programmes, while at the same time entreating the government to institute an investigation on Obayemi's service records in the Nigeria Police Force. He pleads,

> Your Excellency Sir, in line with the high level of transparency of the enviable Government of our dynamic Executive Governor of Edo State, I urge your Excellency to cause an investigation into ascertaining the suitability of the petitioner (Lawrence Obayemi) to have contended the Ọkọgbe Chieftaincy Stool of Ojah ... the petitioner with service No. ... served for 18 years 6 months and 9 days only in the Nigeria Police Force and has been advised by the Federal Government to keep his services to himself. I know that he who seeks equity must go with clean hands. I respectfully therefore urge his Excellency in the interest of sincerity to our Father Land, ask the petitioner (Lawrence Obayemi) to produce his papers of discharge from the Force. On behalf of my community

Ojah, I congratulate the State Government on her unbeatable efforts and wish her more successes in her subsequent programmes.[87]

On 6 June 2011, Mosugu wrote Lawrence Obayemi titled 'Demand for Settlement of Judgment Debts/Costs'[88] in lieu of costs awarded as part of court actions. As we have outlined above, the costs accrued from three court scenarios. First, the sum of N10,000 was awarded against Lawrence Obayemi as part of the judgment delivered on 15 October 2004. Second, on 27 November 2007, the Court of Appeal, Benin City, had struck out three motions filed by Obayemi before that court awarded cumulative cost of N10,000 against him. Third, on 7 March 2011, the Court of Appeal, Benin City, once again struck out two motions brought before it and awarded the sum of N20,000 against Obayemi. The letter warned that the non-payment of the total costs of N40,000 to Okogbe D. S. Lawani was tantamount to contempt of court orders. The letter cautions,

> Take notice, therefore, that if we or our client do not receive the said grand sum of N40,000 (forty thousand Naira) cumulative costs awarded against you in this matter within four weeks of the date of this demand letter, we shall invoke the coercive judicial powers against you and set in motion processes to compel you, a Judgment Debtor, to pay the debt of costs.[89]

It is unclear when and if this warning and payment had been made accordingly until date. It is against backdrop that we can better comprehend how long and complicated this conflict has been and what intended outcomes and unintended consequences the crisis has had on Oza community up until today.

6

Rituals of passage

Ritual processes are complex and multidimensional sequences of symbolic action, routinized according to fluid or fixed patterns and appropriating symbols that may derive from and relate to myths (Adogame 1999: 181). Myths and rituals operate within sacred space and time and occupy a conspicuous place in Ọza religious life. Cosmologies and ritual enactments to the supersensible entities dominate their everyday lives in ensuring *Irẹgumẹ*, good health, good life and human flourishing. Their religious cosmos covers the entire *Ogbẹ* (life) span from the cradle to the grave. Ritual action is very central to the lives of Ọza people in enhancing the relationships to the powers of *Ogbẹ* (life) and *ọfọme egbe/egbia eka* (peace) as a necessary state for the community. This involves actors, action, use of time and space as well as other symbolic agencies. Both sacred space and time are non-homogeneous, that is, not of the same kind as other space and time. What differentiates them is a hierophany, a manifestation of the sacred told in myths and re-enacted in rituals. Sacred spaces, ritual acts and objects are outward, material and symbolic expressions of religious thought and ideas. Rituals, festivals and ceremonies are ways of implementing the values, norms and beliefs of Ọza society. Their ritual structures draw largely upon a philosophy of relationships. The pursuit of health, fertility and a balance between humans and nature constitute some of their basic concerns. Individuals, community or social groupings attain well-being through explanation, prediction and control.

Rites of passage involving birth, puberty, marriage and death are central within Ọza indigenous world views and point to the ritual attitude in maintaining cosmic harmony and balance at individual and collective levels. Rites of passage create a bond between temporal processes and archetypal patterns in order to give form and meaning to human events (Ray 1976: 100). Thus, Ọza people display a pragmatic attitude towards *Ogbẹ*, life; they see *Ogbẹ* as worth living and *iregu*, death, worth dying. An individual's passage through life is monitored, marked and celebrated from pre-birth, parturition, naming and circumcision, puberty and initiation, childhood, transition to adulthood, adulthood, marriage, old age, death and the living-dead. Other rites are associated with planting and harvesting; natural calamities such as drought or rain; and sickness or illness, passing examinations, quest for employment, search for a marriage partner, embarking on a journey and so forth. Whatever natural and unnatural events happen, be it negative or positive, they hardly explain it off to chance. They resort to seeking a prognosis of all situations or conditions, meaning and purpose. They consider life itself as a continuous struggle in a world that hosts the contradictory spiritual forces perpetually out to exterminate one another. They believe that *irimi enẹbẹ*, evil forces, are inimical to human progress, determined to inhibit the human pursuit of *irẹgumẹ* (total well-being, good life) and *ọfọme egbe/egbia eka* (peace). They perceive *irimi eneshi*, the benevolent forces, as more powerful and capable of repressing or restraining *irimi enẹbẹ*, the evil forces, from unleashing venom on humankind. Therefore, this diametrical opposition between the benevolent and malevolent forces trap *agbọ*, human beings, in the middle. The *irimi eneshi* possess the wherewithal with which to provide *irẹgumẹ* for humans. *Irẹgumẹ* thus involves obtaining the 'good things' or blessings in life. The most significant and valuable elements of *irẹgumẹ* to Ọza people are the capability of procreation or having offspring (children), good health, material wealth and long life.

Rites and ceremonies therefore characterize each stage of existence and as circumstances require. The definite intent of the passage rites is to develop fixed and meaningful transformations in the life, ecological and temporal cycles. Some of these rituals of passage help to create rigid and valid renewal in the life cycle. As we shall demonstrate below, rites associated with some major festivals, seasonal changes and individual achievements and sanctity (especially women) highlight the fluidity inherent in ecological and temporal cycles. The rituals associated with these various life stages are vitally significant in Ọza indigenous cultural matrix. The rituals that are either family-individual or community-collective based have significant religious meaning and symbolism, and through them religious ideas are perpetuated and transmitted from one generation to another. Rituals undergird a whole philosophy of how one should conduct oneself towards self, the society and the suprahuman entities. Their veneration, sacrifices, offerings and prayer structures draw largely upon this philosophy of relationships.

Ọza indigenous religious culture recognizes one's pattern of life as it unfolds in progressive stages in the community. The events in the life of the community echo this similar cycle that seeks to engender a distinctive set of roles, responsibilities and privileges. A. van Gennep (1960) suggested a threefold ritual pattern of separation, transition and reincorporation. Victor Turner (1969) posited a liminal phase of transition, serving as an integral ritual phase, which generates a *communitas*, at least on multiple levels as we demonstrate in the next two chapters. We shall explore how a *communitas* emanates from transitional rites that result in *eku* (age grades), but also how aspects of the liminal rites of transition create and reinforce a unique bond and solidarity within the community.

Within this cyclical time-scope, *Ogbo*, 'a human person', traverses through various life stages: *omo, ofale, omo-ofa, omo oleke* (a newborn child) becomes *omuka* (youth), *oburami Ohoshi* (boy), *ubishi oshopa* (girl); a youth boy or youth girl becomes *Ohoshi Orio* (a male adult) and *osami Orio* (a female adult), and upon marriage they become *Ohoshi no osami* (a couple). The deceased persons translate into *eshamai ni di irimi* and *onumai ni di irimi* (revered male and female ancestors). This transmutation does not complete the life cycle of a human person. Any human person who lived a good life, died at a ripe age and accorded a befitting funeral may translate as an ancestor or the living-dead and could be reborn into the world, thus perpetuating the life cycle. Thus, deceased parents or grandparents who attain the status of ancestors return to life in the form of a new baby. Death does not write a finis to life, but death is a transitional phase to another life.

People are metaphysically and sociologically remade into 'new' beings with new social roles, and also seasons transited, marked and celebrated, for instance, from the 'old' *uchi* (month) and *ukpe* (year) into *uchi onofa* (new month) and *ukpe onofa* (new year). The rituals and practices associated with these various stages are both quintessential and vitally significant within Oza cultural matrix. The definite intent of the passage rites is to develop fixed and meaningful transformations in the life, ecological and temporal cycles, and in the accessions of individuals to high office (Ray 1976: 90). The rapidity of these rites and ceremonies in Oza socio-religious milieu lends credence to how often humans strive to be in active touch with the supersensible world. A right relationship with these benevolent powers is a prerequisite for *olo ilami* (human progress), *utanami/efue unemimi* (happiness) and *iregume* (total well-being). Thus, heavy doses of rituals punctuate an individual's entire life span. For instance, starting a new job or business, acquiring a new parcel of land, building a new house, renting a new apartment, buying a new car, planning a journey, sitting for an examination, marrying a new wife and so forth. Each new venture demands a foundational ritual. These rituals and festivals give us insight into how Oza religious cosmology informs and shapes the people's lives and how life shapes their spirituality.

Iyẹsẹmi (ritual sacrifice or offering), as the symbolic presentation of material or physical objects to the spiritual entities through ritual action, operates within sacred space and time and occupies a conspicuous place in Ọza religious life. The act of ritual sacrifice or offering indicates the intersection of the visible and the invisible worlds, and human intent to project into the spiritual cosmos. Ritual symbols or the use of concrete objects plays a very conspicuous role in Ọza cosmology and praxis. Ritual occurs in a sacred space which is set apart by symbols, making that space different from other spaces and hence an appropriate place for the ritual to occur. The hermeneutics and appropriation of these symbols reflect a whole spectrum of their belief system. *Iyẹsẹmi* are enacted mostly at specific ritual times in secluded sacred spaces which vary from family or clan altars to ancestral, village or community shrines, in groves, caves, hills, mountains, rivers, beneath certain trees, sacred forests, road intersections, graveyards and market squares. Ọza people treat these constructed sacred spaces with awe and reverence. Individuals, families or the community engage in *Iyẹsẹmi* both to counteract the evil machinations of the malevolent spiritual beings on humans and to invoke the benevolence of the deities, ancestors and spirits in order to ensure and maintain cosmic balance and cohesion. The import of *Iyẹsẹmi* is partly to avert an impending danger, attract the benevolence of the spiritual entities, ward off evil agencies and evil machinations, a mark of appreciation and thanksgiving for favours received from the benevolent spiritual agencies.

Asa (taboos) are associated with several of these rites and sacred spaces. Integral to several rites within these sacred spaces are *Iyẹsẹmi* appropriating raw and cooked foods; immolation of animals and birds such as fowls, goats, sheep and cows; and household utensils, farm implements, money and clothes. *Iyẹsẹmi* occur at any time during the day or night, middays or midnights. However, people consider *Iyẹsẹmi* at special ritual times as midnights or middays as very potent against the backdrop of their belief that spiritual forces are very mobile and active, thus making humans more vulnerable to their actions. Religious practices usually took the form of ritual processes in which objects are empowered to facilitate the process. Ọza people speak and think of *Iyẹsẹmi* essentially as a religious act, which takes the form of rendering something to a supernatural being or beings, and with various intents and purposes. It could be, for instance, in the decapitation of an animal in honour of an ancestor or divinity. While *Iyẹsẹmi* usually involves the shedding of blood of chicken, goat, cow or sheep, it also includes concrete objects such as foodstuffs, water, money, honey and even farm implements. These materials and victims of sacrifice have symbolic meanings; they are means to an end and not ends in themselves. In most cases, divination ends in the prescription of *Iyẹsẹmi* to the spiritual entities. Through divination, an individual finds out what type of *Iyẹsẹmi* will insure that a predicted good fortune will happen or mitigate the worst effects of a predicted bad fortune. People transmute *Iyẹsẹmi* to usher blessing or wreak havoc on individuals or groups, or to counteract destructive powers and evil machinations. Thus, various types of *Iyẹsẹmi* such as veneration, praise, thanksgiving, votive, propitiatory, preventive and substitutionary and foundational characterize Ọza religious imagination.

People with special religious roles facilitate these elaborate rituals and sacrifices involving processes of explanation, prediction and control. As we discussed in Chapter 3, some of the many special roles in Ọza indigenous religious praxis include that of the shrine priest, diviner, healer, indigenous medical practitioner, sorcerers and witches. In some of the sacred spaces such as communal shrines or sacred groves, there are ritual specialists or priests who undertake special roles in the ritual enactment processes. These religious functionaries serve as caretakers of the communal sacred spaces, as consultants and facilitators of the ritual sacrifices and offerings, but also protect the space from desecration and misappropriation.

Below, we shall demonstrate how myths, often enacted in rites of passage, festivals and ceremonial activities, link the creative powers of the deities, divinities and ancestors with the needs of the people, and how notions of time and ritual cycles are embedded in Ọza religious cosmos. We shall examine, in the next two chapters, how some rituals of passage create rigid and valid renewal in the life cycle – birth, marriage, death and burial – processes in Ọza and highlight the fluidity inherent in their ecological and temporal cycles by examining some rites associated with some major festivals, seasonal changes and individual achievements and sanctity (especially women). Ọza indigenous thought and praxis subsume and reconstruct religious sensibilities and attitude towards ritual praxis and performance at various life stages and community's existence.

Pre-parturition and birthing (naming) rituals

Pre-parturition and childbirth rituals constitute significant aspects of life-cycle events in indigenous Ọza society. Virtually all aspects and stages in everyday life, as we shall briefly discuss in this chapter, are dotted with rituals to ancestors, divinities or the supreme deity. Perhaps the most ritual-inspiring events are birth, marriage and death, commemorations that permeate in Ọza culture, religion and local custom. Ọza people incorporate rituals and ceremonies as an integral part of the pregnancy and birth experience. Procreation is very central and constitutes one of the ingredients of *irẹgumẹ* and a prerequisite for attaining the status of an ancestor. Thus, having an offspring or children is an important outcome of marriage to the extent that they enact special rites during marriage ceremonies to ensure a consummated marriage. Ọza people believe that such ritual performances have potency on women's fertility, protect the parturiency and secure a safe delivery. Thus, rituals and ceremonies form an integral part of pregnancy and birth. Rituals have the power to impact on experiences because of the mythology imbued within them. They anchor bodies and experiences to the cultural beliefs and values behind the rituals in question. The enactment of belief systems through rituals exemplifies core values and connects to family, community, histories, ancestors, divinities and the supreme deity. Enacting rituals as part of the entire period of pregnancy and birth are spiritualizing experiences. The pre-birth and birth ceremonies filled with ritualized encounters help us to understand the underlying religious ideologies and cultural messages these rituals convey.

Many expectant mothers have fears and anxieties about their pregnancy that stem from the belief that *agbọ enẹbẹ* could ensure misfortune in the mysterious loss of the unborn baby, or miscarriage. Pregnancy was one of the important markers for a young bride to become a full member of her husband's family. A couple of months after marriage, extended family, neighbours and friends are anxiously expectant that the young woman would become pregnant subsequently. If the young woman does not become pregnant, people immediately raise suspicion and wonder what the cause of the delay is. Immediate family members usually keep the news of a pregnant woman secret until the pregnancy is advanced or when her belly becomes distinguished. Precaution is taken to keep and protect the woman and unborn child from *agbọ enẹbẹ*, *Efia* and *Egbọ*. Barrenness, childlessness and infertility are considered a major misery for the entire family and could cause psychological, social and emotional discomfort to the spouse (Adogame 1987: 46). They associate cases of sterility with supersensible entities haunting the woman. Thus, in the case of an illness, the family consults a diviner, healer or an indigenous midwife. Through divination, they seek to ascertain the fate and destiny of the unborn, the health of the pregnant woman or exorcise evil spirits from a sterile woman's body. There are several rituals to ensure a normal birth and protect both the unborn child and the mother from the evil eye of sorcerers, witches and wizards. Such rites also aim to protect the evil ones from hijacking or thwarting the course of the destiny of the unborn child.

The preparations for the birth of a child commences from the very beginning of pregnancy. Family members mostly treat the pregnant woman well and ensure that she eats well, maintains good hygiene and refrains from carrying out daily chores, and lifting or carrying heavy objects. The pregnant women must also observe taboos and prohibitions as precautionary measures to ensure a safe birth to a healthy child. For instance, to prevent the pregnant woman and the unborn child from *agbọ enẹbẹ, Egbọ* and *Efia*, she is not allowed to fetch water from the stream or river at noontime under the scorching heat of the sun, go outdoors after sunset, sit down on certain stones, walk over one sitting with legs stretched out or shake hands with non-family members. The expectant mother observes some food taboos as well. Most of these taboos and prohibitions emanate from the people's myths and they hold them dear in their everyday lives. The fact that people believe in the efficaciousness of breaking them clearly reflects the import of indigenous beliefs, rituals, norms and taboos in the Ọza religious landscape.

Rituals of childbirth

Prior to the introduction of western healthcare systems such as maternity homes, clinics and hospitals in Ọza, women mostly gave birth in their family or husband's home. Usually, the family invites a home birthing woman or a skilful midwife to assist in the actual delivery. There are several methods for foretelling the baby's gender, through either a diviner or the skilled indigenous midwife or home birthing woman determining or guessing the gender of the baby by the shape of a mother's belly. The family enacts birthing rituals for the pregnant woman just before she is due to give birth or during labour. Such rites aim at protecting the woman in labour and the infant from evil forces. Such rituals empower the woman, the parent-to-be, as she stands in the liminality between life and death to bring another life into this world, to surrender to the mysteries of labour and birth and to give her strength for the ordeal. It is a very pragmatic ritual affirming that the pregnant person will have a safe birth experience through the guidance of ancestors, divinities and the supreme deity.

There are several *asa* (taboos) to be observed during the childbirth. The process of childbirth is believed to be safer and easier when less people knew about it. In the case of a difficult or delayed delivery, they perform some rites that they believe will induce the baby to come out safely. Immediately after birth, the midwife bathes the baby and wraps it in a quilt to bring warmth and make it feel secured from malevolent spirits. The midwife cuts the umbilical cord, a rite accompanied with the appropriate wishes of a prosperous appearance and a long, happy life for the newborn child. The umbilical cord has a sacral influence on the life of the child; thus, the family jealously protects the umbilical cord. They bury it in *Orosho*, a special place usually around the family compound or within the ancestral home unbeknownst to non-family members (Adogame 1987: 46). People attribute so much power and symbolism to the umbilical cord that the rituals associated with it can mean the difference of life or death for a newborn, his/her family or community. Burying the umbilical cord within the family compound or around the ancestral homeland anchors or binds the child to the land and his/her ancestral heritage. The umbilical cord also symbolizes the attachment of the child to the mother and its roots in the indigenous society, but also the baby's transition from its mother's body into the physical cosmos. The mythology surrounding the umbilical cord brings ritual and ceremony to the fore of the birth experience. The umbilical cord burial is a common ritual and the mythology behind this practice includes the belief that evil spirits can torment the child or enter the family of a newborn child through the umbilical cord. This explains why it is buried secretly and quickly to reduce this potential risk.

The symbolic heralding of a new baby home is the most exciting experience, a time of celebration when the family and community come together to honour and welcome the new child. Thus, rituals and ceremonies that mark the child's birth and survival are rife. These rituals not only celebrate and acknowledge the child but also serve as a significant way for the family to solidify their connection to community, heritage and culture. The birth rituals provide a newborn child with a sense of communal identity. The stages of life determine the life of each individual starting with their birth, the *Ibiemi*. An *Ọbu Evba* intervenes at this decisive point. Through divination, the name, nature of *Ori*, the ancestor or divinity to which the newborn baby is associated with is revealed. Following revelations, the name *Ozu* is given to certain female babies. There are specific rights connected with the name *Ozu*: dancing during the *Agba* festivities in the *orere* (public arena) and being allowed to touch the *Irimi* masks and to speak to them. The birth of a baby, especially if it is the first in the line of *ọmọ Ukpe Akọ*, gives reason for great joy (Lawani 1992: 17).

In Ọza, public announcement and celebration of a newborn baby is marked by shaking with the left hands. The women who already gave birth play bells to the following rhythm: *Oko i Kogo, Yio-k-o-o*. These cries are the expression of their joy and they echo the first cry of the newborn baby (Lawani 1992: 17). The celebration of the birth, the new life, is already linked with death. The intervention of the oracular divination and the ritual celebration function in the same way for children of both sexes; the only difference is that boys are circumcised a few days after their birth. There is no tradition of female circumcision in Ọza. The birth of a new baby is celebrated through certain sociocultural practices. On the morning or day of birth, the senior elder or family relative presents the child to his ancestors and divinities, lowered a number of times over the ancestral altar, accompanied with ritual offerings and incantations that the baby grows up well and safely. In some cases, a specially prepared medicinal potion is rubbed on the child's body and an amulet tied round the baby's wrist or waist for protection and security against evil forces. The circumstances of delivery, for example, can inform the duration of the festivities. *Egbe Ime Fuẹyi*, miscarriage, is seen as a bad omen and suggests that the woman needs to undergo purification. The death of a newborn baby is the starting point of the mother's quarantine at home.

The *ireni ọmọ inami* (naming ritual) or *ọmọ ipami fi okofa di* (outdooring ritual) forms an essential aspect of Ọza social structure. Thus, one conspicuous transitional rite that lubricates passage through life is the naming ritual. A name represents an essential component of human spiritual anatomy and serves as an indicator of destiny. The power of naming is such that an individual does not exist without a name. Every name is imbued with meaning, history and symbolism. A name becomes a religious mark of identification and a sign of honour and respect. Although the form and shape of the rite may vary, the symbolism bears remarkable semblance as a significant constant. As an edifying emblem, parents, grandparents, elders and family members give names to a new child during the naming ritual on the seventh day of birth amid rituals. The significance of the naming ritual on the seventh day lies in the spiritual connection with the ancestors and divinities. The inherent power in the *ori* works to align the spirit of the individual with the ancestors and divinities. Prior to the seventh day of birth, the child engages liminality as he/she remains in limbo between the living and spirit worlds and may even decide to return. The eighth day marks a transition and complete departure from the world of the spirit to the world of the living.

At the naming ritual, the child receives multiple names depending on the occasion and birth circumstances. The power of naming is such that names are chosen for their special meaning, power and source. Names are woven around circumstantial and historical narratives. Newborn children are named based on specific situations surrounding their birth. Naming a child is taken very seriously because it is believed that a name can make or mar a person. For instance, our daughters' indigenous Ọza names are Ọnọshimijẹ (literally meaning 'I have chosen good' or 'God has given me a good choice') and Pamẹhasẹ (literally meaning 'God has lifted me up'), respectively. Such names imbue history, meaning and symbolism which are held dear by the family and recipients.

The naming rite is usually carried out within the family compound with the participation of family members and close relatives (extended family). An elder or a renowned personality in the family conducts the ritual in the presence of both maternal and paternal family relatives seated outside in the family compound. However, at the commencement of the ritual, the eldest male family member lifts the child towards the sky and welcomes him/her to earth. After the symbolic gesture of welcome, with the elder muttering some incantations or prayers, the male elder hands the baby over to a female family member, usually the mother or mother-in-law, charging her to take proper care of the child, while the elder continues the ritual procedure.

Concrete objects, each with its symbolism, facilitate such a symbolic gesture. The symbolic ritual objects include local gin, schnapps, palm wine, corn wine, basket, broom, cutlass and a basin or bottle of water. The cutlass used in the case of a male child signifies hard work. When he grows up, they expect the child to be an industrious person. In the case of a female child, the basket and broom depict her industrious task with domestic chores. The officiating elder also feeds the child symbolically with food items and condiments including palm oil, salt, kolanut, coconut, honey, cassava flakes and cooked beans, thus introducing the child to earthly food. A symbolic drop or touch of each item on the baby's mouth, and mentioning his/her names three times, depicts a taste of the ambiguous reality of life. Libation, in the form of drinks (schnapps or corn drink), is poured to venerate and invoke the blessing of family ancestors on behalf of the newborn baby. The symbolic giving of drinks or sometimes food to the ancestors are tokens of fellowship, hospitality and respect. They are also symbols of family continuity and contact. Pouring of libation coincides with the announcement and blessing of the child's names. The name(s) are repeated three times while the libation is poured. The officiating elder instructs the child, in a symbolic way, to inculcate good moral values. The main naming ritual follows with presentation of money, material objects and gifts to show appreciation of the mother's safe delivery. Such a symbolic gifting helps to commence the life journey and reminds the child of the importance of responsibility with money and material possessions.

The *ireni ọmọ inami* or *ọmọ ipami fi okofa di* ends with feasting and merrymaking, as this is symbolically 'the first time the child is taken out of doors'.

It is an occasion to introduce the newborn baby to the public, the community to which s/he now belongs. The enactment of the naming and outdooring rituals accords the child both individual and social recognition. Through this forum, the officiating elder reminds the gathering that the child is now an integral part of the community, thereby provoking a reciprocal relationship. The community must care for and help in raising the child while the child is also instructed symbolically to take up his/her individual and societal responsibilities. In the last chapter of this book, I shall demonstrate how formal education, religious influences from Christianity and Islam, and modern health institutions have influenced the flavour and texture of naming rituals, although the principles and symbolism have remained largely intact. The symbolism, meaning and power of naming, and several elements of the indigenous naming ritual have been transposed within the African Christian world view, although the agency of propitiation has sharply altered. However, ritual enactments, particularly life-cycle rites such as naming and outdooring, continue to form the core of spirituality in Qza.

From *Osokuru* to *Osọ*: Transitional rituals towards adulthood

Osokuru is the first, initial, male puberty rite that marks the liminal phase between infancy and manhood, the transition from a boy to a man and from boyhood to manhood. This boy-child initiation is not restricted to any specific age but can be performed during the teenage years till a youth becomes a young adult. In Qza community, *Eku* (age grade) system is defined by gender in which case entry is along *Eku Ehọshi* (male age grade) and *Eku Esami* (female age grade) lines. There are currently in existence more *Eku Esami* than *Eku Ehọshi* because the earlier is routinized annually while the latter is either every seven years or occasional as the case may be.[1] Examples of existing *Eku Ehọshi* includes Umagbudume, Okeboye, Azigeloya, Oviruma and Ayabegbe, while *Eku Esami* includes Azama hebenegbeku, Ayabegbe, Azamarogbẹ, Ọgbọdoshemi and Agbọdogbẹ.[2]

Each chosen name is indicative of the symbolic identity, modus operandi and raison d'être of the respective age grades. *Eku Ehọshi* systems formed through *Osokuru, Okutu* and *Osọ* rituals are mainly associated with *Afẹ* lines while the *Eku Esami* group formation through *Ọmọnugere* and *Ibishika* rituals, to be discussed in the next chapter, are usually connected with *Ireme* lines. Each of these social-religious and political processes is often marked by long-drawn rituals and complex initiation preparations. In the case of *Osọ* rites this involves a retreat in a sacred forest, grove or a secluded place. Neophytes are initiated collectively into a more senior age grade, through a progression that is often accompanied by the revelation and control of 'secret' indigenous knowledge, and the engendering of moral compass by older men and women entrusted with the preparation of initiands.

In the first instance, the male initiands register for the *Osokuru* initiation rites by paying some money, cowries in earlier times or two shillings during the colonial era, to the presiding senior age group.³ According to Abiodun Ojisua, the symbolic fee a few decades ago was two shillings, which in monetary terms is the equivalence of N250.00 today. This fee is paid by initiands according to the *Afẹ* they represent. The money collected through registration is summed up and divided equally according to the number of initiands.⁴ Each initiand puts the sum of money in his money bag as he dances to the market square and visits homes of relatives, neighbours and well-wishers, who in turn put money into his bag as a symbol of endorsement, recognition and appreciation. This dance accompanies a popular ritual song rendition: *Ukpagò okpé nè ukpagò oleseme achà okino-obodé* (*ikimeà mini dele nò lesemé achà*).

As part of this ceremony, the initiated boys greet their predecessors and pay their due respect to the senior age grade that is directly above them in ranking. These salutations are characterized by handshakes with the left hand. The initiands can also present a monetary gift to the *Ọpashi*, who will in turn rub palm oil on the back of all new initiands who participated in the rite. Also, the initiand remains confined at home for seven (nine) days; he wears *egere*, traditional costume, apron and beads, and rubs his body with *ovwuru* (*osu*), liquid extract from camwood. Added to this traditional costume is *ugbaro* (a bird's feather) adorning his head. Dressed in this way, he visits people daily until the seventh (ninth) day. At the expiration of the seven (nine) days, all male initiands are free to travel or go out of the town.⁵

The *Osọ* rite is the next mandatory initiation ritual for boys after *Osokuru*, while an intermediate ritual of *Okutu* is common. While *Osokuru* is mostly enacted and linked to the demise of a titled chief or respected elder in the community, *Okutu* is optional and irregular, often enacted by those who have the means and wherewithal to do so. The *Osokuru* is a prerequisite for the *Okutu* rite. This means that only those who previously completed *Osokuru* can aim to enact the *Okutu* after a couple of years, and this event usually involves pomp and celebration spreading across seven days. The blowing of the *Orọtọtọ* (traditional trumpet) symbolizes the enactment and commencement of *Okutu* and takes place around the *Ukpe Ọza* calendar in April/May. The enactment and completion of *Okutu* and *Osọ* rituals vest on *Eku* certain rights and privileges including *agua ivhumi* (chieftaincy title), marks of social respectability and sometimes financial benefits accruing from monies generated through the public performance of *irimi* (masquerades) to the various age grades.[6]

Osọ is rather exclusive, expensive and laborious and important. The initiated age group has specific functions and responsibilities during the demise of an *Ọpashi* (Lawani 1992: 19). Without the *Osọ* ritual, no male can attain the status of *Ọpashi*, a chief/village head, or hold any major chieftaincy title in Qza community. *Osọ* is a routinized ritual that takes place every seven years. Most of the *Osọ* rites take place in a secluded place in the forest. The candidates for initiation are led at dawn by a leading member of the community to a secluded place. During seclusion, they undergo training about male civic duties, endurance, hard work, morality, societal norms, taboos, familial responsibilities, marriage and adulthood. This initiation rite evokes the necessity of the production of masks and the study and mastery of the specialized ritual language of masks. At the end of the ceremony the participants receive a mask that is considered being a natural child of the actors (Lawani 1992: 20).

The initiands engage in *ọkairimi* (sacred dance), sometimes flogged by the masquerades. Those initiands who are able to jump over the long *Agba* (drum) receives full rites of the *Osọ* (see Plates 9a and 9b). It is impossible to attain the status of *Ọpashi* without completion of the *Osọ* initiation rite. The initiating group is also sent to the forest to hunt for a special kind of bird, locally called *okurukutu*. They remain in the forest until they are able to catch this bird, as bringing the bird home is to indicate successful undertaking.[7] At times, they could remain in the forest for up to a month until they hunt the bird down. Thus, while bringing the bird home is a mark of success and achievement to symbolize the *Eku Ehọshi* transition, returning home without the bird is dreaded as a mark of failure and immaturity. The emerging *Eku Ehọshi* return home to pay tribute to the *Eku Ẹrio* (senior age grade) who previously performed the *Osọ* rituals. Each member of the new *eku* contributes or pays *Isuma/Osuma* (tubers of yam), ranging from one hundred to two hundred, according to the ranks attained.

S. N. Eisenstadt (1954) suggests that age-set systems arise and function in those societies in which the basic allocation of roles is not overwhelmingly determined by membership in kinship groups and where some important integrative functions remain to be fulfilled beyond these groups. Elsewhere, Onigu Otite notes in his exploration of continuance and change in an Urhobo age-grade system,

> In traditional forms of societies, it is generally emphasized that an age-grade organization relies on family units for the supply of its man-power. On coming of age and becoming recruited into the age-grade organization, an individual is faced with roles and expectations having the whole town or indigenous state as reference group. Collective rites and ceremonials mark the initiation of age-groups or age-sets and a system of formal or informal education helps to establish traditional local law and custom and to consolidate the spirit of collective responsibility among members. Training to think beyond the immediate kinship units is a vital process of encouraging tolerance and friendship amongst people belonging to the same socio-territorial unit. Also, the fact of belonging to one social system marks members of other systems as constituting out-groups. Thus, though cutting across family, kinship or clan brotherhood, the age-grade organization operates only within the limits of the social system of which it is a vital part. (1972: 302)

The next phase of the ritual is *Egbusio*, lasting four days in the forest. The initiands return home to take part in *Agba* (the dance ritual), adorning colourful traditional attire with painting of their bodies with *ẹsu*, lotion extracts from indigenous camwood tree.[8] Associated with the ritual is wooden sculpture and carving into human effigies by the newly initiated. These masquerade mask sculptures, usually in male or female human form, could be about eight feet tall, well smoothened and designed with good precision. This is the most expensive aspect of the ritual involving food, money and energy. These wooden sculptures are in turn sacralized as masquerade masks and worn by brave initiates, thus transforming the mask bearers temporarily from *agbọ* into *irimi* and back to *agbọ*. This mundane and supramundane manifestation is embodied in the public visibility, performance and retreat of the *irimi* into the forest, the abode of *irimi*, the spirits.

With the ritual fortification of the masquerade mask, costumes and the appropriation of charms and ritual antidotes by those individuals who will put on the huge wooden costumes, the stage is set for the public performance of *irimi* on the appointed day that the *irimi* will make their debut at the *orere*. Following the public display and ritual performance of *irimi* for a couple of days, they retire back into the forest, the spirit world from where they are believed to have emerged. The *irimi* costumes and paraphernalia are then stored in a secluded part of the forest, out of public view. It is *asa* for a woman to behold the *irimi* during their preparation in the forest, their symbolic spirit abode, to visit the community and when they are retiring back into the forest. While the public performance is associated with the visit of the spirits to the human realm, the disappearance of the masquerades also signify their return to the spirit realm. In a sense, the criss-crossing between terrestrial and celestial domains is a way of ensuring and preserving cosmic balance between the world of the living and the world of the spirits and deities, on what the very existence of the land and life crucially depended.

The peak of the *Ọsọ* rite culminates in a major *gbe erẹrẹ ọsọ* (pounding yam for *Ọsọ*) festivity to fully inaugurate and honour the new *Eku Ehọshi*. In former times, the pounded yam would be heaped up to a height of about four feet and about ten yards in circumference, including big pots of drinks, meat, tins of palm oil and the like. The food so prepared was usually very expensive.[9] The climax of the *Ọsọ* ritual is accompanied with elaborate feasting and celebration, and witnessed by the *Ejas*, the representatives of the *Ọpashi*. The *Ejas* hold the highest-ranking titles and serve as advisers to the *Ọpashi*. Thus, their appearance at the *Ọsọ* festivities also marks the end of the ritual. All men who undertake the *Ọsọ* ritual are eligible to attain the status of *Eja*. They could make payments in cowries or money to be considered in future for the position of *Eja*. The fact that no one can become *Ọpashi* without completing this ritual act shows how important and sacred it is.[10] The *Ọsọ* ritual takes place every seven years at which point a new *Eku* is ritually instituted. *Eku* systems have clearly defined rights and privileges within the community. While the different *Eku Ehọshi* share some commonalities, each respective *Eku* carries out definite tasks and its members share common duties, distinctive from those of the other *Eku*. Despite external influences such as Christianity, Islam and western forms of education on Ọza indigenous social systems, the relevance of *Eku* systems cannot be undermined. With modernization processes, *Eku* continue to exist and remain relevant in Ọza social and political organization.

Above, we have briefly described the *Osokuru*, *Okutu* and *Ọsọ* transitional rituals of incorporation which are exclusive for young boys and men. The next chapter will focus on more elaborate, exclusive rituals for the transition of young girls into women, the *Ukpe Iruvie*, *Ọmọnugere* and *Ibishika* ritual festivals, respectively. The last sections of this chapter will focus briefly on marriage and death/funeral rites.

The rites of marriage – *Iruvie Imumi*

Living a good life is one of three important prerequisites for attaining the status of an ancestor, the other conditions being dying a good death and being accorded a befitting funeral. One *sine qua non* for a good, sustainable life is having a consummated marriage consequential in an offspring. Ọza myths of creation ground the institution of marriage as a sacral union between a male and female adult for the main purposes of procreation, mutual companionship and assistance, and for attaining the common good in life. Chief Alonge defined marriage as 'a sort of attainment of independence by the man and the woman to make their own home'.[11] There are also myths illustrating marriage among some local divinities. Such myths underscore the nature of spiritual beings but also help to grasp marriage rites, customs and institution, as integral to Ọza social and religious life (Adogame 1987). Marriage is a necessary choice that all young adults look forward to and it is hardly an individual option. It is a family rather than an individual affair, in that all stages of the marriage from introduction, negotiation and betrothal to marriage, and obsequies involve the nuclear and extended families.

Marriage is a relationship which is socially and legally sanctioned by the society and hence accorded all the rights and duties attached to such a relationship. During the British colonial era, indigenous or traditional marriage was integrated into the colonial legal system as Native Law and Custom. Polygynous and monogamous marital relationships are essentially recognized under Ọza religious practices or customary law; polygamy and polyandry are rare. Polygyny is not a rule but an exception; it is circumstantial. The practice of polygyny seems to fit well into the social structure of indigenous life, although it is no longer prevalent in contemporary era in the face of socio-economic realities (Adogame 1987: 26). The practice instils in people's minds that a big family earns its head great respect in the eyes of the community. Within the indigenous setting, such a practice raises the social status of the family concerned, signifies affluence and is indicative of prestige and social respectability. Alonge (2002: 16) referred to *Isomi*, a form of marriage commonly practised among the Okurosho people where a woman is at liberty to leave her husband at any time, provided she repays the bride price.

Thus, marriage fits well into a larger pattern and web of social relationships in Ọza. In fact, marriage operates within the Ọza social system, and being part of it, the social system determines its essence. As a social institution, marriage is founded on and governed by the social and religious norms of society; it is the root of the family and of society, and a bond between members of the community. It is an activity where all members of a given community – the departed, the living and those yet unborn – meet (Adogame 1987: 16). It therefore strengthens good relationship and cohesion among the families and the society at large. The social, religious and economic import of marriage are so interwoven that they can hardly be separated. In a sense, marriage becomes a duty, a requirement from the corporate society and a passage of life which everyone must participate in except for reasons of impotence. Failure or refusal to get married under normal circumstances, according to John Mbiti, means that 'the person concerned has rejected society and society rejects him in return … to die without getting married and without children is to be completely cut off from the human society, to become disconnected, to become an outcast and to lose all links with mankind' (1969: 133).

Among Ọza people, marriage has a foremost place in their religio-cultural world view and social economy. Marriage looms upon the horizon of every youth as an indispensable function and obligation to be realized with as little delay as possible after attaining puberty. Unmarried persons of either sex, but also couples without children, are often objects of derision by society. Hence, there is recourse to divination rituals for a reversal of such perceived anomalous states in life. Therefore, Ọza people consider marriage as a very important transitional stage in the journey through life, and hence a very high value is set upon it. Generally, marriage among the Ọkpameri, as in other societies, was probably the most significant public event in common life. It did not take place at one single moment of time but came into being across a series of meetings, negotiations and ceremonies (Adogame 1987: 28). In fact, various activities take place in the traditional marriage of the Ọkpameri people. Some of these activities take place long before the time of the actual ceremonies while others take place during and after the actual ceremonies. Central to Ọza life-cycle rituals are those concerned with *Iruvie imumi*, the rites of marriage, that are enacted between her attainment of the state of puberty, betrothment and actual marriage. In the next chapter, indigenous (traditional) marriage ritual ceremonies will be discussed under three categories, namely, preliminary rituals, the marriage (wedding) ceremony and the post-marriage activities, respectively.

Rituals of *Iregu*: Death

We have demonstrated so far that rites of passage are fundamental within Ọza indigenous world view and life cycles, thus illustrating ritual attitude in maintaining cosmic harmony and balance. Life-cycle rituals encompass both rites through life in the human, everyday, mundane existence as well as life in the incorporeal, spirit world and supramundane cosmos. In Ọza society, elaborate rituals accompany death or bereavement. Ọza people believe that *iregu* does not write a finis to *Ogbẹ* but serves as a passage or transition from the *Ogbẹ agbọ* to another phase of living in Ọgbẹ irimi. As a prerequisite for attaining the status of ẹrio adẹ or eshamayi ni inumayi ni di irimi, living a good life, dying a good death and being accorded a befitting funeral are paramount. In other words, they will contend that life is worth living and death worth dying. Ọza people's attitude to death straddles awe, fear and loss, but also joy, gratitude and appreciation for a good life well spent. This is suggestive of a distinction between a good and bad life, a good and bad death, a befitting and unfitting funeral. For instance, a good life and good death is associated with longevity: one who lives a long life up to a ripe age and has an offspring, one who demonstrated good moral standards and was in good health and dies at an advanced age, a death that is considered natural and not of illness/disease or misfortune. Such perceived natural deaths are celebrated and call for rejoicing, merriment and an elaborate, befitting burial. On the other hand, a bad life is characterized by bad moral standards, calamities, evil deeds, incessant illnesses, remaining single and unmarried, a marriage without children, barrenness. A bad death is premature death, that is, death that occurs before a person attains a ripe age, but also death from strange, uncommon illnesses. In fact, all deaths which are considered as unnatural are not accorded a befitting or elaborate funeral.

Each of these life-cycle patterns are consequential in that the path of good life, good death and a befitting funeral would be prerequisite for attaining the status of an ancestor, while the other track of bad life and bad death attracts an unfitting funeral resulting in a precarious afterlife in which they assume malevolent, mischievous spirits. The belief and practice of ancestral veneration is integral in Ọza indigenous society. The burial of the deceased, mostly the aged parents or family members believed to have lived a good life and died a good death, within the family compound hones in this symbolism. They appropriate ancestor-hood with the cyclical concept of time and a life cycle that would entangle birth, death, the ancestral world and reincarnation. Ancestors could also be reborn as children, thus evidencing the belief in reincarnation. Babies considered reborn children are given names of departed ancestors, or they could identify them through distinctive body scarifications or sensual/sensory characteristics.

It is against this backdrop that whatever natural and unnatural events happen, be it negative or positive, nothing is given off to chance. Explanation is sought for all situations or conditions, their meaning and purpose. Life itself is a continuous struggle in a world which hosts the contradictory spiritual forces perpetually out to exterminate one another. The Ẹfia, Egbọ and agbọ enẹbẹ are believed to be inimical to human progress; they are determined to impugn and inhibit human pursuit of total well-being. Thus, the occurrence of death is quickly followed with *orimi unuami* (ritual aetiology, a kind of spiritual autopsy of the dead) to diagnose the cause of death and to prescribe the nature of funeral rituals to be enacted.

Another ritual diagnosis is sought through divination and bringing a petition before the *Ehọ Ẹkẹshi* to ascertain the causality of the death, but also to seek justice in case of mischief and evil machinations. The petition carrier is often seen to visit the shrine in the early morning hours carrying the paraphernalia of sacrifice on her/his head and declaring rhythmically, *Ẹkẹshi gbere o, Ẹkẹshi gbere o…* (literally 'Ẹkẹshi let justice prevail …, Ẹkẹshi let justice prevail …'). Through such ritual enchantment, the petitioner invokes the deities and ancestors to unveil the causes and reasons behind the mysterious death, uncover the culprit(s) and hold accountable whomsoever is responsible. Such ritual act and performance engenders public anticipation of awe, apprehension and suspicion, as they eagerly await the repercussion of that petitioning. It is believed that the deity would respond with instantaneous strokes of justice, often noticeable in a mysterious illness or death befalling the culprit(s), or an unprecedented *Ijọrọmia* (public or private confession of the misdeed). When there is *Ijọrọmia*, ritual antidotes are put in place to avoid instant death or mitigate the nature and extent of catastrophe likely to affect the culprit(s) and their entire families or belongings.

In addition to being a kind of spiritual autopsy mechanism, *orimi unuami* also serves as an accountability check to ascertain whether or not the dead person lived a good life, died a good death, was above or beyond reproach, maintained good ethical standards and was responsible or not for any misfortune or evil deeds while alive. Thus, the *orimi unuami* ritual immediately follows the demise of an individual and departure from the physical world, and the determination of causality or explanation of death facilitates the funeral rites and transitioning into a new supernatural life phase. Death is seen as natural or unnatural depending on the circumstances leading to and surrounding it, and this implicates the ritual purification or defilement of the corpse prior to burial. 'All dead bodies or corpses are subject to a ritual bath or cleansing, depending on the status of *Ọfuegbe* (purity) or *Ọfia* spirit. The journey back to the spirit world begins with a ritual bath for persons of *Ọfuegbe* spirit' (Lawani 1992: 21). The ritual cleansing is followed by *orimi unuami*, which takes place in an open space within the proximity of the deceased's house or family compound. This is a public ritual that is closely observed by family members and the immediate community at large, serving as ritual spectators. Ritual preparation for *orimi unuami* is led by some ritual specialists skilled in such ritual enactments.

The phenomenology of *orimi unuami* involves the ritual specialists cutting off a sample of the deceased's hair and nails, and obtaining a hat (men) or comb (women) of the dead person as ritual paraphernalia. All these concrete ritual objects are placed on top of six young palm fronds that are bound together as a mock coffin. A seventh palm frond will be held by one of the ritual specialists. Other ritual appurtenances involved in this symbolic ritual performance include a bottle gourd and a calabash or clay pot filled with water placed on one end, while farm implements or a stone object are placed horizontally within the ritual space. Two ritual specialists carry the improvised coffin built from six palm fronds, containing the concrete objects of hair, nails and hat or comb, on their heads, standing at both ends of the makeshift ritual casket. The lifting of the substitute casket by the two ritual specialists is accompanied by ritual music. It is believed that as they move forwards and backwards, keeping to the rhythm of the ritual music, they start to slowly move their heads left and right in a frenzy, a somewhat uncontrolled state or mood. This means they are now in a liminal state, *Orimiomuayọ* (possessed by the spirit), in which their body motions and gestures are completely taken over, enchanted and controlled by the *orimi*, the spirit of the dead. The other ritual specialist who is custodian of the seventh palm frond recites incantations, dips the palm leaves into the water-filled gourd, calabash or clay pot, touches first the back and then the front of the other six palm leaves at the spot where the hat or comb is placed. It is believed that through this symbolic communication the spirit of the dead is conjured into action, first on self-disclosure of the deceased in terms of causes of the death and then in deciphering whether the deceased had lived a good life and died a good death.

This involuntary control of the ritual actors by the spirit of the dead serves as a bridge of communication between the visible and invisible. The spirit of the dead is believed to hover around the corpse after death, and thus the ritual attendants invoke the *irimi* with the following words: '*Uke Fu Egbe Ka ha Ame Nwọn; Ukume Fuegbe Ka Su Ikeme Egba*' (literally meaning 'Spirit, if you are pure/honest/morally upright, move and drink water by breaking the gourd; conversely and if you are impure/guilty/immoral, go and bang/strike your head on the rock'). It is revealed through this traumatic spiritual experience whether the cause of death is natural, self-inflicted, unintentional or caused by a deity/ancestor, or inflicted by a malevolent spiritual force or an evil person. The ritual diagnosis or explanation of death causation communicated from the spiritual realm is thus transmitted through the ritual specialists into the human, mundane world.

This ritual drama generates a tense atmosphere and public anxiety as they await the verdict. If the ritual carriers of the improvised coffin are involuntarily swayed by the *Ofuegbe* spirit towards the water-filled gourd, they move closer and break the water gourd in a symbolic manner. This calls for public jubilation and celebration as they exclaim: *Oha amẹ nwọn* (the deceased drank water breaking the water gourd) symbolizing vindication from evil, wrongdoing and an indication of purity and moral uprightness. If the carriers are swayed involuntarily by the *Ofia* spirit towards the rock or farm implements on the adjacent position and symbolically bangs on the rock or concrete objects, that is *ọsu/ọtu ikeme egba* (the deceased bangs/strikes his head on the rock). This outcome is often met with public sigh, silence, shock, disbelief, disgrace, humiliation and disappointment. This result signifies that the deceased is impure, guilty or not morally upright. This could turn out that the deceased is an *Ofia, Ogbọ, Ogbọ ọnọbẹ* or linked to some evil machinations.

If the deceased *Oha amẹ nwọn* (drank water breaking the water gourd), necessary preparations are put in place for an elaborate befitting funeral, in case the deceased is advanced in age and when the death is considered *Iregu obọ Ogbọ* (a good, natural death). Depending on the social status of the deceased, elaborate funeral rituals involving singing, dancing and lavish entertainment is enacted to commemorate a good life well lived and a good death well earned. The tears of joy, gratitude and celebration that follow the burial rituals of an aged person who lived to a ripe age are profound. Such elaborate obsequies are transitional rites believed to usher the deceased into the life of the spirits, the living-dead, thus enhancing the chances of becoming an ancestor. The funeral rituals could take place in phases, with the first phase of the funeral rites culminating in the *orimi ihamishọ* (burial, the laying to the ground of the deceased) amid pomp, commemoration and festivities. A second phase of the funeral rites takes place about four weeks after the initial burial ceremony. These rites take several hours or days, often commencing with an evening wake-keeping and continuing until the morning or entire day, characterized by dancing, music and gift exchanges between the family of the deceased, neighbours and invited guests.

In case of the latter, *ọsu/ọtu ikeme egba* (bangs/strikes his head on the rock), subsequent divination rituals are enacted to reveal the specific details of the act, the victim(s) and the ritual consequences. If the deceased is a victim of the evil intentions of another person, the *Ireme* will make public the name of the guilty person, then necessary ritual remedies and punishment will follow. If it is disclosed that the deceased was *Ofia, Ogbọ* or *Ogbọ ọnọbẹ*, the final disposition of the corpse is done in a shallow dug grave, literally 'thrown away' or 'discarded' in *Ilẹkpẹ* (the designated evil forest) undignifiedly. The victims of *Ehọ* who incurred wrath and punishment by death are also designated for undignified burial in *Ilẹkpẹ*. This is often an unprecedented outcome that brings enormous shame, pain, disgrace and humiliation on the family and offspring of the deceased. Oracular divination may prescribe that some properties and personal belongings of the deceased be discarded in the evil forest or prohibited from public use.

7

Gendering rituals

Performative ritual action, bodily objectification of femininity and the aesthetics of indigenous culture and tradition hardly delimit gendered power of women in Ọza society. Rather, we should situate female ritual power in its broad, indigenous political economy, social, cultural and religious configurations, and against the backdrop of fluid power dynamics, interpersonal relationships and intersubjectivity. It is within these ambiences that gendered power contestation and women's negotiation of their sociality play out in ritualized space and time. Women's contribution, influence and identity-making in Ọza indigenous cultures are linked to their social positioning, that is, how they see and position themselves and how they are seen, as well as religious, economic and political power.

> Ọza social organization is characterized by spaces occupied by *Esami* and *Ehọshi*, both of which are recognized as co-creators and partners in the construction of society. This engagement of women and men in a collective activity is subject to the following rules: sharing of tasks, and respect for the attributes and rights of men and women. These are the two principles that guarantee the continuity of the system. (Lawani 1992: 70)

The political and social role of *Ọdejọ* and her ritual power and function loom large in Ọza community. The *Ọdejọ* serves in an advisory capacity to *Ọpashi* and his *Eja*, and through her political and spiritual responsibility foreground women's involvement in social and political debates. Crucial decisions on matters affecting the community are only taken by *Ọpashi* and *Eja* after due consultation with *Ọdejọ* and her deputies on behalf of the women. Recognition of such gender dynamics is necessary for negotiating social and political equipoise of power. The gendered matrilineality of *Ireme* genealogy unpacks the ritual power, social positionality and cultural locationality of women in Ọza. As highlighted in Chapter 4, women's response to the coloniality of power is remarkable. The political power of women was partly expressed through a dispute regarding the imposition of tax between the colonial native authority and Ọza community. This representative had demanded the payment of taxes for the works done for the development of the Ọza community. The Benin provincial administration through its local district officer had served a letter to the village head and his council of chiefs over payment of tax to the colonial government (Lawani 1992: 73). While the *Ọpashi* deliberated with his *Eja* on the matter, the *Ọdejọ* at the same time gathered her deputies and women to discuss the issue. The women vehemently opposed payment of tax, citing a historical precedence during the reign of Ogundare Lawani when Ọza community received a colonial tax waiver, which was a direct result of women's protest and opposition.

The political consciousness and moral compass of Ọza women is ensconced through the liminal, transitional rites of initiation into *eku*, processes which bring about *communitas*, collective effervescence, social cohesion and social and cultural capital building among each *eku*. Ọza women's political consciousness is also enhanced during the *Ibishika* (*Ọmọnugere*) festivities. The first section of this chapter will focus on preliminary rituals of marriage, *Ukpe Ọza* (Ọza annual festival), the liminal, transitional gendered rituals of *Ibishika* or *Ọmọnugere* and how they are integral to female power production and social identity of women in Ọza. *Ibishika* (*Ọmọnugere*) form part of the social-religious and political processes marked by long-drawn, complex and exclusive rituals of incorporation to transition young girls into women. Such a liminality of ritual spatial time embodies women's political consciousness, engenders ritual empowerment, galvanizes a moral compass and stimulates social responsibility necessary for fostering future domestic, familial tasks and women's sociality.

Preliminary rituals of marriage

In Ọza, marriage is so crucial to a lifeworld that any person who has attained the age of puberty is expected to be engaged. Reiterating the import of marriage among the Ọkpameri peoples generally, Chief Ogunnubi remarked, 'Marriage is so imperative that at the age of puberty, a girl is supposed to be courted, by a man, for at least six months.'[1] If a girl is not courted by any man for a long period, it is assumed that something is amiss. People often speculate that the girl may be of questionable or egregious character, may have inherited some diseases, identified to belong to a bad family, considered a witch or that evil forces are preventing men from approaching her, and so forth. At the same time, when a young man remains single for a while without a wife, people speculate that he is impotent, wicked, may have exchanged marriage for wealth/riches or even believed to be involved in a secret cult that abhors marriage.

Nonetheless, there are marriage-related taboos but also regulations concerning those that one may not marry. These are often people of one's own family, relatives of one's parents up to a certain degree of kinship. Generally, people have cognition of how they are related to others through blood kinship and marriage relationships.

> The structural relationship between a father and his own children is comparatively less important in a matrilineal society. In a matrilineal society like Ojah community, a man's child belongs to the line of his mother. That is, the mother's brothers and sisters will have authority over his own children, as such children could only inherit from their mother's family. In turn, the father has authority over his own sister's children. (Alonge 2002: 37–8)

In other words, any child born into a family belongs automatically to her matrilineal lineage regardless of gender. This system of family arrangement generates, in fathers and men, a feeling of ambivalence towards educating their children, sending them to school or empowering them by investing in trade or professions. This attitude is accompanied by an egregious impression that when a father invests in his children's education, training or trade, he does so to the betterment and advantage of the *Ireme*.

Even when the boy and girl are ignorant of details of such sociocultural and religious taboos, this is where the family serves as the knowledge reservoir; they often know who is a close relative and who they cannot marry. Intra-marriage within the same *Ireme* (matrilineal lineage) is considered a taboo. For instance, a person who belongs to *Ibikira*, one of the seven matrilineal family lineages, is forbidden to marry or be married to a person of the same lineage, but s/he can intermarry from the other *Ireme*. As we noted in Chapter 2, intermarriage between Oza indigenes and *Ilẹmẹ* (Unẹmẹ-Osu peoples) is an egregious taboo insofar as they are considered *ugbọ na adesa* (social outcasts).[2] Such intra-marriages with the same *Ireme*, and intermarriages with *agbọ na adesa*, are not sanctioned by the respective families or the community.

Thus, Oza people have a common belief that broken marriage taboos result in misfortunes, ancestral wrath, untimely death of the couple and their offspring, and social ostracization or banishment from the community. An informant remarked emphatically, 'The man or woman defaulter may be regarded as the cause of any misfortune which befalls his relatives and community' (Adogame

1987: 31). It is also a taboo for parents to engage in incest, marry and have sexual relationships with their children, siblings and grandchildren. Incestuous relationships between siblings, cousins, aunts and nephews are taboo. Such a social norm of marrying outside your *Ireme* or immediate family is a kind of exogamy which helps to preserve blood ties, sustain kinship relationship and genealogies, and facilitate kinship cooperation and alliances with new families. Undisclosed and non-confessed actions may result in similar calamities enumerated above, sometimes evidenced by *idudunemi* (spontaneous swelling of all parts of the body). This condition could lead to *iregu* if the ritual antidote is delayed or denied. Ritual sacrifice which includes *agbi ishiri* (immolation of a goat) is enacted to appease the wrath of the ancestors and divinities.

The courtship and negotiation process is almost similar except for some practices such as the consultation of the oracular diviner or ritual sacrifice which is associated with it. The man's family first consults Ọbu for *evba* to ascertain if the girl he has in mind will be a virtuous wife. Likewise, in the case of the woman, there is also recourse to divination to determine his sincerity and credentials as a potentially wholesome husband. A verbal notice was usually registered between families concerned. When the man thinks that the time has come for him to marry, he makes his intention known to his parents, and, should they have no objections, the girl's family is contacted by one of his uncles or an older relative. Usually, the family of the suitor makes inquiries about the family of the girl and indicates the interest in marriage. The man who wants to get married is not always in the best position to introduce himself and consult directly until the negotiation is consolidated. Thus, the older family relative or representative acts as a 'marriage broker' for him and on the family's behalf. In actual fact, the consent of both families is expedient for a marriage negotiation to be completed. The family's endorsement should not be seen as taking away the agency of the individual man or woman but rather enables it, giving it a familial stamp, mandate and legitimacy. This further underscores the fact that marriage is not an individual affair but that of the entire family and community at large (Adogame 1987: 30).

Due to the centrality of the *Ireme*, the intention and negotiation of marriage is formally done with the maternal family of the girl. If the girl's father is approached in the initial stage, he will immediately refer the family representatives of the boy to the *Ireme* who have the responsibility to give their daughter in marriage. A girl is not given in marriage without the consent and final approval of the *Ireme*. This further underscores the relevance of *Ireme* in Ọza socio-religious life. *Ireme* prescribes the major rules and regulations on which the institution of marriage revolve. Due consent and approval of Ọriọ-Ireme during betrothal, introduction, engagement and actual marriage are paramount. In the first instance, the *Ireme* carefully investigates the family of the suitor to ensure that they are giving their daughter to a good home and family. They exert more impact especially if their daughter is approached for marriage by a man from a different community.

The *Ireme* plays central role in the initiation rituals during the *Oruvie Ukpugbe* and *Ukpe Iruvie*, overseeing and taking enormous responsibilities for ritual enactments, sacrifices and performance. The *Ireme* helps to imbue the *oruvie* with a moral compass and character formation, virtue of chastity, physical development, indigenous knowledge acquisition, hygiene, economic self-reliance, social empowerment and familial responsibility. The *Ireme* has the sole prerogative to prescribe the bride wealth required to consolidate and effectuate a marriage contract. Although the *Afẹ* plays a role in marriage negotiation, the functions and power of the *Ireme* is more pronounced and their influence ubiquitous and entrenched in Ọza society. It is against this backdrop that Ọza is sometimes assumed by some as a matrilineal society than a patrilineal one (Alonge 2002: 46).

There is, however, an exception to this rule as the *Ọpashi* in earlier times could use prerogative to identify a girl he wishes to marry without prior knowledge and negotiations with the girl's parents, family or guardians. Parental or family consent is not sought and they have no right to challenge or object to it because *Ọpashi* is regarded as a 'divine representative of the supreme deity'. Owing to this perception, some family or parents will consider it a social privilege for the *Ọpashi* to take their daughter as a wife. When that happens, she is labelled *ọsami ni Ọpashi o guẹ* (the girl chosen or called by the King or village head). It is necessary that all who wish to be engaged in marriage have attained the age of puberty and undergone the transitional rituals, *Osokuru* and *Osọ* in the case of males, and *Ọmọnugere* and *Ibishika* in the case of females.

Once the family broker conveys the suitor's intention to the girl's family, the head of the *Ireme* or the girl's family summons a meeting to discuss the suitability of the suitor. The *Ireme* gives their consent or disapproval and this is communicated to the man's parents. Following *Ireme* and the immediate parents' confirmation, the bride wealth for their daughter is set and conveyed to the man's family accordingly. The bride wealth is usually a symbolic undertaking transmitted through exchange of cowries, money, goods and services. Its social, cultural and religious value lies in solidifying the new affinal bonds and relationships engendered through marriage, and in legitimizing children born to the union. The economic value of the cowries or money is flexible rather than fixed; it can vary and depend on the families involved. Additional gift items, *Okẹkẹ* (foodstuffs), which forms part of the bride wealth, including tubers of yam, beans, tins of oil, garri, melon and so forth, are presented to the girl's family or *Ireme*. In earlier times, the intending husband volunteers or renders *Ẹrẹsumuna* or *Unwenemi* (help/assistance) to the prospective *osumuna* (parents-in-law) in farm work, house building and roofing. *Ẹrẹsumuna*, as integral to the bride wealth, signifies solemnity, responsibility and commitment to the man's intentionality. Thus, *Okẹkẹ* and/or *Ẹrẹsumuna* are the outward symbols of a serious undertaking by the families concerned. They serve as a familial seal of authority, giving social backing to the would-be husband and wife living together sustainably and bearing children. The *Okẹkẹ* is a mark of gratitude, appreciation for how much the woman's parents or family have cared for her, having been kept in *egbe iruvie*, a pre-marriage practice in which a girl is confined to the house for *Ukpugbe* in preparation.

Consequent upon the provision of the bride wealth, a date for the ceremony is fixed by the bride's family at the convenience of both families. The arranged date must fall within the same period of the annual marriage festivals or ceremonies. Prior to setting aside a date, an *Ọbu* is consulted and *evba* is enacted to ensure that a suitable date for the family ancestors is chosen. Ọza people revere their family ancestors considerably, hence ritual sacrifices are offered to them to guarantee that the couple and their families are alive to witness their marriage and life beyond the ritual event. Girls who attain puberty and undergo *egbe iruvie* are referred to as *Iruvie Afẹ* or *Iruvie Okofa*. They are housebound for a period of one lunar year, a period always calculated with the *uchi* (moon) phases. In the indigenous Ọza calendar, thirteen *uchi* phases make up a year. According to Chief Alonge, 'In the olden times, all the girls to be married in Ọza are confined to the house compulsorily for *Ukpugbe*.'[3] Also, girls who are yet to attain puberty could be kept in the fat-house or fattening house. Another informant conveyed the significance of *egbe iruvie* in this way: 'Girls who attain puberty are kept in seclusion so as to make them "grow-up" and mature for their husbands, they are taught how to perform household duties and most importantly they are kept away from the public, so that no man have sexual relations with them except their intending husbands after marriage.'[4] He suggests that *Ukpugbe* was prescribed by the ancestors and it was in fact an appropriate period for her to become fully matured. Within the indigenous setting, a girl is expected to be chaste before marriage, hence the girl's family feels proud when her husband finds her to be a virgin, unblemished at the time of their daughter's marriage. The strict observance to the retention of a chaste state may be problematic to sustain, just as the one-sided claim of purity demonstrates an inherent bias towards the female gender. In spite of the sociocultural and religious justification for *egbe iruvie*, it is a practice that has ebbed owing to new challenges of western education and modernization.

Prior to the girl being housebound, she is led and made to sit down in *Oroshọ*, the place where the umbilical cord of newborn babies are buried at birth. A symbolic ambush is laid for her; when caught, she is carried shoulder-high by some young men to the *Oroshọ* spot where she is made to sit and given a ritual bath with *Amẹ-Isese* (purificatory water) obtained from *Ẹrẹsha* (see Plate 12). Sitting on *Oroshọ* symbolizes the transition from her youthful stage to womanhood, while the bathing marks the beginning of her home confinement.[5] This is a significant marker in the liminal phase: henceforth she is called and addressed as *Oruvie* or *Oburuvie* (a girl who has attained womanhood). Ọza people believe that if the water obtained from *Ẹrẹsha* is used to bathe her, it refreshes her and keeps her away from all evils throughout the *egbe oruvie* (fattening period).[6] Thus, the significance of the liminal practice of *egbe oruvie* in Ọza's socio-religious imagination cannot be overemphasized. As soon as the ritual bath is completed, she is then led to the house where she will remain confined. Whatever she does throughout the homebound period will be in seclusion from the public. Throughout this period, the intending husband is not allowed to visit her, although the female relatives of the man have the prerogative to do so. Nevertheless, before the girl undergoes confinement, *evba* is consulted and whatever it prescribes in form of *Iyẹsẹmi* is carried out. It is believed that the *Iyẹsẹmi* has the potency in removing any obstacle or misfortune that may occur until the process is completed. Throughout the *Ukpugbe*, apart from being given lessons on domestic duties and personal hygiene, she takes part in indoor games, storytelling, spinning thread and so forth with her family.[7] The *oruvie* learned how to play a certain musical instrument called *Ashekitereke* (idiophone) during this period (Lawani 1992: 26). *Ashekitereke* consists of three parts: a long wooden stick of almost 1.5 metres covered with concentric incisions, a dried, hollow fruit with a hole on each side and a fragment of a pot. Sounds can only be produced by the correct use of all three parts. As contacts with the external world, work and going out are limited during the period of retreat, playing the instrument has the importance of being an antidote to monotony, routine and boredom (Lawani 1992: 26). All these various activities will prepare her for the roles, responsibilities and activities of a housewife and mother.[8]

A. van Gennep defined rites of passage as 'rites which accompany every change of place, state, social position and age' (1960) and shows that all rites of passage or 'transition' are marked by three phases: separation, margin or *limen* ('threshold') and aggregation. One way in which Ọza people ritualize social and cultural transitions of the female gender is through *Imumi Iruvie*. Ritually embodied in this state of transitionality are the phases between a girl's attainment of puberty, initiation, seclusion, betrothment and actual marriage. The first, separation phase embodies symbolic behaviour signifying the detachment of the individual or group from an earlier fixed status from *ubishi/ibishi* to *oruvie/iruvie* or *ọsami/esami* within Ọza social structure, and from a set of religio-cultural conditions. During the intervening 'liminal' period, the characteristics of the ritual subject are ambiguous; she traverses a cultural realm that has few or none of the attributes of the past. Liminal entities are neither here nor there; they are betwixt and between the positions assigned and arrayed by custom, convention and ceremony expressed by a rich variety of symbols. Thus, we can liken liminality in this case to navigating from visibility to invisibility and then back to visibility. Liminal entities, such as *ibishi* in initiation rituals and *oruvie* in puberty rites, may be given a ritual bath, housebound for *Ukpugbe* to demonstrate that as liminal beings they have no status, are yet to be assigned insignia, ranks and position in a kinship system, and have nothing that may distinguish them from their fellow neophytes or initiands. Their behaviour is normally humble and obedient; they must obey their female elder instructors and mothers-in-law implicitly and accept arbitrary punishment without complaint. In marriage initiations with a long period of seclusion as *Ukpugbe*, there is often a robust proliferation of liminal symbols. During the third phase of reaggregation or reincorporation, the passage is consummated. The public show/display during *Ukpe Iruvie* and *Ukpe Ọza* epitomized the readiness and actual marriage that is consequential. The transition from *oruvie* to *ọsami ọnọfa* puts the woman in a relatively stable state once more. The family and community expect *Ọhọshi* and his *ọsami ọnọfa* to behave in accordance with certain customary norms and ethical standards binding on the couple in their new social position and location. The phase of reaggregation in this case comprises the public installation of the *Iruvie* with all pomp and ceremony.

Ukpe Ọza (Ọza annual festival)

Ukpe Ọza, an annual ritual festival enacted usually in the months of April or May, commemorates the indigenous Ọza festival that ushers in *ukpe ọnọfa* (new year). *Ukpe Ọza* marks the climax of the *egbe iruvie* for the *Ukpugbe* period and their first public show or outing signifying their full readiness for marriage. Thus, integral to *Ukpe Oza* is *Ukpe Iruvie*, with several days celebrated with pomp and pageantry. The ritual of *Ifiesemi/Inyesemi* is organized by the parents of the *Iruvie* as part of the *Ukpe Iruvie* ritual ceremonies and lasts for three days. It is symbolized by shaking of hands by the celebrants. The *Oga* (age grade leader) plays a central role in *Inyesemi* (*Ifiesemi*) which brings together *eku* to feast with the celebrant (Alonge 2002: 29). The *Oga* is assisted by his *Ubere* (deputy) and *Evushomi* (errand man). Through their leadership, they are able to mobilize the *eku*, ensure discipline and decorum, instil social compass, galvanize the group for communal work and collective solidarity, and foster reunion, peace and tranquility. The *Ukpe Oza* festival helps the people to recapture their social past. It provides an opportunity for people to relax, play, sing and dance. This introduces an element of variety in the social life of the people (Alonge 2002: 50). *Ukpe Iruvie* and *Ukpe Oza* are indicative of initiation and calendrical rituals of passage. They are events in which rites of marriage engender transitions for individuals and collectivities. Such transitions of liminality are critical to the shaping of both temporal and social experiences of Oza women. The liminal phase of the rituals of marriage characterized by *egbe oruvie*, *Ukpe Iruvie* and *Ukpe Oza* are spatial times where ritual embodiments and ceremonial splendour are also linked to women's bodies, how rituals work on and by means of the body.

Marriage festival rituals are dotted through the Oza four-day market calendar, namely *Ako Ebiene*, *Ako Anumu*, *Ako Afo* and *Ako Akpe*, respectively. These ritual events take place between March and April annually and last for five days including the village four-day market calendar. This four-day market structure is rotatory among neighbouring towns including Oza community. *Ako Anumu* is both Oza market day and a day of leisure and rest from farm work. The next market day, *Ako Afo*, is held in Makeke, while *Ako Akpe* market day is held in Dagbala and the fourth market day, *Ako Ebiene*, takes place in Ososo. These markets are visited and patronized by traders and people from all neighbouring villages as a kind of local economic collaboration. The ritual and festivities vary from one market day to another, just as their import and symbolism bear several distinctions.

On *Ako Akpe*, a day to *Upe Iruvie*, which will be their first outing, all the *Iruvie* are embellished with *ase* (white native chalk) all over their bodies, colourful beads around their necks and white cloth tied around their waists. Through *evba*, they choose a little damsel or adolescent girl from the family of each *oruvie*. In the evening of that day, women accompany all the *Iruvie*, their damsels amid songs to *Eresha* in a ritual called *sesame*, to seek for blessings from the spiritual forces.

A common song rendered goes thus: *Eee ekewewe, Eee ekewewe, aminẹ ukpe, amine onoshemi, eee ekewewe, eee ekewewe* (literally meaning *Eee ekewewe, Eee ekewewe*, we have witnessed another year. We are seeing a good and happy one. *Eee ekewewe, Eee ekewewe*). They take *Amẹ Isese* with them from *Ẹrẹsha* as they undertake the procession back to *Orosho* where they all wash their hands with *Amẹ Isese*, and each of them dance round *Orosho* seven times in the *Ekewewe* ritual (Adogame 1987: 37). The procession to *Ẹrẹsha* and all the rituals involved are indicative of the fact that the *oruvie* is preparing for her first public outing and thus signifies her first outing to fetch water in a stream, a domestic chore she will continue to perform in the husband's house, her new family home (see Plate 12). At this stage, the *oruvie* is only free to go to the stream to fetch water. She is not yet permitted go to the farm unless a diviner is consulted.[9] This shows that she does not have total freedom of movement at this stage. Divination declares whose farm the *oruvie* will visit with her damsel, usually the farm of one of the relatives of the intending husband. At the farm, she receives four tubers of yam as presents to take home. She carries three tubers while the damsel carries the fourth, thus symbolizing the gaining of full freedom of movement and the husband's ability to feed the *oruvie* and care for her adequately.

On *Akọ Ebiene* day, which is their first public outing, all the *Iruvie* are adorned with *Ase* (indigenous white chalk) all over their bodies, their necks and waists full of rows of colourful beads, white cloth around their waists and their hair weaved and festooned with coral beads, a hairstyle referred to as *Ọpia* and *Ugogo*. The *Iruvie* are dressed up with *Egere*, a locally made blue and white cotton cloth, on their waist while their bodies are covered with *Ase* (see Plates 10 and 11). They also have wooden bracelets around their arms with gems and multicoloured pearls. Their front is decorated with crossed jewellery laces made of blue pearls. Each *Oruvie* sits on *apẹtẹ akpa* (wooden stool/box for public display), often looking downwards in a shy, sombre mood with hands crossed on their knees (Lawani 1992: 28 and 108). All *Iruvie* in a particular quarter of the town might sit together in the same *orere*, public square, or individually, holding *uje* and horsewhips, and accompanied by a little maid or girl similarly dressed.

This public display or show, *akpa* or *nya akpa*, the ritual act of sitting on a box-like bridal stool which contains her garb or clothing, is also characterized with calabash or bowls placed in front of each respective *oruvie/ukpelu*, meant for collecting gift items or money presented to them by the public, family, friends, admirers and well-wishers. The *orere* is also the place where the fiancé first appears, although for different reasons. The fiancé or betrothed is usually the first to present money or gift items to his fiancée or would-be-wife, after which relatives, friends and well-wishers follow suit. The presence of a would-be-husband in *orere* is accompanied by a procession, music and dancing. The *Ogiso*, this musical event, is also a way in which the fiancé invites his family, age grade, guests and friends to a meal and drinks reception. Accompanied by drumming, music and dancing, the fiancée is led to the *orere* where her *oruvie* or *ukpelu* sits with her little maid and presents money. His parents play a vital role in this ceremony. First, his mother dances with her age group and offers gift items to members of her age grade in appreciation. Then his father follows with dancing, together with his age grade to *Ukpukpe*, the most important indigenous music and dance for the *iruvie imumi* (Lawani 1992: 29). Through such a symbolic action, the public knows the would-be-husband. On this day, the public will know all the girls who will be married that year. The *Iruvie* who have been initiated on the same day thereby form a new *eku esami*, a female group that will be routinized subsequently.

On the third day, the *Akọ Anumu*, a ritual act and process is routinized as on the second day. The would-be-husband receives and fetes family, friends and guests with food and drinks in their respective homes. The fiancée provides melon and oil which will be baked into *ọfọrẹ* or *efọrẹ*, prepared by the elderly women in the family chosen through divination. According to Alonge, *efọrẹ* is exhibited around the whole community and taken to every nook and cranny where the *Iruvie* are sitting. However, the *Iruvie* are forbidden to see the *efọrẹ* being exhibited around by the *Ọdejọ* or women in charge of the ceremony. The fried melon are usually seven pieces in each *agba* (a small calabash with a lid). The agba, which are also seven in number are placed on a round flat wood called *Eku* (Alonge 2002: 28). The finished product is taken to the marketplace and distributed to all and sundry, while the would-be-husband's share is brought back home. The *onuoruvie*, that is the girl's mother, but also perhaps the 'godmother' takes some portion of the *ọfọrẹ/efọrẹ* home and dispenses it among elderly women while enacting prayer rituals to the ancestors. This melon-cake ritual is significant because it shows that both families are in agreement and hence prayers made to the ancestors are to guide both families (Adogame 1987: 40). At the end of *nya akpa* (public exhibition), *efọrẹ* is taken to the *Ehọ* close to *Erẹsha* and the ritual sacrifice is enacted on behalf of the *Iruvie* to ensure good health and fecundity. The *Iruvie* return home after the ritual and the sacralized *efọrẹ* is shared between the families of the *oruvie* and the suitor, with the former receiving three portions and the latter four portions, respectively (Alonge 2002: 28).

On *Akọ Akpẹ*, all the *Iruvie* to be married will fetch water to the *Ọpashi*. This practice is for the *Ọkọgbe* to know how many girls are going to be married in that year and give them his blessings.[10] On this day the *Iruvie* may also fetch water from the river for *Ọdejọ* and the oldest women in the village who will give them some money as a mark of appreciation (Lawani 1992: 28). The *Ọdejọ*, who is head of all women in the community, plays a great role in *Ukpe Iruvie*. The *Ọdejọ* and her female deputies visit all the girls in *egbe iruvie* for that year, but they also visit them while they observe *nya akpa*, publicly display during the *Ukpe Iruvie* (see Plate 11). In a symbolic gesture, the *Ọdejọ* consecrates or dedicates each of the *Iruvie* by drawing a symbolic circle around their heads with *uje*. This ritual act of incorporation takes place on different occasions of the public appearance of the *oruvie*, thus symbolizing the transition from *ubishi/oruvie* into *ọsami*. On the last night of *Ukpe Iruvie*, the individuals flanked by their families and friends dance around the community as a demonstration of gratitude to all those who showed generosity and presented gifts. Afterwards, they are accompanied to retire to their parents' homes and remain there until the entourage from the would-be-husband's family come to take them to their new homes.

Female initiation processes through marriage ritual festivals is common among Ọkpameri people. For instance, Somorika people enact the *Ogogo, Ofare* and *Omoshele*, all part of female initiation rites. The *Ogogo* festival (festival of girls) is similar to the *Ọmọnugere* and *Ibishika* festival in Ọza. In Lampese, a girl is taken to the *Uhlusho* where after the rituals she becomes an *Ohiuacha* (a cloth tier) who must no longer be seen nude. As Chief Ogunnubi puts it, the significance of nude dancing is for men to choose their future wives and also to know those who are mature.[11] In former times, female initiands danced virtually nude at the *orere* except for beads around their waists and neck, or sat partially nude, *nya akpa*, except for the white cloth around their waists and beads on their necks, at the *orere*, the public space (see Plate 11). While the festival of girls remains resilient, nude dancing or partially nude *nya akpa* are now mostly non-existent owing to modernity and exposure to school education. Although the practice has been in sharp decline, partial or full nudity during the *Ukpe Iruvie, Ọmọnugere* and *Ibishika* festival display and dances highlight embodied experiences and the positionality of girls'/women's bodies in Ọza ritual cosmos.

The selective objectification of female bodies, much more than males, in initiation rituals undercut how femininity is displayed through physical appearance and public performance. Thus, bodily objectification and the social construction of femininity through initiation rituals of the female gender evokes an essential contradiction between femininity and subjective physicality. This renders critical thinking about sexual objectification and its internal and external consequences for measuring feminine beauty and maturity. The works of psychologists such as Barbara Frederickson and Tomi-Ann Roberts (1997) on objectification theory, and Nita Mckinley and Janet Hyde's (1996) objectified body consciousness scale both illuminate how girls'/women's objectified status leads them to internalize an observer's perspective on the self and engage in habitual body monitoring and may feel shame and anxiety about the body. Nonetheless, we have shown how such elaborate preliminary rites and performances of puberty and betrothal are quintessential life-cycle rituals of marriage prior to the actual marriage (wedding) ceremony. The next sections will focus briefly on *Ọmọnugere* and *Ibishika*, then the actual marriage ceremony and post-marriage ritual activities, respectively.

Ibishika

The ritual ceremony of *Ibishika*, held during the last two days of *Ukpe Ọza*, seeks to reunite and reignite the *communitas* and the collective effervescence of all the women in *Orere Ibishika* (public square) on the first day for *ikami* (a public performance). The *Ọmọnugere* dance ritual is held at the *orere* featuring all soon-to-be-initiated girls. Such a vivacity is routinized on the second day, with the festivities held in the respective town quarters in Ọza. When all the females have arrived in the arena, the *Ọdejọ* or the oldest woman who leads and heads the initiation ritual will organize the young girls for a ritual dancing performance. Men are only passive spectators during and throughout this specific ritual celebration (Lawani 1992: 77).

The *Ibishika* ritual is held in the same vicinity where *Orimi Odure* (rituals of silence) is held prior and commences with nine days of silence or peace. Before the *Ọdejọ* announces the commencement of the festivals, rituals are enacted to ensure *egbia eka* (peace) throughout *Ukpe Ọza* and *Ukpe Iruvie* and beyond. Following the directives of *Ọpashi* and his *Eja*, the Ibiovwe family is mandated to perform the necessary ritual sacrifices at specific sacred spaces of *Agbalechi*, *Ekuofa*, *Ogbọmiyan* and *Ẹresha* (Alonge 2002: 50). During the *Orimi Odure* ritual time, no one is to be seen making loud noise, shouting or splitting wood with axe implements. Women are prohibited from work in the farms or in the fields. Even funeral rites and ceremonies are suspended so as to observe the rituals of silence. The ritual of silence is, however, controlled and conditioned by the *irimi* ritual performance. Defaulters and anyone who breaks the rule of silence is sanctioned and fined a certain amount of *ikime* (money). Where the defaulter is unable to make an instant payment of the fine, an alternative ritual sacrifice will be prescribed to appease the *irimi*, the symbolic archetype of *ẹrio adẹ* or *eshamai ni di irimi/onumai no di irimi*.

The *Ibishika* ritual commences immediately following the observance and completion of the rituals of silence. Families, mothers and daughters are involved with the elaborate pre-ritual preparations. As Lawani succinctly described, pearl necklaces are produced during this time. Women also make their *Ohuru* (powder) out of tree roots and the colour of the *Osu/ẹsu* (fruit extracts). *Ohuru* serves to paint the body of the young girls whereas *ẹsu* is used to draw body tattoos (Lawani 1992: 77). The *Ekiẹsu* (tattoo designer) will draw the tattoos with little wooden sticks. In order to gauge the quality of a tattoo, one has to wait until the next day when the lines of the tattoo are most visible after a bath. The bodily objectification and semiotic significance of the *Ibishika* ritual in the form of *ẹsu* (tattoos) attract admiration from their mothers, families and public for the ritual aesthetics but also for their feminine ingenuity and creativity. Three days prior to the commencement of the *Ibishika* festivities, the first layer of *ẹsu* on the female body would have become conspicuous. A second, more detailed layer of *ẹsu* is applied to the body closer to the start of *Ibishika*. The *Iruvie* are bedecked with *Ugogo* and *Ọpia* (hairstyles), before or after the tattooing, as a distinctive symbol for the girls who will be married in that particular year.

On the actual day of the *Ibishika* ritual performance, much effort is put towards the embellishment of female bodies, tattoos, hairstyles, manicures/pedicures and adorning of ensemble attire or clothing in preparation for the public performance of the dance ritual. Such a ritual performance characterized by bodily adornment is of aesthetic, semiotic, symbolic and gendered significance. At the *orere*, the women gather and spread out forming a circle in the middle to create a kind of stage. The girls are arranged according to age brackets and inspected by the *Ọdejọ* or leader of the initiation ritual. The men stay away from the women as mere observers and spectators. To commence the dance ritual, some older women would volunteer to blaze the trail in leading the dance. In this way they pave the way, gestures, steps and rhythms to be emulated by the younger girls. Through such leadership in the dance ritual, the older women reminiscence their own rituals of initiation, routinize the dance performance and transmit the skills to the new female initiands. Such ritual performance generates collective memory to enrich the individual initiands and the community in such a way that galvanizes communal harmony and guarantees female solidarity and women's sociality for future generations. Alonge noted that the *Ọmọnugere* festival was institutionalized to create an opportunity to present girls to the public for eligible bachelors to see. The girls appear stark naked with the design of local black chalk on their body and beads on their necks and waists all exhibiting beauty. 'This is in the form of 'beauty exhibition or beauty parade' which is accompanied with dance that enabled the family of the suitor to spray money on the bride-to-be, in the public' (Alonge 2002: 23).

As Lawani aptly described, the *Ibishika* dance ritual takes place in a rhythmical and coordinated form. The dancing troupe of girls forms a circle under the direction of the ritual leader. Of course, the first dancing steps of the 'initiands' are probationary, not very secure. With several repetitive dancing steps, they will achieve the level of the initiator and will then be *Etesomi* (good dancers) (Lawani 1992: 80). *Ibishika* is an exceptional ritual dance in Oza; its goal is to attain uniformity, regularity and compliance. *Ibishika* concentrates on the voices and the clapping of the hands. The steps follow the melodies, the sound perceived with the ear is gestically translated with the dancers' arms, their feet and the pearl laces around their bodies and ankles. Structured by a model of chorus and responses, the melodies consist of short and simple phrases. The ritual leader leads the chorus while the ritual participants respond with monosyllabic sounds. The different pieces of music are performed in an irregular rhythm. The speed is slow in the beginning and accelerates until the end. Lawani provides a rich taxonomy of ritual songs and music characteristic of *Ibishika*. The *Ibishika* ceremony begins with the *Omonugere* dancing rite usually accompanied by a *Omonugere Ugere Aro…* melody (The dance floor is wating for you …). Then the choice of other melodies and order of appearance of the girls is left open and spontaneous. These include songs/melodies such as *O ya Ugbe, ubishi oshopa …; Osomu Ugogo …; Enishi mo de tutu ma ushe …; Ega o he he he …; Mi cha, mi cha, mi mine ododo pa oyare eke …; Igbadume ibishi yioko …; Oyibo no ra uhuoka …; Oza kino ogegere, ogegere onyama ro …; Beva nu koko …; Oshe makete beraro mi wene wee …; Ode keke semi fine ne Oza e …* (Lawani 1992: 84–97). The melodic aspect of *Ibishika* is *Ivie* (songs). The *Ibishika* melodies are polyphonic. *Ibishika* allows several generations to unite their voices in perfect harmony, translated by polyphony. All other traditional musical manifestations of *Ukpe Oza* are exclusively instrumental (Lawani 1992: 81).

Generally, oral transmissions and sonic and visual representations characterize Oza religious and musical traditions. While myths serve as a pathway for understanding world views and ritual world, music, songs and dance represent another dynamic orature for reconstructing Oza indigeneity and spirituality. Thus, music, songs and dances form a significant source and resource for the reconstruction and self-definition of Oza indigenous spirituality. For instance,

Lawani demonstrated a correspondence between the musical activities like *Agba*, *Ide*, *Ogiso*, *Ibishika* and *Iregede*, and the instruments used for each of them. Their routinization follows a strict schedule and pattern. These ritual activities are mostly linked to the liminal phase of initiation, which plays an essential role in the knowledge-building process of an individual. *Ibishika* takes over a privileged position among these activities, with its melodies beyond the explicit messages, venerating ancestral spirits (Lawani 1992: 100).

Ọza musical cultures

Ukpe Ọza and *Ukpugbe* are structured by different ritual festivities. Most of these are related to rituals of rhythmic music, songs and sounds. This dimension is essential, being men and women's contribution to the musical cultures, sights and sounds that characterize the ritual festivities which take place on a very basic level of society. The choice or preference of essential rhythms of music, songs and musical genres depends on the particular ritual or situation under question. While the rhythmic music and genres are often shared by all the members of society, the onus lies on the ritual adept or music composer to prescribe to the group or audience. The musicality of cultures could also be expressed spontaneously and echoed by each respective group. Beyond the aesthetic, artistic, recreational and performative expressions of music and songs, each retains a specific ritual, ceremonial function.

The tapestry of Ọza musical tradition and genres suggests major functions that straddle cognitive, emotional, social/cultural, ritual/religious and physiological dimensions. Ọza people appropriate music and songs for reverence, devotion, deference, allegiance, appeasement, homage and veneration. Music and songs provide a unique symbolic representation and reflect social and religious values of Ọza culture and cosmology. Ọza music and songs have a social function that fosters bonds, cooperation and empathy between families and peoples, and serves as a communicative tool for ensuring continuity and change, social cohesion, control and coordination, integration and community-building, promoting work ethic and social mores, and impacting moral values and identity. Music and songs could also be used subversively as a social and political critique, counter-critique, defiance, civil disobedience, insubordination, contempt and rebellion, and as a tool with enormous semiotic and symbolic significance.

Lawani provides a robust phenomenology of Ọza musical life, highlighting basic musical elements such as sound, melody, harmony, rhythm, texture, structure and expression, and demonstrating how these elements are not mutually exclusive (Lawani 1992: 58–80 and 84–97).[12] In these detailed works, Lawani highlighted the musical functions, song and dance genres and symbolism of *Agba, Ise, Ide, Ogun, Orimiunuami, Omoukpeako, Ekewewe, Ogiso, Ukpukpe, Olee, Okidogbo, Iregede, Igomi, Iregba, Ishoko, Ikede, Uvieoka, Evieegemi, Uvieakayan* and *Ikidi*, respectively.[13] Other Ọza musical and dance genres include *Alugudu, Igoro, Edukpe* and *Azamarogbẹ*. Lawani makes a useful distinction between ritual, ceremonial, recreational and social musical genres, noting that while each of these genres share commonalities, each has its own peculiarities, meaning, function and symbolism, respectively. One musical genre culled from Lawani is illustrative here of the complexity of the function, meaning and symbolism of Ọza songs: *Ono ku Emo Ne'Mo Di kia Ba* (The ashes will come back to the one who drops them) (Lawani 1992: 68):

1. *Uke ko utosha onoshi* (If you sow a good grain)
   Uda ba utosha onoshi (You will harvest a good fruit)
   Uke ko utosha ọnọbẹ (If you sow a bad grain)
   Uda ba utosha ọnọbẹ (You will harvest a bad fruit)
   Uke ko utosha ọnọbẹ (Don't sow bad grains)
   Utosha ki itosha nake ko (The quality of the grain you sow)
   No yi oda ze ka agbọ ki irimi (Will germinate here on earth and in the spirit world)

2. *Uke ri egue onoshi* (If you do or act good deeds)
   Uda mine e gue onoshi (You will encounter good things/receive good reward in turn)
   Uke ri egue ọnọbẹ (If you do or act bad deeds)
   Uda mine egue ọnọbẹ (You will encounter bad things/receive bad reward in turn)
   Uke ri egue ọnọbẹ (Do not do or engage in bad/evil deeds)
   Egue ki egue ki egue na keri (Whatever actions we take or things we do)
   No yi a da mine kagbo kirimi (We get the result as humans and in the spirit world)

3. *Kadi ma ri onoshi ko* (Come let us unite and do that which is good)
   Shiki ma mino onoshi (In order that we can receive good reward)
   Kadi ma ku egbe gbe gbe (Come let us unite and bond as one)
   Shiki ma ne gu me za (In order that we become strong, a unified force)
   Ọgbo no Ọgbo no demo di kia ba (Whosoever drops ashes will it return)
   Iye ase we ka gbo kirimi (So it was said among the living and the spirit world)

This music/song genre embodies a variety of ritual and social significations that include the inventing of a moral compass with a figurative 'sowing/planting a grain/seed, doing/action indicative of good/bad behaviour, and interpersonal relationship'. It also makes a distinction between this-worldly (human existence) and other-worldly (spirit world) orientations, thus exemplifying a cosmology with a rather fluid nexus between the human and spirit worlds, and locates human quest and prerequisites for attaining the revered status of an ancestor in a kind of cause-effect relationality. This song/music genre also hones in on the power and vitality of *communitas*, a collective effervescence in ensuring and sustaining social bonding, cosmic harmony and human flourishing. Thus, as Lawani aptly argued, besides language as a repository of culture, the different forms and genres of music/songs which accompany ritual ceremonies give Ọza their distinctive musical identity (Lawani 1987). The power of sound, of music and of dance allows what cannot be obtained by violent means. The rhythms and music of the ritual ceremonies serve as some of the most indigenous cultural elements of Ọza. It is an important part of their cultural message because the music, songs and dances recreate and routinize the people's past experiences and expressions. Thus, the centrality of Ọza music, songs and dance cultures is articulated in the local expression, *Eyara Ishimi noi ma kine*, literally meaning 'Our town embodies a dance culture'.

The marriage ceremony

In former times, all marriage ceremonies in a given year were celebrated on the same day. After betrothal, the actual form a girl's marriage takes is usually determined through divination. The prediction might be that the girl is caught unaware on a certain market week day at a particular time and brought to her husband's home. When this happens, all family members are mostly aware except the girl herself. Such an unprecedented action adds anxiety, amusement and jollification to the practice. Alternatively, divination may direct that the marriage be solemnized in an indigenous way. Nonetheless, the consequences of not heeding the injunctions through divination is believed to be very disastrous, in that it could lead to misfortunes ranging from infertility to infant mortality and even to untimely death of the bride or groom as the case may be. Therefore, the key moments of marriage preparations and celebrations are marked with elaborate ritual action and performance (Adogame 1987: 41). The people believe that indigenous marriage is sanctioned by the ancestral spirits; thus, whenever any misfortune happens, or someone took ill, the people mostly attribute it to the wrath of ancestors.

If the diviner's prognostication in reference to the nature of marriage directs that the girl should be caught unaware on a certain day and at a particular place, an ambuscade is laid in a strategic position and she could be sent on an errand that takes her through that part. The prearranged team bushwhack her on the trail and carry her shoulder-high to the husband's house with a retinue of women amid jubilation, singing and dancing. Prior to this event, her mother and female elders would have prepared her personal belongings, which they carry along with the cortege. Although such a practice may mean fun and amusement, it is also a denial of the girl's volition and agency. Nonetheless, such a practice has become unpopular partly due to the exposure to and influence of other marriage forms and social change (Adogame 1987: 42).

On the other hand, if divination prescribes that the marriage be solemnized in the indigenous way, then the man's family prepares greatly to receive *osami ofa* (new wife) to the house. Divination rituals are enacted to ascertain whether the *osami ofa* will bring good luck or adversity into her new home. On the appointed evening, a retinue of female relatives and neighbours are sent to the girl's family home to lead her to the prospective husband's house. Prior to her departure, the parents enact invocatory rituals to the ancestors and an emotional note of felicitation. The cortege of women flanking the *oruvie* is usually accompanied with dancing and singing *osami ofa mayi ma dia pa oo* ... (literally meaning 'We have come to take with us our new wife oo ...') or *Afeomorego mije* ... ('She is going to a wealthy home ...'). Prior to their arrival, the husband is whisked away to a neighbour's house or hidden in a separate room, often not available to welcome his new wife and the entourage. Rather, the *osami ofa* and her cortege are received by members of the family symbolizing the family's hospitality, open-handedness and sociability. This practice further underscores marriage as a family-oriented rather than an individualized enterprise.

Following this warm reception by family members on the behalf of the man, he finally resurfaces from his temporary hideout, amid jubilation, and welcomes his *osami ofa* to their new home. The couple both kneel before the family elders who enact prayer rituals to the family ancestors invoking them to ensure a peaceful married life that will be devoid of calamities and misfortunes. They also engage prayer rituals, sacrifices and pouring of libation to the ancestors and deities to facilitate a consummated marriage with offspring. Through the symbolic act of libation, the ancestors are deemed to share in the feasting that ensues but also witness and sanction the wedding ceremony and marriage. It is for these reasons that elaborate ritual sacrifices embody marriage ceremonies (Adogame 1987: 44). At the end of the prayer rituals, the newly married husband invites his family, relatives, *eku* (age grade), friends and in fact the entire community to a fete. Feasting, drinking, eating and gifts presentation and exchange are ubiquitous in *oruvie imumi*. Some of the prepared food and drinks is offered as libation to the ancestors, while some portion is sent to the *eresumina* (parents-in-law). This is a reciprocal gesture which demonstrates their gaiety and mutuality in sustaining new family ties and an enduring marriage pact. Celebration continues on the following day as the new husband joins his family, *eku* and well-wishers in dancing around the community. However, the pomp and magnanimity of the ceremony depends largely on the man's social status within the community.

Post-marriage rituals

A number of rituals are enacted following the marriage ceremony as an expression of happiness, gratitude to the ancestors and other benevolent spiritual entities, but also as protection from the malevolent spiritual entities and human enemies. Thus, recourse is made to divination subsequently. In former times, the *osami ofa* would not go to the farm or stream until after one year as she was expected to have her first pregnancy and delivery within this period (Adogame 1987: 45). Much importance is attached to the first delivery, hence all care is taken to ensure a successful one. Rituals are enacted all through the period of gestation and the advanced stages of the pregnancy to prevent any misfortunes at child birth. Child birth rites are also rife and ritually expedient. Although now an outmoded practice, when a husband finds his *osami ofa* to be a virgin upon their first sexual encounter after marriage, he sends some gift items to her family as a sign of appreciation for their role in keeping her chaste until marriage. As discussed above, infertility or childlessness is regarded as aberrant, unnatural and a great calamity. In fact, such an anomalous state is the most severe psychological trauma that a woman can suffer. Infertility is mostly interpreted as consequential against the backdrop of ancestral wrath or the couple's failure to heed the injunctions of divination. Pregnancy is therefore a happy omen for the couple, a proof that the union is looked upon with favour by the ancestral spirits and a proof of the couple's, although mostly the woman's, fertility (Adogame 1987: 46). Thus, when the *osami ofa* is not seen to be pregnant in the first few months or first year of her marriage, the parents and parents-in-law generate apprehension. They make recourse to divination and enact ritual sacrifices, where necessary, to appease the ancestors or deities. As a mark of honour and responsibility, the husband sends additional gift items to his parents-in-laws, although these are not part of the bride wealth. The adaptation of *ọsami ofa* to her new home happens progressively. From the foregoing, it is obvious that pre-marriage and marriage rituals and ceremonies occupy a very conspicuous place in the everyday ritual lives of Ọza people and it involves the entire community beyond the immediate families. Therefore, various ritual activities occupy all stages of marriage during the initiation, negotiation, the marriage ceremony and even during the post-marriage ceremony, respectively.

8

The future of Ọza indigeneity in the face of African modernity

This concluding chapter will critically explore the resilience, change and transformation of Ọza indigenous religions and cultures against the backlash of encounters with colonial modernities: British, Nupe, Yoruba and Benin hegemonic incursions and influences, as well as contestations with exogenous religious cultures such as Christianity and Islam that are increasingly engaged in religious competition within contemporary Ọza society. I have written this book through looking back into Ọza historical, cosmological and ritual imaginaries, and this enables me to explore the future of that past and the past of the future, in terms of Ọza contestations of indigeneity and negotiation of modernity. I attempted to interrogate and reconstruct these contestations and negotiations between the colonial enterprise, missionary transmission and indigenous agency and (re)appropriations reflexively.

Therefore, any theorizations of this encounter between the coloniality of power, hegemonic intrusions and indigenous Ọza polity and religious cultures must take due cognisance of instantiations of indigeneity politics and the dynamics of identity, culture, tradition and power. The coercion, manipulation and influence of exogenous hegemonic powers hardly obliterated indigenous polity and agency. Rather, such encounters produced intricate entanglements and negotiations of power, identity and culture that oscillated between resilience, mutual transformation and change. Ọza indigenous cosmologies and rituals constitute a distinctively pattern of religious thought and action. The advent of Islam and Christianity saw the introduction of new religious ideas and practices. The encounter transformed indigenous religious thought and practice but did not supplant it. Ọza indigenous religions preserved some of its beliefs and ritual practices but also adjusted to the new sociocultural milieu. The contact produced new religious imaginaries, with some appropriating indigenous symbols and giving them a new twist. Such initiatives attest to the continuity of Ọza world views and ritual cosmos in the midst of social change.

I have explored indigeneity as a relational concept deriving from colonial and postcolonial milieus, through the prism of Ọza spirituality and indigenous knowledge systems. Any exploration of the concept of indigeneity, at least in Ọza society, that fails to come to terms with inherent dynamism and fluidity will be rather fraught. Ọza indigenous religious cosmologies, world views and culture are hardly static and unchanging; they are dynamic and are constantly in flux. Their indigenous religious cosmologies are living, expressive spiritualities. Ọza people generally celebrate life, their spirituality and their religion; they dance it, sing it and act it. Through rituals, people perform and act out their spiritualities. These are vibrant sources in the lived expressions and experiences of Ọza people. Ọza sociocultural landscape, including their indigenous knowledge and technologies, correlate directly with the dynamics of change and the transformation of individuals' as well as groups' cultural meaning systems and senses of belonging. Therefore, to understand and interpret their complex ritual worlds required methodologies that seek to unearth and conceptualize how and to what their cosmological tradition inform their day-to-day ritual dimension. A self-reflexive approach was therefore quintessential in deciphering the most useful sources and methodologies for the research that resulted in this book.

Competing power contours, multiple loyalties and paradigms of justice

Indigenous cosmologies and ritual imaginaries embody integrated systems for mitigating and managing conflicts, combating social disruptions and checks and balances for ensuring and sustaining norms, values and moral economies. Indigenous methods of conflict resolution include traditional dispute resolution, peacemaking, talking circles, family or community gatherings and mediation, described only by the language of the community. All these refer to the methods of resolving problems and to the methods of restorative and reparative justice. The British coloniality of power, its duplicity, consciously impinged on the indigenous justice system and eroded its power, authenticity and legitimacy, thereby truncating the juridical process. The indigenous paradigm of justice involves the role of *Ẹrio* at the family lineage level, *Eja*, *Ọpashi* and ultimately recourse to *ebu evba, ẹrio adẹ* and *Ehọ* for adjudication, when all other attempts fail. *Ẹrio adẹ* and *Ehọ* such as the deity of justice are frequent reference points. The encounter between the Empire and local power trajectories espouses the intricate politics of indigeneity and induces multiple hegemonies and loyalties, thus demonstrating the upsides and downsides of that experience. Furthermore, the Resident of Benin Province clearly lamented on the collapse of indigenous governance systems as follows,

> Under the indigenous system of government the common people were members of one or other of a series of guilds each of which was a territorial and administrative unit which managed its affairs with a minimum of outside interference. Modern progress has brought in its train the virtual disappearance of the guild, and there has been nothing to replace it.[1]

Although the Resident aptly bemoaned the infringement of 'modern progress' on indigenous governance system, his claim of its extirpation was rather indiscreet and myopic, in light of a mutual negotiation and transformation process that was occurring at the same time.

Nonetheless, such an intrusive amalgam of two justice systems caricatured the indigenous governance systems and paradigms of justice but also minimized its power and legitimacy, while imposing the Native Court and Customary Court as its superior and supreme courts for judicature. The indiscriminate, forced insertion of the indigenous paradigms of justice into a colonial grid of new legal system ensured a monopoly of the coloniality of power but also inculcated an inferiorization and demonization of indigenous structures of justice and conflict resolution mechanisms. Thus, while the Empire was unsuccessful in obliterating and wiping out the indigenous systems of justice, they were nevertheless successful in juxtaposing the British and indigenous structures of justice within a hierarchy of power, influence and authenticity. The hierarchization of power is most consequential in facilitating multiple hegemonies and competing loyalties. Native courts and customary courts are imbrications of a colonial juridical construct and an invented machinery of subjugation, exploitation and expropriation that continue to bear the imprints and vestiges of imperial power. For instance, the District Officer of Kukuruku Division reported,

> The administration of Native Courts passed into the hands of the Divisional Council on October 1st ... It cannot be said that the courts are efficient and dissatisfaction is probably more widespread than is realised. The total number of cases heard in 1954 was 4,247, both civil and criminal, a decrease of 706

compared with the figure for 1953. The large increases in the rates of court fees introduced in May 1954 have undoubtedly resulted in many disputes being adjudicated by Village Heads out of court and the Chairman of the Divisional Council reports that his Council is taking active steps to eradicate the practice. Court revenue has increased from £8,562 in 1953 to £10,252 in 1954. It is of interest to note that in 1954 a total of 4,365 cases were tried in the Native Courts and the revenue amounted to £3,884.[2]

This attempt at infusing and prioritizing a superior colonial legal system, albeit with a minimal recognition of the customary law and a total repudiation of adjudication by village heads, also led to a somewhat commodification of law that fuelled a monetized colonial economy. Revenue generated through court fines and charges was monumental in contributing to the economic base and tax revenues of the colony.

The *Opashi Oza*, vested with temporal power and sacral authority in Oza, had such jurisdiction eroded and debased, as seen in Onobume's incarceration for questionable reasons and the consequent humiliation in which his reinstatement in the Native Court became controversially politicized. Kerr, the Acting District Officer of Kukuruku Division, hinted at reasons for Onobume's imprisonment and negotiated compromise between colonial and village authorities. Offences charged against Onobume were linked to 'his desire for independence both for himself and for the village' and a somewhat 'passive opposition' to the colonial administration. Kerr probably has an outlier personality, while he acquiesced with his superiors in explaining Onobume's resistance to imperial invasion of his political domain and territorial integrity as rather disconcerting for the colonial regime. He hints at their disguised empathy for 'tradition', a certain vulnerability to any ruptures of Oza cultural and sociopolitical imagination, and inherent economic apathy. Kerr's furtive gesture and recognition of Onobume's capability as authoritative village head sends some important signals to his colonial superiors, albeit surreptitiously. At the same time, his ingenuity exemplifies subversion of 'tradition' and traditional authority, and integration into the colonial legal apparatus. Kerr underscored the reverence and angst that *Eho Oza* represents in Oza people's ritual imagination, while a certain perceived fear of the *juju*'s potency was a possible deterrent to any thoughts of the colonial powers about 'blasting' and demolishing *Eho*'s shrine. Thus, dethronement, banishment and demolition of a revered sacred space were delicate options, each of which was likely to precipitate strife and potential crisis for the village, as well as strategic concerns of the colonial powers.

Although the colonial regime reneged on the proposal to destroy the *Ehọ* shrine, one of the most sacred spaces that adumbrates the highest sources of justice and equity in the indigenous system, the mere thought of 'blowing up' the shrine revealed the desperation of the Empire in protecting and sustaining their channels of subjugation, exploitation and expropriation. This entrenchment in and manipulation of the indigenous legal system and paradigms of justice had both intended and unintended consequences. One of such inadvertent after-effect is the protracted legal tussle regarding Ọza chieftaincy leadership succession. In fact, virtually all towns and villages in Akoko Edo LGA of Edo State or even several parts of the country witness the proliferation of court cases regarding chieftaincy leadership succession. The externalization of power sources of justice is a significant variable although not the sole factor. There is, undoubtedly, internal intrigues between the two ruling houses of Ọsuruka prior to the interference of British coloniality of power. However, I contend that such intrusions weaponized and represented the spark that ignited further leadership rivalry and competition that has continued until contemporary era. Thus, while I do not wish to totally externalize the inherent problems that efface succession to chieftaincy leadership in Ọza and elsewhere, it would appear that the colonial experiment of juxtaposing English imperial law with customary law had its merits but also inherent legacies of attendant malcontents.

As I have demonstrated above, a dual justice system came into existence with the coloniality of power, British colonial paradigm of justice apposed with an indigenous justice system. The colonial paradigm, with its roots in an exogenous world view, is based largely on a retributive philosophy that is hierarchical, adversarial, punitive and guided by codified laws and written rules, procedures and guidelines. For instance, in criminal cases, punitive sanctions limit accountability of the offender to the colonial state, instead of to those he/she has harmed or to the community. Unwritten customary laws, traditions and practices, verbally routinized, guide the indigenous justice paradigm, a system based on Ọza world view and a holistic philosophy. Such a holistic perspective galvanizes indigenous justice by connecting everyone involved with a problem or conflict on a continuum, capturing the underlying issues that need to be resolved to attain peace and harmony for the individuals and the community. This continuum represents the entire process, from disclosure of problems, to discussion and resolution, to making amends and restoring relationships. The methodology of restorative and reparative justice depends on principles of healing and living in harmony with all beings and with nature. For Ọza indigenous people, law and justice are part of a whole that prescribes a way of life. Invoking the spiritual realm through prayer rituals and sacrifice is essential throughout the indigenous process. Restoring spirituality and ritual purification are essential to the healing process for everyone involved in a conflict.

In the case of Ọza chieftaincy leadership, the equivocal imploding of the indigenous, microcosmic legal structure into a larger, macrocosmic colonial framework led to its depravity, dependency and subversion of its legitimacy. It also opened up the revered chieftaincy institution to mutual suspicion, unwarranted aversion and increasing competition. As discussed in Chapter 5, the proximity of Lawani Ogundare to the corridors of colonial administration, in his role as interpreter or translator, fanned suspicion especially with the controversial incarceration of Ọkọgbe Adesina. Although a precarious claim, the Ọnọbumẹ family (Ugbọnọkua) within the Ọsuruka royal lineage suspected complicity in the imprisonment of Ọkọgbe Adesina. Such allegations and consequent accusations escalated even after Ọnọbumẹ's release from jail and provoked a backlash of retaliation. It is against this backdrop that the Ọkọkọ royal family lineage deemed the imposition and preference of the regent, Oshioma, as retaliatory. We have shown that although Oshioma's reign was short-lived, this singular deviation from the dual-family rotational system of leadership succession marked a significant watershed that truncated the rotational chieftaincy system within the Ọsuruka royal kindred. The fact that such incriminations that featured in the protracted legal tussle remains resilient today is a matter of conjecture that leaves much to be determined.

Negotiating Nupenization, Yorubanization, Christianization and colonial modernity

The British colonial experiment and experience, sustained encounter and interactions with the Nupe, Yoruba and Bini hegemonies pose a crucial challenge to Ọza indigeneity, and a negotiation process producing and perpetuating new Ọza cultural imaginaries, in transition from tradition to modernity, in an era of social-cultural flux. We highlighted in Chapter 1 that the sociocultural landscape, including indigenous knowledge and technologies of diverse communities and groups, correlates directly with the dynamics of change and the transformation of individuals' as well as groups' cultural meaning systems and senses of belonging. Migration narratives of Ọza from Ife, however remotely linked, and from Benin City towards the northern fringes of the Benin Kingdom, are indeed complex; they engender culture-contact, exchange and impact. Historical and contemporary encounters and relationships between Ọza and her neighbours, cultural hegemonies, incursions and the impact of Christianity and Islam underscore one groundwork in grasping Ọza indigeneity politics within the context and processes of globalization.

Historically, Ọza people enjoyed intermittent epochs of prolonged peace, although with some hiatus at the instance of Yoruba – the Ogedengbe-led Ilesa forces, Nupe-Fulani invasion, raids and occupation that was fed by interethnic wars at the peak of the nineteenth century and British colonization at the turn of the twentieth century. The impact of the Nupe wars and the Islamic Jihad expansionist policies on north-eastern Yorubaland, the Akoko and Afẹnmai were profound. Most of these communities accepted Nupe rule and paid tributes mainly in slaves, often resulting in depopulation, relocation of settlements to hilly terrains and disruption of indigenous industries. Southward expansion threatened established political alliances and economic partnerships. While existing historical sources did not name Ọza among the villages and communities that fell to the Yoruba and Nupe-Fulani raids, narratives of encounter of the Nupe militia and immigrant Fulani Islamic Jihadists by neighbouring communities, however, lend credence to a somewhat oblique encounter with Ọza people. Oral narratives corroborate Ọza people's escape from these external attacks, incursions and exposure to slave raids. Nonetheless, Nupe occupation and hegemony waned with the appearance of the Royal Niger Company in the 1890s, although not without leaving some indelible cultural imprints on Afẹnmai, Akoko and north-eastern Yoruba. These communities pledged their moral and material support to the British forces with the hope of ending the Nupe-Fulani hegemony, and they were supplanted by another hegemonic power.

The relocation from Urogbe to Ọza Okeme settlement probably coincided with the era of interethnic wars and slave raiding that involved Nupe, Yoruba and Benin Kingdoms. Following the era of Yoruba and Nupe raids, internecine wars and the British conquest of Benin in 1897, Ọza people gradually started to move from Ọza Okeme (Ọza settlement in the hills) to settle at the lowlands, the plateau which now forms the present-day settlement. The introduction of primary schools and mission churches enhanced the further migration and settlement on the plateau. Overall, exploring Ọza historical and contemporary encounters and relationships with multiple hegemonies, its immediate and remote neighbours, towns and villages illuminate how and to what extent these proximities may have resulted in mutual religious, political, economic and sociocultural negotiations, exchanges, transformation and impact.

The British, Yoruba and Nupe hegemonies, proximities, incursions, rule, occupation and commerce was consequential in the Christianization, Yorubanization and Nupenization of Ọza social, cultural and religious imagination in profound ways. Language, as a social phenomenon, serves as a significant catalyst and conveyor of power, religion, culture and commerce. Thus, Yoruba and English languages had a deep imprint in the transmission and translation of Christianity, while the Nupe-Fulani-Hausa languages were instrumental in the Islamization process. As we have argued, the languages of Nupenization, Yorubanization, Christianization and, to a lesser extent, Islamization were symbols of social prestige, religious pride, economic opportunism and political elitism.

The Nupe-Fulani onslaught had a profound impact on Afẹnmai communities including Auchi, Agbede and Ikpe (Jattu), thus resulting in new Islamic converts and influence to the extent that the ruling house, the Otaru of Auchi, became Islamized. In spite of these visible instances, a larger part of the Kukuruku Division escaped the process of Islamization. Thus, while the impact of the Nupe-Fulani hegemonic occupation and Islamic influence was more profound in those Afẹnmai towns and villages, also in neighbouring communities in Okene (now part of present Kogi State), Ikare (now part of present Ondo State), there was nevertheless no evidence of direct presence of the Nupe-Filani hegemony but only remote impact on Ọza community. While several oral accounts link the introduction of Islam to Ọza through Alamonu and Adelamomi Agboju, the exact dates are uncertain.[3] Another account suggested that Adesina Agbodere introduced Islam.[4] The impact of Islam has been generally less profound in Ọza with only a few families still bearing that imprint until today.

Chieftaincy titles including *Ọtaru, Dawudu (Daudu), Zaiki (Saiki)* and common names of Ọza individuals and families such as *Lawani, Lawal, Dania, Ali, Musa, Salami, Usman, Sunmonu, Ibrahim* and so forth have Nupe-Fulani and Islamic cultural imprints. Yoruba royal titles such as *Ọba* and *Olọjah of Ọjah* are recent derivatives. Within Ọza royal family lineages, Yoruba-derived names including *Ogundare, Lawani, Adeshina, Obayemi* and *Aiyejina* are replete. Other common adopted Yoruba names include *Balogun, Arishe, Agbabi, Oloriegbe, Ajayi, Ajakaiye, Omotoriogun, Olorife, Aremu, Onikan,*

Ajuwon, Agidiomo, Ojulawo, Onisowo, Obafẹmi, Bosede, Bola, Olusegun, Akin, Kehinde, Taiwo, Olorunfemi, Oloruntoba and so forth. The original name of the community, Ọza, became Yorubanized and Anglicized as Ọzah/Ọja/Ọjah, respectively, *Ọza Okeme* as *Ọjah Oke* (Ọjah uplands), Ọza lowlands as *Ọjah Salẹ* (Ọza lowlands). Town quarters are all characterized by indigenous names and include *Odoshami, Ovopki, Ekpe, Ọdun, Imiejere, Ovoga, Odoyokpe, Ọjaja* and *Ovogbamudu* (see Dania's map). In contrast with Ọza quarters in *Ọza Okeme*, seven new quarters in Ọza lowlands took on mostly Christianized Yoruba names with literal meanings as *Ajoyo* (rejoicing together), *Ileoro* (a rich, peaceful land) formerly Ufa, *Bamishaiye* (coming together to celebrate life), *Oke Iye* (hill of salvation), *Araromi* (I am comforted or satisfied) and *Igodi* (the name of the first settler in the quarter).[5] The seventh quarter, *Agbọkodọ*, was an exception as an indigenous name literally meaning 'People make up a quarter'. Chief Obayemi suggested that the invention and renaming took the following sequence:

> The relocation Bamishaye-Akpara from the uphills to this present site started in 1923 at Ajoyo by one Adeshina, at Ileoro by Lawani Ojope family. At the Bamishaiye by the Uda family. At Araromi by Ọbuẹri family of Okolaba Onikan. At Igodi Olorife of Ọbuẹri family. At Oke Iye by Uka Igbewenhe of Ibiove family. At Agbọkodọ, it was an Osobo exodus of which Mr Ilekha, Olu Abozegha Osobo took the lead.[6]

One informant perhaps best summarized the influence of Yoruba Christian mission agency in the reinvention and naming of town quarters:

> Ọza people give names to people and quarters in Ọza language in those days. We copied Yoruba names from Yoruba pastors that came with the introduction of Christianity to our land. The use of Yoruba names for quarters came directly from Bishop Ojebode when he was an archdeacon not yet a bishop. He visited Christians in Ọza while we were still at Ọza Okeme. Then, he encouraged movement from Ọza Okeme to the lowlands where the CMS church and school were now built. He gave the name Ajoyo to that quarter as the people that will help to stop Ọsọsọ neighbours from encroaching on our land. He named the second quarter, Ileoro, to prevent Makeke people from expanding and moving downwards. The next quarter was named Ileteju, now Araromi along market road. The same man changed Ọza to Ọjah because in their own alphabet, that is in Yoruba language, there is no 'dz' in theirs and therefore changed Ọza to Ọjah. It was in 1936 that we started coming down from our old site, Ọza-Okeme.[7]

While much of the details provided above is not totally corroborated, it is however suggestive of the Yorubanization of Christianity in Ọza. Alleh Ojee aptly remarked, 'The names came into existence based on agreement of the inhabitant of the place. The influence of Yoruba in our language was as a result of education, religion and civilization of the people.'[8] Thus, the renaming of town quarters reinvents cartographical and physiographical maps of Ọza community along the prisms of religion, education, Yorubanization and colonialism. The establishment of mission schools, local authority schools and mission churches led to the preference of English, Yoruba and biblical Christian names, many of whose meanings are imprecise, and the fetishizing and transposing of indigenous names that are replete with meanings, history and symbolism. The adoption of English, Yoruba, Christian and Nupe-Fulani names was also a mark of social respectability, prestige, nobility and what might be termed an emblem of modern 'civilization'.

The British colonial administration, the impact of the missionaries – mostly local Yoruba Christian agents – and traders largely contributed to entrenching the name Ọjah/Ọja from its original derivation, Ọza. The proliferation of mission churches and schools, mostly led by Yoruba catechists and teachers, was instrumental to the Yorubanization of Christianity and naming culture in Ọza and other parts of the region. Church liturgy, Bibles and hymn books were initially with Yoruba as the sole or main language of instruction, a practice that sometimes led communicants to memorize, recite and sing without actually grasping their full meanings. Mission churches conducted catechism, baptism, confirmation, naming, marriage, funeral rituals and ceremonies solely in Yoruba language, and only until recently this was interspersed with Ọza and English languages. Church guilds or societies such as in the Anglican (Church Missionary Society (CMS)) Church bore Yoruba names such as *Ẹgbe Bolorunduro, Ẹgbe Ifeloju, Ẹgbe Toluwalase* and so forth. Liminal rituals of passage such as *ireni ọmọ inami* (naming ritual), *ọmọ ipami fi okofa di* (outdooring ritual) and *Iruvie* (marriage) became Christianized/Yorubanized as *Isọmọluruko* (naming rite) *ikomo* (outdooring rite) and *Igbeyawo* (marriage rite). Besides, Yoruba language preferences and the mode and aesthetics of dress, the normalization of Yoruba dress attires and codes such as *buba, asho* and *gele* (feminine dress form), and *buba, shokoto, agbada* and *fila* (masculine dress form), in contrast to *egere, abuluku* and *agu* (traditional costumes) (see Plates 7, 10 and 11),) are indicative of social-cultural and religious leverage.

Reconfiguring rituals

The interface of Qza indigenous world views with Yoruba, Nupe-Fulani, English, Christian and Islamic cultures resulted in mutual exchange, transformation and change of ritual praxis, processes, symbolism, cosmologies and rites of passage. For instance, the advent of Christianity, Islam and colonial hegemonies occasioned a pluralization of marriage rituals as liminal rituals of passage. Qza people were additionally able to appropriate civil (court), Christian, Islamic marriages in addition to *Ukpe Iruvie*, indigenous marriages or marriages based on native law and custom (Adogame 1987: 48–57). The introduction of Christianity into Ojah community by European missionaries had a profound influence on the indigenous institution of marriage (Alonge 2002: 56). While not denying the influence which these exogenous forms have come to have on the lives of Qza people, indigenous marriage continues to have a tremendous impact on their everyday religious, social, economic and political existence (Adogame 1987: 48–57).

These dimensions contribute to a fuller understanding of Qza imagination, dynamism and symbolism of marriage ritual systems. At the same time, a number of factors that militate against the enactment of indigenous marriage rites include the influence of Western education, mission Christianity, colonial legal paradigms, urbanization, moribund marriage rites, economic factors and changing attitude of the youths (Adogame 1987: 58–72). Although some families continue to accord primacy to indigenous rituals of marriage, there is a somewhat decline. While some families were attracted to one of these exogenous marriage systems, thus jettisoning the indigenous forms, others explored a synthesis of the rituals, combining the indigenous with the civil (customary law) and Christian marriage ritual ceremonies. In fact, some Christian churches consider the enactment of indigenous marriage rituals as a prerequisite for solemnizing marriage or wedding in the church. It is common practice that the couple receives traditional approval, consent or blessing from their parents prior to church or civil marriage. Parents, elders and family members invoke the spirit of ancestors and deities through ritual sacrifice, including libation, to attain consent and endorsement prior to marriage. People believe that to omit such an important ritual aspect is to incur the wrath and displeasure of the benevolent spiritual forces consequential in calamity, misfortune upon marriage.

Some Qza people now increasingly contest core aspects of life-cycle rituals, especially ritual enactments associated with *Iruvie imumi*, between the liminal phases of puberty, betrothment and actual marriage. Initiation rituals of the *Oruvie Ukpugbe*, *Ọmọnugere*, *Iviesemi* and *Ibishika* ritual obsequies that are pivotal to *Ukpe Qza* and *Ukpe Iruvie* are negotiated. *Ẹrẹsumuna* or *Unwenemi* to the prospective *osumuna* in farm work, house building and roofing, a practice which is integral to the bride wealth, signifying solemnity, responsibility and commitment to the man's intentionality has become optional. The strict observance of *Oruvie Ukpugbe*, *Ọmọnugere/Iviesemi/Ibishika*, *Ẹrẹsumuna/Unwenemi* and so forth has become discretionary especially in view of school education and modernity. As F. Alonge remarked, 'Today, Christianity and westernization have affected marriage ceremony, most especially the Ọmọnugere festival that serves as a prerequisite to the real initation ceremony into woman-hood (Ukpe Iruvie) ... Also, the normal one year fattening ceremony has been reduced to three day as a result of education of the female child' (2002: 56).

Iruvie Imumi have been increasingly Christianized where some churches such as the Anglican and Catholic churches have adapted and routinized marriage rituals as a nexus to alternative age-grade formation. By so doing, they evade indigenous ritual processes while retaining the symbolism of age-grade and marriage systems. Some churches continue to recognize aspects of indigenous marriage rituals, so that some Christians who take part in selective indigenous ritual enactments return to church for blessings. As Father Bane noted, 'when parties validly married according to native law and custom are baptized, their former "pagan" marriage still holds (as natural law is above ecclesiastical law)'.[9] Such a synthesis of marriage rites and practices hones in the centrality, deep-rootedness and resilience of indigenous cosmologies in people's everyday lives, including the institution of marriage as a liminal, life-cycle ritual (Adogame 1987: 70). In spite of any ritual modification, synthesis, transformation and change, indigenous rituals of marriage will continue to be relevant in the cosmological and everyday life of Qza people.

The more Qza people assumed the Christian identity and professed Christianity, the more some of them became ostracized from their indigenous world views and ways of life. Thus, the encounter between Qza indigenous religions and exogenous religions of Christianity and Islam produced complex levels of religious identities. The first level is those who switch religious affiliation, 'converted' to Christianity or Islam and through that process attempt to relegate and repudiate their indigenous religious identity. Others cling to their indigenous religious tradition and resist switching or 'converting' to the exogenous religions. A third category navigates multiple religious affiliations and multiple religious allegiance such as adherence to Christianity and the indigenous religions contemporaneously.

The interplay of mission Christianity, colonial education and indigenous knowledge production

The annual report of Benin Province 1939[10] indicated the principal Missions functioning in Benin Province as the CMS and the Roman Catholic Mission (RCM). Others that are active are the American Baptist, the Apostolic, the United African and the Salvation Army. The report noted further,

> Friendly relations continue between the Administration and the Missions, and Missionaries are always most helpful in aiding proposals for cultural progress of the people. Christians and Animists continue to display friendly tolerance and live happily side by side. In the Kukuruku Division, Christianity makes only slow progress and Mohammedanism is popular, but elsewhere in the Province most of the educated youth profess some form of the Christian faith.[11]

Late Chief Ogundare Lawani first introduced mission Christianity into Ọza in 1918 but it did not survive. In 1920, Daniel Ogundare reintroduced Christianity into Ọza through the CMS, today known as St. Paul's Anglican Church. 'Again, the new church met with difficulties including persecution, ordeal, punishment, suffering and frustration. In spite of all the difficulties, the church survived and now we are enjoying the fruits of his labour.'[12] A variant of this narrative suggested that 'Christianity was introduced in Ọza in the year 1914 by Lawani Ogundare the name was Church Missionary Society (CMS). The King did not accept it because he saw it as foreign culture, so Christianity died off. In 1920, another Daniel Ogundare introduced it. That was when Christianity stood firm till date.'[13] According to a second source, 'everybody were adherents of the indigenous religion until Chief Lawani Ogundare brought Christianity through his in-law from Ogori in 1914. This could not stand, in 1918 another man Ajelu reintroduced it and still could not stand. In 1920 Daniel Idadashi Ogundare Eberemu brought it the third time and some people accepted the offer and they became Christians till date.'[14] Chief Obayemi even suggested that the CMS, now the St. Paul's Anglican Church, came earlier, by around 1916, while the RCM came later by around 1920.

Late Ogundare was the head of the Anglicans while the late Balogun Akowe (Akukonaye's father) was head of the Catholics.[15]

Nonetheless, virtually all oral accounts corroborate the view that Christianity made its debut in Ọza through the CMS, although the dates vary between 1914 and 1920. One oral source linked to the founder of the CMS even asserted,

> My father was the only child born of his parents. He was four months old when his father left Ọza to Idah. He never knew his father until he got married. Then came a day when he decided to go in search of his father. He vowed never to return to Ọza until he found his father. When he received a message at Okene that his mother was seriously ill because of his absence, this sad news forced him to return to Ọza in 1920, the same year he introduced Christianity in Ọza. Because of the little knowledge he had, the tax was not too much for him and he was able to convince many people. That was how Christianity started till today.[16]

With the relative success of the CMS, other Christian missions followed subsequently by establishing branches in Ọza. Other churches founded in the early 1920s and 1930s are the St. John the Baptist Catholic Church in 1923, the Christ Apostolic Church in 1935 and the Cherubim and Seraphim Oke Iye in 1943,[17] respectively. Pa Alleh remarked, "Baba Egbe (the father of Abogun Ogundare) introduced Christianity to Ọza ... the Catholic Church was introduced in Ọjah by Pa William (Olaja's father). Christ Apostolic Church (C.A.C) was introduced by Pastor J.O. Omolola, while the Cherubim and Seraphim was introduced by Eli Samuel."[18] Other oral accounts indicated that Alu and Sunday Alagabu founded the Cherubim and Seraphim Church.[19] Ọza religious landscape has become more diverse in recent times with the establishment of the Deeper Life Bible Church in 1981, Assemblies of God in 1991 and the Lord's Chosen Charismatic Revival Movement Church in 2002. Other churches that have now established branches in Ọza include the Redeemed Christian Church of God, Winners Chapel and so forth.

We can also understand the politics of indigeneity in Ọza against the backdrop of the sociocultural ferment and the negotiation of knowledge production. The encounter between Ọza, the British coloniality of power, Nupe-Filani and Yoruba colonialisms resulted in a clash of knowledge production in which indigenous knowledge systems negotiated asymmetrical powers of knowledge production. With the introduction of schools, the colonial and missionary machineries foisted new, dominant ways of knowing and meaning-making, thus entrenching alien forms of reasoning that lay claims to a 'civilizing mission'. The European knowledge paradigm assumed a dominant epistemology while diabolizing indigenous world views as subaltern knowledge systems. In the face of these sociocultural entanglements, Oza indigenous epistemologies negotiated the power dynamics that ensued from multiple discourses, knowledge-production and meaning-making processes. Nonetheless, such contestation had dire implications for Oza indigenous epistemologies.

During the immediate colonial era, three primary schools were established in Oza, with the highest class being Primary III. The earliest, St. Paul's CMS Anglican School, was founded on 18 January 1932 under the proprietorship of Miss J. V. Herklots.[20] She became renowned for her pioneer education work in the CMS Anglican Benin Diocese for several years. The Catholic School was established with Bishop P. J. Kelly as proprietor. The Resident of Benin Province noted in his *Annual Report 1950* that the RCM, under the Right Reverend Bishop Kelly, continued to expand its activities within the Benin Province.[21] The third was the Local Authority School, under the board of management of the local colonial authority. This meant that early Western education took the investments of church missions and the colonial government authority, respectively. However, during the early years of existence, funding was a major constraint in sustaining these schools. Inadequate funding and poor infrastructure have remained a perennial feature in management of schools. In the last few decades, the Edo State government established a government secondary school, Oza Grammar School, in 1980. Utter government neglect and inadequate funding resulted in Oza community's involvement, investments and management of the secondary school, later renamed as 'Oza Comprehensive High School'.

While the introduction of mission and local authority schools was an important attraction for some Oza people, others found it objectionable and suspect. During their formative years, schools were not particularly attractive to some people as a viable alternative to farming and hunting. In fact, some parents were hesitant in sending their wards or children to school as they posed a potential threat to their vocation and means of livelihood through farming and hunting. As I have argued earlier, there is a gender twist to this contempt that shaped some parent's training of their children. The primacy of *Ireme* within the Oza socio-religious compass instils a certain bias and sentiment in some men who think, although erroneously, that training a child benefits the maternal family line disproportionately as compared to the paternal family. Such an astern, retrogressive attitude continues to bear some resilience in its perception of educational development today. Pa Dania aptly remarks on people's ignorance, aversion, reluctance and frigidity that characterized early years of mission and local authority schools,

> There is no effect of school teaching on the village with regard to farming, because the village school is not at an advantage to make farm. The school is yet very young to teach farming practically. The schools do not do farming at all … The schools have not played any noticeable pleasing part in the village. There are no teacher-parent associations. The reasons are: the schools are just existing, not living. The parents do not understand education. They have no interest in the school. They are all illiterates. Frankly speaking, the chief aim of parents sending children to the school is purposely to acquire wealth, this is rather very incorrect considering the aim of education.[22]

He also highlights some attendant challenges and difficulties that the school faced during its infancy, as well as potential benefits that served as attraction for parents to send their children to school or enrol for adult literacy program for themselves. Pa Dania explains,

> There is no prejudice against religion but there is difficulty concerning fees. There is also economic difficulty. The children attending school live in the village. At present the proportion of teachers to children is about 1 to 30. Almost all the children leave the school without completing the junior or senior primary courses. The reasons for this are: there is financial difficulty. There is no complete Primary Six course at Ojah. The difficulty in going to distant towns is very outstanding … There are attempts to relate the school curriculum to the needs of the village, through the Adult Literacy … There is a class of the Adult Literacy recently formed. There is no success yet … The school teaching has certain effects on the village e.g. the few children at school are taught personal cleanliness, this they practice and they appear neater than those not at school, and as a result, other children practice personal cleanliness.[23]

He highlights possible remedies to teach the villagers farming through an adult literacy programme where the school could 'make a garden and an experimental farm under the supervision of a trained agriculturist'.[24]

Since its inception, the British colonial power introduced an educational policy that placed primary emphasis on primary- and secondary-level education. The proliferation and investments in schools link these colonial projects with reduction of literacy, knowledge production, revenue generation and generating a work force to serve the colonial administration. In 1940, the Resident of Benin Province reported that the Benin Province, with ten government primary schools, was fortunate in possessing a larger number than any other Province in Nigeria.[25] According to this report,

> 'All of these schools are full primary schools going up to Standard VI ... There are 21 Government aided Mission schools – the Church Missionary Society having 8, the Roman Catholic Mission 12, and the American Baptist Mission 1. Despite financial difficulties these schools have maintained their efficiency, and Government regulations have, on the whole, been satisfactorily observed, although few of them have been in a position to advance beyond minimum requirements.[26]

The report also notes, 'There are 213 unassisted primary schools, which with a few notable exceptions, are inefficient. Denominational rivalry often results in the failure of two schools in a village where one might succeed. Usually the staff is poorly paid and buildings and equipment are poor.'[27]

The Resident of Benin Province's *Annual Report 1939* was very instructive, while his figurative adumbration of the prospects of Native Administration was indeed self-evident.

> The machinery of Native Administration has been assembled in most of the Province and it is in course of being tested and run in. A few parts require modification or renovation for the machine was not constructed entirely with new parts. As with all new machinery it is unwise to give it the full throttle until the machine has been thoroughly run in. Youth is all for speed and finds irksome the brake of conservatism applied by his elders. The administration has attempted, with some degree of success to find the happy mean.[28]

The Resident was indeed ingenious in mirroring the complexity of the encounter process between the coloniality of power and indigenous polity and social compass.

More than a decade later, a new Resident of Benin Province reporting on Kukuruku Division remarked,

> Preparations for the introduction of universal free education in January 1955 took second place only to political developments in the minds of the people. 1955 will see 306 schools established compared with 134 in 1954; fifteen years ago there were fewer than 40 schools in the Division. Of the 172 new schools under construction during 1954 it is estimated that 90% will be ready for occupation in January 1955, while 16,000 children have been registered for year 1.[29]

The introduction of universal free education was an added impetus in the proliferation of colonial education. As the report noted in its introduction, 'the most outstanding event of importance during 1954 was undoubtedly the conduct of Local Government elections in the Kukuruku and Asaba Divisions consequent upon the application of the Local Government Law, and the Federal elections held throughout the Province in November'.[30] In the course of 1954, the Local Government Law was successfully applied to the Asaba and Kukuruku Divisions, while statutory inquiries were held in the Benin and Ishan Divisions. This supplanted the old colonial administrative structure of the Native Authorities, which the Resident contrasted as follows, 'There is no doubt in my mind that the new Councils in the Asaba and Kukuruku Divisions are markedly superior to the old Native Authorities in these Divisions.'[31] This political development, the application of the Local Government Law of 1952, led to the establishment of three District Councils: Etsako (Afẹnmai), Akoko-Ẹdo and Ivbiosakon within the Kukuruku Division.

In retrospect, Benin Province a few years earlier had already encountered some political turbulence and uncertainty. As his predecessor Resident of Benin Province reported,

> Politically, 1949 was described as lying between the waves. This was certainly prophetic so far as Benin was concerned: 1950 has been a stormy year of personal antagonisms and ill-considered recrimination on which excessive time, energy and money have been wasted. The Native Administration machine came almost to a standstill ... The Kukuruku Division Native Authorities pulled themselves together after the near-bankruptcy of 1949.[32]

The so-called Second World War dealt a crucial political, economic and strategic blow on the British imperial project, witnessing a backlash in the aftermath of the global debacle. Thus, the touted political disruptions and economic strangulations in Benin Province was shaped partly by this war catastrophe and its unintended consequences. In summing up his annual report in 1954, the Resident of Benin Province H. L. M. Butcher could not but reveal his somewhat ambivalent, apparent pessimism and disdain for anti-colonial, nationalistic feelings that were brewing within Benin Province and what was to become the nation state, Nigeria. He remarked,

> The old order changeth giving place to new – that I think sum up the work of the year 1954. The people have experienced new forms of Local Government, new forms of election, a vast programme of preparation for educational expansion, new buildings going up for schools and hospitals. New Councils have been elected, this time by Secret ballot, and they have already shown themselves eager to accept their new responsibilities. Old Councils whose lives are drawing

> to a close have, in some instances, continued to display the old bad qualities of intolerance, greed and partiality. There is a feeling of uncertainty in the minds of some sections of the public about the future. They feel rather like the passengers in a plane about to take off which they know is controlled by a new and inexperienced pilot. Yet they appreciate very much the fact that the Ballot box has put more real power into their hands, and the elections have shown that the present system is far more likely than any of the old methods to bring forward men of good character and ability.[33]

He went further,

> There is no doubt that there are men with the ability to provide good Local Government. The question must always be asked, however, whether in all cases there is also the will to put the interests of the people first, and to give disinterested efficient service to those who elected them. There is still far too great a tendency to nepotism, pomp and display, and an inclination to leave to the District Officer most of the more tedious and less spectacular duties of local Government.[34]

Butcher expressed his unbridled sarcasm in his scepticism about the necessity and sustainability of political independence. 'The attitude of quite a fair proportion of even the newly elected councillors reminds me irresistibly of the old Irish woman during the last war who was heard to say "Down with the British." When asked what then would happen if the German came, she replied, "Sure, the British will protect us!"'[35] Undoubtedly, Butcher's subjectivity deserves a fuller critical interrogation, just as the immediate political and economic antecedents to the demise of colonial rule and the attainment of Nigeria's independence in 1960 need better treatment. Such a detailed elucidation goes beyond the scope of this book and forms the immediate research tasks of a follow-up book. Suffice to mention here that the development, alluded to above, points to the fact that agitations, negotiations and transitions towards self-rule, decolonization and the quest for political independence were already taking place and, in some cases, reaching a crescendo by the late 1950s.

In sum, the advent of mission Christianity, colonial education and governance saw the introduction of new religious ideas, practices and knowledge systems. Christian missionaries, Yoruba indigenous clergy and agency, and hegemonic British, Yoruba, Nupe and Benin structures served as cultural brokers, particularly in terms of language, epistemology, aesthetics, political and religious reimagination. The negotiation between the coloniality of power and indigenous political logic led to an indiscriminate subversion, undermining of Ọza indigenous political systems, the power and authority of the *Ọpashi*, the routinization of chieftaincy and the *Eja* hierarchical system, and established political institutions in Ọza. The transmission and translation of Christianity but also of Islam is indicative of how the prioritization and hierarchization of exoglossic, non-indigenous languages of English and Yoruba have the powering potentiality of caricaturing, endangering and fossilizing indigenous Ọza language to their very extinction. Ọza indigenous peoples were hardly passive receptors and consumers in negotiating these cognitive processes and competing knowledge hierarchies. The encounter transformed indigenous religious thought, praxis and knowledge-based systems but did not supplant it. Ọza indigenous cosmologies and spiritualities preserved some of its beliefs, ritual practices and knowledges but also adjusted to the new sociocultural milieu. The contact produced new religious imaginaries and multiplex epistemological reproduction with some appropriating indigenous symbols and giving them a new twist. Such initiatives attest to the politics of indigeneity; shifting allegiances, fluid identities, competing loyalties and solidarities; cultural, political and religious reimagination; and the resilience, continuity and transformation of Ọza cosmologies, world views and ritual sensibilities amid social change.

Perhaps the best way to illustrate the imagined future of Ọza indigeneity in the face of modernity is by invoking their popular indigenous songs and aphorisms. The first renders as *Ọza kino ogegere, ogegere ọnyama ro* (literally 'Ọza has gone through a mutation, and has become the wonderful *Ogegere*'). The aphorism renders as follows: *Uvie na supẹ omẹdẹ munu ibiẹhẹmi* (The song prelude makes the refrain or response intelligible). In these transitional, liminal states of social change, two popular Igoro and Azamarogbe cultural song rhythms in Oza (Lawani 1992: 66, 69) that also evoke good memory and rekindle hope for the future are worth concluding with.

> **Ọzah mai ọdẹ shemi mayi** (Azamarogbe rhythm)
> *Ọzah mai eọda shemi ma yio* (Ozah, our home will be prosperous for us).
> *Ọnọshi ọnọshi oshikunu ọgumusẹ mayio* (the supreme deity will remain benevolent)
> *Ọnọshi ọnọshi o'made a mi nẹ egbe* (we will continue to meet and reunite well)
> *iyoruba we pade wa bi oyin* (The Yoruba say that reunions are like honey)
> *Oyibo* says 'safe journey' (coloured Europeans says safe journey)
> *Oyibo* says 'we shall meet again' (coloured Europeans says we shall meet again)

Kẹrẹdi (Igoro rhythm)
Kẹrẹdi, Kẹrẹdi ọmọ menọ (Come back quickly, come back quickly my child)
Ukẹ tọsẹ shi riri (Don't stay out long)
Umẹ sho, umẹ sho, kẹrẹdi (You can hear me, you can hear me, come back quickly)
Okẹ bise we tia musẹ owọ (Don't stay out at night, if too late sleep there)
Uke ibiriki kia (Don't walk in the dark)
Kẹrẹdi (Come back quickly)

Notes

1 Decolonizing history, memory and method

1 The original name is spelt as 'Ọza', while its anglicized forms are 'Oja' or 'Ojah'. We will retain and use these spellings interchangeably throughout this book, especially as extant works appropriated them.
2 The International African Institute, London, has been engaged in the preparation and publication of an ethnographic survey of Africa since 1945, the objective being to present information on the various peoples of Africa in terms of location, natural environment, economy, crafts, social structure, political organization, religious beliefs and cults. Bradbury's book (co-published with P. C. Lloyd) is one of the several volumes of *Ethnographic Survey of Africa*, published by the International African Institute, to briefly document 'a summary of available information concerning the different peoples of Africa with respect to location, natural environment, economy and crafts, social structure, political organization, religious beliefs and cults' (Bradbury 1957: v). A Committee of the Institute set up under the chairmanship of Professor Radcliffe Brown undertook the editing of the survey with the generous collaboration of research institutions, anthropologists, the British Colonial Development and Welfare Funds and the Belgian authorities through the Commission d'Ethnologie of the Institute Royal Colonial Belge.
3 See Fela Anikulapo Kuti (1938–1997). Available online: https://felakuti.com/.
4 See 'Yellow Fever' (1976) MP3/WAV/FLAC/Vinyl song lyrics. First reissued by Knitting Factory Records as part of Fela Kuti Box Set #4 curated by Erykah Badu in 2018. Originally released by Decca Afrodisia. Available online: https://felakuti.com/releases/156575-fela-kuti-yellow-fever-(1976) (accessed 5 December 2020).
5 See full text: 'Rev. Al Sharpton Delivers Eulogy at George Floyd's Memorial'. Available online: https://www.youtube.com/watch?v=QAvPo5DVHOk (accessed on 5 June 2020).
6 *Contending Modernities*' new series is devoted to generating new knowledge and greater understanding of the ways that religious and secular forces interact in the modern world. See *Contending Modernities*, 'Decoloniality and the Study of Religion', February 2020. Available online: https://contendingmodernities.nd.edu/decoloniality/introdecolonial/ (accessed 23 October 2020).

7 This refers to the plantation economy introduced by the colonial hegemony to generate raw materials such as rubber, cocoa, timber, palm produce, crude oil and cotton to feed and service the metropole, the colonial economy and European industries. This indiscriminate exploitation and expropriation of raw materials resulted in land grabbing, politicization and commodification of ancestral lands and consequently fueled family conflicts and interethnic land disputes which has continued in several local contexts till date.

8 This is one of the inscriptions attributed to Archbishop Desmond Tutu on the exhibit walls of Freedom Park, Pretoria, South Africa. See also A. W. Oliphant, M. W. Serote and P. G. Raman (eds), *Freedom Park: A Place of Emancipation and Meaning* (Pretoria: Freedom Park Publishers, 2014).

9 UN General Assembly Resolution 45/163. Passed 21 December 1993 and proclaiming the International Decade of the World's Indigenous People. See, for instance, José R. Martínez Cobo, 'Study of the Problem of Discrimination against Indigenous Populations', United Nations Department of Economic and Social Affairs, 1986. Available online: https://www.un.org/development/desa/indigenouspeoples/publications/martinez-cobo-study.html; Department of Economic and Social Affairs, 'Workshop on Data Collection and Disaggregation for Indigenous Peoples | UN Doc. E/CN.4/Sub.2/1986/7', United Nations, 2004. Available online: http://www.scribd.com/doc/236735001/Study-on-the-Problem-of-Discrimination-against-Indigenous-Populations-Workshop-Data-Background-UN-Doc-E-CN-4-Sub-2-1986-7. See also Johan S. McGuinne, 'Official Definitions of Indigeneity', Indigeneity, Language and Authenticity. Available online: http://johansandbergmcguinne.wordpress.com/official-definitions-of-indigeneity/ (accessed 23 July 2017).

10 Jacob Olupona, 'The Spirituality of Africa', Harvard Gazette, 6 October 2015. Available online: http://news.harvard.edu/gazette/story/2015/10/the-spirituality-of-africa/. Olupona succinctly puts it, 'Though larger religions have made big inroads, traditional belief systems, which are based on openness and adaptation endure.'

11 One instance of a detailed academic focus on and treatment of indigenous knowledge systems is *Indilinga: African Journal of Indigenous Knowledge Systems* in Pietermaritzburg, South Africa (http://www.indilinga.org.za/). For especial focus, see contributions, for instance, by J. A. Loubser, 'Unpacking the Expression "Indigenous Knowledge Systems"', pp. 74–88; and L. Dondolo, 'Intangible Heritage: The Production of Indigenous Knowledge in Various Aspects of Social Life', pp. 110–26. For one of the most authoritative reference sources for recent scholarly research on the importance of knowledge and value systems, see the two edited volumes by Patrick Ngulube (2016, 2017). Both volumes provide a unique perspective on alternative knowledge systems through interdisciplinary research on knowledge management, sharing and transfer among indigenous communities.

2 Historical origins, migration narratives, relationship with neighbours

1. H. L. M. Butcher, Resident, *Annual Report 1954: Benin Province*, National Archives, File: Ben Prof. 1 (1954–5), p. 29.
2. Personal Interview with Pa P. A. Dania, Ojah, 29 August 2004. See also P. A. Dania, Individual project (unpublished), St. David's College, Evboneka, Benin, n.d., p. 2, that corroborated this claim. He noted that there is a street in Benin City still called Oza until date.
3. Google Maps gleaned showed the existence of Oza Street, Avbiama, off Sakponba Road, Benin City; Oza Primary School, Oza-Nisi. Oza-nogogo and Idumu-Oza are located in Agbor, Ika South LGA of Delta State. Oza is the language spoken by the people of Oza-nogogo community. See Isaac Ogbeiwi Omo-Aghe, *Oza History, Nigeria: Oza History in Delta and Edo State, Nigeria*. 1st edition (Benin City: Omo-Aghe Ogbeiwi Isaac, 2016). See also: O. W. Ogbomo, 'Oza-Nogogo: A Peripheral Edo Community', *Nigeria Magazine*, vol. 57, nos. 3–4 (July–December 1989). Orhionmwon River separates Oza-nogogo from its sister community, Oza-Aibiokunla, in Orhionwon LGA of Edo State.
4. Isaac Omo-Aghe traced the origin of the mentioned Oza peoples to Egbarevba's (1968: 11) assertion and reference to the Akpanigiakon war of 1287 during the reign of Oba Oguola of Benin in 1280. He noted that several migrations resulting in fuller formation or expansion of Oza took place during the reign of many other Obas (Kings) of Benin such as the harsh decrees of Oba Ewuare the Great. However, it was Army General Oza who founded Oza in 1290 when he refused to surrender to constituted authority. For more details of this history, see Omo-Aghe, *Oza History, Nigeria*.
5. Dania, Individual project, pp. 1–2.
6. Oral interview with Dania Okoko, Ojah, 29 August 2004.
7. The extensive Benin moats encircled the old perimeter precincts of the ancient City and were constructed as a defensive barrier in times of war. It was claimed that Oba Oguola (c. 1280–95) decreed the digging of the first and second moats to fortify the City from invaders, including the imperial European invaders, who were at the time hunting for African slave labourers. Other Benin Obas expanded the building of the moats considerably.
8. Oral interviews with Dania Okoko, Uka Joseph, Lawrence Obayemi, Aremu Omomikashie and Pa Omosunmoje, Ojah, 29 August 2004 and 30 August 2004. See also Plates 1a–1c.
9. The second version suggests that Ogbomiyan mentioned nine days to germinate.
10. Oral interview with Abogun Ogundare, Kole Ureshemi, Hezekiah Olorunfemi and Ijenozah Victor Anojie, Ojah, 30 August 2004.

11 See also Dania, Individual project, p. 3.
12 Interview with Jonathan Alonge as recorded in Felix Alonge, *Traditional Marriage Ceremony in Ojah, Akoko-Ẹdo LGA of Edo State. A Historical Approach*, BA Long Essay, Department of History, University of Ibadan, Ibadan, September 2002. p. 5.
13 Oral interview with Chief Otaru, Ojah, 23 August 2004.
14 Oral Interview with Pa Hezekiah Olorunfemi, Ojah, 19 August 2004.
15 Oral interviews with Pa Hezekiah Olorunfemi and Pa Omosunmoje, Ojah, 19 August 2004.
16 Dania, Individual project, p. 45.
17 Dania, Individual project, p. 46.
18 Focus group interviews with Chief Abiodun Joshua, Chief Abiodun Alleh, Barrister Ignatius Afẹ Oshiomogwe and Segun Joshua. Ojah, 20 October 2020.
19 Oral interview with Chief Abiodun Joshua. Ojah, 10 August 2020. Ọsọsọ's remarkable encroachment on Ọza physical land mass up until Ojah-Ajoyo Quarters is now increasingly consequential in boundary disputes and land litigation (see Google images that delineated the geographical expansion). The recent court case between Lewis Ashore (Ojah-Ajoyo Quarters) and the former Justice Joshua A. Omoluabi (Ọsọsọ) is a case in point.
20 Oral interview with Chief Abiodun Joshua, 10 August 2020.
21 Oral Interview with Chief Alleh, an elder in the Osu family, Ojah, 4 November 2020.
22 Oral Interview with Chief Alleh, 4 November 2020.
23 Oral Interview with Chief Alleh, 4 November 2020.
24 Letter to the Okogbe of Ojah signed for and on behalf of the Obueri paternal family Ojah by Alabi Usabemo (head of the Obueri paternal family), Ezekiel Dalu, Joseph Igodi, Aiyela Ajakaiye (members of the Obueri paternal family) titled 'Donation of Land between the Anglican Church and Ufa Quarters Ojah to the Entire Ojah Community for Communal Development', 3 January 1977.
25 Oral Interview with Chief Alleh, 4 November 2020.
26 Rowling served a note of caution that in the absence of first-hand research inquiry, the information provided in this report relied upon documentary evidence submitted to the W. A. Lands Committee 1912; Ward Price's Yoruba Land Tenure: Part IV; Provincial and Divisional Files; a selection of Native Courts Records; and Appeal cases, respectively.
27 See Letter of Complaint from Ufeshi-Ọza family, 'Land Dispute – Ojah/Okpella' to the Sole Administrator, Akoko Edo Local Government, Igarra, 22 October 1984. The letter signed by the following family representatives – Ugah Ufeshi, Ojagun Ufeshi, Udeh Ufeshi and Ogisua Ufeshi – chronicled early contested land boundaries and litigations involving the Ufeshi-Ọza family with Okpella and Ọsọsọ peoples around 1939–48. The Ufeshi clan lay claim to ownership of the

land until Iduru River, which forms a natural boundary with Okpella. The Ufeshi family asserted that the original boundary between Okpella and Ọza stretches from Owouyemi, Utofamogbe, Erema, Uki and to Ọbu.

28 The Ọsọsọ operate a confederation of quarters in which each quarter is headed by an Otaru. Every Ọsọsọ quarter is further divided into kindreds headed by Ivies. The most cohesive association in Ọsọsọ is the age grade, which is formed in brackets of seven years.
29 See also *British Intelligence Political Report on Nigeria*, no. 38, 1919.
30 He suggested that the name of these people seems to derive from *Ileme*, a rarely used and possibly archaic Benin word for 'blacksmith'.
31 According to Bradbury,

   The Northern Ineme living away from the rivers, depend for subsistence upon farming and palm-oil production. A large proportion of the men are blacksmiths and they are to be found widely scattered among the towns of Kukuruku and Ishan and farther afield among the Igbira of Kabba Province, in Kabba town and in other parts of Yoruba country. Formerly they smelted their own ore, but they no longer do so. (1957: 123)

32 According to Lewis, Northern Uneme is composed of Uneme-Osu, Eturu, Uneme-Ekpe (largest and most northerly), Uneme-Ogbe and Enegi. See Lewis (2013: 13).
33 Little is known of their subsequent history or of the manner or order in which the present settlements were formed. See Bradbury (1957: 124).
34 Some of the Ineme village names as represented by Bradbury have probably changed. For instance, Egeni probably refers to present-day Uneme-Nekhua while Osi refers to present-day Ayegunle. Ineme Ekpe is now called Ekpẹdo, while Ineme Osu is now Uneme Osu. Eturu is now known as Uneme Erhurun.
35 The author, identified in the book's foreword as a non-Uneme, was commissioned, mobilized and funded by the Executive Committee of the Uneme National Development Association (UNDA) to write for and on behalf of the Association (p. xxiii). Harunah noted that 'the UNDA Executive Committee, (a pan-Uneme sociocultural organisation) invited me to be a member and leader of a 2-man team, which it commissioned in 1995 to carry out research into the history and culture of the Uneme' (p. xxvii). The 'Foreword' indicated that the author 'satisfied the yearnings of the UNDA for a book that will place Uneme history and culture in correct perspectives … The book has also filled a yawning gap in the literature on the Edoid-speaking peoples of south-western Nigeria' (p. xxiv). However, the author is mostly subjective, far from being thorough and unbiased in many respects as its 'Foreword' claims. The fact that its contents were censored or redacted by the UNDA renders the book less historically reliable and accurate.
36 See Michael Ogunu, 'Foreword', in Harunah (2003: xxiii–xxiv).

37 In comparison to Bradbury's list of Northern Ineme, Harunah mentions two new names, Uneme Akpama and Uneme Aiyetoro. The others were Uneme Aki-Osu (Harunah)/Ineme-Osu (Bradbury), Uneme Erhurun (Harunah)/Eturu (Bradbury), Uneme Nekhua (Harunah)/Egeni (Bradbury) and Uneme Ekpẹdo (Harunah)/Ineme-Ekpe (Bradbury). Bradbury mentioned Ineme-Ogbe but this is missing in Harunah's list. Compare Harunah (2003: 212) and Bradbury (1957: 123), respectively.

38 See oral narratives by the Ọza-Osu family above.

39 See Extract from Map of Nigeria, London War Office 1910, Map E, as in Plates 2a and 2b.

40 Map of Benin Province, published under the direction of the Inspector General of Surveys Nigeria (n.d) (endorsed by Directorate of Military Survey May Library, 26 November 1954). Obtained from British Library, London, 11 December 2017. See Plates 3a–3c.

41 See Plates 4a–4c.

42 See details of their history of migration and settlement in Harunah (2003: 212–29).

43 Harunah (2003: 215–17). Throughout the book, the author refers to Uneme Osu as Uneme Aki-Osu. It is unclear why the latter is preferred even when the former is recognized and used in contemporary time.

44 Harunah (2003: 215). The *Afe-Osu* and *Afẹ Osobo* families continue to exist in Ọza and Dagbala until today. Both continue to recognize and maintain their land ownership as stretching between Ọza and Dagbala, and concur that both families originally own the land that Uneme-Osu currently inhabits. Virtually all my interlocutors have corroborated these claims to land ownership.

45 See Harunah (2003: xxv–xxvi). See also extensive elaboration on the caste prejudice and intermarriages in the third section of the book, Chapter 4, pp. 147–78, and Chapter 14, pp. 523–43.

46 See, for instance, the examination of Nupe administration of the Yagba people and the people's disenchantment with their Nupe overlords (Omoniyi 2003: 16–24).

47 For a brief treatment of the Akoko societies and Afenmai peoples with respect to the Nupe wars and Jihad of the early nineteenth century, see Crowder (1962: 91), Mason (1970: 193–209; 1977: 63–76); Mohammed (1990: 142–57) and Kolapo (1999, 2012).

48 Cf. Oshiedu (1980: 28).

49 For the early history of Yoruba and Edo-speaking peoples, Obayemi relied entirely on non-written sources of various kinds. Of these, oral tradition is probably the most important. It was supplemented with the findings of archaeological and linguistic research, and with inferences drawn from the results of ethnographic mapping of present-day cultures and sociopolitical organizations. He drew on the

various types simultaneously, and by constantly cross-checking one against another, built some semblance of a coherent and probable narrative. This methodological approach is quite informative for this present book.
50 The launching of a biography by the Benin monarch in 2004, where he narrated the Bini origin of the Ife monarchy, had furthered a controversial debate in royal and academic circles. See Omo N'Oba Erediauwa, *I Remain, Sir, Your Obedient Servant* (Ibadan: Spectrum, 2004). See also Omo N'Oba N'Edo UkuAkpolo Kpolo Oba Erediauwa, 'The Benin-Ife Connection', *Sunday Vanguard*, 14 May 2004; and Oba Sijuade, Ooni of Ifé, 'How Oba of Benin Goofed', *Vanguard*, 16 May 2004.
51 Lewis observed that while there appears to be some consensus in both Bini and Ife oral traditions that a prince of Ifé went to rule Bini in the twelfth century AD, controversy surrounds the lineage of the said prince and whether his ascension to the throne was the origin of the Bini or a mere change of dynasty (2018: 5).
52 As Lewis explained, the kinds of pots restricted to the Edoid have traditional functionality. They are designed with little aesthetic character and have deep cultural relevance. Such traditionally functional pots are absent in Ijaye pottery, where the pots are more ornamental and made as artefact rather than household tools (2018: 15).

3 World views, religious cosmologies, spiritual agency

1 Interview with Chief Abiodun Joshua, Ojah, 10 October 2020.
2 Interview with Chief Abiodun Joshua, Ojah. 10 October 2020.
3 The abode of *Odumu* (lion) is located at *Onya Odumu* (*Odumu* hill), the entrance to present-day Uneme Osu from the driving direction of Dagbala. This corroborates the fact that the Oza landmass extends to that location since it originally had a geographical boundary with Dagbala prior to giving part of their land to the Ileme immigrants, now known as Uneme Osu.
4 Interview with Chief Abiodun Joshua, Ojah, 10 October 2020.
5 Interview with Chief Abiodun Joshua, Ojah, 10 October 2020.
6 P. A. Dania, Individual project (unpublished), St. David's College, Evboneka, Benin, n.d., p. 33.
7 Interview with Segun Joshua, Ojah, 20 October 2020.
8 See also photo image no. 9 (Lawani 1992: 109).
9 Interview with Chief Abiodun Alleh, Ojah, 20 October 2020. He embodies an indigenous *Obu Evba* and *Obu Ikumu* who has several *Ebu* trainees under his tutelage.

4 Genealogies of kinship and sacral kingship

1 The agnatic (patrilineal) descent group is a basic social unit that contrasts with cognatic elements with descent traced through the apical ancestor in both male and female lines.
2 See later usage by Kunstadter (1963: 56–65) and the 'matrifocal family' as a comparative category (Randolph 1964: 628).
3 See Olupona (1991: 58–85), Chapter III – 'Ǫdun Oba: The Ideology and Rituals of Sacred Kingship'.
4 See a detailed discussion of the *Upe Iruvie, Ibishika* and *Ǫmǫnugere* festivals in Chapter 7.
5 See Olupona (1991: 130–57), Chapter VI – 'Ǫdun Obitun/Aje: Women's Rituals of Reproduction and Wealth'.
6 See 'Edo State Arts and Craft', Edo State Ministry of Arts, Culture, Tourism & Diaspora Affairs EBlog. Available online: https://edostateministryofartsandculture.wordpress.com/edo-state-arts-and-craft/.
7 Northcote W. Thomas was a British colonial government anthropologist and a remarkable figure in the early history of anthropological research in Nigeria from 1909 to 1913. During the early part of the century, his collections remained a largely untapped source for scholars interested in Edo- and Igbo-speaking areas. He made a major contribution to the study of both anthropology proper and related fields such as linguistics, ethnobotany and ethnomusicology. Thomas's particular areas of study were the Edoid-speaking areas north of Benin City and the Igbo areas around Awka. However, the collection of materials from Edoid areas such as Sabongida-Ora, Agenebode, Otuo and Okpe are virtually unique, as no other major museum collections in Nigeria or elsewhere have focused on this region. For more details, see Blench (1995: 20–8).
8 The expression 'coloniality of power' was coined by Anibal Quijano to depict the colonial structures of power, control and hegemony that have emerged during the modernist era, the era of colonialism, which stretches from the conquest of the Americas to the present. See, for instance, Quijano (2000: 533–80; 2007: 168–78). Walter Mignolo built on the concepts 'Modernity/coloniality' to refer to the way in which modernity and coloniality are inseparable – two sides of the same coin. See Mignolo (2007: 449–514).
9 P. A. Dania, Individual project (unpublished), St. David's College, Evboneka, Benin, n.d., p. 43.
10 Dania, Individual project, p. 50.
11 See Letter from R. B. Kerr, Acting District Officer, Kukuruku Division, titled 'Chief Ǫnǫbumę of Ǫja' to the Resident, Benin Province, Benin City. No. K.B. 205/2. The Divisional Office, Kukuruku Division, Auchi, 13 October 1934. Provincial

Administration Department, Ben Prof. 1 File No. BP926/1 converted from File No. B.P. 120/1931. This letter with the subject 'Chief Ọnọbumẹ of Ọja' was in respect of circumstances surrounding Chief Ọnọbumẹ's release from incarceration. G. S. Huges served as Resident for Benin Province from January to September 1933 and was succeeded by Acting Resident G. B. Williams (1933, 1934–5). For a fuller detail of some of the Residents of Benin Province, see Egharevba (1953: 117–18).

12 Kerr, 'Chief Ọnọbumẹ of Ọja'.
13 Kerr, 'Chief Ọnọbumẹ of Ọja', p. 4.
14 Kerr, 'Chief Ọnọbumẹ of Ọja', p. 5.
15 Resident-Benin Province, *Annual Report on the Benin Province for 1939*, National Archives, Ibadan. File: Ben Prof. 1, vol. 1, 11 March 1940, p. 9.
16 Resident-Benin Province, *Annual Report on the Benin Province for 1939*, p. 9.
17 Cf. Resident-Benin Province, *Annual Report on the Benin Province for 1939*, p. 9.
18 H. L. M. Butcher, Resident, *Annual Report 1954: Benin Province*, National Archives, File: Ben Prof. 1 (1954–5), p. 2.
19 Butcher, Resident, *Annual Report 1954: Benin Province*, p. 2.
20 See Resident-Benin Province, *Annual Report Benin Province 1931–33*, for Prison Statistics, Criminal Returns, Table of Sentences at the Provincial Court, and Native Court Cases, Benin Province. National Archives, File: Ben Prof. 1. Memorandum No. B.P. 40/1, 24 February 1933.
21 Butcher, *Annual Report 1954: Benin Province*, p. 5.
22 Butcher, *Annual Report 1954: Benin Province*, p. 6.
23 Butcher, *Annual Report 1954: Benin Province*, p. 6.
24 Butcher, *Annual Report 1954: Benin Province*, p. 35.
25 Butcher, *Annual Report 1954: Benin Province*, p. 75.
26 Butcher, *Annual Report 1954: Benin Province*, p. 34.
27 Butcher, *Annual Report 1954: Benin Province*, p. 32.
28 Butcher, *Annual Report 1954: Benin Province*, p. 33.
29 Butcher, *Annual Report 1954: Benin Province*, p. 33.
30 Kerr, 'Chief Ọnọbumẹ of Ọja', p. 2.
31 *Ọdumu* also literally means 'lion' to symbolize the power and potency of the royal appurtenance.
32 Dania, Individual project.
33 Kerr, 'Chief Ọnọbumẹ of Ọja', p. 4.
34 Resident-Benin Province, *Annual Report on the Benin Province for 1939*, p. 29.
35 Kerr, 'Chief Ọnọbumẹ of Ọja', p. 4.
36 Kerr, 'Chief Ọnọbumẹ of Ọja', p. 4.
37 Resident-Benin Province, *Annual Report on the Benin Province for 1939*, p. 12.
38 Resident-Benin Province, *Annual Report on the Benin Province for 1939*, p. 11.
39 Resident-Benin Province, *Annual Report on the Benin Province for 1939*, p. 11.

40 Resident-Benin Province, *Annual Report - Benin Province 1950–51*, National Archives, Ibadan. Ben Prof. 1: File: B.P. 40 vol. XIV, 1951, p. 14.
41 Resident-Benin Province, *Annual Report - Benin Province 1950–51*, p. 14.
42 Resident-Benin Province, *Annual Report on the Benin Province for 1939*, p. 27.
43 Resident-Benin Province, *Annual Report on the Benin Province for 1939*, p. 12.
44 Resident-Benin Province, *Annual Report on the Benin Province for 1939*, p. 21.
45 Resident-Benin Province, *Annual Report Benin Province 1939*, p. 13.
46 Resident-Benin Province, *Annual Report - Benin Province 1950–51*, p. 5.
47 Resident-Benin Province, *Annual Report - Benin Province 1950–51*, p. 15.
48 Resident-Benin Province, *Annual Report - Benin Province 1950–51*, p. 15.
49 Butcher, *Annual Report 1954: Benin Province*, p. 71.
50 Butcher, *Annual Report 1954: Benin Province*, p. 38.
51 Resident-Benin Province, *Annual Report - Benin Province 1950–51*, p. 6.
52 Resident-Benin Province, *Annual Report - Benin Province 1950–51*, p. 6.
53 Resident-Benin Province, *Annual Report - Benin Province 1950–51*, p. 11.
54 Kerr, 'Chief Ọnọbumẹ of Ọja', p. 5.
55 See Acting Resident, Benin Province, "Ọnọbumẹ of Ọja. Your letter No. K.B. 205/2 of the 13th of October, 1934", to the District Officer, Kukuruku Division, Auchi. B.P. 926/7. 19 January 1935. I. R. Dickins served as Acting Resident, Benin Province, from January to March 1935 and was then succeeded by H. P. James as Acting Resident from March to May 1935, followed by H. F. M. White from May 1935 to May 1936. See Egharevba (1953: 118).
56 See Acting Resident, 'Ọnọbumẹ of Ọja. Your letter No. K.B. 205/2 of the 13th of October, 1934'.
57 The District Officer, 'Ọnọbumẹ of Ọja', Letter from the Divisional Office, Kukuruku Division, Auchi to the Resident, Benin Province, Benin City. No. K.B. 205/12, 16 May 1935.
58 The District Officer, 'Ọnọbumẹ of Ọja', p. 1.
59 *Juju* or *Ju-ju*, originally coined from French vocabulary *joujou*, literally meaning 'plaything' to denigrate indigenous African belief systems that incorporate concrete objects, such as charms and amulets used in ritual practice. Generally, the term also appeared in connection with the Priest-Kings of towns in West Africa. See Talbot (1915: 79–112). P. A. Talbot was a district commissioner in Southern Nigeria. See also Frazer (1900). The wrong appropriation of this colonial invented term '*ju-ju*' to African indigenous religions has continued to gain traction in contemporary Africa and by armchair scholarship till date.
60 The District Officer, 'Ọnọbumẹ of Ọja', p. 2.
61 Private family communication from Chief D. S. Lawani, on behalf of the Okoko ruling house, Osuruka royal kndred, to Segun Lawani (Paris, France), 16 August 2005, p. 2.

62 The District Officer, 'Ọnọbumẹ of Ọja', p. 2.
63 Resident-Benin Province, *Annual Report on the Benin Province for 1939*, p. 5.
64 Resident-Benin Province, *Annual Report on the Benin Province for 1939*, p. 6.
65 R. B. Kerr, Acting District Officer, Kukuruku Division "Chief Ọnọbumẹ of Ọja" to the Resident, Benin Province, Benin City (No. K.B. 205/2, The Divisional Office, Kukuruku Division, Auchi, 13 October 1934).
66 This table was adapted from the letter by Kerr, 'Chief Ọnọbumẹ of Ọja' (No. K.B. 205/2, pp. 2–3) without any redaction. However, it should be observed that some names were incorrectly spelt (see asterisk *) in the letter such as Obuese (Oburese), Iviovie (Ibiovie), Obuele (Obueri), Odosame (Odosami), Okora (Okara), Oboro (Obuoro) and so forth, and 'family' used instead of 'kindred'.
67 Official letter by Kerr, "Chief Ọnọbumẹ of Ọja" (No. K.B. 205/2), p. 3.
68 Butcher, *Annual Report 1954: Benin Province*, p. 29.
69 Butcher, *Annual Report 1954: Benin Province*, p. 29.
70 P. A. Alonge, 'How Ọjah Is Ruled', Letter sent to the Chieftaincy Committee, Akoko Oke District Council, Igarra by Ọjah Royal Family, 28 August 1961. The letter was signed by Alonge as Secretary for the Ọjah Royal Family.
71 Alonge, 'How Ọjah Is Ruled'.
72 The titles 'Saiki' and 'Otaru' were assimilated and adopted into Ọza royal vocabulary through the Nupe-Fulani hegemonic influence and expansion in the region.
73 Alonge, 'How Ọjah Is Ruled', p. 2.
74 See Letter from Osuruka Ruling Family (c/o Chief Kilani Ishineka Eroko, the Obuoro of Ọjah), 'An Amendment to the Research conducted on June 3rd 1970 into Ọjah Chieftaincy at Customary Court, Dagbala in Okuloso Clan', to the Permanent Secretary, Ministry of Local Government and Chieftaincy Affairs, Benin City, 27 June 1970. The letter was signed by the following: Samuel Okoko, Chief Obuoro – Kilani Ishineka Eroko, Adebayo Lawani, Philip Adegboyega, P. A. Alonge and P. A. Dania. Additional copies of the letter were sent to the following: Chief Adeshina Ọnọbumẹ, The Okogbe of Ọjah; The Sole Administrator, Akoko-Ẹdo Division, Igarra; The Secretary, Akoko-Ẹdo Division, Igarra; The Permanent Secretary, Ministry of Local Government and Chieftaincy Affairs, Benin City; The Research Officer in charge of Chieftaincy Affairs, Ministry of Local Government and Chieftaincy Affairs, Benin City.
75 The Ugbonokua family lineage trace their genealogical tradition of royal chieftainship succession from Asoka. See more details below.
76 Letter from Osuruka Ruling Family, 'An Amendment to the Research Conducted on June 3rd 1970 into Ọjah Chieftaincy at Customary Court, Dagbala in Okuloso Clan', to the Permanent Secretary, Ministry of Local Government and Chieftaincy Affairs, Benin City, 27 June 1970.

5 Kingship myth, leadership succession and legal imbroglios (1991–2011)

1 This may partly explain the feeling of family abandonment, as society separates persons with contagious diseases, such as leprosy, and quarantines them in a leprosarium. In the case of Imodafe, in his capacity as *Ọpashi*, it is improbable that he ended up in a leprosarium. Most probably his palace was deserted.
2 P. A. Dania, Individual project (unpublished), St. David's College, Evboneka, Benin, n.d., p. 47.
3 See Table with names of the Ọkọgbe of Ọjah and their respective quarters, in Dania, Individual project, p. 55.
4 Dania, Individual project, p. 47.
5 There is no record of how long Ọkọkọ Aiyejina reigned as Ọkọgbe of Ọza. The duration of his reign and that of most of his successors is a matter of conjecture.
6 Full text of Judgement, Ọkọkọ & Lawani v. Ọnọbume & Ọbayemi, Suit No. HIG/11/91. In the High Court of Justice, Edo State of Nigeria, In the Igarra Judicial Division Holden at Igarra Before His Lordship Hon. Justice P. I. Imoedemhe – Judge on Friday, 15 October 2004, p. 5.
7 Text of Judgement, Okoko & Lawani v. Ọnọbumẹ & Obayemi, Suit No. HIG/11/91, p. 6.
8 Text of Judgement, Okoko & Lawani v. Ọnọbumẹ & Obayemi, Suit No. HIG/11/91, p. 6.
9 Text of Judgement, Okoko & Lawani v. Ọnọbumẹ & Obayemi, Suit No. HIG/11/91, p. 6.
10 Dania, Individual project, p. 56.
11 Dania, Individual project, pp. 47–51.
12 Dania, Individual project, p. 52.
13 Text of Judgement, Okoko & Lawani v. Ọnọbumẹ & Obayemi, Suit No. HIG/11/91, p. 7.
14 Text of Judgement, Okoko & Lawani v. Ọnọbumẹ & Obayemi, Suit No. HIG/11/91, p. 8.
15 Text of Judgement, Okoko & Lawani v. Ọnọbumẹ & Obayemi, Suit No. HIG/11/91, p. 8.
16 Text of Judgement, Okoko & Lawani v. Ọnọbumẹ & Obayemi, Suit No. HIG/11/91, p. 8.
17 Text of Judgement, Okoko & Lawani v. Ọnọbumẹ & Obayemi, Suit No. HIG/11/91, p. 6.
18 Text of Judgement, Okoko & Lawani v. Ọnọbumẹ & Obayemi, Suit No. HIG/11/91, p. 6.

19 Text of Judgement, Okoko & Lawani v. Ọnọbumẹ & Obayemi, Suit No. HIG/11/91, p. 8.
20 Text of Judgement, Okoko & Lawani v. Ọnọbumẹ & Obayemi, Suit No. HIG/11/91, p. 6.
21 Text of Judgement, Okoko & Lawani v. Ọnọbumẹ & Obayemi, Suit No. HIG/11/91, p. 8. They also claimed that 'these three Okogbes were brothers and the sons of one Oriere while Okoko and Olowu Eruko were their half brothers'.
22 Text of Judgement, Okoko & Lawani v. Ọnọbumẹ & Obayemi, Suit No. HIG/11/91, p. 7.
23 Text of Judgement, Okoko & Lawani v. Ọnọbumẹ & Obayemi, Suit No. HIG/11/91, p. 9.
24 Text of Judgement, Okoko & Lawani v. Ọnọbumẹ & Obayemi, Suit No. HIG/11/91, p. 9.
25 Minutes of meeting held between Ọza Solidarity Movement, Ọjah (Lagos Branch) and the Osuruka ruling house, 21 September 1993.
26 Letter 'Ruling in Osuruka Family' from the Okoko ruling house to the Divisional Police Officer (D.P.O), Divisional Police Office, Igarra, 18 June 1991. Twelve representatives from the Okoko ruling house signed this memorandum, namely Adebayo Lawani, P. A. Dania, J. A. Ogundare, James Dania, Felix Obuoro, James Samari, Felix Kilani, Adewole Daudu, Aliu Lawani, Andrew Lawani, Daniel S. Lawani and Jonathan Alonge.
27 Letter 'Ruling in Osuruka Family'.
28 Interview with P. A. Dania, Ọjah, 21 November 2004.
29 Text of Judgement, Okoko & Lawani v. Ọnọbumẹ & Obayemi, Suit No. HIG/11/91, p. 6.
30 Writ of Summons filed and dated 2 July 91. See full text of Judgement, Okoko & Lawani v. Ọnọbumẹ & Obayemi, Suit No. HIG/11/91.
31 See Letter from the Okoko ruling house, 'Action Likely to Cause the Breach of the Peace in Ọjah', to the Chief Security Officer, Nigerian Security Office, Igarra, 9 October 2002. This was following a complaint made to the State Government regarding a purportedly forged letter by Mr Sunday S. Alonge, 'Re: Save Our Souls', on 10 October 2001, which was tantamount to escalating conflict. The letter described S. S Alonge and his agents as a group of persons with a hidden agenda on Ọjah Chieftaincy dispute and called on the government's quick intervention to 'save the big havoc this group of persons that have no regard for the court could cause'.
32 See 'The Disolution of Ọjah Town Council', Letter from the National Executive Council, OCDM National Secretariat, Ọjah to the Chairman, Ọjah Town Council, Ọjah, 28 September 1991. This letter was signed by twenty-three attendees: the National President (J. A. Ogundare), Vice President (James Ashore), the Secretary (L. A. Olorunfemi), Treasurer (R. S. Adogame), Publicity Secretary (Leo Lawani),

Financial Secretary (F. O. Fashola); and OCDM branch representatives from Lagos, Ibadan, Ilorin, Kaduna, Kano, Maiduguri, Ogun, Ondo, Igarra, Etsako, Akure, Warri/Sapele, Ajaokuta/Okẹkẹ, Benin, Abuja, Owan, Home and copied to all OCDM branches, Quarter Heads/Elders of Ọjah, respectively.

33 OCDM National Committee, 'Appointment of Community Leader in Ọjah', Official letter addressed to Chief Bokeshimi, Chairman of Akoko Edo Local Government Area, 2 October 1992. This letter was copied to Edo State Governor, Chairman of the Traditional Council of Akoko Edo LGA, Divisional Police Officer, Igarra, Officer in charge at Ọsọsọ Police Station and Chief B. A Arishe. Twenty-seven members comprising the OCDM National Executive Committee and members including F. A. Edward (National President), Lewis Ashore (General Secretary), James Ashore (Auditor), R. U. Ijejeme (National Auditor) and twenty-two other members duly signed the letter.

34 OCDM National Committee, 'Appointment of Community Leader in Ọjah'.

35 Ọjah Community Development Movement, 'Attention: Chief F.L. Bokeshimi', Official Letter addressed to the Chairman, Akoko Edo Local Government Council, Igarra, 5 May 1993.

36 Personal interview with Pa Rufus Adogame, Ọjah, 25 July 2019.

37 R. S. Adogame (Immediate Past Community Leader), 'Resignation Letter As a Community Leader', Letter through the President, National OCDM, Lagos to all OCDM Branches in the Federation, 27 September 2002.

38 See Letter from the OSMO President (Lagos), 'Request for Peace within Osuruka Kindred Ọjah', to the Osuruka Family, Ọjah, 3 December 1996.

39 See Letter from Chief Lawani to the OSMO President (Lagos), 'Request for Peace within Osuruka Kindred Ọjah', 20 December 1996; and Letter from the Okoko Ruling House, The Osuruka Royal Kindred of Ọjah, 'Succession of the Okogbe Chieftaincy, Ọjah', to the OCDM Lagos, 22 December 1996, respectively.

40 See Letter from Chief Lawani to the OSMO President (Lagos), 'Request for Peace within Osuruka Kindred Ọjah'.

41 See Letter from Chief Lawani to the OSMO President (Lagos), 'Request for Peace within Osuruka Kindred Ọjah'.

42 Letter from the Okoko Ruling House, The Osuruka Royal Kindred of Ọjah 'Succession of the Okogbe Chieftaincy, Ọjah'. The second letter was endorsed by Chief J. O. Lawani, P. A. Dania (Okoko), J. A Ogundare, D. S. Lawani and Felix K. Kilani on behalf of the Okoko ruling house; as well as Chief P. A. Alonge (Osuruka royal kindred) and Mr Felix I. A. Ajayi (OSMO representative) listed as coordinators.

43 See *Minutes of the Reconciliation Meeting of Osuruka Royal Kindred, Ọjah*, held on 20, 22 and 24 January 1997.

44 *Minutes of the Reconciliation Meeting of Osuruka Royal Kindred*, p. 1.

45 *Minutes of the Reconciliation Meeting of Osuruka Royal Kindred*, p. 2. The six-man reconciliation committee members comprised P. A. Dania and J. A. Ogundare (Okoko ruling house), Pa Michael Aiyede Ọnọbumẹ and Adebayo Ọnọbumẹ (Ugbonokua ruling house), and Paul Agbalajobi and Abudu Daudu (great-grandchildren of Oshioma), respectively. There appears to be a discrepancy between the dates mentioned on the minutes title (20, 22, and 24 January1997) and those indicated as subsequent meeting dates (22 and 24 January 1998). It is most improbable that the Osuruka family would allow a full year to deliberate on a crisis matter that required such an urgency.

46 *Minutes of the Reconciliation Meeting of Osuruka Royal Kindred*, p. 3.

47 *Minutes of the Reconciliation Meeting of Osuruka Royal Kindred*, p. 3.

48 *Minutes of the Reconciliation Meeting of Osuruka Royal Kindred*, p. 1.

49 *Minutes of the Reconciliation Meeting of Osuruka Royal Kindred*, p. 3.

50 The 1st-3rd defendants (respectively listed as Executive Governor of Edo State; Attorney General of Edo State; Commissioner of Local Government and Chieftaincy Affairs, Edo State), with leave of court, entered appearance and filed a joint statement of defence but took no further part in the proceeding. The 4th defendant (Akoko-Ẹdo Traditional Rulers Council) took no part in the proceeding although it was duly served.

51 Text of Judgement, Okoko & Lawani v. Ọnọbumẹ & Obayemi, Suit No. HIG/11/91, p. 3.

52 Text of Judgement, Okoko & Lawani v. Ọnọbumẹ & Obayemi, Suit No. HIG/11/91, pp. 3-4.

53 Text of Judgement, Okoko & Lawani v. Ọnọbumẹ & Obayemi, Suit No. HIG/11/91, pp. 4-5.

54 A regent is a person appointed to administer a kingdom because the monarch or king is a minor or is absent or incapacitated.

55 Text of Judgement, Okoko & Lawani v. Ọnọbumẹ & Obayemi, Suit No. HIG/11/91, p. 5.

56 Text of Judgement, Okoko & Lawani v. Ọnọbumẹ & Obayemi, Suit No. HIG/11/91, p. 12.

57 Text of Judgement, Okoko & Lawani v. Ọnọbumẹ & Obayemi, Suit No. HIG/11/91, pp. 13-14. Table 1 and 2 were adapted here from the original judgement text.

58 Text of Judgement, Okoko & Lawani v. Ọnọbumẹ & Obayemi, Suit No. HIG/11/91, p. 16.

59 Text of Judgement, Okoko & Lawani v. Ọnọbumẹ && Obayemi, Suit No. HIG/11/91, pp. 20-1.

60 Text of Judgement, Okoko & Lawani v. Ọnọbumẹ & Obayemi, Suit No. HIG/11/91, p. 21.

61 Text of Judgement, Okoko & Lawani v. Ọnọbumẹ & Obayemi, Suit No. HIG/11/91, p. 21.
62 Text of Judgement, Okoko & Lawani v. Ọnọbumẹ & Obayemi, Suit No. HIG/11/91, pp. 21–2.
63 Text of Judgement, Okoko & Lawani v. Ọnọbumẹ && Obayemi, Suit No. HIG/11/91, p. 22.
64 Hon. Commissioner (signed by Mrs B. M. Momoh), 'Appointment of Chief Daniel Suru Lawani as the Village Head (Okogbe) of Ọjah in Akoko-Ẹdo Local Government Area', Letter Ref. CH. 768/200, Ministry of Local Government and Chieftaincy Affairs, Office of the Commissioner, Benin City, Edo State of Nigeria, 14 March 2006.
65 *Edo State of Nigeria Gazette (Extraordinary)*, published by Authority, vol. 16, no. 14 (2 April 2006), published as Edo State Legal Notice No. 3 of 2006 (E.S.L.N. 3 of 2006, p. B5). It is cited under the theme 'Traditional Rules and Chiefs Law, 1979', Appointment of Chief Daniel Suru Lawani as the Village Head (Okogbe) of Ọja in Okuloso Federated Clan, Akoko-Ẹdo Local Government Area, Benin City, dated 13 March 2006, and signed by Osagie Ize-Iyamu Esq., Secretary to the State Government, Edo State.
66 Philip Okoko Anor (Respondent) v. Lawrence Obayemi (Applicant), Motion filed in the Court of Appeal Holden at Benin City on Tuesday the 27th day of November, 2007 Before Their Lordships Hon. Justice Saka A. Ibiyeye (presiding), Hon Justice Stanley Shenko Alagoa and Hon. Justice Abu Abubakar Gumel (Court of Appeal), File CA/B/229/06, 27 November 2007.
67 Philip Okoko Anor (Respondent) v. Lawrence Obayemi (Applicant), Motion filed in the Court of Appeal Holden at Benin City on Tuesday the 27th day of November, 2007 Before Their Lordships Hon. Justice Saka A. Ibiyeye (presiding), Hon Justice Stanley Shenko Alagoa and Hon. Justice Abu Abubakar Gumel (Court of Appeal), File CA/B/229/06, 27 November 2007.
68 Lawrence Obayemi v. Okoko & Lawani, 'Reply to Further Affidavit Filed on 3/11/08', in the Court of Appeal, in the Benin Judicial Division Holden at Benin City. Appeal No: CA/B/229/2006; Suit No.: HIG/11/91, 18 May 2009; and Lawrence Obayemi v. Okoko & Lawani, 'Counter Affidavit In Opposition to the Application for the Committal of Appellant for Contempt', in the Court of Appeal, in the Benin Judicial Division Holden at Benin City. Appeal No: CA/B/229/2006; Suit No.: HIG/11/91, 18 May 2009.
69 Lawrence Obayemi & Anor v. The Executive Governor of Edo State & ORS. In the Court of Appeal Holden at Benin City – Edo State on Monday the 7th Day of March 2011 Before Their Lordships Hon. Justice A. Sanusi (presiding), Hon. Justice O. F. Omoleye, Hon. Chioma E. Nwosu-Iheme (Justice, Court of Appeal), File CA/B/229/2006, 7 March 2011.

70 Lawrence Obayemi & Anor v. The Executive Governor of Edo State & ORS. In the Court of Appeal Holden at Benin City – Edo State on Monday the 7th Day of March 2011 Before Their Lordships Hon. Justice A. Sanusi (presiding), Hon. Justice O. F. Omoleye, Hon. Chioma E. Nwosu-Iheme (Justice, Court of Appeal), File CA/B/229/2006, 7 March 2011.

71 B. A. Alegbe Esq., Petition 'Acting in Dual Capacity as a Village Head of Ojah and as a Civil Servant and Receiving Remuneration for both Positions', to His Excellency, The Deputy Governor Edo State, Osadebey Avenue GRA, Benin City [Ref. BAA/J/2011/VOL 11/32], 12 March 2011.

72 Alegbe Esq., Petition 'Acting in Dual Capacity as a Village Head of Ojah and as a Civil Servant and Receiving Remuneration for both Positions'.

73 Alegbe Esq., Petition 'Acting in Dual Capacity as a Village Head of Ojah and as a Civil Servant and Receiving Remuneration for both Positions'.

74 V. O Okhuasuyi, Director (on behalf of Permanent Secretary), Petition 'Acting in Dual Capacity as a Village Head of Ojah and as a Civil Servant and Receiving Remuneration for both Positions', Letter from the Office of the Deputy Governor to the Honourable Commissioner, Ministry of Local Government and Chieftaincy Affairs, Benin City [Our Ref. No. ODG 13/1/68], 14 March 2011.

75 Dr S. E. Mosugu, Re: Response to Petition: 'Acting in Dual Capacity as a Village Head of Ojah and as a Civil Servant and Receiving Remuneration for both Positions', Letter to His Excellency, the Deputy Governor of Edo State of Nigeria, Benin City, 23 May 2011, p. 7.

76 Mosugu, Re: Response to Petition: 'Acting in Dual Capacity as a Village Head of Ojah and as a Civil Servant and Receiving Remuneration for both Positions', p. 1.

77 Mosugu, Re: Response to Petition: 'Acting in Dual Capacity as a Village Head of Ojah and as a Civil Servant and Receiving Remuneration for both Positions', p. 1.

78 Mosugu, Re: Response to Petition: 'Acting in Dual Capacity as a Village Head of Ojah and as a Civil Servant and Receiving Remuneration for both Positions', p. 2.

79 Mosugu, Re: Response to Petition: 'Acting in Dual Capacity as a Village Head of Ojah and as a Civil Servant and Receiving Remuneration for both Positions', p. 2.

80 The Traditional Rulers and Chiefs Law was enacted on 24 August 1979 to regulate all matters pertaining to Traditional Rulers and Chiefs in the then Bendel State, now applicable to Edo state. The Law in its preliminary sections (Section 2) defined a 'Traditional Ruler' as 'the traditional head of an ethnic unit or clan who is for the time being the holder of the highest traditional authority within the ethnic unit or clan', and 'Traditional Chief' as 'the holder of a Chieftaincy title to which traditional functions are attached'. See *The Traditional Rulers and Chiefs Edicts No 16 of 1979. Law of Bendel State of Nigeria, applicable in Edo State.*

81 Mosugu, Re: Response to Petition: 'Acting in Dual Capacity as a Village Head of Ojah and as a Civil Servant and Receiving Remuneration for both Positions', p. 3. See *Edo State of Nigeria Gazette (Extraordinary)*.
82 Mosugu, Re: Response to Petition: 'Acting in Dual Capacity as a Village Head of Ojah and as a Civil Servant and Receiving Remuneration for both Positions', p. 4.
83 *Traditional Rulers and Chiefs Edicts No 16 of 1979*, Section 30 (1–4).
84 Mosugu, Re: Response to Petition: 'Acting in Dual Capacity as a Village Head of Ojah and as a Civil Servant and Receiving Remuneration for both Positions', p. 5.
85 HRH D. S. Lawani, Ifiabeka II, the Okogbe of Ojah, ' "Re" Settlement of Stipends', Letter to the Permanent Secretary, Ministry of Local Government and Chieftaincy Affairs, Benin City, April 2007 (n.d.).
86 Mosugu, Re: Response to Petition: 'Acting in Dual Capacity as a Village Head of Ojah and as a Civil Servant and Receiving Remuneration for both Positions', p. 6.
87 HRH D. S. Lawani, Ifiabeka II, the Okogbe of Ojah, 'Re: Acting in Dual Capacity as a Village Head of Ojah and as a Civil Servant and Receiving Remuneration for both Positions', Letter to His Excellency, The Deputy Governor of Edo State, 1 June 2011, p. 4.
88 Dr. S. E. Mosugu, SAN, 'Demand for Settlement of Judgment Debts/Costs-Now', Letter addressed to Mr. Lawrence Obayemi, Ojah, 6 June 2011.
89 Mosugu, SAN, 'Demand for Settlement of Judgment Debts/Costs-Now'.

6 Rituals of passage

1 Interview with Chief Abiodun Joshua and Shegun Joshua, Ojah, 12 October 2020.
2 Interview with Shegun Joshua, Ojah, 20 October 2020.
3 P. A. Dania, Individual project (unpublished), St. David's College, Evboneka, Benin, n.d., p. 27.
4 Interview with Chief Abiodun Joshua, Ojah, 10 October 2020.
5 Dania, Individual project, n.d., p. 27.
6 Interview with Chief Abiodun Joshua, Ojah, 10 October 2020.
7 Dania, Individual project, n.d., p. 28.
8 Dania, Individual project, n.d., p. 28.
9 Dania, Individual project, n.d., p. 30.
10 Dania, Individual project, n.d., p. 30.
11 Personal interview with Chief P. A. Alonge, Ojah, 28 December 1986.

7 Gendering rituals

1 Personal Interview with Chief J. O. Ogunnubi, the Onibillo of Ibillo, Royal Palace, Ibillo, 8 November 1986.
2 Cf. subsection 'Ọza People and Ileme (Uneme-Osu)' in Chapter 2 of this book.
3 Personal interview with Chief P. A. Alonge, Ojah, 28 December 1986.
4 Personal interview with Oke Afemiye, Ojah, 5 October 1986.
5 Personal interview with Chief Alonge, Ojah, 28 December 1986.
6 Personal interview with Madam Ojulawo Omotoriogun, Ojah, 16 December 1986.
7 Personal interview with Madam Omotoriogun, Ojah, 16 December 1986.
8 Personal interview with Gabriel Ajumoh, Ojah, 28 October 1986.
9 Personal interview with Chief Alonge, Ojah, 28 December 1986.
10 Personal interview with Chief Alonge, Ojah, 28 December 1986.
11 Personal interview with Chief Ogunnubi, the Onibillo of Ibillo, Royal Palace, Ibillo, 8 November 1986.
12 See also O. A. Lawani, L'Inscription Sociale et La Fonction De La Musique Chez Les Ọzah. Nigeria. Departement de Musicologie, Universite Paris 8, Vincennes Saint-Denis; and O. A. Lawani and J. N. Bertrand, Filmographie 'Quand les gens d'Ọzah dansent'. Centre Culturel Francais (Lagos, Nigeria), 1987.
13 See, for instance, the full description in Lawani, L'Inscription Sociale et La Fonction De La Musique Chez Les Ọzah, pp. 54–102.

8 The future of Ọza indigeneity in the face of African modernity

1 Resident, *Annual Report Benin Province 1939*, 11 March 1940, p. 5.
2 Resident, Benin Province, *Annual Report Benin Province 1954–1955*, p. 38.
3 Interviews with Aremu Courage Omomikashie, Pa Hezekiah Olorunfemi, Pa Omosunmoje and Kole Ureshemi, 19–23 August 2004.
4 Interview with Ijenọzah Victor Anojie, 19 August 2004.
5 Interviews with Pa Okoko Dania, Elder Alleh Ojee, Abase F. Peter, Kole Ureshemi, Pa Otaru, Uka Joseph, Chief Obayemi, Aremu Omomikashie, Pa Omosunmoje and Pa Olorunfemi, Ojah, August 2004.
6 Interview with Chief L. A. Obayemi, Ojah, 19 August 2004.
7 Interview with Clement Afaya, Ojah, 19 August 2004.
8 Interview with Elder Alleh Ojee, Ojah, 20 August 2004.
9 Rev. Father Bane, 'Blessing of Marriage', Letter from the District Office, Kukuruku Division to the Resident, Benin Province, Benin City, 2 September 1937.

10 Resident, *Annual Report Benin Province 1939*, 11 March 1940, p. 28.
11 Resident, *Annual Report Benin Province 1939*, p. 28.
12 Interview with Pa Okoko Dania, Ojah, 20 August 2004. This narrative was corroborated by several informants including Pa Hezekiah Olorunfemi, Courage Omomikashie, Pa Omosunmoje, Clement Afaya, Daniel Agbabi, Kole Ureshemi, Elder J. D. Igodi, Chief Otaru, Ijenozah Victor Anojie, Jonathan Abogun Ogundare, John Afeshemime Albert (interviews held at Ojah, August 2004) and so forth.
13 Interview with Pa Hezekiah Olorunfemi, Ojah, 20 August 2004.
14 Interview with Clement Afaya, Ojah, 23 August 2004.
15 Interview with Chief Lawrence A. Obayemi, Ojah, 22 August 2004.
16 Interview with John Afeshemime Albert, Ojah, 22 August 2004.
17 Interview with Pa Otaru, Ojah, 24 August 2004.
18 Interview with Elder Alleh Ojee, Ojah, 24 August 2004.
19 Interviews with Pa Otaru and Michael Aiyemibo, Ojah, 19 August 2004.
20 P. A. Dania, Individual project (unpublished), p. 37.
21 The Resident, Benin Province, *Annual Report 1950 Benin Province*, 1950, p. 32.
22 Dania, Individual project, p. 39.
23 Dania, Individual project, pp. 37–9.
24 Dania, Individual project, p. 39.
25 Resident, *Annual Report Benin Province 1939*, 11 March 1940, p. 18.
26 Resident, *Annual Report Benin Province 1939*, p. 18.
27 Resident, *Annual Report Benin Province 1939*, p. 19.
28 Resident, *Annual Report Benin Province 1939*, p. 29.
29 Resident H. L. M. Butcher, *Annual Report 1954 Benin Province*, Ben Prof 1, 26 June 1954, p. 4.
30 Resident H. L. M. Butcher, *Annual Report 1954 Benin Province*, p. 1.
31 Resident H. L. M. Butcher, *Annual Report 1954 Benin Province*, p. 10.
32 Resident, Benin Province, *Annual Report 1950 Benin Province*, p. 33.
33 Resident H. L. M. Butcher, *Annual Report 1954 Benin Province*, p. 85.
34 Resident H. L. M. Butcher, *Annual Report 1954 Benin Province*, p. 86.
35 Resident H. L. M. Butcher, *Annual Report 1954 Benin Province*, p. 86.

Oral Sources

Interview with Pa Omole Bamidele, Lampese, 6 August 1986.
Interview with Ezekiel Omogun, Somorika, 16 August 1986.
Interview with Oke Afemiye, Ojah, 5 October 1986.
Interview with Gabriel Ajumoh, Ojah, 28 October 1986.
Interview with HH Oba J. O. Ogunnubi, Ibillo, 8 November 1986.
Interview with Madam Ojulawo Omotoriogun, Ojah, 16 December 1986.
Interview with Chief P. A. Alonge, Ojah, 28 December 1986.
Interview with Micheal A. Stephen, Ojah, 17 August 2004.
Interview with Peter F. Abase, Ojah, 17 August 2004.
Interview with Chief Otaru, Ojah, 19 August 2004.
Interview with Ijenozah Victor Anojie, Ojah, 19 August 2004.
Interview with Benedicta B. Lawani, Ojah, 20 August 2004.
Interview with Janet O. Salami, Ojah, 20 August 2004.
Interview with Patricia O. Clement, Ojah, 20 August 2004.
Interview with See Me Happy Otaru, Ojah, 20 August 2004.
Interview with Chief Otaru, Ojah, 23 August 2004.
Interview with Abogun Ogundare, Ojah, 25 August 2004.
Interview with Agnes Agbabi, Ojah, 25 August 2004.
Interview with Jonathan Alonge, Ojah, 25 August 2004.
Interview with Mr S. Akarele, Ojah, 25 August 2004.
Interview with Uka Joseph, Ojah, 25 August 2004.
Interview with Anthony Imeriayo, Ojah, 29 August 2004.
Interview with Aiyemibo Michael, Ojah, 29 August 2004.
Interview with Chief Lawrence Obayemi, Ojah, 29 August 2004.
Interview with Dorcas G. Dania, Ojah, 29 August 2004.
Interview with Elizabeth Aliu, Ojah, 29 August 2004.
Interview with Ijenozah Victor Anojie, Ojah, 29 August 2004.
Interview with Kole Ureshemi Destiny, Ojah, 29 August 2004.
Interview with Pa P. A. Dania, Ojah, 29 August 2004.
Interview with Remi O. Oloruntoba, Ojah, 29 August 2004.
Interview with Uka Joseph, Ojah, 29 August 2004.
Interview with Aremu Omomikashie, Ojah, 30 August 2004.
Interview with HRH Thompson Lawani, the Okogbe of Ojah, 24 July 2019.
Interview with Pa Rufus Adogame, Ojah, 25 July 2019.
Interview with Barrister Ignatius Afe Oshomogwe, Abuja, 14 August 2020.

Interview with Shadrach Oladungbehin, Abuja, 14 August 2020.
Interview with Chief Abiodun Joshua, Ojah, 10 September 2020.
Interview with Shegun Joshua, Ojah, 10 September 2020.
Interview with Chief Abiodun Alleh, Ojah, 20 October 2020.

Select Bibliography

Adesina, J., 'Re-appropriating Matrifocality: Endogeneity and African Gender Scholarship'. *African Sociological Review*, 14, no. 1 (2010): 2–19.

Adjoto, G. O., 'The Traditional Beliefs of Okpameri People in Akoko-Edo Division, Bendel State'. A research paper in Headmasters' Institute, Benin City, 1976.

Adogame, A., *Traditional Marriage among the Okpameri People*. BA diss., Bendel State University, Ekpoma. Nigeria, June 1987.

Adogame, A., *Celestial Church of Christ. The Politics of Cultural Identity in a West African Prophetic-Charismatic Movement*. Frankfurt am Main: Peter Lang, 1999.

Adogame, A., 'Calling a Trickster Deity a "Bad" Name in Order to Hang It? Deconstructing Indigenous African Epistemologies within Global Religious Maps of the Universe'. In S. D. Brunn (ed.), *The Changing World Religion Map: Sacred Places, Identities, Practices and Politics*. Dodrecht: Springer Netherlands, 2015. pp. 1813–26.

Agbi, J., 'Okpameri Culture', *The Nigerian Observer*, 4 November 1986. p. 6.

Ajibolu, S. I., An Annual message of the Editor, (Okpameri Calendar) to the Okpameri People, 1985.

Akintoye, S. A., 'The North-Eastern Yoruba Districts and the Benin Kingdom'. *Journal of the Historical Society of Nigeria* 4, no. 4 (June 1969): 539–53.

Alonge, F., *Traditional Marriage Ceremony in Ojah, Akoko-Edo LGA of Edo State. A Historical Approach*. BA Long Essay, Department of History, University of Ibadan, Ibadan, September 2002.

Amadiume, I., *Male Daughters, Female Husbands: Gender and Sex in an African Society*. London: Zed Books, 1987.

Assmann, J., *Religion and Cultural Memory*. Stanford, CA: Stanford University Press, 2006.

Austin, J. L., 'Performative Utterances'. In J. O. Urmson and G. J. Warnock (eds), *Philosophical Papers*. Clarendon Press, 1961. pp. 233–52.

Austin, J. L., *How to Do Things with Words*. Oxford: Clarendon Press, 1962.

Avalos, N., '*Decolonial Approaches to the Study of Religion: Teaching Native American and Indigenous Religious Traditions*'. In S. Jacoby and J. Tinklenberg (eds), *Teaching Religion as Anti-Racism Education: Spotlight on Teaching*. Religious Studies News. American Academy of Religion, Available online: https://rsn.aarweb.org/spotlight-on/teaching/anti-racism/decolonial-approaches (accessed 26 June 2021).

Avalos, Natalie, 'Taking a Critical Indigenous and Ethnic Studies Approach to Decolonizing Religious Studies'. *Contending Modernities: Exploring How Religious and Secular Forces Interact in the Modern World*, 14 October 2020. Available online: https://contendingmodernities.nd.edu/decoloniality/critical-indigenous-approach/ (accessed 23 October 2020).

Ballard, J. A., 'Historical Inferences from the Linguistic Geography of the Nigerian Middle Belt'. *Africa: Journal of the International African Institute* 41, no. 4 (1971): 294–305.

Barnard, A., 'Kalahari Revisionism, Vienna and the "Indigenous" Debate'. *Social Anthropology* 14, no. 1 (2006a): 7.

Barnard, A., '"Rejoinder" Mathias Guenther et al., "Discussion: The Concept of Indigeneity"'. *Social Anthropology* 14, no. 1 (2006b): 29–31.

Barnes, B. R., 'Decolonising Research Methodologies: Opportunity and Caution'. *South African Journal of Psychology* 48, no. 3 (2018): 379–87.

Beier, U., *Decolonising the Mind: The Impact of the University on Culture and Identity in Papua New Guinea*, 1971–74. Canberra: Pandanus Books, 2005.

Bhabha, H. K., *The Location of Culture*. London: Routledge, 1994.

Bhambra, G. K., *Postcolonial and Decolonial Reconstructions in Connected Sociologies*. London: Bloomsbury Academic, 2014.

Blench, R. M., 'The Work OF N.W. Thomas as Government Anthropologist in Nigeria'. *The Nigerian Field* 60 (1995): 20–8.

Bradbury, R. E., *The Benin Kingdom and the Edo-Speaking Peoples of South-Western Nigeria Including the Ishan, the Northern Edo, the Urhobo and Isoko of the Niger Delta*. London: International African Institute, 1957.

Bradbury, R. E., 'Chronological Problems in the Study of Benin History'. *Journal of the Historical Society of Nigeria* 1, no. 4 (1959): 263–87.

Carsten, J., *After Kinship*. Cambridge: Cambridge University Press, 2003.

Césaire, A., *Discourse on Colonialism: A Poetics of Anticolonialsim* (trans.). New York: Monthly Review Press, [1955] 1972.

Chidester, D., *Savage Systems: Colonialism and Comparative Religion in Southern Africa*. Charlottesville: University Press of Virginia, 1996.

Chidester, D., *Empire of Religion. Imperialism and Comparative Religion*. Chicago: University of Chicago Press, 2013.

Chilisa, B., *Indigenous Research Methodologies*. 2nd edition. London: Sage, 2019.

Conrad, J., *Heart of Darkness and Other Stories*. Hertfordshire: Wordsworth Editions. 1993.

Crenshaw, K., 'Mapping the Margins: Intersectionality, Identity Politics, and Violence against Women of Color'. *Stanford Law Review* 43, no. 6 (1991): 1241–99.

Crowder, M., *The Story of Nigeria*, London: Faber, 1962.

Dania, P. A., Individual project (unpublished), St. David's College, Evboneka, Benin, n.d.

Delgado-P, G., and J. B. Childs (eds), *Indigeneity: Collected Essays*. Santa Cruz, CA: New Pacific Press, 2012.

Denzin, N. K., Y. S. Lincoln and L. T. Smith (eds), *Handbook of Critical and Indigenous Methodologies*. Thousand Oaks, CA: Sage, 2008.

Dillard, C. B., *Learning to (Re)member the Things We've Learned to Forget: Endarkened Feminisms, Spirituality, and the Sacred Nature of Research and Teaching*. New York: Peter Lang, 2012.

Dunbar-Ortiz, R., *An Indigenous Peoples' History of the United States*. Boston: Beacon Press, 2014.

Dupigny, E. G. M., *Gazetteer of Nupe Province*. London, 1920.

Egbarevba, J. U., *A Short History of Benin*. Ibadan: Ibadan University Press, 1947.

Egbarevba, J. U., *A Short History of Benin*. 3rd edition. Ibadan, 1968.

Egbarevba, J. U., *A Short History of Benin*. 4th edition. Ibadan: University of Ibadan Press, [1934] 1968.

Egharevba, J. U., *A Short History of Benin*. 2nd edition. Ibadan: Ibadan University Press, 1953.

Eisenstadt, S. N., 'African Age Groups: A Comparative Study'. *Africa* 24, no. 2 (1954): 100–13.

Elugbe, B. O., 'Some Tentative Historical Inferences from Comparative Edoid Studies'. *Kiabara Journal of the Humanities* 2, no. 1 (1979): 82–101.

Elugbe, B. O., *Comparative Edoid Phonology and Lexicon*. Delta Series, No. 6. Port Harcourt: University of Port Harcourt Press, 1989.

Erediauwa, O. N'Oba, *I Remain, Sir, Your Obedient Servant*. Ibadan: Spectrum, 2004.

Erediauwa, O. N'Oba N'Edo UkuAkpolo Kpolo Oba, 'The Benin-Ife Connection'. *Sunday Vanguard*, 14 May 2004.

Eweka, E. B., *A History of Benin*. Ibadan: Ethiope, 1989.

Eweka, E. B., *Evolution of Benin Chieftaincy Titles*. Benin City: University of Benin Press. 1992.

Falola, T., 'The Amistad's Legacy: Reflections on the Spaces of Colonization', *Africa Update Newsletter* 14, no. 2 (Spring 2007). Available online: https://web.ccsu.edu/afstudy/upd14-2.html#Amistad.

Fanon, F., *Black Skin, White Masks* (trans.). New York: Grove Books, [1952] 2008.

Fanon, F. *The Wretched of the Earth* (trans.). New York: Grove Weidenfeld, [1961] 1963.

Fitzgerald, G., 'Introduction to Decoloniality and the Study of Religion'. *Contending Modernities: Exploring How Religious and Secular Forces Interact in the Modern World*. Available online: https://contendingmodernities.nd.edu/decoloniality/introdecolonial/ (accessed 24 February 2020).

Forde, C. D., *The Yoruba-Speaking Peoples of South-Western Nigeria*. London: International African Institute, 1951.

Forde, D., 'Foreword'. In R. E. Bradbury, *The Benin Kingdom and the Edo Speaking Peoples of South Western Nigeria*, 1957. pp. v–vi.

Fortes, M., *Kinship and the Social Order: The Legacy of Lewis Henry Morgan*. Chicago: Aldine, 1969.

Frazer, J. G., *1854–1941: The Golden Bough: A Study in Magic and Religion*. 2nd edition, 3 volumes. London: Macmillan, 1900.

Frederickson, B. L., and T. Roberts, 'Objectification Theory: Toward Under- standing Women's Lived Experiences and Mental Health Risks'. *Psychology of Women Quarterly* 21 (1997): 173–200.

Geertz, C., *The Interpretation of Cultures: Selected Essays*. New York: Basic Books, 1973.

Glass, R. L., *London: Aspects of Change*, vol. 3. London: MacGibbon & Kee, 1964.

Gomes, A., 'Anthropology and the Politics of Indigeneity'. *Anthropological Forum: A Journal of Social Anthropology and Comparative Sociology* 23, no. 1 (2013): 5–15.

González, E. M., and Y. S. Lincoln, 'Decolonizing Qualitative Research: Nontraditional Reporting Forms in the Academy'. In N. K. Denzin and M. Gardina (eds), *Qualitative Inquiry and the Conservative Challenge*. Walnut Creek, CA: Left Coast Press, 2006. pp. 193–214.

Griaule, M., *Conversations with Ogotemmeli: An Introduction to Dogon Religious Ideas*. Oxford: Oxford University Press, 1965.

Guenther, M., 'Discussion: The Concept of Indigeneity'. *Social Anthropology* 14, no. 1 (February 2006): 17–32.

Guesmi, Haythem, 'The Gentrification of African Studies'. Africa Is a Country, 22 December 2018. Available online: https://africasacountry.com/2018/12/the-gentrification-of-african-studies (accessed 5 January 2021).

Halbwachs, M., *On Collective Memory*, ed. and trans. Lewis A. Coser. Chicago: University of Chicago Press, [1925] 1992.

Hamilton, C., '"Living by Fluidity": Oral Histories, Material Custodies and the Politics of Archiving'. In C. Hamilton, V. Harris, M. Pickover, G. Reid, R. Saleh and J. Taylor (eds), *Reconfiguring the Archive*. Cape Town: David Philip, 2002. pp. 209–28.

Harunah, H. B., *A Cultural History of the Uneme: From the Earliest Times to 1962*. Lagos: The Book Company, 2003.

Hoppers, O. C., 'Culture, Indigenous Knowledge and Development: The Role of the University. Centre for Educational Policy Development'. *Occasional Paper* No. 5 (2005).

Idrees, A. A., 'Collaboration and the British Conquest of Bida in 1897: The Role and Achievement of the Indigenous Interest Groups'. *African Study Monographs* 10, no. 2 (August 1989): 69–82.

Jackson, C., 'Modernity and Matrifocality: The Feminization of Kinship?' *Development and Change* 46 (2014): 1–24.

Jansen, J. C., and J. Osterhammel, *Decolonization: A Short History*. Princeton, NJ: Princeton University Press, 2017.

Kaplan, F., and S. Edouwaye, 'Understanding Sacrifice and Sanctity in Benin Indigenous Religion, Nigeria: A Case Study'. In Jacob. K. Olupona (ed.), *Beyond Primitivism: Indigenous Religious Traditions and Modernity*. London: Routledge, 2003. pp. 181–99.

Keane, M., C. Khupe and M. Seehawer, 'Decolonising Methodology: Who Benefits from Indigenous Knowledge Research?' *Educational Research for Social Change* 6 (2017): 12–24.

Keikelame, M. J., and L. Swartz, 'Decolonising Research Methodologies: Lessons from a Qualitative Research Project'. *Global Health Action* 12, no. 1 (2019). DOI: 10.1080/16549716.2018.1561175.

Khupe C., and M. Keane, 'Towards an African Education Research Methodology: Decolonising New Knowledge'. *Educ Res Soc Change* 6 (2017): 25–37.

Kolapo, F. J, 'Military Turbulence, Population Displacement and Commerce on a Southern Frontier of the Sokoto Caliphate: Nupe c.1810–1857'. PhD diss., York University, 1999.

Kolapo, F. J., 'The Dynamics of Early 19th Century Nupe Wars'. *Scientia Militaria – South African Journal of Military Studies* [S.l.] 31, No. 2 (February 2012). Available online: http://scientiamilitaria.journals.ac.za/pub/article/view/151 (accessed 14 June 2018).

Kovach, M., *Indigenous Methodologies: Characteristics, Conversations and Contexts*. Toronto: University of Toronto Press, 2009.

Kunstadter, T. S., 'A Survey of the Consanguine or Matrifocal Family'. *American Anthropologist* 65, no. 1 (June 1963): 56–65.

Kuper, A., 'The Return of the Native'. *Current Anthropology* 44, no. 3 (2003): 389–402.

Kuper, A., 'Discussion: The Concept of Indigeneity'. *Social Anthropology* 14, no. 1 (2006): 21–2.

Lawani, O. A., *Ibishika: La Musique et La Danse des Femmes D'Ozah. Nigeria* (English trans. Ibishika: Music and Dance of Ozah Women. Nigeria). Maitrise de Musique. Université de Paris VIII. Session d'Octobre, 1992.

Lawani, O. A., *L'Inscription Sociale et La Fonction De La Musique Chez Les Ozah. Nigeria*. Département de Musicologie, Université Paris 8, Vincennes Saint-Denis, 1997.

Lawani, O. A., and J. N. Bertrand, *Filmographie "Quand les gens d'Ozah dansent."* Lagos, Nigeria: Centre Culturel Francais, 1987.

Leach, E. 'Ritualization in Man in Relation to Conceptual and Social Development'. *Phil. Trans. R. Soc. B* 251 (1966): 247–526.

Lewis, A. A., *North Edoid Relations and Roots*. Unpublished PhD diss. submitted to the Department of Linguistics and African Languages. Ibadan: University of Ibadan, June 2013.

Lewis, D., *North Edoid Relations and Roots*. PhD diss., University of Ibadan, 2013.

Lewis, D., 'Linguistic Prehistory and Identity in Nigeria's Bini-Ife Pre-Eminence Contestation'. *Multilingual Margins* 5, no. 1 (2018): 2–23.

Lincoln, Y. S., and E. M. G. González, 'The Search for Emerging Decolonizing Methodologies in Qualitative Research: Further Strategies for Liberatory and Democratic Inquiry'. *Qualitative Inquiry* 14, no. 5 (July 2008): 784–805.

Ludwig, F., and A. Adogame (eds), *European Traditions in the Study of Religion in Africa*. Wiesbaden: Harrassowitz Verlag, 2004.

Lugard, F. D., *Report on the Amalgamation of Northern and Southern Nigeria, and Administration, 1912–1919*. London: H.M. Stationery Office, 1920.

Lugones, M. 'Toward a Decolonial Feminism'. *Hypatia* 25, no. 4 (2010): 742–59.

Maldonado-Torres, N., 'On the Coloniality of Being: Contributions to the Development of a Concept'. *Cultural Studies* 21, nos 2–3 (2007): 240–70.

Mason, M., 'The Jihad in the South: An Outline of Nineteenth Century Nupe Hegemony in North-Eastern Yorubaland and Afenmai'. *Journal of the Historical Society of Nigeria* 5, no. 2 (June 1970): 193–209.

Mason, M., 'The Antecedents of Nineteenth-century Islamic Governments in Nupe'. *International Journal of African Historical Studies*, 10, no. 1 (1977): 63–76.

Mbiti, J. S., *African Religions and Philosophy*. London: Heinemann, 1969.

McKinley, N. M., and J. S. Hyde, 'The Objectified Body Consciousness Scale: Development and Validation'. *Psychology of Women Quarterly* 20 (1996): 181–215.

Memmi, A., *The Colonizer and the Colonized*. Boston: Beacon Press, [1957] 1965.

Merlan, F., 'Indigeneity: Global and Local'. *Current Anthropology* 50, no. 3 (June 2009): 303–33.

Mignolo, W. D., and C. E. Walsh, *On Decoloniality: Concepts, Analytics, Praxis*. Durham: Duke University Press, 2018.

Mignolo, W. D., 'Delinking: The Rhetoric of Modernity, the Logic of Coloniality and the Grammar of De-Coloniality'. *Cultural Studies* 21, no. 2 (2007): 449–514.

Mohammed, A. R., 'The Sokoto Jihad and Its Impact on the Confluence Area and Afenmai'. In Ahmad Mohammad Kani and Kabir Ahmed Gandi (eds), *State and Society in the Sokoto Caliphate*. Sokoto: Usmanu Danfodiyo University, 1990, pp. 142–57.

Nadel, S. F., *A Black Byzantium: The Kingdom of Nupe in Nigeria*. London: Oxford University Press, 1942.

Nair, M., *Defining Indigeneity: Situating Transnational Knowledge*. World Society Focus Paper Series. Zurich: World Society Foundation, 2006.

Nel, P. J., 'Indigenous Knowledge: Contestation, Rhetoric and Space'. *Indilinga: African Journal of Indigenous Knowledge Systems* 4, no. 1 (2005): 2–14.

Nel, P. J., 'Indigenous Knowledge Systems: Conceptualization and Methodology'. Unpublished lecture, 21 October 2008.

Ngulube, P. (ed.), *Handbook of Research on Social, Cultural, and Educational Considerations of Indigenous Knowledge in Developing Countries*. 1st edition. Hershey: IGI Global, 2016.

Ngulube, P. (ed.), *Handbook of Research on Theoretical Perspectives on Indigenous Knowledge Systems in Developing Countries*. Hershey: IGI Global, 2017.

Nye, M., 'Modernity and the Disciplinary Formation of Religious Studies'. *Religion Bites Blog*, 27 June 2017. Available online: https://medium.com/religion-bites/

modernity-and-the-disciplinary-formation-of-religious-studies-1cbe73070cf5 (accessed 25 January 2021).

Nye, M., 'Decolonising the Study of Religion'. *Open Library of Humanities* 5, no. 1 (2019): 1–45.

Obayemi, A., 'The Yoruba and Edo-Speaking Peoples and Their Neighbours before 1600'. In J. F. A. Ajayi and M. Crowder (eds), *History of West Africa*, vol. 1. Ibadan: Longman, 1971. pp. 255–322.

Obayemi, A., 'The Sokoto Jihad and the "O-kun" Yoruba: A Review'. *Journal of the Historical Society of Nigeria* 9, no. 2 (1978): 61–87.

Ogunnaike, O., *Deep Knowledge: Ways of Knowing in Sufism and Ifa, Two West African Intellectual Traditions*. University Park: PennState University Press, 2020.

Ohimai, O. J., and E. Okunna, 'Traditional Pottery: Example of Innovation and Adaptation of Ojah Pots in Modern Usage'. *Tropical Built Environment Journal* 1, no. 5 (2016): 77–87.

Ohimai, O. J., I. B. Kashim and T. L. Akinbogun (eds), 'Development of a Prototype Pots and Potsherds Kilns for Facilitating Ceramic Wares Firing in Tertiary Institutions in Nigeria'. *Creative Education* 4, no. 8 (2013): 475–83.

Okogie, C. G., *Ishan Native Laws and Customs*. Yaba: Okwesa, 1960.

Olomola, I., 'The Eastern Yoruba Country before Oduduwa: A Re-assessment'. In I. A. Akinjogbin and G. O. Ekemode (eds), *Proceedings of the Conference on Yoruba Civilization*. Ile-Ife: University of Ife, 1976. pp. 34–73.

Olupona, J. K., *Kingship, Religion, and Rituals in a Nigerian Community: A Phenomenological Study of Ondo Yoruba Festivals*. Volume 28 of Acta Universitatis Stockholmiensis: Stockholm Studies in Comparative Religion. Stockholm: Almqvist & Wiksell International, 1991.

Olupona, J. K. (ed.), *African Spirituality: Forms, Meanings and Expressions*. New York: Crossroad, 2001.

Olupona, J. K. (ed.), *Beyond Primitivism: Indigenous Religious Traditions and Modernity*. New York: Routledge, 2004.

Olupona, J. K., *City of 201 Gods: Ilé-Ifè in Time, Space, and the Imagination*. Oakland: University of California Press, 2011.

Olupona, J. K., *African Religions: A Very Short Introduction*. Oxford: Oxford University Press, 2014.

Omo-Aghe, I. O., *Oza History Nigeria: Ọza History in Delta and Edo State, Nigeria*. Kindle Edition, 2016.

Omoniyi, J. O., 'Literacy and Historical Reflections on the Yagba Protest Movement against Nupe Hegemony before 1939'. In A. Olukoju, Z. O. Apata and O. Akinwumi (eds), *Northeast Yorubaland. Studies in the History and Culture of a Frontier Zone*. Ibadan: Rex Charles Publications in association with Connel Publications, 2003. pp. 16–24.

Osadolor, O. B., *The Military System of Benin Kingdom, c. 1440–1897*. PhD thesis, University of Hamburg, Germany, 2001.

Oshiedu, A.B., *Historical Facts on Ogori*. 2nd edition. Ilorin: Kwara State Printing and Publishing Co, 1980.

Osman, E. A., 'Indigenous Knowledge in Africa: Challenges and Opportunities'. *An inaugural lecture, Centre for African Studies, University of the Free State, South Africa*, 4 November 2009.

Otite, O., 'Continuance and Change in an Urhobo Age-Grade Organization in Nigeria'. *Cahiers d'Études Africaines* 12, no. 46 (1972): 302–15.

Oyewumi, O., *The Invention of Women: Making an African Sense of Western Gender Discourses*. Minneapolis: University of Minnesota Press, 1997.

Platvoet, J., J. Cox, and J. Olupona (eds), *The Study of Religions in Africa: Past, Present and Prospects*. Cambridge: Roots & Branches, 1996.

Quijano, A., 'Coloniality of Power, Eurocentrism, and Latin America'. *Nepantla: Views from South* 1, no. 3 (2000): 533–80.

Quijano, A., 'Coloniality and Modernity/Rationality'. *Cultural Studies* 21, no. 2 (2007): 168–78.

Randolph, R., 'The "Matrifocal Family" as a Comparative Category'. *American Anthropologist* 66 (1964): 628.

Ray, B. C., *African Religions: Symbol, Ritual, and Community*. Englewood Cliffs: Prentice-Hall, 1976.

Rowling, C. W., *Notes on Land Tenure in the Benin, Kukuruku, Ishan and Asaba Divisions of Benin Province*. Lagos: Government Printer, 1948.

Saba, F. O., 'Inter-Group Relations among Akoko Communities in the Pre-Colonial Times'. In A. Olukoju, Z. O. Apata and O. Akinwumi (eds), *Northeast Yorubaland. Studies in the History and Culture of a Frontier Zone*. Ibadan: Rex Charles Publications in association with Connel Publications, 2003. pp. 7–15.

Said, E. W., *Orientalism*. New York: Vintage Books, 1978.

Scauso, M. S., *Intersectional Decoloniality: Reimagining International Relations and the Problem of Difference*. London: Routledge, 2020.

Schneider, D., *American Kinship: A Cultural Account*. Chicago: University of Chicago Press, 1968.

Sefa Dei, G. J., and C. S. Jaimungal (eds), *Indigeneity and Decolonial Resistance. Alternatives to Colonial Thinking and Practice*. Gorham, ME: Myers Education Press, 2018.

Sijuade, Oba, Ooni of Ife, 'How Oba of Benin Goofed'. *Vanguard*, 16 May 2004.

Smith, J. Z., *On Teaching Religion: Essays by Jonathan Z. Smith*, ed. Christopher I. Lehrich. New York: Oxford University Press, 2013.

Smith, L. T., *Decolonizing Methodologies: Research and Indigenous Peoples*. 2nd edition. London: Zed, [1999] 2012.

Smith, R. T., *The Negro Family in British Guiana: Family Structure and Social Status in the Villages*. London: Routledge & Paul, 1956.

Smith, R. T., *The Matrifocal Family: Power, Pluralism, and Politics*. London: Routledge, 1996.

Spickard, J., 'Why Reflexive Ethnography Matters to the Study of World Christianity'. *Journal of World Christianity* 11, no. 2 (2021): 180–94.

Spivak, G., 'Can the Subaltern Speak?'. In Patrick Williams and Laura Christman (eds), *Colonial Discourse and Postcolonial Theory: A Reader*. New York: Colombia University Press, 1998. pp. 66–109.

Strathern, M., *After Nature: English Kinship in the Late Twentieth Century*. Cambridge: Cambridge University Press, 1992.

Tachine, A. R., E. Y. Bird and N. L. Cabrera, 'Sharing Circles. "An Indigenous Methodological Approach for Researching with Groups of Indigenous Peoples'. *International Review of Qualitative Research* 9, no. 3 (Fall 2016): 277–95.

Talbot, P. A., 'A Priest King in Nigeria'. *Folk-Lore, A Quarterly Review of Myth, Tradition, Institution, and Custom* Being the Transactions of the Folk-Lore Society and Incorporating the Archaeological Review and *The Folk-Lore Journal* 26 (March 1915): 79–112.

Tambiah, S. J., 'The Magical Power of Words'. *Man* (New Series) 3, no. 2 (June 1968): 175–208.

Tambiah, S. J., *A Performative Approach to Ritual*. London: British Academy, 1979.

Tambiah, S. J., *Culture, Thought, and Social Action*. Cambridge, MA: Harvard University Press, 1985.

Tambiah, S. J., *Magic, Science, Religion, and the Scope of Rationality*. Cambridge: Cambridge University Press, 1990.

Tanner, N., 'Matrifocality in Indonesia, in Africa and among Black Americans'. In M. Rosaldo and L. Lamphere (eds), *Women, Culture and Society*. Stanford, CA: Stanford University Press, 1974. pp. 129–56.

Tayob, Abdulkader, 'The Promise of Decolonization for the Study of Religions'. *Contending Modernities: Exploring How Religious and Secular Forces Interact in the Modern World*, 10 March 2020. Available online: https://contendingmodernities.nd.edu/decoloniality/promise-of-decolonization/ (accessed 23 October 2020).

Temple, C. L., *Notes on the Tribes, Provinces, Emirates and States of the Northern Provinces of Nigeria*. Cape Town: Argus, 1919.

Temple, O., *Notes on the Tribes, Provinces, Emirates and States of the Northern Provinces of Nigeria*. 2nd edition. London: Frank Cass, 1965.

Thomas, N. W., *Anthropological Report on the Edo-Speaking Peoples of Nigeria*. Part 1: Law and Custom. London: Harrison and Sons, 1910a.

Thomas, N. W., *Anthropological Report on the Edo-Speaking Peoples of Nigeria*. Part II: Linguistics. London: Harrison and Sons, 1910b.

Thomas, N. W., 'The Edo-Speaking Peoples of Nigeria'. *Journal of the Royal African Society* 10, no. 37 (1910c): 1–15.

Thomas, N. W., 'Pottery-Making of the Edo Speaking peoples of Southern Nigeria'. *Man: The Journal of the Royal Anthropological Institute of Great Britain and Ireland* 10, no. 53 (1910d): 97–8.

Turner, V., *The Ritual Process: Structure and Anti-Structure*. Chicago: Aldine, 1969.

United Nations, 'Study of the Problem of Discrimination against Indigenous Populations'. United Nations Economic and Social Council, 1981. Available online: https://www.un.org/esa/socdev/unpfii/documents/MCS_intro_1981_en.pdf (accessed 26 June 2021).

United Nations, 'Report of the Working Group on Indigenous Populations'. United Nations Commission on Human Rights, 11 March 1986. Available online: https://www.refworld.org/docid/3b00f0b948.html (accessed 26 June 2021).

United Nations, 'Report of the Workshop on Data Collection and Disaggregation for Indigenous Peoples'. United Nations Digital Library, 2004. Available online: https://digitallibrary.un.org/record/517063?ln=en (accessed 26 June 2021).

van Gennep, A., *The Rites of Passage*. Chicago: University of Chicago Press, 1960.

Weaver, H. N. 'Indigenous Identity: What Is It, and Who Really Has It?' *American Indian Quarterly* 25 (2001): 240–55.

Westerlund, D., 'Preface' to Jacob K. Olupona, *Kingship, Religion, and Rituals in a Nigerian Community*, 1991.

Willett, F., *African Art*. London: Thames and Hudson, 2002.

Williamson, K., and R. Blench, 'Niger-Congo'. In B. Heine and D. Nurse (eds), *African Languages. An Introduction*. Cambridge: Cambridge University Press, 2000. pp. 11–42.

Wilson, Carla, 'Review of Linda T. Smith, *Decolonizing Methodologies: Research and Indigenous Peoples* (London: Zed Books, 1999)'. *Social Policy Journal of New Zealand*, no. 17 (2001): 214–17. Available online: https://www.msd.govt.nz/about-msd-and-our-work/publications-resources/journals-and-magazines/social-policy-journal/spj17/decolonizing-methodologies-research-and-indigenous-peoples.html (accessed 13 November 2020).

Windchief, S., and T. San Pedro (eds), *Applying Indigenous Research Methods: Storying with Peoples and Communities*. London: Routledge, 2019.

Wynter, S., 'Unsettling the Coloniality of Being / Power / Truth / Freedom: Towards the Human, After Man, Its Overrepresentation – An Argument'. *CR: The New Centennial Review* 3, no. 3 (2003): 257–337.

Zavala, M., 'What Do We Mean by Decolonizing Research Strategies? Lessons from Decolonizing, Indigenous Research Projects in New Zealand and Latin America'. *Decolonization: Indigeneity, Education & Society* 2 (2013): 55–71.

Index

Africa as Object and Africa as Subject 4, 6
African Diaspora 20, 29
African religions and spiritualities 3–9, 16–22, 29–30
African religious beliefs and ritual systems 3
Alberto Gomes 34
Anibal Quijano 22, 25, 115

Benin/ Bini- Edo Kingdom/Province x, 2–5, 41–62, 71–5, 112–35, 161–7, 213–19, 225–31
   Ọba of Benin 48, 51, 54, 60, 107–8, 220
Benin kingdom/city 2, 47–51, 58–9, 73–5, 115, 124, 219
Black 12–17, 29
British x, 5, 11–12, 24, 37–42, 50, 58–9, 62–70, 107, 115–17, 213–31
burial/funeral 38, 48, 83–5, 120–1, 138–40, 171–6, 183–90, 203, 222
   Royal funeral 48, 120–1

Catherine Walsh 26
chief/chieftaincy roles and chiefdoms 37, 51–3, 75, 86, 99, 105, 151, 181
Christian mission 4, 29, 36, 39, 4, 50, 213, 219–26, 231–2
Christianity 5, 20–1, 29, 36, 39–41, 51, 93, 93, 107, 179, 183, 213, 219–26, 231–2
colonization, colonialists 5, 7, 18–19, 25–8
   anti-colonial 28, 230
   British coloniality, colonization 37, 50, 58, 219
   colonial education and Christian mission 225–33
   colonial knowledge hegemony 7
   coloniality of power 12–18, 25, 27, 37, 100, 115–17, 120, 123, 130–1, 191, 213–17, 226, 231
   coloniality 24

colonization of memory 6
colour/colourless 14–17, 22, 204, 232
cosmology/cosmologies 29, 31, 77–8, 99, 169, 224
   African cosmologies 91
   Ọza indigenous cosmologies 31, 89, 171–2, 206, 208

David Chidester 29–30
death 35, 38, 43, 63, 79–97, 106, 119–20, 127–77, 183–93, 203
decolonizing knowledges/decolonization 3, 9–10, 20–1, 25–6, 29, 36
   decolonial feminism 26–7
   decoloniality turn 25
   decoloniality 24–7
   decolonizing methodologies 23, 27, 29, 32
   decolonizing the study of religion 5, 18, 21–2
   history of 23–30
Desmond Tutu 32
diviners and divination 29, 35, 46, 84, 89–92, 106, 120–1, 138, 173–7, 185–94, 200–1, 208–10
Dunbar-Ortiz 27, 29

Edo/Akoko-Edo 41, 43
emic/etic 3, 17–18, 33, 36

family and social life 97
   courtship and sexual relationships 194
   indigenous culture 80
   marriage ceremony 11, 181, 185, 196–8, 208–11, 224
festival 2, 85
   harvest 97
   marriage festival 97
   new yam festival 85
   Ọza festival 198–203
   ritual festivals 86

gender 9, 38, 18–38, 80–109, 116–19, 170–99, 202–4
    gender and spirit possession/mediumship 88
    gender power 9, 18–20, 38, 109, 191
gentrification 19–20
gentrification of African studies 18
globalization 7, 20, 41, 219

Hausa 14, 21, 70, 220
healers, healing, and healing systems 35–6, 49, 88–93

Idoma 71, 73
Igala 42–6, 64, 67–8, 71–3
Ilé-Ifè 29, 45–6, 47, 74
indigeneity/indigenous 1, 20–1, 30–9, 76, 100, 213–15, 219, 229, 232
indigenous epistemologies 3–6, 7–8, 22, 35
indigenous epistemologies 3, 6–8, 22, 28, 30, 35
indigenous knowledge systems 3, 6–7, 22, 30–5, 214, 231–2
insiders'/outsiders' discourses 3, 17
intersectionality 18, 26, 127
Islam 5, 29, 36, 41, 64–5, 70, 85–8, 93, 100–13, 179, 183, 213, 219–24, 232, 262

Jacob Olupona 29, 103
Jan Platvoet 4

Kanuri 70
kingship/rulership 75, 99–100, 104, 107–11, 119–21, 100, 140
    deity king 107
    kingship myth 37, 107, 136–7
    sacral kingship 109–12, 123
kinship 36, 101–9, 193, 198
    kindred, lineage 100–5, 120, 132–45, 218
    lineage group 36, 99–105
    Oza kinship system 36–7, 99–109, 115, 121, 129–31
    royal kindred 138, 145–59, 166, 218
Kukuruku Division x, 42–4, 54–5, 59–62, 215–30, 116–33

etymology 42
Kukuruku Council 43, 133, 230
population 42, 44, 59, 62

land 32
    ancestral land 32–3, 105, 176
    bounded/unbounded 33, 35
    commodification/commoditization 32–3, 55
    land contestation 7, 33, 61
    land rights 23, 55–7, 61
    Oza land tenure system 33, 52, 54
language 38, 14, 25–6, 31–2, 44–6, 71–8, 208, 220–2, 231–2
    Edo language 46, 59, 71–4

Malory Nye 10, 20–2, 32
Marcus Scauso 26
market days and market square 85, 112, 172, 180, 199, 221
masquerades 82–7, 106, 121, 181, 183
matrifocality 103
matrilineal/patrilineal 36, 53, 99, 101–2, 104, 193
memory 1, 3, 6, 9, 10, 31, 35–6, 52, 204, 232
    politics of memory/remembering 9–10, 25, 36
    repositories of memory 9–10
migration 47–69, 73–4, 219
modernization 7, 23, 183, 197
myths 2, 9–12, 29, 36–8, 41–7, 63, 79, 99–108
    Oza myths of origin/creation myths 2, 36, 41, 45–7, 77–9, 184

Native Court 37, 119, 122–31, 215
Nigeria x, 1–2, 5, 10–11, 15–18, 21, 41–7, 51, 60–1, 70–1, 108, 112–16, 134–5, 144–5, 160–6
Nupe, Nupenization 64, 107

Oludamini Ogunnaike 29–30
Olusegun A. Lawani 80–97, 104–10, 128–66, 200–32
Omo-Aghe Isaac 47
oral traditions and texts 2–3, 9, 35, 83, 93
Oza (Oja/Ojah), 1, 41–2, 45, 50, 62, 221–2
    etymology, 50

music/musical life and culture 206–8
social norms 102, 106, 169, 181, 184, 214
social organization 2, 36, 73–7, 99–109, 183, 191
traditional crafts 37, 45, 112–15
traditional setting, 111–12

pantheon of deities 79–80, 99
  gender and 80–2
  guardian spirit 84, 87
  Supreme being/Deity 33, 36, 79–80, 92, 107–8, 121
postcolonial 5, 9, 24–6, 30, 214

race, racialization/racializing 14–17
Ray E. Bradbury 2, 5, 43, 45, 55–75, 100–12
religion
  in Africa 4–9
  female religious leaders 86
  Ọza indigenous religions 36, 38, 77–80, 88–92, 132, 170, 178, 186, 213–14, 232
  Ọza religious cultures 21, 31, 321
  Ọza religious epistemology 36, 79
  religious identities 31, 224, 232
  religious specialist 88, 111, 173
  and spirituality 34, 79, 218
research methodologies 20, 23, 27, 32, 28–9, 214
rites of passage 35, 38, 169–89, 197–9, 223
  adulthood 179–83
  airth and naming 169, 173–9
  death 185–90
  marriage 183–5
  puberty rites 198
rituals and taboos 84, 88, 93
  birth/birthing 173–5
  of childbirth 175–7
  of death 185–90

of marriage 183–5, 192–8
of naming 177–9
post-marriage rituals 210–11
and sacrifice 88
specialists 188
symbols 88–9

social anthropology 5
spirit cosmos/religious world 79–88
  ancestors 33–6, 49, 53, 74, 79, 80–99, 171–8, 186–7, 201–23
  and religion 29–30, 100, 108, 111, 114, 174, 213–28
  spirit world 84
  witches and wizards 81–4, 91–2, 175
spirituality/spiritualties 3, 7–8, 20–1, 30, 34, 77–9, 89, 214, 232

Victor Turner 5, 171

Walter Mignolo 23, 25–6
women 36–7, 88, 97–8
  collective ritual 203–6
  ingenuity 112–15
  initiation process 202–3
  objectification of bodies 202–3
  political power/consciousness 110–11, 191–2
  ritual power and sacral kingship 109–12
  role and status of Ọza women 37–8, 81–114, 170–6, 191–206
  village heads 109
world Christianity 20–1
world views 6–7, 10, 20, 31
  Ọza world views 1, 17, 31–6, 77, 169, 205, 214, 223–4, 232

Yoruba/Yorubanization 47, 51, 64–6, 71–5, 107

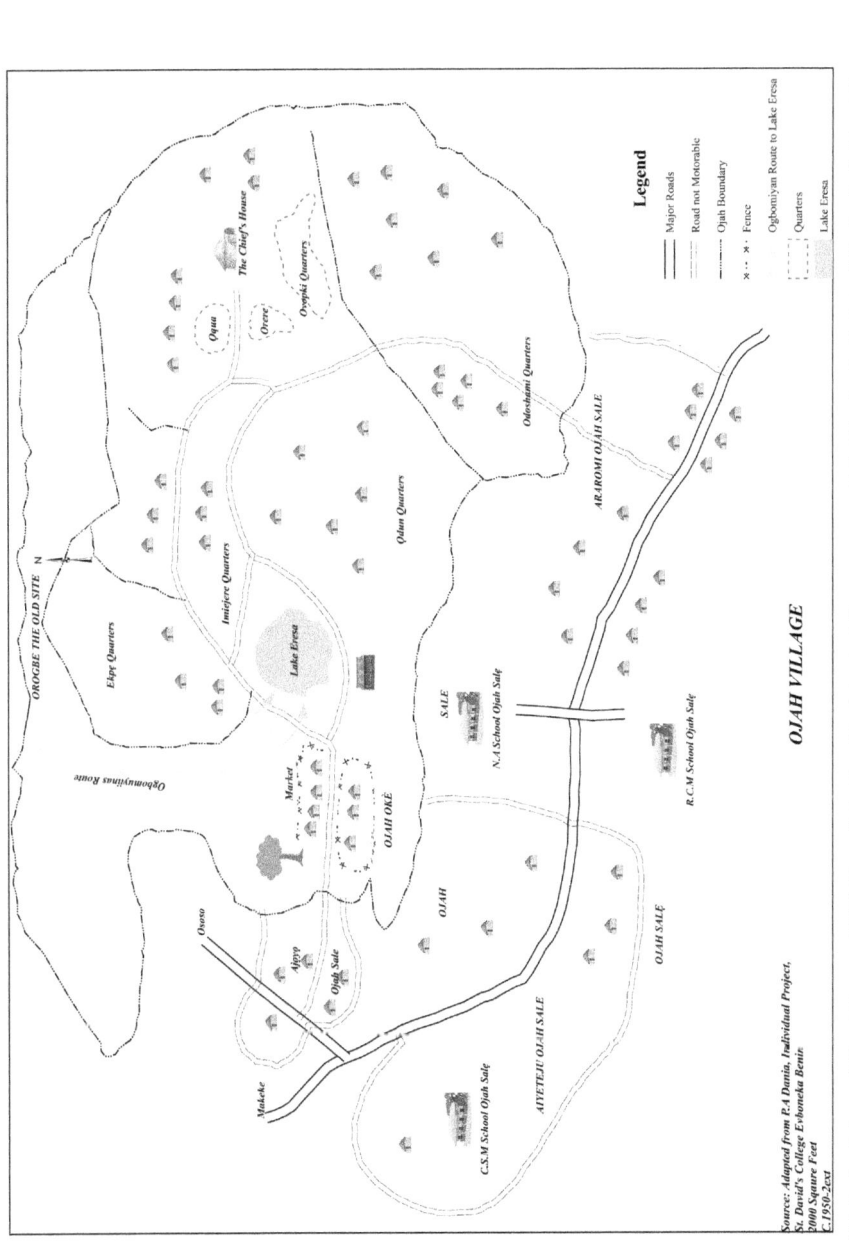

Plate 1a (Map of Ọza Okeme (Old Ọza site). Credit: Adapted from source: P.A. Dania, Individual Project, St. David's College, Evboneka, Benin, c. 1950–2.

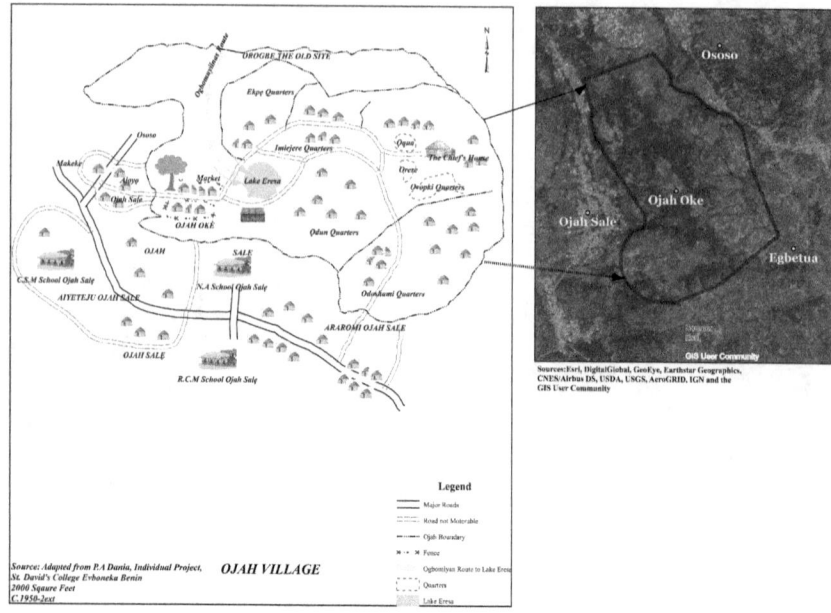

Plate 1b Map of Ọza Okeme. Credit: Map recreated by Amidu Elabo from: Esri, DigitalGlobal, GeoEye, Earthstar Geographics, CNES/Airbus DS, USDA USGS, AeroGRID].

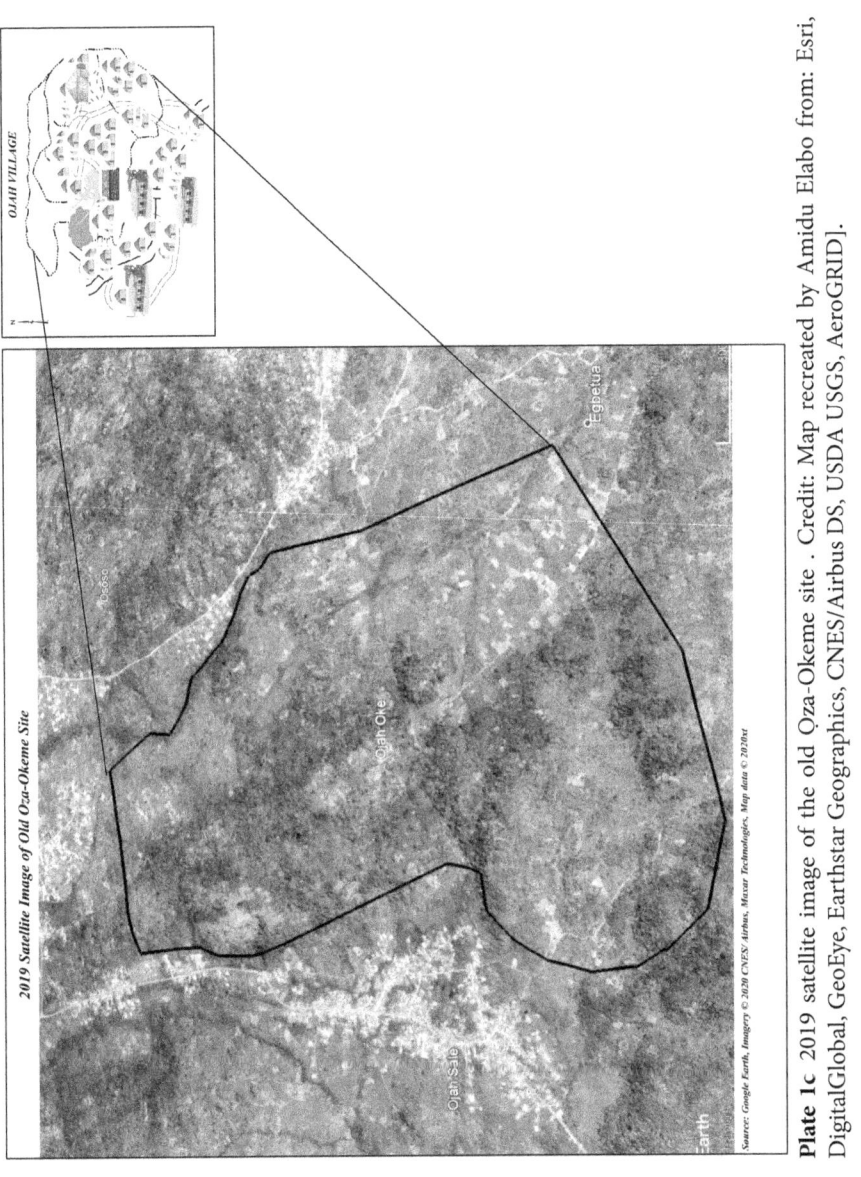

Plate 1c 2019 satellite image of the old Ọza-Okeme site. Credit: Map recreated by Amidu Elabo from: Esri, DigitalGlobal, GeoEye, Earthstar Geographics, CNES/Airbus DS, USDA USGS, AeroGRID].

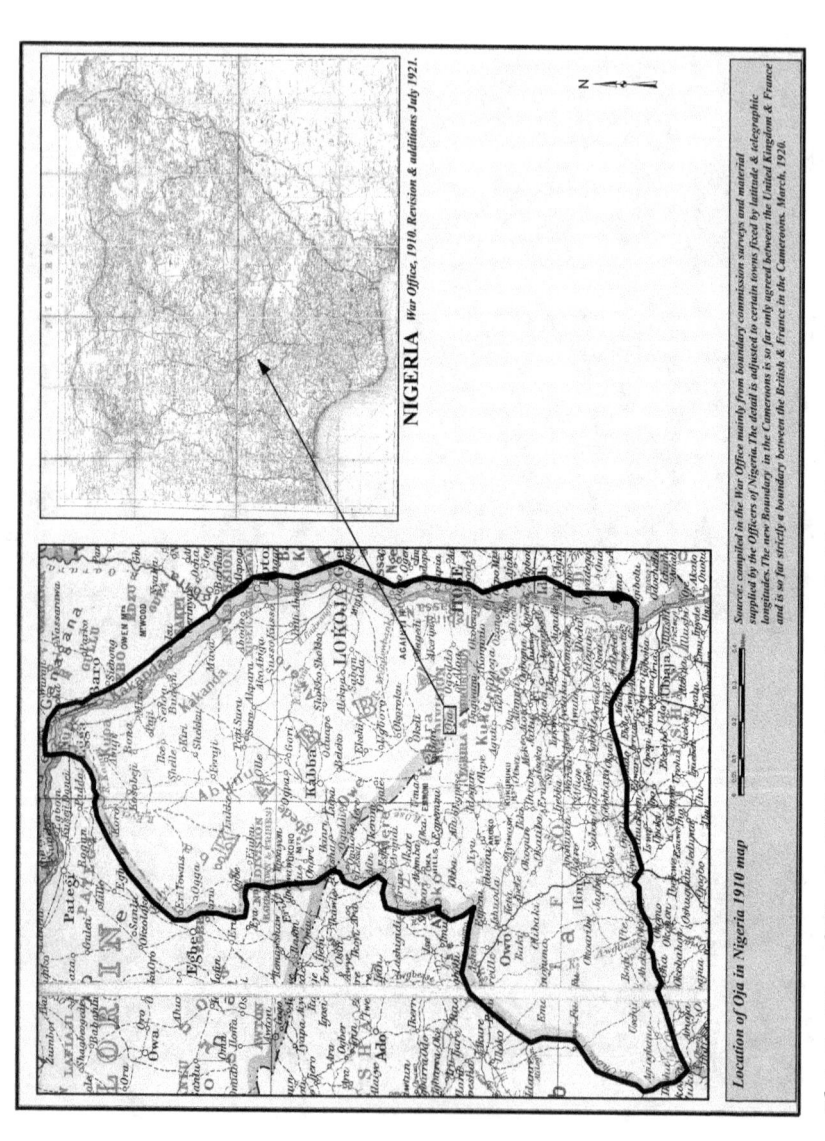

Plate 2a Map of Nigeria 1910, London National Archive. Credit: © 2018 Barry Lawrence Ruderman Antique Maps Inc.

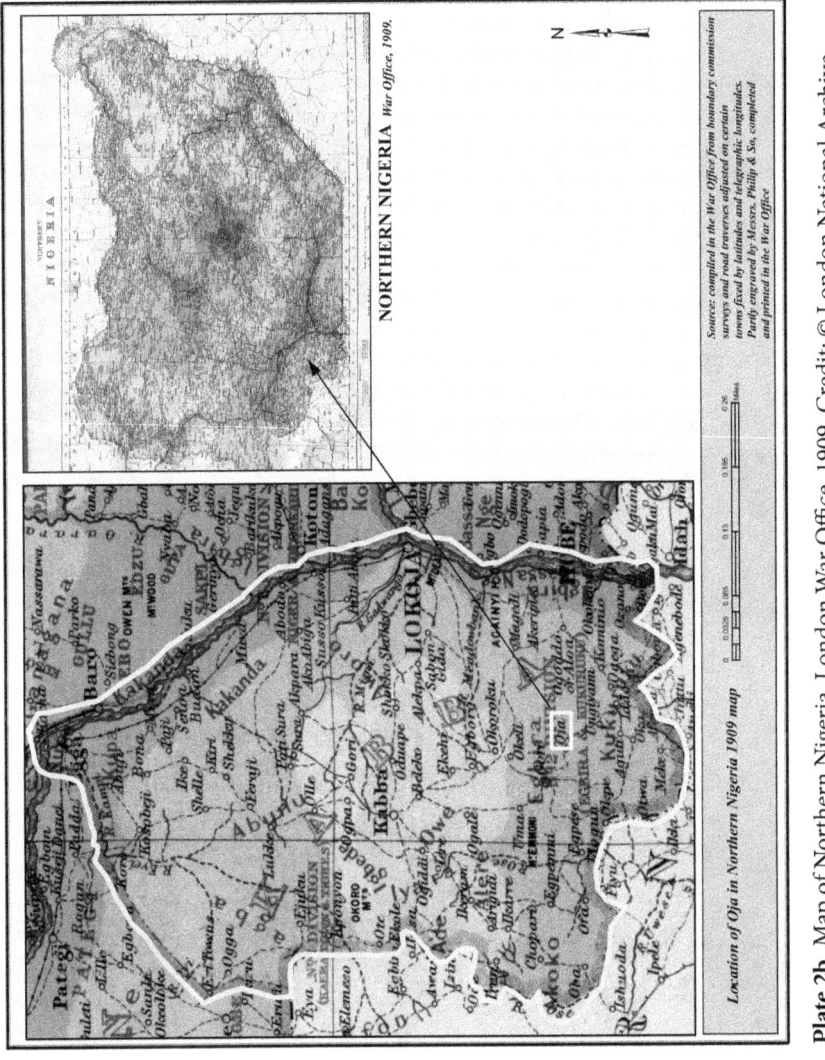

Plate 2b Map of Northern Nigeria, London War Office, 1909. Credit: © London National Archive.

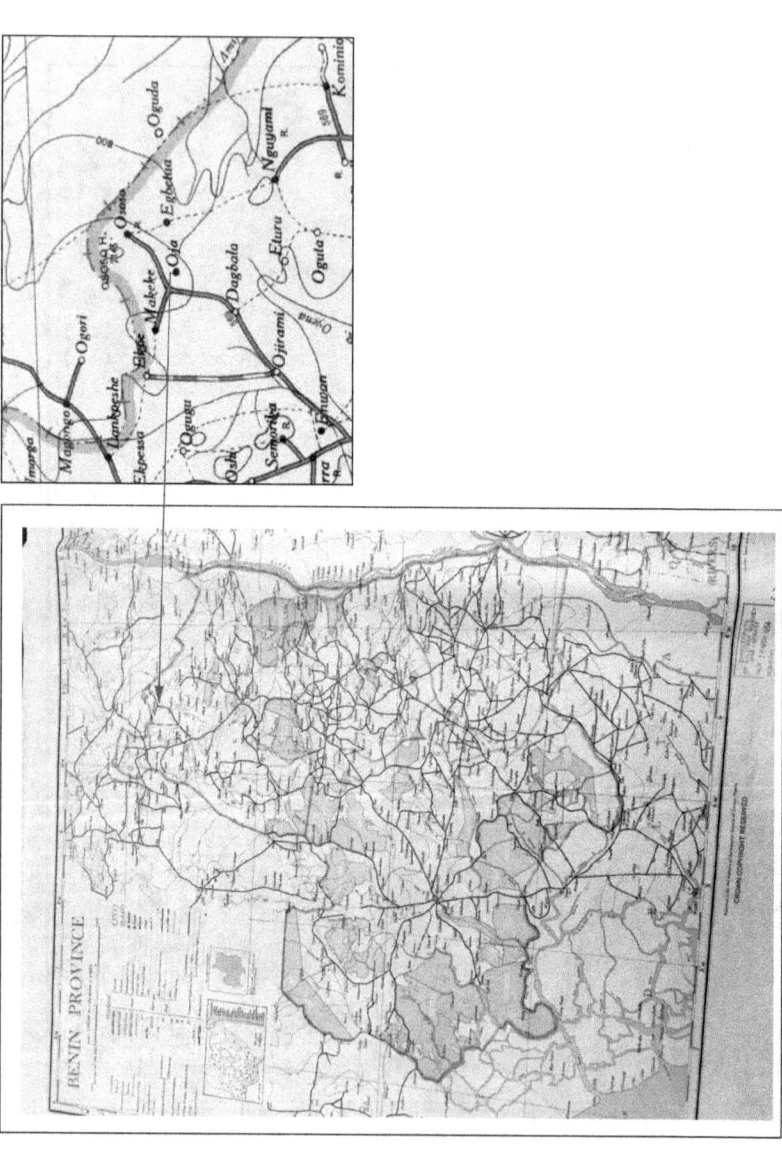

Plate 3a, 3b Map, Benin Province. Published under the direction of the Inspector General of Surveys Nigeria (n.d). Endorsed by Directorate of Military Survey May Library, 26 November 1954. Credit: Permission from

(b)

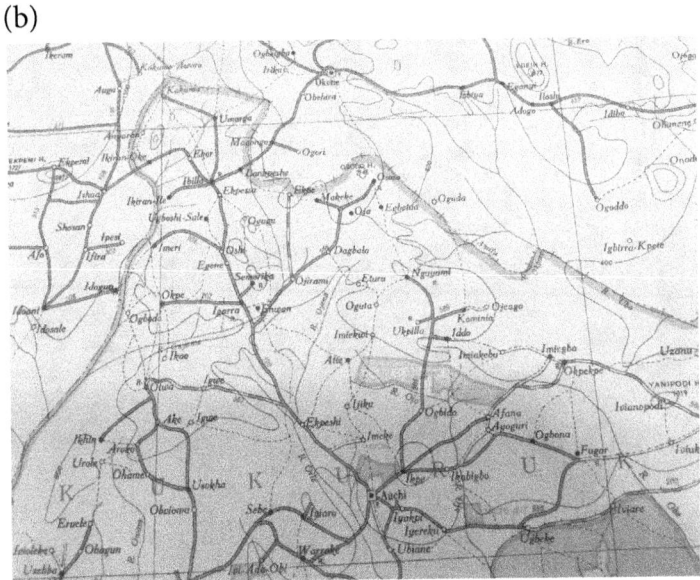

Plate 3 (Continued)

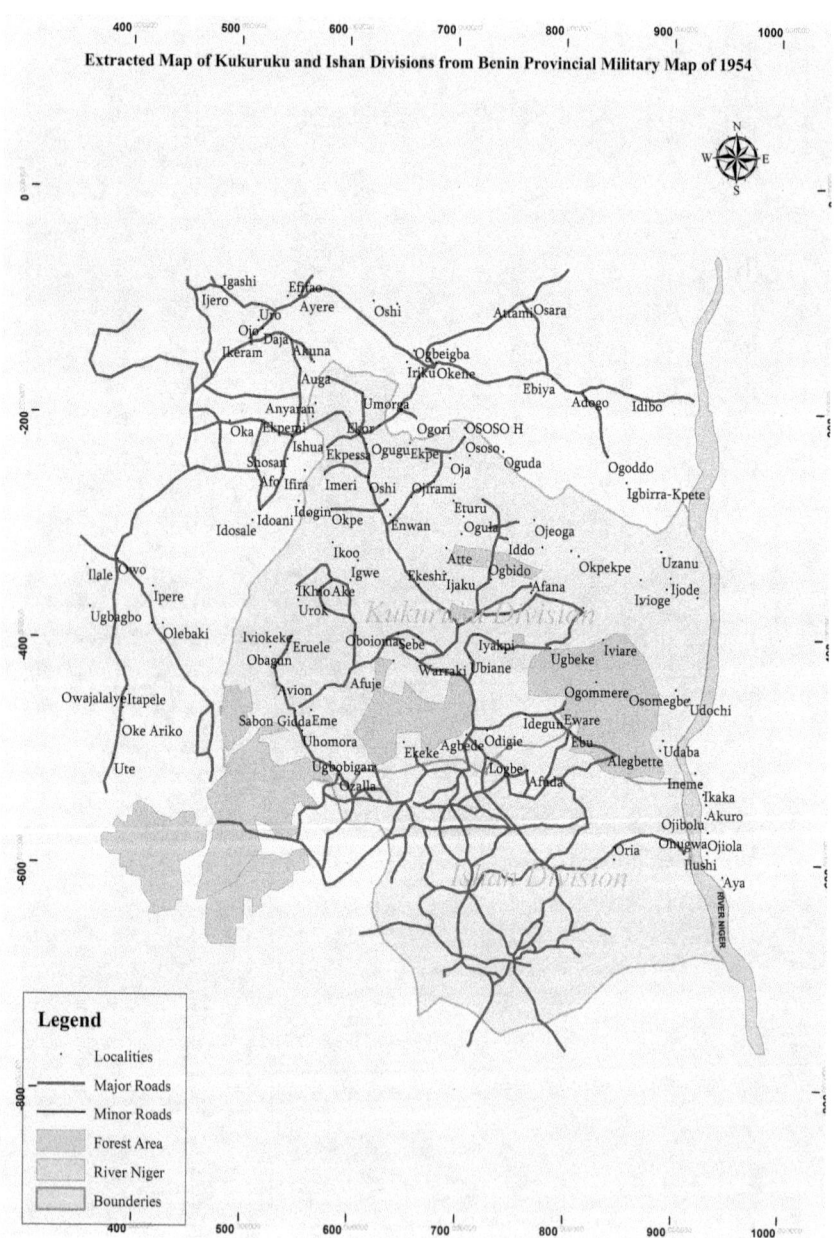

Plate 3c Extracted Map of Kukuruku and Ishan Divisions from Benin Provincial Military, 1954. Map of 1954 by Amidu Elabo.

(a)

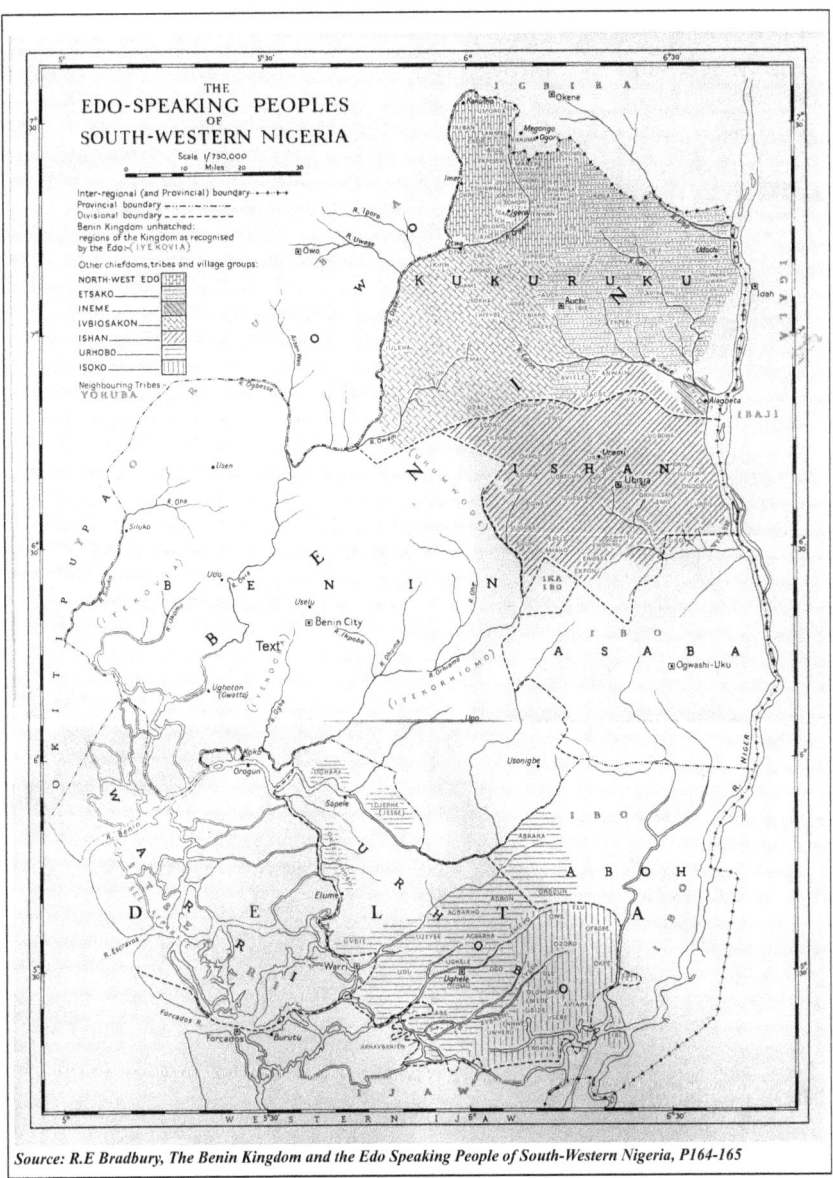

Plate 4a, 4b, 4c The Edo-speaking peoples of South-Western Nigeria. Credit: R. E. Bradbury, *The Benin Kingdom and the Edo Speaking Peoples of South-Western Nigeria*, 1957 (Ethnographic Survey Africa). Permission © Taylor & Francis, April 16, 2021.

(b)

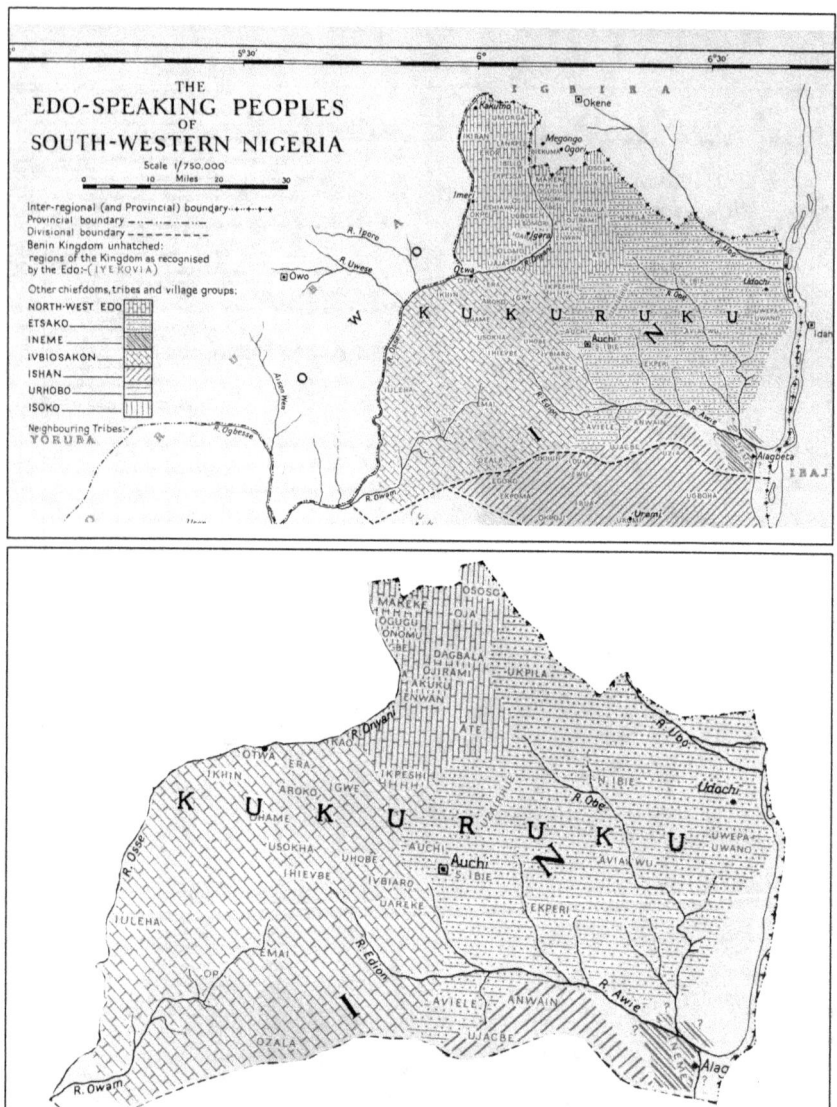

Plate 4 (Continued)

(c)

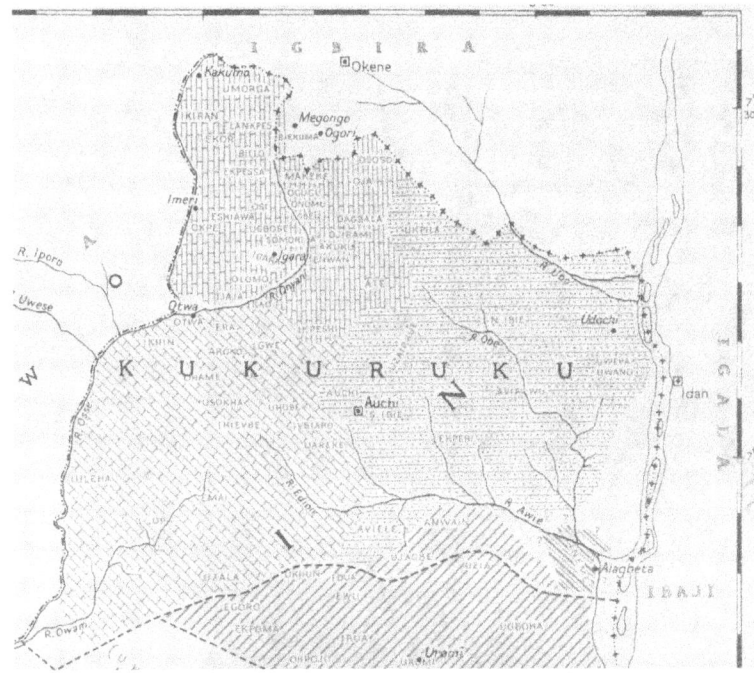

Plate 4 (Continued)

Plate 5 *Ọbu Evba* (diviner) with paraphernalia and client. Credit: Shegun Joshua.

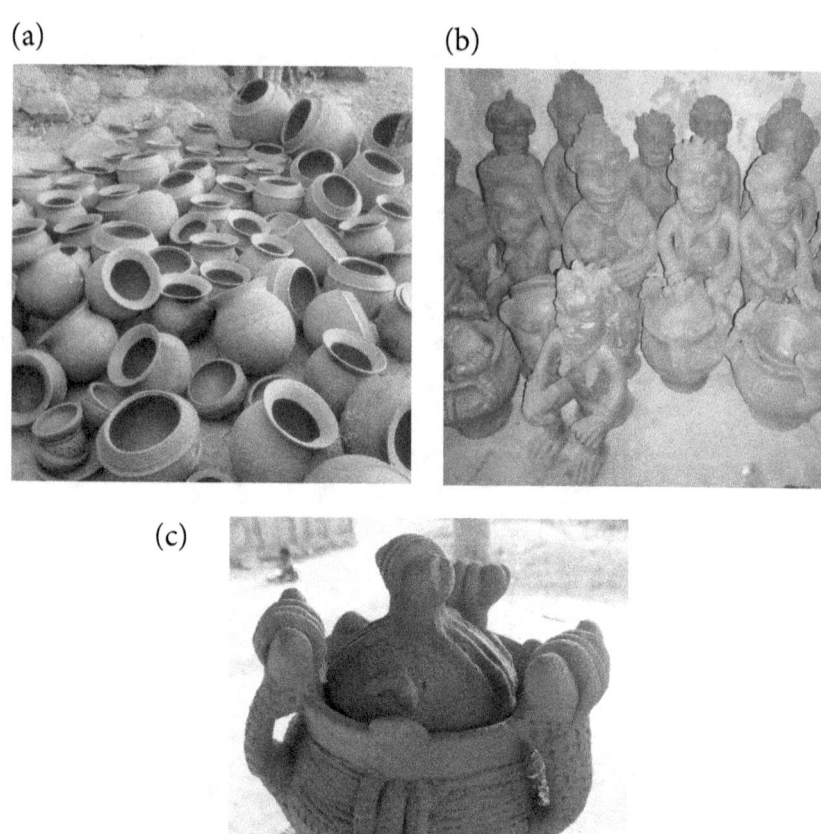

Plate 6a, 6b, 6c, 6d, 6e, 6f, 6g Variations of *Ẹrẹma* clay products for domestic and aesthetic purposes. Credit: Shegun Joshua.

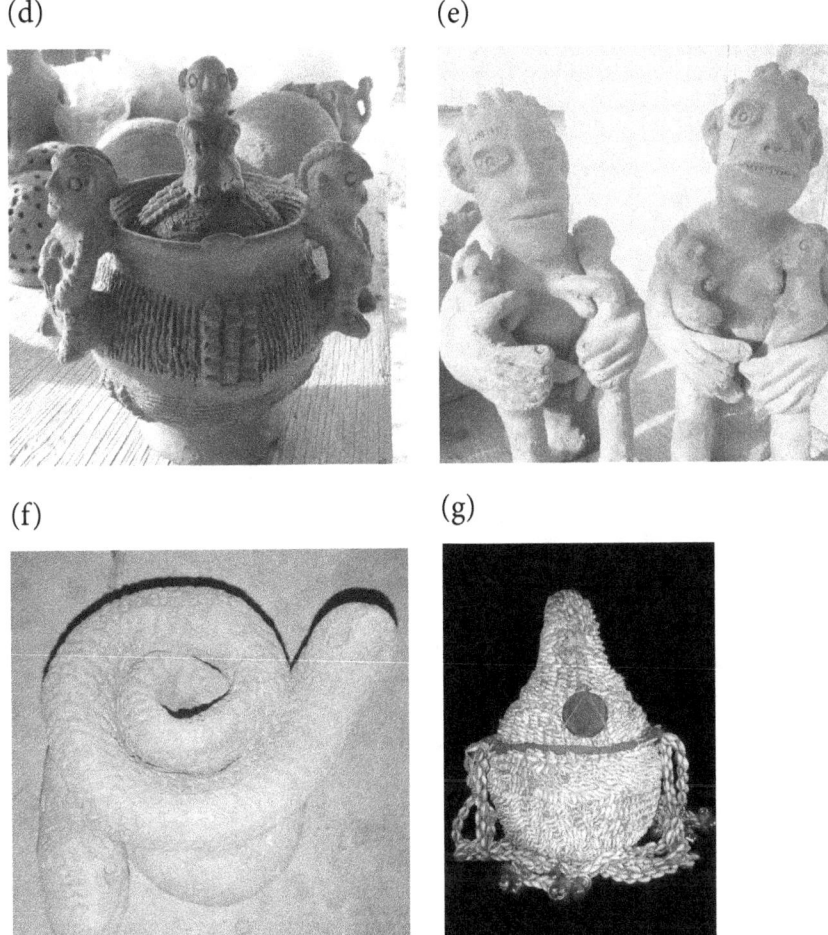

Plate 6 (Continued)

Plate 7 A male *osokuru* initiate with *egere*, traditional outfit. Credit: Shegun Joshua.

(a)   (b)

Plate 8a, 8b *Irimi/Erimi* (masquerade(s) in their ritual paraphernalia). Credit: Shegun Joshua.

Plate 9a, 9b The long *Agba* (drum) used during the *Oso̩* rite. Credit: Shegun Joshua.

Plate 10 A female *oruvie/ibishika* initiate with *egere*, traditional outfit during *Ukpe Oruvie/Ukpe O̩za*. Credit: Esther Adogame.

Plate 11 A female *oruvie/ibishika* initiate during *nya akpa* (public appearance of oruvie) during *Ukpe Iruvie/Ukpe Ọza*. Credit: Shegun Joshua.

Plate 12 *Ẹrẹsha* (Ẹrẹsa) sacred lake in Ọza Okeme. Credit: Shegun Joshua.

www.ingramcontent.com/pod-product-compliance
Lightning Source LLC
Chambersburg PA
CBHW052214300426
44115CB00011B/1680